A HANDBOOK OF INTERNATIONAL ORGANISATIONS

A HANDBOOK OF INTERNATIONAL ORGANISATIONS

SONU TRIVEDI

Foreword by

PROF. DR. K. MATHEWS

Professor of International Relations, Addis Ababa University, Ethiopia.

and

Formerly, Professor of African Studies and Head of the Department, Faculty of Social Sciences, University of Delhi, India.

Published by

B-2, Vishal Enclave, Opp. Rajouri Garden,
New Delhi-110027
Phones : 25413460, 25429987, 25466842

Sales Office
7/22, Ansari Road, Darya Ganj,
New Delhi-110002
Phones : 23273880, 23275880, 23280451
Fax : 91-11-23285873
web : www.atlanticbooks.com
e-mail : info@atlanticbooks.com

ISBN 81-269-0431-3

Printed in India
at Nice Printing Press, Delhi

CONTENTS

FOREWORD

International Organisations are institutional mechanisms for transnational cooperation and collective action to promote common security and welfare. The process of organization takes place through formal Inter-governmental Organisations such as the United Nations (UN) and the Bretton Woods Institutions or through informal group arrangements among countries such as the G-7, G-15, G-20, G-24, and G-77. In the absence of a world government, these are the only such institutions that can create mechanisms, rules and practices for much needed global governance. The adaptation of existing institutions and the creation of new institutions, as circumstances and times change, are a critical component of global governance.

International organisations can play three different, though not mutually exclusive, roles in world politics. First, they can be used by states as instruments of foreign policy in accordance with the traditional state-centric view; second, they can serve to modify states' behaviour; and third, they can achieve a measure of autonomy and operate as actors in their own right. These three roles are usually expressed through three images, *viz.*, 'instrument', 'arena' and 'actor'. The most common image of the role of international organizations is that of an instrument being used by its members for particular ends. This is the case particularly with Inter-governmental Organisations (IGOs) where the members are sovereign states with powers to limit independent action by international organisations instead of using them for pursuance of their foreign policy objectives. Thus, IGOs become tools to be used by their member states. The United Nations, for example, in its first decade of existence was largely used by the United States as an instrument of its diplomacy. Secondly, the international organisations are seen as arenas or forums within which action can take place. In this case the organisation provide meeting places for members to come together to discuss, debate, cooperate or disagree in the more open and public forum than that provided by bilateral diplomacy. During the 1970s, for example, the U.N. and its agencies were used by the Third World countries to air their views on the subject of New International Economic Order (NIEO). Thirdly, as 'independent' actors, they affect the course of world events. When this happens, the international organizations become actors in the international arena and competitors of the nation-state. Many well-known International Non-Governmental Organisations (INGOs) display a strong corporate identity showing the organization to be stronger than the sum total of its membership and also act effectively on the world stage. The International Committee of the Red Cross (ICRC), Amnesty International (AI), etc. provide useful examples in this respect.

It may also be noted that the international organisations have come to assume increasingly important roles in the contemporary world. The present-day world of the early 21st century is vastly different from the world half a century or so ago. With the revolution in information and communications technology the world has greatly shrunk and has become truly a global village. The idea of 'One World' has, indeed, become a reality today. But it is artificially divided into some 200 or so 'sovereign' nations-states. Moreover, with the intensification of economic globalization, the world has become one global market. The process of globalization in the world economy has brought about profound changes in the international context. Besides, problems in any part of the world are not only one's own. They impinge on the rest of the world, be they political, economic, ecological, strategic, demographic, or those entailing terrorism and drug trafficking. Therefore, solutions to problems anywhere in the world must be found and administered by the world as a whole collectively. In other words, the need for global governance and global institutions has become imperative.

The United Nations and the Bretton Woods Institutions were at the core of the international system for global governance that was set up in 1945. The nation state remained the foundation of both the conception and the design of these institutions. Even if they were unequal partners, nation states were not only actors on stage but also the directors backstage. Now, more than half a century later new developments, particularly, globalization have constrained the role of the nation state. The autonomy of the nation state is much reduced in matters economic if not political. For another, there are significant new players apart from nation states. International terrorist organizations like the al-Qaeda have become more powerful than states. The system of institutions and rules for global governance created in 1945 have become incompatible and inadequate to meet the present-day challenges in the international system. Recent crises in the world, particularly the Iraq war in 2003, seem to indicate that unilateralism and anti-diplomacy may destroy the United Nations. In the wake of the Iraq war many even started writing obituaries of the UN. There is an ongoing debate on the role of the Security Council and the future of the United Nations. The present US President George Bush has even said that the UN has become irrelevant. Today the U.N. is marginalized by unilateralism and unipolarism.

In the emerging New World Order, there are two main elements to be considered: one is globalisation and the other is the role of the U.N. The intensification of globalization is generating new and unprecedented problems and crises, notably international terrorism, increasing poverty and the globalisation of finance. The fact that we are confronted by new problems means there is a need for a drastic change in the U.N. The world today needs a third generation of international organisations to succeed the U.N., just as it succeeded the League of Nations in 1945. This third generation of international organisation will not come about by changing the composition of the Security Council, or revolutionizing the operation of the General Assembly, or reinforcing the Economic and Social Council. The third generation must be the result of a drastic change in the overall concept. It may take years of hard work to materialize.

The world continues to be in its 'state of nature'. It is important to note here that in Europe the nation state system has been undergoing a major transformation through the formation of the European Union (EU) in 1993. In Africa, a radical change has taken place in recent years in the form of replacing the ineffective Organization of African Unity (OAU) established in 1963 with the new African Union established in 2001. The crucial difference between the erstwhile OAU and the present AU is the ability of the latter to intervene in the domestic affairs of the member states under certain circumstances. The intervention of the AU in the on-going Darfur (Sudan) Crisis (2004) is a case in point. It is also to be stressed that the U.N. exists to find solutions to a myriad of problems through the common endeavour of all states. It is the one indispensable global organization in our globalizing world, though with many imperfections. As Dag Hammarskjoeld, the UN's great second Secretary-General put it, the UN was not created to take humanity to heaven, but to save it from hell. It has done so in the last six decades of its existence. As it attempts to face the post-Cold War world of the 21st century, the United Nations provides an indispensable forum to bring states together to tackle great problems of our time. In short, experience has shown that the international organizations are assuming increasingly important roles in world affairs despite all setbacks and shortcomings. Although the nation-states may not go so far as to surrender sovereign powers to international organisations, they do find them indispensable for other purposes. New nations demonstrate this in their eagerness to be admitted to the United Nations or to concerned regional organisations.

Ms. Sonu Trivedi's comprehensive study in this book is a valuable contribution to the understanding of the complex nature, structure and role of international organisations in the world today. The book provides much useful information and insights about a great variety of international organizations particularly the United Nations and related agencies, other major international organizations like the Amnesty International and the G-77, the International Criminal Court, etc., and major regional organizations all over the world. The book would be of enormous value not only to students of international organizations and international relations in various universities, but also to practitioners, policy-makers and observers involved and interested in international affairs and global developments. I strongly recommend the book to all concerned.

PROF. DR. K. MATHEWS
Professor of International Relations
Addis Ababa University, Ethiopia.
and
Formerly, Professor of African Studies
and Head of the Department
Faculty of Social Sciences
University of Delhi, India.

ACKNOWLEDGEMENT

The present highly informative, voluminous, book would not have been possible without the help and co-operation of a number of persons. I convey my heartfelt gratitude to all those who have directly or indirectly extended their co-operation in the making of this book.

I express my sincere thanks to the Secretariats and Regional Offices of the various International Organisations for being kind enough to provide the wide range of pamphlets and folders on all aspects of the works of their respective organisations.

I am also grateful to Prof. K. Mathews, currently Professor of International Studies, Addis Ababa University and the former Head of the Department of African Studies, University of Delhi, for writing a Foreword for the book. Despite his busy schedule and overseas assignment, he has been kind enough to spare his valuable time for us.

I am also indebted to my friends without whose help and encouragement this book could not have been completed.

Finally, my sincere gratitude goes to Dr. K.R. Gupta, Chairman of the Atlantic Publishers and Distributors, New Delhi, who has been primarily responsible for publishing this book in the shortest possible time. Without his help, the book would not have seen the light of the day.

Although utmost care has been taken to make the book faultless and precisely clear in its details, yet there may be some errors of facts or interpretation that might have inadvertently crept into the first edition of this book. Any suggestions regarding the improvement of the book would be of great importance to us and gratefully acknowledged.

SONU TRIVEDI

PREFACE

Over and over again history has shown us that, once a single nation becomes uncomfortably strong, its next-door neighbours start joining together in self-defense. In the early days these groups of nations—or alliance as historians call them—often sprang up and died with bewildering speed. Looking back over the past four hundred years we can see as to how the rise to power of France, Spain, the Austro-Hungarian Empire, Prussia, Nazi Germany, and most recently Russia and China, have caused other states to unite together to protect themselves. We can also see how Britain time and again has done to ensure that no single country on the mainland ever dominate Europe.

Until the start of the first Great War in 1914, the Grand Alliance against Emperor Napoleon I of France had been the earliest and one of the most important example of the world international organisations. The victory at Waterloo was a victory of the British policy for maintaining a balance of power in Europe; just as the outbreak of war in August 1914 was a defeat of that same policy.

Apart from the death and suffering it caused, the First Great War changed many things. It was truly the First World War in which people of the entire world got affected since every continent got involved. Indians too were one among them. The bombs and artillery attacks were extensively made in this war. By the time the battles ended, men had realized that the world had shrunk. It was feared that in future if ever a local war between the major European powers breaks out, then it could be hardly kept within its boundaries. As Litvinov, the Soviet representative at the League of Nations, put it: "Peace is indivisible."

In the new world of America there was a growing impatience because of Europe's continuing quarrels. In Europe itself, after four years of fighting, there was a desperate wish that such horrors should never occur again. The sacrifice of several millions in the four years of war necessiated creation of a truly International Organisation—the League of Nations.

The first aim of the League—and of the United Nations, which later took its place—was to establish and maintain peace all over the world. But as we shall see, both these bodies aimed at doing more than that. All the nations belonging to these organisations pledged themselves to get rid of poverty and starvation, and to provide education to millions of people all over the world. The League and the United Nations have also battled to wipe out disease; to eradicate the drug running; to make air travel safer; to improve agriculture; to help regional organisation and so forth.

Over the past few years there has been a significant increase in the efforts of developing countries to achieve regional economic integration. In various parts of the developing world, the existing regional arrangements have been revitalised or expanded and new groupings formed. Examples include the Association of South East Asian Nations (ASEAN), which now has an agreed trade liberalisation agenda; Mercosur in Latin America; the West African Economic and Monetary Union (WAEMU); and the Southern African Development Community (SADC), which has formulated a new strategy for market integration. These initiatives have coincided with new and deepened regional integration involving industrialised nations—as exemplified by the Treaty on European Union (EU), the enlargement of the EU, and the creation of the North American Free Trade Area (NAFTA). On top of all this, the successful conclusion of the Uruguay Round has led to the creation of the World Trade Organisation (WTO), thereby strengthening the multilateral trading system.

No matter we realize it or not, the fact remains that everything that these international organisations have done and are doing, affect each of us in our daily lives. Hence, being a part of this world we should know about their work.

This book is not intended as a general history of international organisations. Such histories are already available, in much greater details than it could be attempted here. It is rather a description and a brief overview of the United Nations system and that of other major International and Regional Organisations of the world.

The book has been divided into two major sections. The first part deals with the International Organisations in general. The first chapter begins with the conceptual analysis of the term 'international organisation', and the pre-requisites for its establishment. It further looks into the functions performed by these organisations and their evolution and growth. The most obvious Global International Organisation *viz.*, the United Nations finds place in the second chapter. This chapter also describes the various specialized agencies and autonomous institutions working under the United Nations. The third chapter gives a brief sketch of the other major international organisations of the world, such as, APEC, OECD, OPEC, NAM, The Commonwealth, WCO, etc.

The second part of the book studies the process of regional co-operation and integration in general, and its growth and evolution. This is described in the fourth chapter. And the last chapter deals with the major regional organisations of the world. This has been categorized on the basis of different regions, *viz.*, African, Asian and Pacific, Central and Latin American, European and the Middle East.

It is expected that such a comprehensive analysis of the various International and Regional Organisations of the world would be beneficial for the students and scholars pursuing research in this field.

SONU TRIVEDI

LIST OF ACRONYMS

ADB	—	Asian Development Bank
ADF	—	African Development Fund
AI	—	Amnesty International
ALADI	—	Asociación Latinoamericana de Integración (Latin American Integration Association)
AMU	—	Arab Maghreb Union
ANZUS	—	Australia, New Zealand and United States
APEC	—	Asia-Pacific Economic Cooperation
ARF	—	ASEAN Regional Forum
ASEAN	—	Association of South-East Asian Nations
ASEM	—	Asia Europe Meeting
AU	—	African Union
BIMST-EC	—	Bangladesh-India-Myanmar-Sri Lanka-Thailand Economic Cooperation (Bay of Bengal Initiative for Multi-Sectoral, Technical and Economic Cooperation)
BIST-EC	—	Bangladesh, India, Sri lanka, Thailand-Economic Cooperation
CACM	—	Central American Common Market
CARICOM	—	Caribbean Community
CET	—	Common External Tariff
CIS	—	Commonwealth of Independent States
COMECON	—	Council For Mutual Economic Assistance
COMESA	—	Common Market for Eastern and Southern Africa
EAC	—	East African Community
EADB	—	East African Development Bank

EALAF	—	East Asia-Latin American Forum
ECOWAS	—	Economic Community of West African States
EU	—	European Union
FAO	—	Food and Agriculture Organisation
G-15	—	Group-15
G-20	—	Group-20
G-77	—	Group-77
G-8	—	Group-7/8
GATT	—	General Agreement on Tariffs and Trade
GCC	—	Gulf Cooperation Council
IAEA	—	International Atomic Energy Agency
IBRD	—	International Bank for Reconstruction and Development
ICAO	—	International Civil Aviation Organisation
ICC	—	International Criminal Court
ICD	—	Islamic Corporation for the Development of Private Sector
ICIEC	—	Islamic Corporation for Insurance of Investments and Export Credits
ICSID	—	International Centre for Settlement of Investment Disputes
IDA	—	International Development Association
IDB	—	Islamic Development Bank
IDCP	—	United Nations International Drug Control Programme
IFAD	—	International Fund for Agricultural Development
IFC	—	International Finance Corporation
IFRC	—	International Federation of the Red Cross
ILO	—	International Labour Organisation
IMF	—	International Monetary Fund
IMO	—	International Maritime Organisation

INTERPOL	—	International Criminal Police Organisation
IOM	—	International Organisation for Migration
IORAG	—	Indian Ocean Rim Academic Group
IOR-ARC	—	Indian Ocean Rim Association for Regional Cooperation
IORBF	—	Indian Ocean Rim Business Forum
IOTO	—	Indian Ocean Tourism Organisation
IPU	—	Inter-Parliamentary Union
IRTI	—	Islamic Research and Training Institute
ISA	—	International Seabed Authority
ISO	—	International Organisation for Standardisation
ITU	—	International Telecommunications Union
IUCEA	—	Inter-University Council for East Africa
LAFTA	—	Latin American Free Trade Area
LVFO	—	Lake Victoria Fisheries Organisation
MERCOSUR	—	Mercado Común Del Sur (Southern Common Market)
MIGA	—	Multilateral Investment Guarantee Agency
NAFTA	—	North American Free Trade Agreement
NAM	—	Non-Aligned Movement
NATO	—	North Atlantic Treaty Organisation
NGO	—	Non-Governmental Organisation
NIB	—	Nordic Investment Bank
NTF	—	Nigeria Trust Fund
UDHR	—	Universal Declaration of Human Rights
OAS	—	Organisation of American States
OECD	—	Organisation for Economic Cooperation and Development
OIC	—	Organisation of Islamic Countries
OPEC	—	Organisation of Petroleum Exporting Countries

OSCE	—	Organisation For Security And Cooperation In Europe
PTA	—	Preferential Trade Area for Eastern and Southern Africa
SADC	—	South Asian Association for Regional Cooperation
SADC	—	Southern African Development Community
SAFTA	—	South Asian Free Trade Area
SAPTA	—	SAARC Preferential Trading Arrangement
SPA	—	SADC Programme for Action
TAC	—	Treaty of Amity and Cooperation
TEAM-9	—	Techno Economic Approach for Africa-India Movement
TRIMS	—	Trade Related Investment Measures
TRIPS	—	Trade Related Intellectual Property Rights
UNCTAD	—	United Nations Conference on Trade and Development
UNDP	—	United Nations Development Programme
UNEP	—	United Nations Environment Programme
UNESCO	—	United Nations Educational, Scientific and Cultural Organisation
UNFPA	—	United Nations Population Fund
UN-Habitat	—	United Nations Human Settlements Programme
UNHCR	—	United Nations High Commissioner for Refugees
UNICEF	—	United Nations International Children's Emergency Fund
UNIDO	—	United Nations Industrial Development Organisation
UNRWA	—	United Nations Relief and Works Agency for Palestine Refugees
UN	—	United Nations

UPU	—	Universal Postal Union
WCO	—	World Customs Organisation
WEF	—	World Economic Forum
WFP	—	World Food Programme
WHO	—	World Health Organisation
WIPO	—	World Intellectual Property Organisation
WMO	—	World Meteorological Organisation
WTO	—	World Trade Organisation
WWF	—	World Wide Fund for Nature

Part I

International Organisation

1

INTERNATIONAL ORGANISATION: AN OVERVIEW

Nations do cooperate from time to time without the use of set forms of procedure and without creating or using any common organs and even, perhaps, without adopting common legal foundations or limitation for their action. Contributions of famine relief by one nation to another would provide an example. And such cooperation has its value. It is, however, very slight in extent, very unstable in duration, very ambiguous in quality. It is organised international cooperation which counts most and in organised international cooperation it is the institutions—organs and procedures—which forms the distinctive element and which determine to a large degree the effectiveness of the action. These institutions embody and reflect the motives of the nations, their most strongly felt convictions. They are, moreover made up, of living and striving individuals who embody vital human and national and international purposes and demands[1].

The idea of an International Organisation is the outcome of an attempt to bring order into international relations by establishing lasting bonds across frontiers between Governments or social groups wishing to defend their common interests, within the context of permanent bodies, distinct from national institutions, having their own individual characteristics, capable of expressing their own will and whose role is to perform certain functions of international importance[2].

1. Potter, P.B., *Introduction to the study of International Organisation*, New York, 1948.
2. Gerbet, G., "Rise and Development", *International Social Science Journal*, Vol. 29, No.1 (1977).

In the lexicon of International relations the words international, multi-national, and trans-national are often misunderstood. Hence, an attempt is made to clear the confusion at the very outset. The terms 'international' 'multinational' and 'transnational' have been variously used to refer to the control of an organisation, the composition of its staff and the scope of its operation. An organisation is 'transnational' rather than 'national' if it carries on significant centrally directed–operation in the territory of two or more nation states. Similarly, an organisation will be called international rather than national only if control of the organisation is explicitly shared among representatives of two or more nationalities. And an organisation is 'multinational' rather than 'national' only if people from two or more nationalities participate significantly in its operations. These distinctions are important because almost any combination of internationalism, multi-nationalism, and trans-nationalism or their national opposites could exist in practice. The World Bank, for example, is formally international in control, highly multinational in personnel and clearly transnational in its operations.

The science of international organisation is relatively new. International relations in general have been observed and studied in a more or less unscientific way, for over two thousand years, and international law has been studied as a branch of general jurisprudence for well over three centuries, but the scientific study of international organisation dates from the latter part of the nineteenth, or the early years of the twentieth, century.

International organisations constitute the principle feature of international relations today. They grow up and are created by the means of certain objective factors or the conditions of fact—nations, international intercourse—and certain elements of felt needs or purpose—national and international interests and policies—as the foundations thereof and in response to these factors.

Memberships of the international organisations consist of nations with widely divergent physical–geologic, geographic, and climatic—situations, and are composed of more or less divergent racial and cultural strains. As a result, the nations individually develop divergent needs and interests, and these divergent needs and interests give rise to divergent foreign policies or programs of action towards other nations. Hence there need arises for social control, among states than among individuals. For this purpose the procedure and agencies of international organisation must facilitate communication of information and policy and opinion by one nation to another. Communication, agreement and cooperation are the fundamental forms of action which international organisation must facilitate, in order that the national policies may be reconciled with one another, socially synthesised and executed.

Pre-requisites for the Growth of International Organisation

The principal pre-requisites for the appearance and the growth of International organisation must be noted at the outset.

Existence of Separate States. There must exist a number of separate states or nation states so as to make available certain potential members of a community of nations. There could be no international intercourse, law or organisation if a large number of Free states cease to exist in the world. The existence of independent nations is absolutely indispensable to the existence of the international organisation.

Multiplicity of units is desirable, rather than a bare plurality, for, just as the multiplicity of specimens provides a better foundation for the development of general principles of law in the field of physical sciences. Therefore, multiplication of independent states is conducive to a rapid growth of the law of nations.

Homogeneity. A certain degree of homogeneity among the states is equally necessary for the growth of international organisation. A moderate amount of homogeneity is indispensable as a basis for law among units of any order. If there are no common interests and standards, there can be no legal community. A substantial international spiritual unity or community must precede any effective international organisation, and the denial of any such thing exists today, must be accepted.

There could be very little international law or practice in a world of one great state, or a restricted number of states, or of states immeasurably at variance in character. Retardation in the growth of international law and organisation in the past can often be traced directly to the suppression of independent states or to the fact that national practices and views have differed so widely that agreement was impossible.

Stability. The intercourse and the elaboration of the legal and institutional connections among the states will be rendered increasingly difficult if the rise and fall of the states in the world is too rapid. If the process of modification of the old states is too swift, it becomes difficult to determine the degree of independence enjoyed by the given states. Too much rapid changes in the political map of the world, is not conducive to the development of an orderly international system.

Equality. It is increasingly desirable that every state shall be free to manage its own affairs and able to do so effectively. Independent action is essential for the expression of the individuality of each nation. Domination of one state by another impairs the operation of the process of free international cooperation. Irrespective of the relative power, the nations are entitled to live independent lives in so far as they so desire. The smaller nations must have freedom to live their own lives and to receive satisfaction for their national rights in the face of the more powerful members of the international community.

Territorial possession. A nation must possess a certain territorial domain in order to be a state. Throughout history, states or other organisations of the people lacking a territorial basis have failed to contribute greatly to the international life. To deprive a state of its territorial basis means to deprive it of existence. Modern international law and diplomacy are the products of a system of territorial states, in contrast to an earlier system of personal jurisdictions.

General secular character. If the law and practice of the nations is to reach its fullest fruition, the states must be general in character, *i.e.*, they must be comprehensive in their activities and aims and not exclusively religious, industrial, scientific or aesthetic. Members of the community of nations with only special interest would contribute little to the law of nations outside their own interest. If the states have only special interests, relations with other states becomes difficult and dependent on the chance that there will be other states with the similar interests.

External historical conditions. Certain external historical conditions are also requisite to the growth of any considerable system of international relations and government.

First, there must be sufficient degree of contact among the existing states. Unless two states make contact they can have no economic, political or legal relations. National isolation results in paralysis of international growth. As means of communication increases and are exploited among the nations, the intercourse upon which the whole system is founded grows in volume and complexity. More needs arise for, and more facilities are provided for creating, an international legal and governmental system.

Second, a science of international relations must be developed to explain existing conditions and suggest the elaboration of new legal and political institutions. For want of mature science of international relations, the Greek state-system went down before Macedon and Rome. The first and the second World Wars were fought for the want of an adequate science and art of an international government. With all the materials for international organisation present, the world still lacked a statesmanship equal to the task of ensuring justice and keeping peace.

Functions and Role of International Organisation

The functions to be performed by the international organisation are analogous to those performed by the national Governments such as the making and execution of laws in the individual state. In international organisation, the task is to secure enactment or the adoption of the international law (out of national policies synthesised into international), its revision as the needs of the time change, and to secure its execution or administration by national or international agencies, including, logically, enforcement if need arises.

The general objective of the international organisation is the promotion of the welfare of the nations. This is to be accomplished in the first place by preventing aggression by one state upon another and promoting security and peaceful settlement of controversies. It is to be accomplished mainly by erecting and constantly revising standards of conduct whereby justice shall be done among the nations, and seeing that these standards are observed. Finally, securing international cooperation where necessary for the service of mutual needs is the objective which completes the schedule; pacification or the protection, the doing of justice and the promotion of cooperation constitute the tasks performed by the international organisation.

The functions of international organisation range over all aspects of human life and cover about the same range as is covered by the scope of activity of the individual state. Maintenance of order and safety, protection of life and property and the facilities of communication and transit, promoting the development of those communications and of the economic and social welfare of the nations are some of the general functions of international organisation.

Traditional views of international organisations consider them to be a part of institutionalised relationship between states and governments. They have a state-centric view of the political world and have little interest in international non-governmental organisations. Their starting point was the existence of the present state system in which there is no common authority over and above the sovereign state and where there is international anarchy in the sense of a lack of government at the international level.

A noticeable development in the international relations literature since the World War II has been the movement away from the state centric view towards one that admits the importance of international organisations as international actors in their own right rather than as meeting places fur or instruments of their member states. This view is represented by the functionalists and differs with the traditional view of international organisations based on the State centric model. The functional approach focuses on inter-governmental organisations and allows for a network of specialised agencies. It favours the weakening of the importance and power of the sovereign states as a middleman between the individual and the world community. The neo functionalists or integrationists have assigned a major role to international organisation as active agents of task expansion as opposed to the passive recipient of new task.

International organisations have been viewed as potential dispensers of collective legitimacy. In this regard, the capacity of the United Nations to elicit world wide approval for national policies has emerged as one of its major functions. The function of legitimating in the international realm has tended in recent years to be increasingly conferred upon international political institutions. International organisations because of their universality are the major venue within which the global legitimating struggle over international regimes are carried out. These institutions also act as the vehicle in international politics for agenda formation. They also provide for the forums for the creation of trans-governmental coalitions as well as instrument of trans-governmental policy coordination as well as means through which global dominance structure is enhanced or can possibly be undermined.

The most usual image of the role of international organisation is that of an instrument being used by its members for a particular end. This is particularly true of the United Nations in its first few years of its existence. Till early 50s the United States used UN as a Cold war implement. This role of the UN could not be sustained for long with the emergence of the third world and change in the nature of Cold War, particularly due to the nuclear arms race between the US and the Soviet Union.

International organisations like the UN have often become an arena or forum for a more open and public debate than that provided by bilateral diplomacy. During the 70s, the UN and its specialised agencies were used by the third world countries for a New International Economic Order (NIEO). The earlier Bretton Woods system was based on the United States economic hegemony. A large number of developing countries found this system as unsympathetic to their economic aspirations. Subsequently, the Oil Crises of the 70s gave a death blow to the economic strength of the western industrialised nations.

Another role attributed to the international organisations in the international system is that of an independent actor. However, this role of the international organisation is subject to a number of limitations, the most significant being the role played by the Super Powers during the Cold war and the emergence of United States hegemony in the post-Cold War era. In today's interdependent world, it is not possible for the international organisations to work without being influenced by the outside forces.

These roles are however, not mutually exclusive. The importance of each of these roles depend upon the changes brought about in the international politics—be it the Cold War, détente or the end of the Cold War. More recently the emergence of globalisation and liberalisation of the third world economies has brought about the marginalisation of developing world. The developing countries are under the heavy debt burden of the international financial institutions such as the World Bank and the IMF. They have to undergo the Structural Adjustment Programmes (SAP) and adhere to the conditionality attached to these loans. This greatly undermines the independent functioning of the international organisations and as a result they become subservient to the monopolistic role of the economic Super Power of the world.

Evolution of International Organisations

Since the beginning of the nineteenth century, each of the major wars—Napoleonic War, the First and the Second World Wars—have been followed by the attempts to establish international organisations viz. the Concert of Europe, the League of Nations and the United Nations. Historically international organisations have been permeated by the power relations. During the Concert of Europe (1815-1914) 'the golden age of diplomacy', the conquest of colonies became the symbol of great power status.

The League of Nations was a step forward in international society. The league, however, displayed a conspicuous disparity of power with the Great Powers holding a controlling influence on the organisation. The Great Powers by virtue of their special status in the council and owing to the rule of the unanimity could always and actually did frustrate any action of the League in cases where their vital interests were at stake. This made the League of Nations totally ineffective in dealing with the overt acts of aggression.

The United Nations is in many ways a superior type of international organisation. However, the Charter bears the imprint of the power realities prevailing at that time. But the actual working of the United Nations has revealed that it is also not free from the influence of the Great Powers. The independent working of the UN has always been subjected to the domination by the US hegemony in the Post-Cold War era. In recent years, the American doctrine of pre-emptive military intervention poses a fundamental challenge to the world peace and stability on which the UN has rested since last 58 years. The recent Gulf War II has raised doubts about the relevance and creditability of the World Body.

One of the remarkable features of the present day international system is the growing part played by the international organisations. Before the Second World War, they had no established role and their activities were confined to few specialised areas such as transport, health etc. In the post World War II period, it is not only the quantitative growth but new qualitative features have also been added in the world scene which have made international organisations an important element of international relations. The collapse of colonialism and the emergence of a large number of Afro-Asian nations have changed the power equation of the international politics. Not only the United Nations but a number of international organisations representing the interests of the third world nations (NAM, UNCTAD, and G-77 etc.) have been established. Furthermore, the end of the Cold War and the emergence of a Unipolar world has necessitated a change in the objectives and functioning of most of the international organisations. This was particularly seen in the transformation of GATT into WTO and reviewing and self-assessment by a number of other organisations such as the UN, NAM, and G-7 etc.

Another significant development was the emergence of a number of regional organisations. The emergence of regional cooperation's and organisations after the second world were initially the consequence of fear & security but latter on, particularly after the demise of the Soviet Union, these organisation were based on economic cooperation and mutual prosperity. The revival of interest in regionalism is due to its spectacular development, which has affected all continents. Even the United States was finally won over to the virtues of regionalism when it initiated a series of free trade agreements in 1988. Today's regionalism differs from the previous wave in the 1960s by its being embedded in a different international economic and political context, characterised by the end of the Cold War and its bipolarity, a strengthened multilateral trading system epitomised by the WTO, and the globalisation of world economy. Not only new organisations have been established (European Union, African Union, NAFTA, IOR-ARC, BIMST-EC etc.), but a number other organisations have undergone restructuring and enlargement such as the transformation of SADCC into SADC, PTA into COMESA and the revival of the EAC and revision of the ECOWAS Treaty.

One major characteristic of the contemporary international politics is the emergence of scientific and technological revolution. Particularly, in this regard mention can be made of the TRIPS and TRIMS working under the aegis of WTO. Besides, there are a host of other problems of global nature which calls for broad international cooperation. These can be summarised as the threat of nuclear arms race; environmental degradation; star wars etc. A number of organisations are particularly working in these fields.

The Identity Crises

International organisations proliferated faster than nations in the quarter-century after World War II although, the birthrate of new nations itself hit a record. They grew in numbers, in activities, in personnel at work for or with them, and in budgets. The United Nations itself more than doubled in membership and has taken on many new tasks. On the basis of reproductive capacity, this new breed of political institution would appear potent and destined for a decisive role in the conduct of international affairs[3].

3. Jacob, Atherton and Wallenstein, *The Dynamics of International,* Dorsey Press, 1972.

However, there are those who argue that high birthrate does not assure a healthy population (in fact, it may signal that a lot of babies will die off before maturity); and spending more money no more guarantees soundness of performance than an inflationary increase in GNP reflects a sound economy. In fact, protagonists of international organisations of every variety are confronting a lapse of confidence so severe that one would be tempted to forecast imminent bankruptcy, were it not that alternatives of unilateral and bilateral action in coping with major world problems have already gone into receivership.

The truth is that we, the peoples and the governments of the nation states have yet to learn how to live in the kind of a world that is here, or even to understand and admit what kind of a world it is. This being so, we are not effectively using the international institutions that in a strange and expediential manner have been invented to deal with crises in interstate relations. Since they were conceived piecemeal, with little relationship to each other, and as a kind of appendage to the existing state system, awareness of the truly innovative nature of these institutions has come very slowly to statesmen as well as the general public.

They have, indeed been seriously misconceived—sometimes as super governments and more often as alliances under a different name. When used as a super-government, they have failed in most of the instances because we stand committed to a pluralistic, politically divided world, with decentralised authority. This is one of the inescapable realities. But alliances haven't worked either. They have failed to effectively recognise the realities of global interdependence. When international organisations have been used as alliances, and their conduct manipulated to serve the national interests of only one segment of the world, they have exacerbated international conflict and rigidified political and social cleavages across the world.

Experiences suggest that international organisations are usually incapable of performing the customary functions of the government. Whenever they have been asked to perform them, they have failed in the immediate task and are weakened for other assignments. They should not be expected to legislate in the sense of mandating rules binding on their constituent states or on persons under national jurisdiction. They should rarely be called upon to adjudicate conflicts in the sense of rendering a verdict that the parties are obliged to accept. Above all, they are basically disqualified for the enforcement function of the executive, whether in the traditional form or through the device of the "collective security".

For international organisations to fulfill the vital role required of them in the management of international relations, it is necessary first, to strip away from the delusion that they can govern and to thwart any attempt to misuse them as though they were governments. They are the machinery to give the appearance of legitimacy to a power play by one group of states, seeking to impose its will on others. They are in fact, as best the expression of a voluntary consensus reached by a group of autonomous decision makers. In the 21st century, these institutions should emerge as an instrument of political integration and reconciling political pluralism with technological and social interdependence in the world arena.

2

UNITED NATIONS

2.1 UNITED NATIONS: AN INTRODUCTION

United Nations is a centre for harmonizing the actions of nations. Established 58 years ago, UN has helped the world to move towards the path of peace and cooperation. The bitter experiences of the World War II and the failure of the League of Nations put together paved the way for the formation of the United Nations in October 24, 1945.

The Charter revealed the actual role of the World Body. The objectives enshrined in the Preamble to the Charter envisages a better and peaceful life to the people of the world through practicing tolerance and living together in peace and harmony with one another. This spirit has facilitated the emergence of peaceful coexistence among the states despite political, economic and ideological differences prevailing between them.

The purposes of the United Nations as set forth in Article 1 of the Charter include maintenance of international peace and security; development of friendly relations among nations; cooperation in solving international problems; and to act as a centre for harmonizing the actions of the nations to achieve the above ends. For the attainment of the above purposes the UN acts in accordance with certain principles such as: the the sovereign equality of the member nations; settle international disputes by peaceful means; refrain from threat or use of force in international relations; to assist the UN in any action within the UN charter and no intervention in domestic affairs of member nations.

History of the United Nations

The name "United Nations", coined by the President of United States Franklin D. Roosevelt, was first used in the "Declaration by United Nations" of 1 January 1942, during the Second World War, when representatives of 26 nations pledged their Governments to continue fighting together against the Axis Powers.

One of the intial examples of International Organisations established to cooperate on specific matters is the International Telecommunication Union founded in 1865 and the Universal Postal Union established in 1874. Both are now United Nations specialized agencies. In 1899, the International Peace Conference was held in Hague to elaborate instruments for settling crises peacefully, preventing wars and codifying rules of warfare. It adopted the Convention for the Pacific Settlement of International Disputes and established the Permanent Court of Arbitration, which began work in 1902.

The forerunner of the United Nations was the League of Nations, an organisation conceived in similar circumstances during the first World War, and established in 1919 under the Treaty of Versailles "to promote international cooperation and to achieve peace and security." The International Labour Organisation was also created under the Treaty of Versailles as an affiliated agency of the League. The League of Nations ceased its activities after failing to prevent the Second World War.

In 1945, representatives of 50 countries met in San Francisco at the United Nations Conference on International Organisation to draw up the United Nations Charter. The delegates deliberated on the basis of proposals worked out by the representatives of China, the Soviet Union, the United Kingdom and the United States at Dumbarton Oaks (United States) in August-October 1944. The Charter was signed on 26 June 1945 by the representatives of the 50 countries. Poland, which was not represented at the Conference, signed it later and became one of the original 51 Member States.

The United Nations officially came into existence on 24 October 1945, when the Charter had been ratified by China, France, the Soviet Union, the United Kingdom, the United

States and by a majority of other signatories. This day is celeberated as United Nations day each year.

The UN Family

The UN as such is made of six main organs—the General Assembly, the Security Council, the Economic and Social Council, the Trusteeship Council, the International Court of Justice and the Secretariat. All are based at UN headquarters at New York, except for the Court, which is at Hague, the Netherlands.

The UN, its programmes and funds, and the specialized agencies compose the "UN system". As a family of organisations, the UN performs a vast range of duties that affect us all in myriad ways. These range from the decision of the Security Council to dispatch a peacekeeping operation in response to a dispute, to setting standards for air safety and communications compatibility; from rushing emergency supplies to victims of natural disaster, to coordinating the response to the AIDS pandemic; from helping countries to carry out free and fair elections, to securing low interest loans to develop the infrastructures of the developing countries. Ultimately, its work is about making a healthier, more stable world with enhanced opportunities and justice for all of us.

The UN specialized agencies and analogous bodies, working in such diverse areas such as health, agriculture, international aviation and meteorology are related to the UN through special agreements. The specialized agencies coordinate their work with UN but are separate, autonomous organisations.

Rationale of the UN

It is often said that if we did not have the United Nations, it would have to be invented. In a world plagued by conflict, the UN permits instant consultations among governments and provides the forum for dealing with long-term problems. The UN is a catalyst for action on major global issues, such as the environment and illicit drug, and provides the best mechanism available to mobilize and sustain international cooperation to tackle these issues. The UN and its agencies help build economies and stabilize financial markets. They help eradicate disease, expand food production and increase longevity. They protect refugees, deliver food aid respond quickly to natural disasters. It protects vulnerable groups, like children, refugees, displaced persons, minorities, indigenous people and the disabled. The UN and its agencies also provide the machinery for setting technical and legal standards in vital areas of global interactions-from air safety standards to human rights. No organisation in the world is better suited to pursue these goals, because no other possesses the UN's universality and legitimacy.

The UN in Practice

The members of the UN are Sovereign Nations, and the UN Charter is one of the strongest safeguards of sovereignty, enshrining this principle as one of its central pillars. At the same time, most of the problems that world faces today, are of such complexity that they cannot be addressed by any single nation acting alone. The UN is where the world's countries come together to address common problems. Working with other countries is an exercise of sovereignty, not a limitation of it. By cooperating in specific areas through the United Nations, States build the structures that make international life possible. Countries voluntarily decide to work together because they feel it is in their best interest. The universality and impartiality of the UN provides the common ground where countries can achieve maximum benefits from cooperation, while guaranteeing that their sovereignty will be protected.

The United Nations is the instrument of all its Members States, who shape its policies by discussing and voting on major issues. In the General assembly, all members have the same voting rights, making it the most democratic of international institutions. Even in the Security Council, the United States and the other four powerful, veto wielding members, though able to stop any action with which they agree, must take the views of other States into account and cannot impose their will. No country, however powerful, is able to dictate UN policies single handedly.

Although the UN is the world organisation of States, its framework provides opportunities to involve other actors whose cooperation is increasingly vital for the solution of the global cooperation. Various expressions of civil society contribute to the work of the UN—Non-Governmental Organisations (NGOs), the business community, trade unions, professional associations—and their involvement with the UN is growing. The UN has also expanded its cooperation with research and academic institutions, youth groups and other associations.

Among the most important players at the UN are the NGOs. Some 2,100 NGOs active in economic and social development have "consultative status" with the Economic and the Social Council—the main policy making body on economic and social matters—and their representatives may be invited to address its meetings. On addition, some 1,670 NGOs carrying out information programmes on matters of concern to the UN are accredited with the UN Department of Public Information. Many NGOs have official representative at the UN headquarter, providing the UN with the valuable links to the world's people.

NGOs speak for broad international and national constituencies and have increasing influence on the UN's work. They play a prominent role at UN conferences, advancing the views of the constituencies on issues ranging from women's rights to food security. They were instrumental to the adoption of the 1997 Convention banning landmines and the establishment in 1998 of an International Criminal Court to deal with genocide, war crimes and crime against humanity. In the poorer countries, NGOs work hand in hand with the UN to assist people in need.

The United Nations has played a crucial role in the economic and social advancement of the people. In the early Cold War era, UN's efforts concentrated on relationship between nations and the issues of war and peace. It was also confronted with the challenges arising from global interdependence and social and economic inequalities. These new realities served to broaden the scope of UN activities and chart the future course of its global involvements. With the end of the Cold War, international concerns expanded to include the increasing economic competition between developed countries, problems of development, environmental degradation, population growth, and the threat of nuclear proliferation, the violation of human rights, and the political fragmentation of civil wars within national boundaries. It is the UN that is called upon to confront these new challenges and to develop solutions.

2.2 THE ORGANS

General Assembly

The General Assembly is the main deliberative organ of the United Nations. It is composed of representatives of all Member States, each of which has one vote. Decisions on important questions, such as those on peace and security, admission of new Members and budgetary matters, require a two-thirds majority. Decisions on other questions are reached by a simple majority.

Functions and Powers

Under the Charter, the functions and powers of the General Assembly include:

- to consider and make recommendations on the principles of cooperation in the maintenance of international peace and security, including the principles governing disarmament and arms regulation;
- to discuss any question relating to international peace and security and, except where a dispute or situation is being discussed by the Security Council, to make recommendations on it;
- to discuss and, with the same exception, make recommendations on any question within the scope of the Charter or affecting the powers and functions of any organ of the United Nations;
- to initiate studies and make recommendations to promote international political cooperation, the development and codification of international law, the realization of human rights and fundamental freedoms for all, and international collaboration in economic, social, cultural, educational and health fields;
- to make recommendations for the peaceful settlement of any situation, regardless of origin, which might impair friendly relations among nations;

- to receive and consider reports from the Security Council and other United Nations organs;
- to consider and approve the United Nations budget and to apportion the contributions among Members;
- to elect the non-permanent members of the Security Council, the members of the Economic and Social Council and those members of the Trusteeship Council that are elected;
- to elect jointly with the Security Council the Judges of the International Court of Justice; and, on the recommendation of the Security Council, to appoint the Secretary-General.

Sessions

The General Assembly's regular session usually begins each year in September. The 2004-05 session, for example, is the fifty-ninth regular session of the General Assembly. At the start of each regular session, the Assembly elects a new president, 21 Vice-Presidents and the Chairspersons of the Assembly's six Main Committees. To ensure equitable geographical representation, the presidency of the Assembly rotates each year among five groups of States: African, Asian, Eastern European, Latin American and Caribbean, and Western European and other States.

In addition to its regular sessions, the Assembly may meet in special sessions at the request of the Security Council, of a majority of Member States, or of one Member if the majority of Members concurs. Emergency special sessions may be called within 24 hours of a request by the Security Council on the vote of any nine Council members, or by a majority of the United Nations Members, or by one Member if the majority of Members concurs.

At the beginning of each regular session, the Assembly holds a general debate, often addressed by heads of state and government, in which Member States express their views on the most pressing international issues.

Main Committees

Most questions are then discussed in its six Main Committees:

First Committee - Disarmament and International Security Committee

Second Committee - Economic and Financial Committee

Third Committee - Social, Humanitarian and Cultural Committee

Fourth Committee - Special Political and Decolonization Committee

Fifth Committee - Administrative and Budgetary Committee

Sixth Committee - Legal Committee

Some issues are considered only in plenary meetings, rather than in one of the Main Committees. All issues are voted on through resolutions passed in plenary meetings, usually towards the end of the regular session, after the committees have completed their consideration of them and submitted draft resolutions to the plenary Assembly.

Voting in Committees is by a simple majority. In plenary meetings, resolutions may be adopted by acclamation, without objection or without a vote, or the vote may be recorded or taken by roll call.

While the decisions of the Assembly have no legally binding force for governments, they carry the weight of world opinion, as well as the moral authority of the world community. The work of the United Nations year-round derives largely from the decisions of the General Assembly that is to say, the will of the majority of the Members as expressed in resolutions adopted by the Assembly. The work is carried out:

- By the committees and other bodies established by the Assembly to study and report on specific issues, such as disarmament, peacekeeping, development and human rights;
- in international conferences called for by the Assembly and
- by the Secretariat of the United Nations - the Secretary-General and his staff of international civil servants.

The Security Council

The Security Council has primary responsibility, under the Charter, for the maintenance of international peace and security. It is so organized as to be able to function continuously, and a representative of each of its members must be present at all times at United Nations Headquarters. On 31 January 1992, the first ever Summit Meeting of the Council was convened at Headquarters, attended by Heads of State and Government of 13 of its 15 members and by the Ministers for Foreign Affairs of the remaining two. The Council may meet elsewhere than at Headquarters; in 1972, it held a session in Addis Ababa, Ethiopia, and the following year in Panama City, Panama.

When a complaint concerning a threat to peace is brought before it, the Council's first action is usually to recommend to the parties to try to reach agreement by peaceful means. In some cases, the Council itself undertakes investigation and mediation. It may appoint special representatives or request the Secretary-General to do so or to use his good offices. It may set forth principles for a peaceful settlement.

When a dispute leads to fighting, the Council's first concern is to bring it to an end as soon as possible. On many occasions, the Council has issued cease-fire directives which have been instrumental in preventing wider hostilities. It also sends United Nations peace-keeping forces to help reduce tensions in troubled areas, keep opposing forces apart and create conditions of calm in which peaceful settlements may be sought. The Council may decide on enforcement measures, economic sanctions (such as trade embargoes) or collective military action.

A Member State against which preventive or enforcement action has been taken by the Security Council may be suspended from the exercise of the rights and privileges of membership by the General Assembly on the recommendation of the Security Council. A Member State which has persistently violated the principles of the Charter may be expelled from the United Nations by the Assembly on the Council's recommendation.

A State which is a Member of the United Nations but not of the Security Council may participate, without a vote, in its discussions when the Council considers that the country's interests are affected. Both Members of the United Nations and non-members, if they are parties to a dispute being considered by the Council, are invited to take part, without a vote, in the Council's discussions; the Council sets the conditions for participation by a non-member State.

The Presidency of the Council rotates monthly, according to the English alphabetical listing of its member States.

Under the Charter, the functions and powers of the Security Council are:

- to maintain international peace and security in accordance with the principles and purposes of the United Nations;
- to investigate any dispute or situation which might/ lead to international friction;
- to recommend methods of adjusting such disputes or the terms of settlement;
- to formulate plans for the establishment of a system to regulate armaments;
- to determine the existence of a threat to the peace or act of aggression and to recommend what action should be taken;
- to call on Members to apply economic sanctions and other measures not involving the use of force to prevent or stop aggression;
- to take military action against an aggressor;
- to recommend the admission of new Members;
- to exercise the trusteeship functions of the United Nations in "strategic areas";
- to recommend to the General Assembly the appointment of the Secretary-General and, together with the Assembly, to elect the Judges of the International Court of Justice.

The Economic and Social Council

The Economic and Social Council (ECOSOC), under the overall authority of the General Assembly, coordinates the economic and social work of the United Nations and the UN family of organisations. As the central forum for discussing international economic and social issues and for formulating policy recommendations, the Council plays a key role in fostering international cooperation for development and in setting priorities for action. It coordinates the economic and social work of the UN specialized agencies, programmes and funds, and also plays a key role in formulating follow-up mechanisms to the major UN conferences, to ensure implementation. It also consults with non-governmental organisations (NGOs), thereby maintaining a vital link between the United Nations and civil society.

The Council has 54 members, elected by the General Assembly for three-year terms. It meets throughout the year and holds a major session in July, during which a special meeting of Ministers discusses major economic, social and humanitarian issues.

The Council's subsidiary bodies meet regularly and report back to it. The Commission on Human Rights, for example, monitors the observance of human rights throughout the world. Other bodies focus on such issues as social development, the status of women, crime prevention, narcotic drugs and environmental protection. Five regional commissions promote economic development and cooperation in their respective regions.

ECOSOC has seen a revitalized role in recent years as it has taken the lead in tackling many of the major challenges presented by globalization. Along with coordinating the works of the Commissions that deal with such topics as population, sustainable development and social development, it has led efforts to meet new challenges—such as closing the "digital divide" between the developed and developing countries through its work on information and communication technologies. The Council has also emerged as a forum of major importance for policy dialogue, bringing key representatives from the World Bank and the International Monetary Fund together with the diplomatic community at the UN to forge new policy directions.

Trusteeship Council

The Trusteeship Council suspended operation on 1 November 1994, with the Independence of Palau, the last remaining United Nations trust territory, on 1 October 1994.

By a resolution adopted on 25 May 1994, the Council amended its rules of procedure to drop the obligation to meet annually and agreed to meet as occasion required—by its decision or the decision of its President, or at the request of a majority of its members or the General Assembly or the Security Council.

In setting up an International Trusteeship System, the Charter established the Trusteeship Council as one of the main organs of the United Nations and assigned to it the task of supervising the administration of Trust Territories placed under the Trusteeship System. Major goals of the System were to promote the advancement of the inhabitants of Trust Territories and their progressive development towards self-government or independence. The Trusteeship Council is made up of the five permanent members of the Security Council—China, France, Russian Federation, United Kingdom and United States.

The aims of the Trusteeship System have been fulfilled to such an extent that all Trust Territories have attained self-government or independence, either as separate States or by joining neighbouring independent countries.

Under the Charter, the Trusteeship Council is authorized to examine and discuss reports from the Administering Authority on the political, economic, social and educational advancement of the peoples of Trust Territories and, in consultation with the Administering Authority, to examine petitions from and undertake periodic and other special missions to Trust Territories.

The International Court of Justice

The International Court of Justice is the principal judicial organ of the United Nations. Its seat is at the Peace Palace in The Hague (Netherlands). It began work in 1946, when it replaced the Permanent Court of International Justice which had functioned in the Peace Palace since 1922. It operates under a Statute largely similar to that of its predecessor, which is an integral part of the Charter of the United Nations.

The Court is composed of 15 judges elected to nine-year terms of office by the United Nations General Assembly and Security Council sitting independently of each other. It may not include more than one judge of any nationality. Elections are held every three years for one-third of the seats, and retiring judges may be re-elected. The Members of the Court do not represent their governments but are independent magistrates.

The judges must possess the qualifications required in their respective countries for appointment to the highest judicial offices, or be jurists of recognized competence in international law. The composition of the Court has also to reflect the main forms of civilization and the principal legal systems of the world. When the Court does not include a judge possessing the nationality of a State party to a case, that State may appoint a person to sit as a judge *ad hoc* for the purpose of the case.

The Court has a dual role: to settle in accordance with international law the legal disputes submitted to it by States, and to give advisory opinions on legal questions referred to it by duly authorized international organs and agencies.

The Court is competent to entertain a dispute only if the States concerned have accepted its jurisdiction in one or more of the following ways:

- by the conclusion between them of a special agreement to submit the dispute to the Court;
- by virtue of a jurisdictional clause, *i.e.*, typically, when they are parties to a treaty containing a provision whereby, in the event of a disagreement over its interpretation or application, one of them may refer the dispute to the Court. Several hundred treaties or conventions contain a clause to such effect;
- through the reciprocal effect of declarations made by them under the Statute whereby each has accepted the jurisdiction of the Court as compulsory in the event of a dispute with another State having made a similar declaration. The declarations of 64 States are at present in force, a number of them having been made subject to the exclusion of certain categories of dispute.

In cases of doubt as to whether the Court has jurisdiction, it is the Court itself which decides.

The procedure followed by the Court in contentious cases is defined in its Statute, and in the Rules of Court adopted by it under the Statute. The latest version of the Rules dates from 5 December 2000. The proceedings include a written phase, in which the parties file and exchange pleadings, and an oral phase consisting of public hearings at which agents and counsel address the Court. As the Court has two official languages (English and French) everything written or said in one language is translated into the other.

After the oral proceedings the Court deliberates in camera and then delivers its judgment at a public sitting. The judgment is final and without appeal. If one of the States involved fail to comply with it, the other party may have recourse to the Security Council of the United Nations.

The Court discharges its duties as a full court but, at the request of the parties, it may also establish a special chamber. The Court constituted such a chamber in 1982 for the first time, formed a second one in 1985, constituted two in 1987 and two more in 2002. A Chamber of Summary Procedure is elected every year by the Court in accordance with its Statute. In July 1993 the Court also established a seven-member Chamber to deal with any environmental cases falling within its jurisdiction

Since 1946 the Court has delivered 78 Judgments on disputes concerning inter alia land frontiers and maritime boundaries, territorial sovereignty, the non-use of force, non-interference in the internal affairs of States, diplomatic relations, hostage-taking, the right of asylum, nationality, guardianship, rights of passage and economic rights.

Sources of Applicable Law

The Court decides in accordance with international treaties and conventions in force, international custom, the general principles of law and, as subsidiary means, judicial decisions and the teachings of the most highly qualified publicists.

Advisory Opinions

The advisory procedure of the Court is open solely to international organisations. The only bodies at present authorized to request advisory opinions of the Court are five organs of the United Nations and 16 specialized agencies of the United Nations family.

On receiving a request, the Court decides which States and organisations might provide useful information and gives them an opportunity of presenting written or oral statements. The Court's advisory procedure is otherwise modelled on that for contentious proceedings, and the sources of applicable law are the same. In principle the Court's advisory opinions are consultative in character and are therefore not binding as such on the requesting bodies. Certain instruments or regulations can, however, provide in advance that the advisory opinion shall be binding.

Since 1946 the Court has given 24 Advisory Opinions, concerning inter alia admission to United Nations membership, reparation for injuries suffered in the service of the United Nations, territorial status of South-West Africa (Namibia) and Western Sahara, judgments rendered by international administrative tribunals, expenses of certain United Nations operations, applicability of the United Nations Headquarters Agreement, the status of human rights rapporteurs, and the legality of the threat or use of nuclear weapons.

The Secretariat

The Secretariat—an international staff working in duty stations around the world—carries out the diverse day-to-day work of the Organisation. It services the other principal organs of the United Nations and administers the programmes and policies laid down by them. At its head is the Secretary-General, who is appointed by the General Assembly on the recommendation of the Security Council for a five-year, renewable term.

The duties carried out by the Secretariat are as varied as the problems dealt with by the United Nations. These range from administering peacekeeping operations to mediating international disputes, from surveying economic and social trends and problems to preparing studies on human rights and sustainable development. Secretariat staff also informs the world's communications media about the work of the United Nations; organize international conferences on issues of worldwide concern; and interpret speeches and translate documents into the Organisation's official languages.

The Secretariat has a staff of about 8,900 under the regular budget drawn from some 170 countries. As international civil servants, staff members and the Secretary-General answer to the United Nations alone for their activities, and take an oath not to seek or receive instructions from any Government or outside authority. Under the Charter, each Member State undertakes to respect the exclusively international character of the responsibilities of the Secretary-General and the staff and to refrain from seeking to influence them improperly in the discharge of their duties.

The United Nations, while headquartered in New York, maintains a significant presence in Addis Ababa, Bangkok, Beirut, Geneva, Nairobi, Santiago and Vienna, and has offices all over the world.

The Secretary General is the top official of the United Nations and its Chief Administrative Officer—the symbol of the Organisation to the world, particularly the foremost international mediator and peacemaker. The Secretary General draws world attention to major global issues, from development to disarmament to human rights, and is empowered to bring to the attention of the Security Council any problem that threatens international peace and security. To help resolve international disputes, the Secretary General may carry out mediation or exercise quiet diplomacy behind the scenes.

The impartiality of the Secretary General is one of the UN's most important assets. In recent years, the Secretary General has intensified the exercise of preventive diplomacy to keep the international disputes from arising, escalating or spreading. The Secretary General has also taken the lead in efforts to reorganize and streamline the works of the UN. Working closely with the General Assembly and other bodies of the UN, it ensures that reforms are far reaching and coordinated, so that the UN may respond effectively to the needs of the Member States.

The Secretary General is also the Chairman of the United Nations System Chief Executives Board for Coordination (CEB), which meets twice annually to ensure the coordination of activities in pursuit of the common goals of Member States across a wide range of issues. It comprises of the Executive

Heads of 27 organisations, including UN funds, programmes and specialized agencies, as well as the International Atomic Energy Agency (an autonomous agency under the aegis of the UN) and the World Trade Organisation—representing the entire UN system

2.3 UNITED NATIONS SYSTEM

The UN specialized agencies and autonomous bodies have their own governing bodies, budgets and secretariats. Together with the United Nations, they are known as the UN family, or the UN system. Together, they provide technical assistance and other forms of practical help in virtually all economic and social areas.

The International Monetary Fund, the World Bank and 12 other independent organisations known as "specialized agencies" are linked to the UN through cooperative agreements. These agencies, among them the World Health Organisation and the International Civil Aviation Organisation, are autonomous bodies created by intergovernmental agreement. They have wide-ranging international responsibilities in the economic, social, cultural, educational, health and related fields. Some of them, like the International Labour Organisation and the Universal Postal Union, are older than the UN itself.

In addition, a number of UN offices, programmes and funds—such as the Office of the UN High Commissioner for Refugees (UNHCR), the UN Development Programme (UNDP) and the UN Children's Fund (UNICEF)—work to improve the economic and social condition of people around the world. They report to the General Assembly or the Economic and Social Council.

UN System at a Glance

The UN system Chief Executive Board for Coordination (CEB) is chaired by the Secretary General of the United Nations. Its members include the Secretary General and the heads of the following organisations:

- ❖ Food and Agriculture Organisation (FAO)
- ❖ International Atomic Energy Agency (IAEA)
- ❖ International Civil Aviation Organisation (ICAO)

- International Fund for Agricultural Development (IFAD)
- International Labour organisation (ILO)
- International Maritime Organisation (IMO)
- International Monetary Fund (IMF)
- International Telecommunications Union (ITU)
- United Nations International Children's Emergency Fund (UNICEF)
- United Nations Conference on Trade and Development (UNCTAD)
- United Nations Development Programme (UNDP)
- United Nations Educational, Scientific and Cultural Organisation (UNESCO)
- United Nations Environment Programme (UNEP)
- United Nations High Commissioner for Refugees (UNHCR)
- United Nations Human Settlements Programme (UN-HABITAT)
- United Nations Industrial Development Organisation (UNIDO)
- United Nations International Drug Control Programme (IDCP)
- United Nations Population Fund (UNFPA)
- United Nations Relief and Works Agency for Palestine Refugees (UNRWA)
- Universal Postal Union (UPU)
- The World Bank Group
- World Food Programme (WFP)
- World Health Organisation (WHO)
- World Intellectual Property Organisation (WIPO)
- World Meteorological Organisation (WMO)
- World Trade Organisation (WTO)

FOOD AND AGRICULTURE ORGANISATION (FAO)

The Food and Agriculture Organisation of the United Nations was founded in 1945 with a mandate to raise levels of nutrition and standards of living, to improve agricultural productivity, and to better the condition of rural populations.

Today, FAO is one of the largest specialized agencies in the United Nations system and the lead agency for agriculture, forestry, fisheries and rural development. An intergovernmental organisation, FAO has 187 member countries plus one member organisation, the European Union.

Since its inception, FAO has worked to alleviate poverty and hunger by promoting agricultural development, improved nutrition and the pursuit of food security—defined as the access of all people at all times to the food they need for an active and healthy life.

Food production has increased at an unprecedented rate since FAO was founded in 1945, outpacing the doubling of the world's population over the same period. Since the early 1960s, the proportion of hungry people in the developing world has been reduced from more than 50 percent to less than 20 percent. Despite these gains, however, more than 790 million people in the developing world—more than the total population of North America and Western Europe combined—still go hungry.

A specific priority of the Organisation is encouraging sustainable agriculture and rural development, a long-term strategy for increasing food production and food security while conserving and managing natural resources. The aim is to meet the needs of both present and future generations by promoting development that does not degrade the environment and is technically appropriate, economically viable and socially acceptable. The Food and Agriculture Organisation of the United Nations leads international efforts to defeat hunger. Serving both developed and developing countries, FAO acts as a neutral forum where all nations meet as equals to negotiate agreements and debate policy. FAO is also a source of knowledge and information.

FAO's activities comprise four main areas:

Putting information within reach. FAO serves as a knowledge network. It uses the expertise of--agronomists, foresters, fisheries and livestock specialists, nutritionists, social scientists, economists, statisticians and other professionals—to collect, analyse and disseminate data that aid development. It also publishes hundreds of newsletters, reports and books, distribute several magazines, create numerous CD-ROMS and host dozens of electronic fora.

Sharing policy expertise. FAO lends its years of experience to member countries in devising agricultural policy, supporting planning, drafting effective legislation and creating national strategies to achieve rural development and hunger alleviation goals.

Providing a meeting place for nations. Dozens of policy-makers and experts from around the globe convene at headquarters or in the field offices to forge agreements on major food and agriculture issues. As a neutral forum, FAO provides the setting where rich and poor nations can come together to build common understanding.

Bringing knowledge to the field. The wide field of knowledge is put to the test in thousands of field projects throughout the world. FAO mobilizes and manages millions of dollars provided by industrialized countries, development banks and other sources to make sure the projects achieve their goals. FAO provides the technical know-how and in a few cases is a limited source of funds.

FAO is governed by the Conference of Member Nations, which meets every two years to review the work carried out by the Organisation and approve a Programme of Work and Budget for the next biennium.

The Conference elects a Council of 49 Member Nations to act as an interim governing body. Members serve three-year, rotating terms. The Conference also elects the Director-General to head the agency.

FAO is composed of eight departments: Administration and Finance, Agriculture, Economic and Social, Fisheries, Forestry, General Affairs and Information, Sustainable Development and Technical Cooperation.

It employs more than 3450 staff members—1450 professional and 2000 general service staff—and maintains five regional offices, five sub-regional offices, five liaison offices and over 78 country offices, in addition to its headquarters in Rome.

Since 1994, FAO has undergone the most significant restructuring since its founding to decentralize operations, streamline procedures and reduce costs. Savings of $50 million a year have been realized. Highlights of the reforms include:

- increased emphasis on food security
- the transfer of staff from headquarters to the field
- increased use of experts from developing countries and countries in transition
- broadened links with the private sector and non-governmental organisations
- greater electronic access to FAO statistical databases and documents

INTERNATIONAL ATOMIC ENERGY AGENCY (IAEA)

The IAEA is the world's center of cooperation in the nuclear field. It was set up as the world's "Atoms for Peace" organisation in 1957 within the United Nations family. The Agency works with its Member States and multiple partners worldwide to promote safe, secure and peaceful nuclear technologies.

The IAEA's mission is guided by the interests and needs of Member States, strategic plans and the vision embodied in the IAEA Statute. Three main pillars—or areas of work—underpin the IAEA's mission:

- Safety and Security;
- Science and Technology and
- Safeguards and Verification.

Promoting Safeguards & Verification

The IAEA is the world's nuclear inspectorate, with more than four decades of verification experience. Inspectors work to verify that safeguarded nuclear material and activities are not used for military purposes. The Agency is additionally responsible for the nuclear file in Iraq as mandated by the UN Security Council.

The main areas of activities are:

Safeguards. The IAEA inspects nuclear and related facilities under safeguards agreements with more than 140 States. Most agreements are with States that have internationally committed themselves not to possess nuclear weapons. They are concluded pursuant to the global Treaty on the Non-Proliferation of Nuclear Weapons (NPT), for which the IAEA is the verification authority.

Verification in Iraq. Under UN Security Council resolutions, the IAEA is the inspectorate for nuclear-related monitoring and verification in Iraq. Activities are carried out through the IAEA's Iraq Nuclear Verification Office (INVO).

Additionally, the IAEA assists the international community in nuclear disarmament efforts. Under a Trilateral Initiative with the Russian Federation and United States, the IAEA is supporting steps to verify weapon-origin and other fissile materials that these two countries have released from their defense programmes.

The IAEA Department of Safeguards is the organisational hub for the IAEA's safeguards work, with INVO responsible for the Iraq nuclear file relevant to UN Security Council resolutions.

Promoting Safety & Security

The IAEA helps countries to upgrade nuclear safety and to prepare for and respond to emergencies. Work is keyed to international conventions, standards and, guidance. The main aim is to protect people and the environment from harmful radiation exposure.

Two sets of activities target priorities:

In the safety area, they cover nuclear installations, radioactive sources, radioactive materials in transport, and radioactive waste. A core element is setting and promoting the application of international safety standards for the management and regulation of activities involving nuclear and radioactive materials.

In the security area, they cover nuclear and radioactive materials, as well as nuclear installations. The focus is on helping States prevent, detect, and respond to terrorist or other malicious acts—such as illegal possession, use, transfer, and trafficking—and to protect nuclear installations and transport against sabotage.

The IAEA's work has set the framework for cooperative efforts to build and strengthen an international safety and security regime. This framework includes advisory international standards, codes, and guides; binding international conventions; international peer reviews to evaluate national operations, capabilities, and infrastructures; and an international system of emergency preparedness and response.

Also in place are targeted measures to address specific needs or concerns—two examples are the Action Plan for Protection Against Nuclear Terrorism and the Action Plan on the Safety of Radiation Sources and Security of Radioactive Materials.

The IAEA Department of Nuclear Safety and Security is the organisational hub for this pillar of the IAEA's work.

Promoting Science & Technology

The IAEA works to mobilize peaceful applications of nuclear science and technology for critical needs in developing countries. The IAEA is the world's focal point for scientific and technical cooperation in nuclear fields. The work contributes to fighting poverty, sickness, and pollution of the earth's environment, and to other global "Millennium Goals" for a safer and better future.

The main areas of activities are:

Technical Cooperation. The IAEA supports cooperative projects achieving tangible social and economic benefits for people in developing countries. Many channels and partnerships provide expert services, specialized equipment, training, and other types of support.

Research & Development. Jointly with institutes and laboratories worldwide, the IAEA supports research and development on critical problems facing developing countries. Work targets food, health, water, and environmental areas where nuclear and radiation technologies can make a difference.

Energy & Electricity. The IAEA helps countries assess and plan their energy needs, including nuclear generation of electricity. Major emphasis is placed on the role of "innovative" and advanced technologies vital to meeting the world's rising energy needs.

Where they hold comparative advantages, nuclear science and technology have become preferred solutions—and sometimes the only solutions—to many problems hindering development in poorer countries. They have made significant contributions valued at more than US $400 million to the world's major goals of sustainable development.

Three IAEA Departments lead programmes in fields of nuclear science and technology: Department of Technical Cooperation; Department of Nuclear Sciences and Applications; and Department of Nuclear Energy.

IAEA programmes and budgets are set through decisions of its own policymaking bodies—the 35-member Board of Governors and the General Conference of all Member States.

The General Conference is the highest policymaking body of the IAEA. It is composed of representatives of all Member States of the Agency. The General Conference meets annually, typically in September, to consider and approve the Agency's programme and budget and to decide on other matters brought before it by the Board of Governors, the Director General, or Member States. High-ranking officials and representatives from IAEA Member States considered a range of issues.

The IAEA convenes a Scientific Forum in conjunction with its General Conference. Forum sessions bring together international experts to examine selected topics influencing nuclear developments and the IAEA's work.

The Board of Governors is composed of 35 Member States, as designated and elected by the General Conference. The Board of Governors generally meets five times per year—in March and June, twice in September (before and after the General Conference) and in December. At its meetings, the Board examines and makes recommendations to the General Conference on the IAEA's accounts, programme, and budget and considers applications for membership. It also approves safeguards agreements and the publication of the IAEA's safety standards and has the responsibility for appointing the Director

General of the IAEA with the approval of the General Conference.

The IAEA Secretariat is headquartered at the Vienna International Center in Vienna, Austria. Operational liaison and regional offices are located in Geneva, Switzerland; New York, USA; Toronto, Canada; and Tokyo, Japan. The IAEA runs or supports research centers and scientific laboratories in Vienna and Seibersdorf, Austria; Monaco; and Trieste, Italy.

The IAEA Secretariat is a team of 2200 multi-disciplinary professional and support staff from more than 90 countries. The Agency is led by Director General and six Deputy Directors General who head the major departments.

IAEA programmes and budgets are set through decisions of its policymaking bodies—the 35-member Board of Governors and the General Conference of all Member States. Reports on IAEA activities are submitted periodically or as cases warrant to the UN Security Council and UN General Assembly. IAEA financial resources include the regular budget and voluntary contributions.

The IAEA has 137 Member States. Eighteen ratifications were required to bring the IAEA's Statute into force.

INTERNATIONAL CIVIL AVIATION ORGANISATION (ICAO)

The constitution of ICAO is the Convention on International Civil Aviation, drawn up by a conference in Chicago in November and December 1944, and to which each ICAO Contracting State is a party. According to the terms of the Convention, the Organisation is made up of an Assembly, a Council of limited membership with various subordinate bodies and a Secretariat. The chief officers are the President of the Council and the Secretary General.

The Assembly, composed of representatives from all Contracting States, is the sovereign body of ICAO. It meets every three years, reviewing in detail the work of the Organisation and setting policy for the coming years. It also votes a triennial budget.

The Council, the governing body which is elected by the Assembly for a three-year term, is composed of 33 States. The Assembly chooses the Council Member States under three headings: States of chief importance in air transport, States which make the largest contribution to the provision of facilities for air navigation, and States whose designation will ensure that all major areas of the world are represented. As the governing body, the Council gives continuing direction to the work of ICAO. It is in the Council that Standards and Recommended Practices are adopted and incorporated as Annexes to the Convention on International Civil Aviation. The Council is assisted by the Air Navigation Commission (technical matters), the Air Transport Committee (economic matters), the Committee on Joint Support of Air Navigation Services and the Finance Committee.

The Secretariat, headed by a Secretary General, is divided into five main divisions: the Air Navigation Bureau, the Air Transport Bureau, the Technical Co-operation Bureau, the Legal Bureau, and the Bureau of Administration and Services. In order that the work of the Secretariat shall reflect a truly international approach, professional personnel are recruited on a broad geographical basis.

ICAO works in close co-operation with other members of the United Nations family such as the World Meteorological Organisation, the International Telecommunication Union, the Universal Postal Union, the World Health Organisation and the International Maritime Organisation. Non-governmental organisations which also participate in ICAO's work include the International Air Transport Association, the Airports Council International, the International Federation of Air Line Pilots' Associations, and the International Council of Aircraft Owner and Pilot Associations.

INTERNATIONAL FUND FOR AGRICULTURAL DEVELOPMENT (IFAD)

The International Fund for Agricultural Development (IFAD), a specialized agency of the United Nations, was established as an international financial institution in 1977 as one of the major outcomes of the 1974 World Food Conference. The Conference was organized in response to the food crises of the early 1970s that primarily affected the Sahelian countries of Africa. The Conference resolved that "an International Fund for Agricultural Development should be established immediately to finance agricultural development projects primarily for food production in the developing countries". One of the most important insights emerging from the Conference was that the causes of food insecurity and famine were not so much failures in food production, but structural problems relating to poverty and to the fact that the majority of the developing world's poor populations were concentrated in rural areas.

In this context, IFAD was created to mobilize resources on concessional terms for programmes that alleviate rural poverty and improve nutrition. Unlike other international financial institutions, which have a broad range of objectives, the Fund has a very specific mandate: to combat hunger and rural poverty in developing countries. Under the terms of the Strategic Framework for IFAD 2002-2006, the Fund will continue to work towards *enabling the rural poor to overcome poverty*—as perceived by the poor themselves—by fostering social development, gender equity, income generation, improved nutritional status, environmental sustainability and good governance. Concretely, this implies: developing and strengthening the organisations of the poor to confront the issues they define as critical; increasing access to knowledge so that poor people can grasp opportunities and overcome obstacles; expanding the influence that the poor exert over public policy and institutions; and enhancing their bargaining power in the marketplace. All IFAD's strategic choices (as reflected in regional, country and thematic strategies; loan and grant activities; involvement in poverty reduction strategy papers; policy dialogue; and choice of development partners) will be made with these principles in mind.

The Fund's target groups, therefore, are the poorest of the world's people: small farmers, the rural landless, nomadic pastoralists, artisanal fisherfolk, indigenous people and rural poor women.

In line with the Fund's special focus on the alleviation of rural poverty in developing countries, the bulk of its resources are made available to low-income countries on highly concessional terms, repayable over 40 years, including a grace period of ten years and a 0.75% service charge per annum.

Loans may also be provided on intermediate and ordinary terms, which are less concessional.

Since its establishment, IFAD has financed 653 projects in 115 countries and independent territories, to which it has committed USD 8.1 billion in project financing. Governments and other financing sources in the recipient countries—including project beneficiaries—have contributed USD 8.0 billion to these projects. External co-financiers have provided USD 6.7 billion in co-financing of which bilateral donors contributed USD 1.1 billion, multilateral USD 5.3 billion and various international and northern NGOs USD 30.2 million. These projects have aimed at assisting approximately 50 million rural poor households, equivalent to approximately 250 million people.

Membership in the Fund is open to any state that is a member of the United Nations or any of its specialized agencies, or of the International Atomic Energy Agency. The Fund's highest authority is its Governing Council, on which all 163 Member States are represented by a Governor and an Alternate Governor. Sessions of the Governing Council are held annually and special sessions may be called when necessary. The Executive Board, consisting of 18 Members and 18 Alternate Members, oversees the Fund's operations, particularly the approval of its programme of work. The President, elected by the Governing Council for a four-year term that is renewable for one further term, is the Fund's chief executive officer and chairperson of the Executive Board.

INTERNATIONAL LABOUR ORGANISATION (ILO)

The International Labour Organisation is the UN specialized agency which seeks the promotion of social justice and internationally recognized human and labour rights. It was founded in 1919 and is the only surviving major creation of the Treaty of Versailles which brought the League of Nations into being and it became the first specialized agency of the UN in 1946.

The ILO formulates international labour standards in the form of Conventions and Recommendations setting minimum standards of basic labour rights: freedom of association, the right to organize, collective bargaining, abolition of forced labour, equality of opportunity and treatment, and other standards regulating conditions across the entire spectrum of work related issues. It provides technical assistance primarily in the fields of:

- vocational training and vocational rehabilitation;
- employment policy;
- labour administration;
- labour law and industrial relations;
- working conditions;
- management development;
- cooperatives;
- social security;
- labour statistics and occupational safety and health.

Objectives of ILO

- Promote and realize standards and fundamental principles and rights at work;
- Create greater opportunities for women and men to secure decent employment and income;
- Enhance the coverage and effectiveness of social protection for all;
- Strengthen tripartism and social dialogue;
- Cross-cutting activities.

It promotes the development of independent employers' and workers' organisations and provides training and advisory services to those organisations. Within the UN system, the ILO has a unique tripartite structure with workers and employers participating as equal partners with governments in the work of its governing organs.

The ILO accomplishes its work through three main bodies, all of which encompass the unique feature of the Organisation: its tripartite structure (government, employers and workers).

International Labour Conference. The member States of the ILO meet at the International Labour Conference in June of each year, in Geneva. Each member State is represented by two government delegates, an employer delegate and a worker delegate. They are accompanied by technical advisors.

It is generally the Cabinet Ministers responsible for labour affairs in their own countries who head the delegations, take the floor and present their governments' points of view. Employer and worker delegates can express themselves and vote according to instructions received from their organisations. They sometimes vote against each other or even against their government representatives. The Conference plays a very important role. It establishes and adopts international labour standards. It acts as a forum where social and labour questions of importance to the entire world are discussed. The Conference also adopts the budget of the Organisation and elects the Governing Body.

Executive Council. The Governing Body is the Executive Council of the ILO and meets three times a year in Geneva. It takes decisions on ILO's policy. It establishes the programme and the budget which it then submits to the Conference for adoption. It also elects the Director-General. It is composed of 28 government members, 14 employer members and 14 worker members. Ten of the government seats are permanently held by States of chief industrial importance. Representatives of other member countries are elected at the Conference every three years, taking into account geographical distribution. The employers and workers elect their own representatives respectively.

International Labour Office. The International Labour Office is the permanent secretariat of the International Labour Organisation and focal point for the overall activities that it prepares under the scrutiny of the Governing Body and under the leadership of a Director-General, who is elected for a five-year renewable term. The Office employs some 1,900 officials of over 110 nationalities at the Geneva headquarters and in 40 field offices around the world. In addition, some 600 experts undertake missions in all regions of the world under the programme of technical cooperation. The Office also constitutes a research and documentation centre and a printing house issuing a broad range of specialized studies, reports and periodicals.

INTERNATIONAL MARITIME ORGANISATION (IMO)

Shipping is perhaps the most international of all the world's great industries and one of the most dangerous. It has always been recognized that the best way of improving safety at sea is by developing international regulations that are followed by all shipping nations and from the mid-19th century onwards a number of such treaties were adopted. Several countries proposed that a permanent international body should be established to promote maritime safety more effectively, but it was not until the establishment of the United Nations itself that these hopes were realized. In 1948 an international conference in Geneva adopted a convention formally establishing IMO (the original name was the Inter-Governmental Maritime Consultative Organisation, or IMCO, but the name was changed in 1982 to IMO). The IMO Convention entered into force in 1958 and the new Organisation met for the first time the following year.

The purposes of the Organisation, as summarized by Article 1(a) of the Convention, are "to provide machinery for cooperation among Governments in the field of governmental regulation and practices relating to technical matters of all kinds affecting shipping engaged in international trade; to encourage and facilitate the general adoption of the highest practicable standards in matters concerning maritime safety, efficiency of navigation and prevention and control of marine pollution from ships". The Organisation is also empowered to deal with administrative and legal matters related to these purposes.

IMO's first task was to adopt a new version of the International Convention for the Safety of Life at Sea (SOLAS), the most important of all treaties dealing with maritime safety. This was achieved in 1960 and IMO then turned its attention to such matters as the facilitation of international maritime traffic, load lines and the carriage of dangerous goods, while the system of measuring the tonnage of ships was revised.

But although safety was and remains IMO's most important responsibility, a new problem began to emerge—pollution. The growth in the amount of oil being transported by sea and in the size of oil tankers was of particular concern and the Torrey Canyon disaster of 1967, in which 120,000 tonnes of oil was spilled, demonstrated the scale of the problem.

During the next few years IMO introduced a series of measures designed to prevent tanker accidents and to minimize their consequences. It also tackled the environmental threat caused by routine operations such as the cleaning of oil cargo tanks and the disposal of engine room wastes—in tonnage terms a bigger menace than accidental pollution.

The most important of all these measures was the International Convention for the Prevention of Pollution from Ships, 1973, as modified by the Protocol of 1978 relating thereto (MARPOL 73/78). It covers not only accidental and operational oil pollution but also pollution by chemicals, goods in packaged form, sewage, garbage and air pollution.

IMO was also given the task of establishing a system for providing compensation to those who had suffered financially as a result of pollution. Two treaties were adopted, in 1969 and 1971, which enabled victims of oil pollution to obtain compensation much more simply and quickly than had been possible before. Both treaties were amended in 1992, and again in 2000, to increase the limits of compensation payable to victims of pollution.

IMO also developed a number of other legal conventions, most of which concern liability and compensation issues.

Shipping, like all of modern life, has seen many technological innovations and changes. Some of these have presented challenges for the Organisation and others have presented opportunities. The enormous strides made in communications technology, for example, have made it possible for IMO to introduce major improvements to the maritime distress system.

In the 1970s a global search and rescue system was initiated. The 1970s also saw the establishment of the International Mobile Satellite Organisation (IMSO), which has greatly improved the provision of radio and other messages to ships.

In 1992 a further advance was made when the Global Maritime Distress and Safety System began to be phased in. In February 1999, the GMDSS became fully operational, so that now a ship that is in distress anywhere in the world can be virtually guaranteed assistance, even if the ship's crew do not have time to radio for help, as the message will be transmitted automatically.

Other measures introduced by IMO have concerned the safety of containers, bulk cargoes, liquefied gas tankers and other ship types. Special attention has been paid to crew standards, including the adoption of a special convention on standards of training, certification and watchkeeping.

The adoption of maritime legislation is still IMO's most important concern. Around 40 conventions and protocols have been adopted by the Organisation and most of them have been amended on several occasions to ensure that they are kept up to date with changes taking place in world shipping.

But adopting treaties is not enough—they have to be put into effect. This is the responsibility of Governments and there is no doubt that the way in which this is done varies considerably from country to country.

IMO has introduced measures to improve the way legislation is implemented, by assisting flag States (the countries whose flag a ship flies) and by encouraging the establishment of regional port State control systems. When ships go to foreign ports they can be inspected to ensure that they meet IMO standards. By organizing these inspections on a regional rather than a purely national basis resources can be used more efficiently.

IMO has also developed a technical co-operation programme which is designed to assist Governments which lack the technical knowledge and resources that are needed to operate a shipping industry successfully. The emphasis of this programme is very much on training and perhaps the best example is the World Maritime University in Malmö, Sweden, which was established in 1983 and provides advanced training for the men and women involved in maritime administration, education and management.

Two initiatives in the 1990s are especially important. On 1 July 1998 the International Safety Management Code entered into force and became applicable to passenger ships, oil and chemical tankers, bulk carriers, gas carriers and cargo high speed craft of 500 gross tonnage and above. It became applicable to other cargo ships and mobile offshore drilling units of 500 gross tonnage and above not later than 1 July 2002.

On 1 February 1997, the 1995 amendments to the International Convention on Standards of Training, Certification and Watchkeeping for Seafarers, 1978 entered into force. They greatly improve seafarer standards and, for the first time, give IMO itself powers to check Government actions.

It is expected that these two measures, by raising standards of management and shipboard personnel, will greatly improve safety and pollution prevention in the years to come. The emphasis on the so-called "human element" remains paramount for IMO. Meanwhile, IMO has seen a renewed focus on security issues since the terrorist atrocities in the United States in September 2001.

A new, comprehensive security regime for international shipping is set to enter into force in July 2004 following the adoption by a week-long Diplomatic Conference in December 2002 of a series of measures to strengthen maritime security and prevent and suppress acts of terrorism against shipping. The Conference was of crucial significance not only to the international maritime community but the world community as a whole, given the pivotal role shipping plays in the conduct of world trade.

With a staff of 300 people, IMO is one of the smallest of all United Nations agencies. But it has achieved considerable success in achieving its aim of "safer shipping and cleaner oceans". Ship casualty rates have declined and the amount of oil entering the sea from ships has been cut.

The challenge now facing IMO and its 163 Member States is how to maintain this success at a time when shipping is changing more rapidly than ever before.

INTERNATIONAL MONETARY FUND (IMF)

The IMF is an international organisation of 184 member countries. It was established to promote international monetary cooperation, exchange stability, and orderly exchange arrangements; to foster economic growth and high levels of employment; and to provide temporary financial assistance to countries to help ease balance of payments adjustment.

The International Monetary Fund—also known as the "IMF" or the "Fund"—was conceived at a United Nations conference convened in Bretton Woods, New Hampshire, U.S. in July 1944. The 45 governments represented at that conference sought to build a framework for economic cooperation that would avoid a repetition of the disastrous economic policies that had contributed to the Great Depression of the 1930s.

The purposes of the International Monetary Fund are:

- To promote international monetary cooperation through a permanent institution which provides the machinery for consultation and collaboration on international monetary problems.
- To facilitate the expansion and balanced growth of international trade, and to contribute thereby to the promotion and maintenance of high levels of employment and real income and to the development of the productive resources of all members as primary objectives of economic policy.
- To promote exchange stability, to maintain orderly exchange arrangements among members, and to avoid competitive exchange depreciation.
- To assist in the establishment of a multilateral system of payments in respect of current transactions between members and in the elimination of foreign exchange restrictions which hamper the growth of world trade.
- To give confidence to members by making the general resources of the Fund temporarily available to them under adequate safeguards, thus providing them with opportunity to correct maladjustments in their balance of payments without resorting to measures destructive of national or international prosperity.
- In accordance with the above, to shorten the duration and lessen the degree of disequilibrium in the international balances of payments of members.

The Fund shall be guided in all its policies and decisions by the purposes set forth in the Charter of the IMF.

Since the IMF was established its purposes have remained unchanged but its operations—which involve surveillance, financial assistance, and technical assistance—have developed to meet the changing needs of its member countries in an evolving world economy.

Surveillance involves the monitoring of economic and financial developments, and the provision of policy advice, aimed especially at crisis-prevention.

The IMF also lends to countries with balance of payments difficulties, to provide temporary financing and to support policies aimed at correcting the underlying problems; loans to low-income countries are also aimed especially at poverty reduction.

Third, the IMF provides countries with technical assistance and training in its areas of expertise. Supporting all three of these activities is IMF work in economic research and statistics.

In recent years, as part of its efforts to strengthen the international financial system, and to enhance its effectiveness at preventing and resolving crises, the IMF has applied both its surveillance and technical assistance work to the development of standards and codes of good practice in its areas of responsibility.

INTERNATIONAL TELECOMMUNICATIONS UNION (ITU)

In today's increasingly wired world, it is hard to imagine life without telecommunications. As a result of cooperative efforts between nations spanning more than a century, telecommunication networks now underpin almost every aspect of day-to-day life and are becoming increasingly important to the economic prosperity of all nations.

As the world's oldest international organisation, ITU can take much of the credit for developing the vast, interconnected web of networks which have grown to become the planet's largest man-made artifact. Established in 1865 to manage the first international telegraph networks, the Union has worked tirelessly to ensure that the latest technological advances have been rapidly integrated into the telecommunication networks of countries all around the world.

Over the last 135 years, the Union's mandate has expanded to cover the invention of voice telephony, the development of radio communications, the launch of the first communications satellites, and, most recently, the technological convergence that heralds the dawn of a new, telecommunications-based information age.

With a membership which includes almost all the world's countries and over 500 private members from the telecommunication, broadcasting and information technology sectors, ITU can boast a long and highly successful track record in developing and managing our telecommunication resources. An international organisation which is, at heart, a community of its members, today's ITU remains unsurpassed in its ability to combine an impartial, global perspective and cooperative approach with a solid technical foundation built on the expertise of hundreds of leading manufacturers, carriers and service providers.

Through the work of its study groups and its extensive programme of international and regional conferences and meetings, ITU provides a multilateral forum where governments and the private sector can meet to broker agreements in areas of mutual interest. Together, in an atmosphere of cooperation and constructive debate, ITU members forge the standards and policies which will help shape tomorrow's world.

The explosive growth of the telecommunication industry over the last two decades has increased the value of ITU membership many-fold. Through its unique, global network, the Union helps its members make the key business contacts essential to success in an increasingly competitive environment, and provides an unparalleled forum for forging alliances among an ever-widening range of players.

As the winds of change continue to sweep through the industies, transforming and reshaping the world around us, ITU's role in developing and managing essential communication resources, combined with its unique ability to bring the industry together in a spirit of partnership and cooperation, will be more important than ever before.

As it has successfully done many times in the past, ITU is committed to reviewing its procedures, its activities and its priorities to ensure it remains at the forefront of the industry it has nurtured, with the aim of serving the needs of its members even more effectively into the new millennium.

Every time someone, somewhere, picks up a telephone and dials a number, answers a call on a mobile phone, sends a fax or receives an e-mail, takes a plane or a ship, listens to the radio, watches a favourite television programme or helps a small child master the latest radio-controlled toy, they benefit from the work of the International Telecommunication Union.

The Union was established last century as an impartial, international organisation within which governments and the private sector could work together to coordinate the operation of telecommunication networks and services and advance the development of communications technology. Whilst the organisation remains relatively unknown to the general public, ITU's work over more than one hundred years has helped create a global communications network which now integrates a huge range of technologies, yet remains one of the most reliable man-made systems ever developed.

As the use of telecommunication technology and radio communication-based systems spreads to encompass an ever-wider range of activities, the vital work carried out by ITU is taking on growing importance in the day-to-day lives of people all around the world.

The Union's standardization activities, which have already helped foster the growth of new technologies such as mobile telephony and the Internet, are now being put to use in defining the building blocks of the emerging global information infrastructure, and designing advanced multimedia systems which deftly handle a mix of voice, data, audio and video signals.

Meanwhile, ITU's continuing role in managing the radio-frequency spectrum ensures that radio-based systems like cellular phones and pagers, aircraft and maritime navigation systems, scientific research stations, satellite communication systems and radio and television broadcasting all continue to function smoothly and provide reliable wireless services to the world's inhabitants.

Finally, ITU's increasingly important role as a catalyst for forging development partnerships between government and private industry is helping bring about rapid improvements in telecommunication infrastructure in the world's underdeveloped economies.

Whether in telecommunication development, standards-setting or spectrum sharing, ITU's consensus-building approach helps governments and the telecommunication industry confront and deal with a broad range of issues which would be difficult to resolve bilaterally.

The result is real-life, workable agreements which benefit not only the telecommunication industry as a whole but, ultimately, telecommunication users everywhere.

The purposes of ITU are:

- To maintain and extend international cooperation between all its Member States for the improvement and rational use of telecommunications of all kinds.
- To promote and enhance participation of entities and organisations in the activities of the Union, and to foster fruitful cooperation and partnership between them and Member States for the fulfilment of the overall objectives embodied in the purposes of the Union.
- To promote and offer technical assistance to developing countries in the field of telecommunications, and also to promote the mobilization of the material, human and financial resources needed to improve access to telecommunications services in such countries.
- To promote the development of technical facilities and their most efficient operation, with a view to improving the efficiency of telecommunication services, increasing their usefulness and making them, so far as possible, generally available to the public.
- To promote the extension of the benefits of new telecommunication technologies to all the world's inhabitants.

- To promote the use of telecommunication services with the objective of facilitating peaceful relations.
- To harmonize the actions of Member States and promote fruitful and constructive cooperation and partnership between Member States and Sector Members in the attainment of those ends.
- To promote, at the international level, the adoption of a broader approach to the issues of telecommunications in the global information economy and society, by cooperating with other world and regional intergovernmental organisations and those non-governmental organisations concerned with telecommunications.

The International Telecommunication Union is unique among international organisations in that it was founded on the principle of cooperation between governments and the private sector. With a membership encompassing telecommunication policy-makers and regulators, network operators, equipment manufacturers, hardware and software developers, regional standards-making organisations and financing institutions, ITU's activities, policies and strategic direction are determined and shaped by the industry it serves.

The three Sectors of the Union—Radiocommunication (ITU-R), Telecommunication Standardization (ITU-T), and Telecommunication Development (ITU-D)—work today to build and shape tomorrow's networks and services. Their activities cover all aspects of telecommunication, from setting standards that facilitate seamless interworking of equipment and systems on a global basis to adopting operational procedures for the vast and growing array of wireless services and designing programmes to improve telecommunication infrastructure in the developing world. ITU's work has provided the essential background that has enabled telecommunications to grow into a US$1 trillion industry worldwide.

Each of the three ITU Sectors works through conferences and meetings, where members negotiate the agreements which serve as the basis for the operation of global telecommunication services.

Study groups made up of experts drawn from leading telecommunication organisations worldwide carry out the technical work of the Union, preparing the detailed studies that lead to authoritative ITU Recommendations. ITU-R draws up the technical characteristics of terrestrial and space-based wireless services and systems, and develops operational procedures. It also undertakes the important technical studies which serve as a basis for the regulatory decisions made at radiocommunication conferences.

In ITU-T, experts prepare the technical specifications for tele-communication systems, networks and services, including their operation, performance and maintenance. Their work also covers the tariff principles and accounting methods used to provide international service.

ITU-D experts focus their work on the preparation of recommendations, opinions, guidelines, handbooks, manuals and reports, which provide decision-makers in developing countries with 'best business practices' relating to a host of issues ranging from development strategies and policies to network management.

There are currently 24 study groups spanning the Union's three Sectors (7 in ITU-R, 14 in ITU-T, 2 in ITU-D), which together produce around 550 new or revised Recommendations every year. All ITU Recommendations are non-binding, voluntary agreements.

Each Sector also has its own Bureau which ensures the implementation of the Sector's work plan and coordinates activities on a day-to-day basis.

In 1996 ITU initiated the World Telecommunication Policy Forum (WTPF), an informal international gathering convened on an ad hoc basis to harmonize telecommunication policies on issues which extend beyond the domain of any single country. The frequency of forums is determined by ITU's top policy-making body, the Plenipotentiary Conference, while the topic of each forum is determined by the Council, ITU's annual governing body.

ITU is also responsible for organizing Telecom, the world's largest and most influential telecommunication exhibition and forum. World Telecom is held every four years, with two regional events held each year in the intervening years, covering Asia, Africa, the Americas and the Arab States on a rotating basis. Designed as a service to ITU members, Telecom showcases the latest technologies and promotes in-depth discussion of key issues facing the industry through a comprehensive, wide-ranging forum programme.

UNITED NATIONS INTERNATIONAL CHILDREN'S EMERGENCY FUND (UNICEF)

UNICEF was established on 11 December 1946 by the United Nations to meet the emergency needs of children in post-war Europe and China. Its full name was the United Nations International Children's Emergency Fund.

In 1950, its mandate was broadened to address the long-term needs of children and women in developing countries everywhere. UNICEF became a permanent part of the United Nations system in 1953, when its name was shortened to the United Nations Children's Fund. However, UNICEF retained its original acronym.

UNICEF works in 158 countries around the world. Some 84 per cent of the organisation's approximately 7,100 posts are located in the field. There are eight regional offices and 125 country offices worldwide, as well as a research centre in Florence, a supply operation in Copenhagen and offices in Tokyo and Brussels. UNICEF headquarters are in New York.

The heart of UNICEF's work is in the field, with 126 country offices, some serving several countries. Each country office carries out UNICEF's mission through a unique programme of cooperation developed with the host government. This five-year programme focuses on practical ways to realize the rights of children and women. Their needs are analyzed in a situation report produced at the beginning of the programme cycle. Regional offices guide this work and provide technical assistance to country offices as needed. UNICEF's work is fully part of other United Nation's activities in a country.

Overall management and administration of the organisation takes place at headquarters in New York, where global policy on children is shaped. Specialized offices include the Supply

Division, based in Copenhagen, which provides such essential items as the majority of life-saving vaccine doses for children in developing countries.

UNICEF also operates the Innocent Research Centre in Florence and Offices for Japan and Brussels, which assist with fund-raising and liaison with policy makers.

UNICEF works through the 37 National Committees for UNICEF. These non-governmental organisations promote children's rights, raise funds, sell UNICEF greeting cards and products, create key partnerships, and provide other invaluable support. The Committees raise a third of UNICEF's resources. Well known National Committee campaigns include Check Out for Children, where guests add a donation to UNICEF to their room bill when checking out; Change For Goods, which enables passengers on international airlines to donate their leftover foreign coins and notes; and 'Trick or Treat for UNICEF,' in which millions of children in the United States, Canada, Mexico and Ireland raise funds for UNICEF.

UNICEF is supported entirely by voluntary funds. Governments contribute two thirds of our resources; private groups and some 6 million individuals contribute the rest through our National Committees.

Guiding and monitoring all of UNICEF's work is a 36-member Executive Board made up of government representatives. They establish policies, approve programmes and decide on administrative and financial plans and budgets. Members are elected by the United Nations Economic and Social Council, usually for three-year terms.

With its strong presence in 158 countries, UNICEF is the world's leading advocate for children. UNICEF is the driving force that helps build a world where the rights of every child are realized. It has the global authority to influence decision-makers, and the variety of partners at grassroots level to turn the most innovative ideas into reality. That makes it unique among world organisations, and unique among those working with the young. UNICEF consists of more than 7,000 people working in 158 countries around the world.

UNICEF believes that nurturing and caring for children are the cornerstones of human progress. UNICEF was created with this purpose in mind to work with others to overcome the obstacles that poverty, violence, disease and discrimination place in a child's path. It believes that along with its Member States it can, together, advance the cause of humanity.

UNICEF advocates for measures to give children the best start in life, because proper care at the youngest age forms the strongest foundation for a person's future. It promotes girls education ensuring that they complete primary education as a minimum, because it benefits all children, both girls and boys. It also carries out the immunization programmes against common childhood diseases, so that children are well nourished, because it is wrong for a child to suffer or die from a preventable illness.

UNICEF also works to prevent the spread of HIV/AIDS among young people. It helps children and families affected by HIV/AIDS to live their lives with dignity.

UNICEF helps involve everyone in creating protective environments for children. It is present to relieve suffering during emergencies, and wherever children are threatened, because no child should be exposed to violence, abuse or exploitation.

UNICEF upholds the Convention on the Rights of the Child. It works to assure equality for those who are discriminated against, girls and women in particular. It works for the Millennium Development Goals and for the progress promised in the United Nations Charter. UNICEF strives for peace and security and works to hold everyone accountable to the promises made for children.

It is a part of the Global Movement for Children—a broad coalition dedicated to improving the life of every child. Through this movement, and events such as the United Nations Special Session on Children, it encourages young people to speak out and participate in the decisions that affect their lives.

UNITED NATIONS CONFERENCE ON TRADE AND DEVELOPMENT (UNCTAD)

Established in 1964, the United Nations Conference on Trade and Development (UNCTAD) aims at the development-friendly integration of developing countries into the world economy with 192 countries as its member.

UNCTAD is the focal point within the United Nations for the integrated treatment of trade and development and the interrelated issues in the areas of finance, technology, investment and sustainable development. It is a forum for inter-governmental discussions and deliberations, supported by discussions with experts and exchanges of experience, aimed at consensus-building.

UNCTAD undertakes research, policy analysis and data collection in order to provide substantive inputs for the discussions of experts and government representatives. In co-operation with other organisations and donor countries, UNCTAD provides technical assistance tailored to the needs of the developing countries, with special attention being paid to the needs of the least developed countries, and countries with economy in transition.

UNCTAD's work is focused on four areas of activity: globalization and development; investment enterprise development and technology; trade in goods and services and commodity issues; and services infrastructure for development trade efficiency and human resources development. In each of these areas priority is attached to providing assistance to developing countries in particular least-developed countries, small Island developing States, landlocked developing countries. Structurally weak and vulnerable economies and economies in transition are also be taken into account.

The UNCTAD Secretariat provides substantive and technical services to the intergovernmental bodies of UNCTAD in their discussions and deliberations. Since its inception in 1964, the secretariat has thus serviced 11 sessions of the United Nations Conference on Trade and Development, meeting every four years. The UNCTAD XI summit was held in Sao Paulo, Brazil in June 2004. It has also fully serviced three United Nations Conferences on the Least Developed Countries, meeting every 10 years with the third Conference having taken place in Brussels, Belgium, in May 2001.

In performing its functions, the Secretariat works together with member Governments and interacts with organisations of the United Nations system and regional commissions, as well as with governmental institutions, non-governmental organisations, the private sector, including trade and industry associations, research institutes and universities worldwide.

The Bangkok Declaration and Plan of Action, adopted in February 2000 at the tenth session of UNCTAD, provide the main thrust for the current work of UNCTAD, which relates to:

International trade. Identifying international trade policy tools supportive of development efforts in a globalizing economy; suggesting ways and means to address the constraints faced by developing countries in deriving full benefits from the multilateral trading system; providing technical support to developing countries in understanding trade-related negotiation issues; addressing issues related to competition law and policy; development and diversification of the commodity sector; promoting risk management against commodity price fluctuations; addressing constraints faced by the developing countries in responding to environmental challenges.

Investment, enterprise and technology. Analyzing trends in foreign direct investment and its impact on development; understanding issues involved in international investment agreements so as to attract and benefit from foreign direct investment; enhancing interaction between domestic and foreign investment; assisting capacity-building efforts and the development of small and medium-size enterprises in a globalizing economy; supporting efforts to respond to technological and scientific changes; developing policy instruments to facilitate technology transfer.

Globalization, interdependence and development. Conducting research on the broad trends and prospects in the world economy and examining successful development experiences to help promote policies and strategies at the national and international level that are conducive to development; analysing the causes and effects of financial crises and contributing to the debate on measures for the prevention, management and resolution of such crises; providing technical assistance for the management of external debt and suggesting solutions to the debt problem of developing countries; contributing to the implementation of the United Nations New Agenda for the Development of Africa (UN-NADAF).

Services infrastructure for development, trade efficiency, and human resources development. Facilitating international trade through better use of information technologies and management systems in trade-supporting services; carrying out capacity-building activities and training in these areas; analysing the challenges and opportunities for developing countries of using e-commerce for development; enhancing multimodal transport and trade logistics, with special attention to the particular difficulties encountered by landlocked developing countries and transit developing countries.

Least developed, landlocked and small island developing countries. Assisting in the implementation of the United Nations Programme of Action for the Least Developed Countries for the Decade 2001-2010, adopted in Brussels, Belgium, in May 2001, with particular attention to the special handicaps of landlocked developing countries and small island developing States.

Technical cooperation activities. An important element in achieving the objectives and policies outlined in the Bangkok Declaration and Plan of Action, UNCTAD's technical co-operation emphasizes knowledge sharing and enhancement, human resources development, productive capacity building, as well as support to trade facilitation and logistics, as instruments to facilitate a more equitable integration of developing countries into the global economy and to enhance their economic growth and development prospects.

UNITED NATIONS DEVELOPMENT PROGRAMME (UNDP)

UNDP is the UN's global development network, advocating for change and connecting countries to knowledge, experience and resources to help people build a better life. On the ground in 166 countries, UNDP uses its global network to help the UN system and its partners to raise awareness and track progress, while it connects countries to the knowledge and resources needed to achieve these goals.

The substantive focus is on helping countries build and share solutions to the challenges of:

Democratic Governance. More countries than ever before are working to build democratic governance. Their challenge is to develop institutions and processes that are more responsive to the needs of ordinary citizens, including the poor. UNDP brings people together within nations and around the world, building partnerships and sharing ways to promote participation and effectiveness at all levels. It uses the support of Information and Communications Technology (ICT) to improve government accountability. It helps countries strengthen their electoral and legislative systems, improve access to justice and public administration, and develop a greater capacity to deliver basic services to those most in need.

Poverty Reduction. Developing countries are working to create their own national poverty eradication strategies based on local needs and priorities. UNDP advocates for these nationally owned solutions and helps ensure their effectiveness. We sponsor innovative pilot projects, including those relying on ICT to help enhance service delivery; connect countries to global best practices and resources; promote the role of women in development; and bring governments, civil society and outside funders together to coordinate their efforts.

Crisis Prevention and Recovery. Many countries are increasingly vulnerable to violent conflicts or natural disasters that can erase decades of development and further entrench poverty and inequality. Through its global network, UNDP seeks out and shares innovative approaches to crisis prevention, early warning and conflict resolution. And UNDP is on the ground in almost every developing country—so wherever the next crisis occurs, we will be there to help bridge the gap between emergency relief and long-term development.

Energy and Environment. Energy and environment are essential for sustainable development. The poor are disproportionately affected by environmental degradation and lack of access to clean affordable energy services. These issues are also global as climate change, loss of biodiversity and ozone layer depletion cannot be addressed by countries acting alone. UNDP helps countries strengthen their capacity to address these challenges at global, national and community levels, seeking out and sharing best practices, providing innovative policy advice and linking partners through pilot projects that help poor people build sustainable livelihoods.

HIV/AIDS. To prevent the spread of HIV/AIDS and reduce its impact, developing countries need to mobilize all levels of government and civil society. As a trusted development partner, UNDP advocates for placing HIV/AIDS at the centre of national planning and budgets; helps build national capacity to manage initiatives that include people and institutions not usually involved with public heath; and promotes decentralized responses that support community-level action. Because HIV/AIDS is a world-wide problem, UNDP supports these national efforts by offering knowledge, resources and best practices from around the world.

In each of these five practices, UNDP advocates for the protection of human rights and especially the empowerment of women. Through our global network, we seek out and share ways to promote gender equality as an essential dimension of ensuring political participation and accountability; economic empowerment and effective development planning; crisis prevention and conflict resolution; access to clean water, sanitation and energy services; the best use of new technologies for development purposes; and society-wide mobilization against HIV/AIDS.

UNDP also engages in extensive advocacy work. The annual Human Development Report 2003, commissioned by UNDP, focuses the global debate on key development issues, providing new measurement tools, innovative analysis and often controversial policy proposals. It is guided by the belief that development is ultimately "a process of enlarging people's choices", not just raising national incomes. The independent team of experts who write the Report draw on a worldwide network of leaders from academic, government and civil society who contribute data, ideas, and best practices. Developing countries and their international partners use the Report to gauge results and shape new policies.

The global Report's analytical framework and inclusive approach carry over into regional, national and local Human Development Reports, also supported by UNDP. So far, more than 420 National Human Development Reports have been published in 135 countries. These Reports are created by national experts and intellectuals who draw on UNDP's global network for advice and inspiration; their success shows how quality research and advocacy can spur policy debates, draw political attention to pressing issues, and help countries build their own development solutions.

In each country office, the UNDP Resident Representative normally also serves as the Resident Coordinator of development activities for the United Nations system as a whole. Through such coordination, UNDP seeks to ensure the most effective use of UN and international aid resources.

It integrates information and communications technology for development into its work in democratic governance and poverty reduction, helping developing countries improve government accountability and service delivery. UNDP helps countries attract and use aid effectively. In all the activities, UNDP promotes the protection of human rights and the empowerment of women.

UNDP delivers most of its services through its more than 130 country offices but it also engages in global and regional advocacy and analysis to increase knowledge, share best practices, build partnerships, mobilize resources, and promote enabling frameworks including international targets for reducing poverty. In addition, UNDP supports Technical Cooperation Among Developing Countries.

UNDP has helped more than 120 developing countries produce their own National Human Development Report 2003, which provides a basis for informed local debate about priorities and policies. These reports also help donor governments to measure the impact of their aid dollars, and to communicate the way in which aid is making a positive difference both to direct beneficiaries and to electorates at home.

UNITED NATIONS EDUCATIONAL, SCIENTIFIC AND CULTURAL ORGANISATION (UNESCO)

UNESCO—the United Nations Educational, Scientific and Cultural Organisation—was born on November 16, 1945. For this specialized UN agency, it is not enough to build classrooms in devastated countries or to restore world heritage sites (to publish scientific breakthroughs). Education, Social and Natural Science, Culture and Communication are the means to a far more ambitious goal: to build peace in the minds of men. Today, UNESCO works as a laboratory of ideas and a standard-setter to forge universal agreements on emerging ethical issues. The Organisation also serves as a clearinghouse—that disseminates and shares information and knowledge—while helping Member States to build their human and institutional capacities in diverse fields. In short, UNESCO promotes international co-operation among its 190 Member States and six Associate Members in the fields of education, science, culture and communication.

UNESCO works to create the conditions for true dialogue, based upon respect for commonly shared values and the dignity of each civilization and culture. This role is critical, particularly in the face of terrorism, which constitutes an attack against humanity. The world urgently requires global visions of sustainable development based upon observance of human rights, mutual respect and the alleviation of poverty, all of which lie at the heart of UNESCO's mission and activities.

The General Conference is the primary decision-making body, comprising representatives of all Member States. It meets every two years to determine the policies and main lines of work of the Organisation. Following the principle of one vote per country, it approves UNESCO's programme and budget. Every four years, it appoints the Director-General based upon the recommendation of the Executive Board. The Executive Board, composed of 58 Member States, meets twice a year to ensure that decisions taken by the General Conference are implemented. It is also responsible for preparing the work of the General Conference and examining the Organisation's programme and budget.

The Secretariat consists of the Director-General and staff. The Director-General is the executive head of the Organisation. He or she formulates proposals for appropriate action by the Conference and Board and prepares a draft biennial programme and budget. The staff implements the approved programme. As a result of a new decentralization policy, more than 640 staff members work in UNESCO's 53 field offices around the world.

UNESCO is the only UN agency to have a system of National Commissions in 190 Member and Associate States. The Commissions form a vital link between civil society and the Organisation. They provide valuable insight concerning the Organisation's programme and help implement many initiatives including training programmes, studies, public awareness campaigns and media outreach. The Commissions also develop new partnerships with the private sector, which can provide valuable technical expertise and financial resources.

UNESCO plays an integral role in the UN system and works closely with a wide range of regional and national organisations. Some 330 non-governmental organisations (NGOs) maintain official relations with UNESCO and hundreds more work with the Organisation on specific projects.

The regular two-year budget is financed by Member States through assessed contributions also benefits from substantial extra-budgetary funding to strengthen its programmes, especially in the field, and to increase its outreach activities. In 2002-2003, these extra-budgetary resources amounted to some US $400 million.

Three main strategic thrusts:

- Developing and promoting universal principles and norms, based on shared values, in order to meet emerging challenges in education, science, culture and communication and to protect and strengthen the "common public good";
- Promoting pluralism, through recognition and safeguarding of diversity together with the observance of human rights;
- Promoting empowerment and participation in the emerging knowledge society through equitable access, capacity-building and sharing of knowledge.

Twelve strategic objectives:

Education

- Promoting education as a fundamental right in accordance with the Universal Declaration of Human Rights;
- Improving the quality of education through the diversification of contents and methods and the promotion of universally shared values;
- Promoting experimentation, innovation and the diffusion and sharing of information and best practices as well as policy dialogue in education.

Sciences

- Promoting principles and ethical norms to guide scientific and technological development and social transformation;
- Improving human security by better management of the environment and social change;
- Enhancing scientific, technical and human capacities to participate in the emerging knowledge societies.

Culture

- Promoting the drafting and implementation of standard-setting instruments in the cultural field;
- Safeguarding cultural diversity and encouraging dialogue among cultures and civilizations;
- Enhancing the linkages between culture and development, through capacity-building and sharing of knowledge.

Communication and Information

- Promoting the free flow of ideas and universal access to information;
- Promoting the expression of pluralism and cultural diversity in the media and world information networks;
- Access for all to information and communication technologies, especially in the public domain.

UNESCO deploys its action in the fields of Education, Natural Sciences, Social and Human Sciences, Culture,

Communication and Information. Through its strategies, UNESCO is actively contributing to the achievement of the United Nations Millenium Development Goals. Overall, it is formulated around a single unifying theme—UNESCO contributing to peace and human development in an era of globalization through education, science, culture and communication. Thus, it seeks to create a link between UNESCO's mandate and role on the one hand and globalization with a human face on the other hand.

UNITED NATIONS ENVIRONMENT PROGRAMME (UNEP)

The mission of the United Nations Environment Programme is to provide leadership and encourage partnership in caring for the environment by inspiring, informing, and enabling nations and peoples to improve their quality of life without compromising that of future generations.

UNEP, established in 1972, is the voice for the environment within the United Nations system. UNEP acts as a catalyst, advocate, educator and facilitator to promote the wise use and sustainable development of the global environment. To accomplish this, UNEP works with a wide range of partners, including United Nations entities, international organisations, national governments, non-governmental organisations, the private sector and civil society.

UNEP work encompasses:

- Assessing global, regional and national environmental conditions and trends.
- Developing international and national environmental instruments.
- Strengthening institutions for the wise management of the environment.
- Facilitating the transfer of knowledge and technology for sustainable development.
- Encouraging new partnerships and mind-sets within civil society and the private sector.

UNEP's global and cross-sectoral outlook is reflected in its organisational structure, its activities and its personnel. Being based in Africa gives UNEP a clear advantage in understanding the environmental issues facing the world's developing countries.

To ensure its global effectiveness UNEP supports six regional offices, plus a growing network of centres of excellence such as the Global Resource Information Database (GRID) centres and the UNEP World Conservation Monitoring Centre (UNEP-WCMC). UNEP also has major offices in Geneva and Paris, where its Division of Technology, Industry and Economics is situated.

UNEP also hosts several environmental convention secretariats including the Ozone Secretariat and the Montreal Protocol's Multilateral Fund, CITES (the Convention on International Trade in Endangered Species of Wild Fauna and Flora), the Convention on Biological Diversity, the Convention on Migratory Species, and a growing family of chemicals-related agreements, including the Basel Convention on the Transboundary Movement of Hazardous Wastes and the recently negotiated Stockholm Convention on Persistent Organic Pollutants (POPs).

UNEP was the driving force behind the 1987 Montreal Protocol on Substances that Deplete the Ozone Layer. As a result of this global agreement, industrialized countries ceased production and consumption of a significant proportion of all ozone depleting substances in 1996. The diminishing worldwide consumption of ozone-depleting substances—nearly 75% in the last seven years led to a simultaneous decline in the growth rate of these substances in the atmosphere. An estimated 1.5 million cases of melanoma skin cancer due to the sun's UV-B radiation will be averted by the year 2060 as a result of the Protocol.

UNEP is the leading force for the global sound management of hazardous chemicals and to reduce or eliminate risks they pose to human health and the environment. UNEP jointly with FAO successfully facilitated the negotiation of an international legally binding instrument on the Prior Informed Consent Procedure for Certain Hazardous Chemicals and pesticides in International Trade. UNEP is currently managing the negotiation of a legally binding instrument on persistent Organic Pollutants. Through the Chemical programme of information dissemination and capacity building, UNEP has helped to close the gap between the world's technical knowledge and expertise on hazardous chemicals management and the people who need to use it.

UNEP is actively promoting the Global Reporting Initiative developed in partnership with leading multi stakeholder organisations to encourage voluntary environmental reporting by companies around the world. A global set of guidelines for corporate sustainability reporting has been developed and over 20 corporations from around the world have agreed to actively pilot test the guidelines.

UNEP is a driving force to engage private sector leaders in a change of course towards sustainability, in particular through the voluntary initiatives developed in the field of mining, telecommunication, tourism and financial services.

UNEP is the leading force for the global sound management of hazardous chemicals and to reduce or eliminate risks they pose to human health and the environment. UNEP jointly with FAO successfully facilitated the negotiation of an international legally binding instrument on the Prior Informed Consent Procedure for Certain Hazardous Chemicals and pesticides in International Trade. UNEP is currently managing the negotiation of a legally binding instrument on persistent Organic Pollutants. Through the Chemical programme of information dissemination and capacity building, UNEP has helped to close the gap between the world's technical knowledge and expertise on hazardous chemicals management and the people who need to use it.

UNEP has been at the forefront of efforts to protect the world's biological diversity by forging the Convention on Biological Diversity. By administering the Convention on International Trade in Endangered Species of Wild Fauna and Flora (CITES), UNEP helps protect over 30,000 of the world's endangered species. As a result, the elephant has been brought back from the brink of extinction, thanks to the ban on international trade in ivory and other elephant products. UNEP's key role led to an increase in the number of rhinoceroses in Kenya, Namibia, South Africa, peninsular Malaysia and India.

UNITED NATIONS HIGH COMMISSIONER FOR REFUGEES (UNHCR)

The Office of the United Nations High Commissioner for Refugees was established on December 14, 1950 by the United Nations General Assembly. The agency is mandated to lead and co-ordinate international action to protect refugees and resolve refugee problems worldwide. Its primary purpose is to safeguard the rights and well-being of refugees. It strives to ensure that everyone can exercise the right to seek asylum and find safe refuge in another State, with the option to return home voluntarily, integrate locally or to resettle in a third country.

UNHCR is one of the world's principal humanitarian agencies, its staff of more than 5,000 personnel helping some 20 million people in more than 120 countries. During its half century of work, the agency provided assistance to at least 50 million people, earning two Nobel Peace Prizes in 1954 and 1981.

UNHCR's programmes, its protection and other policy guidelines, are approved by an Executive Committee of 64 member states which meets annually in Geneva. A second 'working group' or Standing Committee meets several times a year. The High Commissioner reports on the results of the agency's work annually to the U.N. General Assembly through the Economic and Social Council.

As a humanitarian, non-political organisation, UNHCR has two basic and closely related aims i.e. to protect refugees and to seek ways to help them restart their lives in a normal environment.

International protection is the cornerstone of the agency's work. In practice that means ensuring respect for a refugee's basic human rights and ensuring that no person will be returned involuntarily to a country where he or she has reason to fear persecution—a process known as refoulement.

UNHCR promotes international refugee agreements and monitors government compliance with international refugee law. Its staff work in a variety of locations ranging from capital cities to remote camps and border areas, attempting to provide the above mentioned protection and to minimize the threat of violence, including sexual assault, which many refugees are subject to, even in countries of asylum.

The organisation seeks long-term or 'durable' solutions by helping refugees repatriate to their homeland if conditions warrant, by helping them to integrate in their countries of asylum or to resettle in third countries.

UNHCR's first mandate was of limited geographical scope and time—a three-year programme to help principally European refugees. In the intervening decades the problem of displaced people became both more complex and took on a global dimension. UNHCR changed along with the problem. It expanded from a relatively small, specialized agency to an organisation with offices in more than 120 countries, a $1 billion annual budget, the capacity to provide not only legal protection but also material relief in major emergencies, and the ability to help increasingly diverse groups of dispossessed people.

The term refugee is a very specific definition covering only people who have fled their homeland and sought sanctuary in a second country. However, there are millions of people in similar desperate circumstances but who do not legally qualify as refugees and are therefore not eligible for normal relief or protection. Increasingly, UNHCR has provided assistance to some of these groups.

Globally, there are an estimated 20-25 million so-called internally displaced persons (IDPs), people who have fled their homes, generally during a civil war, but have stayed in their home countries rather than seeking refuge abroad. UNHCR helps 6.3 million of these internally displaced, but as the new millennium began an international debate was underway on how the humanitarian community could provide more sustained and comprehensive assistance to this group.

UNHCR assists people who have been granted protection on a group basis or on purely humanitarian grounds, but who have not been formally recognized as refugees and assists and monitors the reintegration of refugees who have returned to their own countries.

UNHCR can only offer effective legal protection if a person's basic needs—shelter, food, water, sanitation and medical care—

are also met. The agency therefore coordinates the provision and delivery of such items and has designed specific projects for vulnerable women, children and the elderly who comprise 80 percent of a—normal' refugee population. Makeshift tents made from UNHCR blue plastic sheeting became immediately recognizable symbols in major emergencies which in the last decade included operations to help millions of people in Kosovo, Timor, Africa's Great Lakes region, West Africa, the Balkans and in the aftermath of the Gulf War. In Central America, and later in other parts of the world, UNHCR developed the concept of Quick Impact Projects or QIPs. These projects, usually small-scale programmes to rebuild schools and clinics, repair roads, bridges and wells, were designed to bridge the gap between emergency assistance provided to refugees and people returning home and longer-term development aid undertaken by other agencies.

In the aftermath of World War II, UNHCR concentrated on resettling the bulk of the refugees under its mandate in new countries. But as the number of displaced people increased dramatically worldwide, so did both the attitudes of countries receiving refugees and the uprooted peoples themselves. Many states remain willing to help civilians fleeing conflicts such as Bosnia and Kosovo, but only on a temporary basis. The great majority of today's refugees would themselves prefer to return home once the situation stabilizes.

In these circumstances, UNHCR encourages voluntary return by providing transportation, financial incentives and practical help such as seeds, farming equipment and building materials. When Quick Impact Projects (QIPs) are approved, they are designed not only to help returning refugees, but also members of local communities which, in developing countries, are often as poor and deprived as the refugees themselves.

When it is sometimes impossible for refugees to go home, UNHCR helps them either to integrate in countries where they first sought asylum or to go to one of around a dozen states which regularly accept refugees for permanent resettlement.

While UNHCR has strengthened its ability to handle major emergencies, it devotes more resources to trying to avert these crises by anticipating and preventing huge population movements from global trouble spots. One approach is to put in place a so-called early warning system—establishing an international monitoring presence to confront problems before conflict breaks out. UNHCR, for instance, undertook the preventive deployment of staff to five former Soviet republics in Central Asia which were experiencing serious internal tensions following Independence.

Such humanitarian initiatives are helpful, but governments and international political bodies must ultimately make political decisions to solve refugee and other human displacement problems. Regional initiatives such as the International Conference on Central American Refugees (1989), the International Conference on Indo-Chinese Refugees (1989) and a later Commonwealth of Independent States (CIS) Conference in Geneva were important steps in this direction.

As humanitarian crises have become more complex, UNHCR has expanded both the number and types of organisations it works with. United Nations sister agencies include the World Food Program (WFP), which supplies food and basic commodities to refugees, the U.N. Children's Fund (UNICEF), the World Health Organisation (WHO), the U.N. Development Program (UNDP), the Office for the Coordination of Humanitarian Affairs (OCHA) and the U.N. High Commissioner for Human Rights.

Other organisations include the International Committee of the Red Cross (ICRC), the International Federation of Red Cross and Red Crescent Societies (IFRC), the International Organisation for Migration (IOM) and more than 500 non-governmental organisations.

More unorthodox, and at times controversial partners, have included U.N. peacekeepers in the former Yugoslavia, Kosovo and Timor, various militaries which provided logistical support in Rwanda and Kosovo and financial institutions such as the World Bank with which UNHCR has signed a Framework of Cooperation.

UNHCR is funded almost entirely by voluntary contributions, principally from governments but also from intergovernmental organisations, corporations and individuals.

It receives a limited subsidy of under two percent of its budget from the United Nations regular budget for administrative costs and accepts—in kind' contributions including such things as tents, medicines, trucks and air transportation.

As the number of persons of concern to UNHCR jumped to a high of 27 million in 1995, its budget rose accordingly, from $564 million in 1990 to more than $1 billion for most of the 1990s. The budget until recently was divided into two parts: general programmes supporting ongoing, basic operations such as refugee protection and assistance, and special programmes covering emergencies, voluntary repatriation and non-refugee programmes. Starting January 1, 2000, programmes were consolidated into a unified budget—the Annual Programme Budget—which will provide a more transparent and comprehensive picture of the totality of the organisation's work and financial needs.

UNITED NATIONS HUMAN SETTLEMENTS PROGRAMME (UN-HABITAT)

The United Nations Human Settlements Programme, UN-HABITAT, is the United Nations agency for human settlements. It is mandated by the UN General Assembly to promote socially and environmentally sustainable towns and cities with the goal of providing adequate shelter for all. It was established in 1978 after Vancouver Agreement and was known as Habitat-I. From 1978 to 1997, with meagre support and an unfocused mandate, Habitat struggled almost alone among multi-lateral organisations to prevent and ameliorate problems stemming from massive urban growth, especially among cities of the developing world. From 1997 to 2002, by which time half the world had become urban, UN-HABITAT—guided by the Habitat Agenda and the Millennium Declaration—underwent a major revitalisation, using its experience to identify emerging priorities for sustainable urban development and to make needed course corrections.

In 1996, the United Nations held a second conference on cities, *Habitat II,* in Istanbul, Turkey to assess two decades of progress since Vancouver and set fresh goals for the new millennium. Adopted by 171 countries, the political document that came out of this "City Summit" is known as the *Habitat Agenda* and contains over 100 commitments and 600 recommendations.

On 1 January 2002, the agency's mandate was strengthened and its status elevated to that of a fully fledged programme of the UN system in UN General Assembly Resolution A/56/206. Key recommendations and fine tuning of the agenda are now underway as strategy clusters for achieving the urban development and shelter goals and targets of the *Millennium Declaration*—the United Nations' development agenda for the next 15 to 20 years. The revitalisation has placed UN-HABITAT squarely in the mainstream of the UN's development agenda for poverty reduction with a more streamlined and effective structure and staff, and more relevant and focused set of programmes and priorities.

It is through this agenda that UN-HABITAT contributes to the overall objective of the United Nations system to reduce poverty and promote sustainable development. Its partners range from governments and local authorities to a wide international cross-section of Non-Governmental Organisations and civil society groups.

Strategic Vision

Urban poverty reduction strategies derive from an understanding of current conditions and trends (e.g., urbanization, globalization, the growth of slums and the gross inequities in urban life) and from the norms and principles that guide the United Nations response to these conditions. These norms and principles include, among others, sustainable urban development, adequate shelter for all, improvement in the lives of slum dwellers, access to safe water and sanitation, social inclusion, environmental protection and the various human rights. With experience and understanding also comes the recognition that urban and shelter finance mechanisms are essential to poverty reduction and, also, that very little may be achieved without collaborative effort as expressed in partnerships.

With these imperatives in mind and with a sharper focus on urban poverty and, in particular, slums as the most visible manifestation of urban poverty within the overall urbanization process, the UN-HABITAT strategic vision has been further refined, giving more attention to knowledge management, the financing of housing and human settlements and, particularly, to strategic partnerships. The expanded strategic vision is both forward looking and pragmatic, being consistent with social norms and political principles as well as with UN-HABITAT mandates, capabilities and partners' objectives. Its main elements are:

- Knowledge management and reporting, expanding the global understanding of urban development, shelter and poverty, and tracking progress in implementing the Habitat Agenda;
- Advocacy of norms for sustainable urbanization and urban poverty reduction, carried forward through two global campaigns and a number of global programmes;
- Technical cooperation in linking norms and campaign/ programme goals to urban poverty reduction activities on the ground;
- Innovative financing for urbanization and specific shelter needs of the urban poor and
- Strategic partnerships to leverage resources and coordinate international programme activities that work toward similar ends.

Organisational Structure

The Executive Director of UN-HABITAT is United Nations under Secretary-General. Headquartered in Nairobi, Kenya, with a team of some 200 international and local staff, the agency has regional offices for Asia and the Pacific in Fukuoka, Japan, for Latin America and the Caribbean in Rio de Janeiro, Brazil, and for Africa and the Arab States in Nairobi. The regional office for Eastern Europe and Transition Countries is also based in Nairobi.

The agency has three main divisions which each oversee a set of programmes:

The Shelter and Sustainable Human Settlements Development Division. It coordinates the agency's global advocacy functions. Its departments are the Shelter Branch which focuses on the Global Campaign for Secure Tenure;

the Water, Sanitation and Infrastructure Branch which promotes access to basic services and raises awareness on water and sanitation mainly through the *Water for African Cities* programme, and the *Water for Asian Cities* programme; the Training and Capacity Building Branch which helps strengthen local authority and civil society management capacity through training and organisation development; and the Urban Development Branch which runs UN-HABITAT's *Global Campaign on Urban Governance.* It also runs the Safer Cities Programme, the Urban Management Programme, the Risk and Disaster Management Programme, and a programme called *Localising Agenda 21* which seeks to ensure crucial environmental issues are brought into urban development planning.

The Monitoring and Research Division. Also known as the Urban Secretariat, this division runs three programmes. The Monitoring Systems Branch that keeps a closely documented watch over the conditions of human settlements ranging from rights and policy issues, to the lessons learned through the Best Practices Programme and the Local Leadership Programme; the Policy Analysis, Synthesis and Dialogue Branch, which focuses on enhancing the agency's policies and produces its two flagship reports; and the Urban Economy and Finance Branch which looks at employment issues in urban areas, especially the informal sector in developing nations, and ways of developing municipal and housing finance systems.

The Regional and Technical Cooperation Division. It is responsible for implementing the agency's technical cooperation programmes and projects around the world. It oversees the regional offices.

UN-HABITAT runs two major worldwide campaigns—the *Global Campaign on Urban Governance,* and the *Global Campaign for Secure Tenure.* Through these campaigns and by other means, the agency focuses on a range of issues and special projects which it helps implement.

These include a joint UN-HABITAT/World Bank slum upgrading initiative called the *Cities Alliance,* promoting effective housing development policies and strategies, helping develop and campaigning for housing rights, promoting sustainable cities and urban environmental planning and management, post-conflict land-management and reconstruction in countries devastated by war or natural disasters. Others take in water and sanitation and solid waste management for towns and cities, training and capacity building for local leaders, ensuring that women's rights and gender issues are brought into urban development and management policies, helping fight crime through UN-HABITAT's *Safer Cities Programme*, research and monitoring of urban economic development, employment, poverty reduction, municipal and housing finance systems, and urban investment. It also helps strengthen rural-urban linkages, and infrastructure development and public service delivery.

UN-HABITAT also has some 154 technical programmes and projects in 61 countries around the world, most of them in the least developed countries. These include major projects in post-war societies such as Afghanistan, Kosovo, Somalia, Iraq, Rwanda, and the Democratic Republic of Congo, to name a few. The agency's operational activities help governments create policies and strategies aimed at strengthening a self-reliant management capacity at both national and local levels. They focus on promoting shelter for all, improving urban governance, reducing urban poverty, improving the living environment and managing disaster mitigation and post-conflict rehabilitation.

A key function of UN-HABITAT in fulfilling its mandate is the monitoring of global trends and conditions and the assessment of progress in implementing the Habitat Agenda at the international, regional, national and local levels. The monitoring function is done through two main instruments: Global Urban Observatory and Statistics and Best Practices. By working at all levels and with all relevant stakeholders and partners, the agency contributes to linking policy development and capacity-building activities with a view to promoting cohesive and mutually reinforcing social, economic and environmental policies. On the request from the Human Settlements Commission the agency has devised a monitoring system. The UN-HABITAT monitoring system has three main components:

The Statistics Programme which regularly collects data from member countries and cities.

The Urban Indicator Programme which regularly collects indicators from more than 200 cities.

The Best Practices Programme, which has compiled over 1,100 best practice cases in 600 cities.

The agency is participating in tracking Millennium Declaration goals by providing 4 indicators and slum index based on them for Goal 7, target 11. Those indicators are:

- Percentage of people with access to sanitation.
- Percentage of people with access to safe water.
- Percentage of people with secure tenure.
- Percentage of people in permanent housing/dwelling.

Every two years, UN-HABITAT's work and relationships with its partners are examined in detail by a Governing Council composed of 58 member states. It is a high-level forum of governments at the ministerial level during which policy guidelines and the organisation's budget are established for the next two-year period.

The Governing Council reports to the General Assembly through the Economic and Social Council (ECOSOC) which coordinates the work of the subsidiary bodies of the General Assembly. The governments have representatives in Nairobi with whom senior UN-HABITAT officials meet regularly throughout the year in the Committee of Permanent Representatives (CPR).

UNITED NATIONS INDUSTRIAL DEVELOPMENT ORGANISATION (UNIDO)

UNIDO was set up in 1966 and became a specialized agency of the United Nations in 1985. As part of the United Nations common system, UNIDO has responsibility for promoting industrialization throughout the developing world, in cooperation with its 171 Member States. Its headquarters are in Vienna, and it is represented in 35 developing countries. This representation and a number of specialised field offices, for investment and technology promotion and other specific aspects of its work, give UNIDO an active presence in the field.

It helps developing countries and countries with economies in transition in their fight against marginalization in today's globalized world. It mobilizes knowledge, skills, information and technology to promote productive employment, a competitive economy and a sound environment. Carlos Magariños, the Director-General of UNIDO, describes the Organisation as a specialized United Nations agency that focuses its efforts on relieving poverty by fostering productivity growth.

UNIDO has three policy-making organs: the Programme and Budget Committee; the Industrial Development Board; and the General Conference.

- The chief policy-making organ of the Organisation, the General Conference, comprising representatives of all Member States, takes place every two years.
- The Programme and Budget Committee, consisting of 27 Members elected by the General Conference for a two-year term, is a subsidiary organ of the Board, and assists it in preparing work programmes and budgets.
- The Industrial Development Board of 53 Members reviews the implementation of the work programme, the regular and operational budgets and, every four years, recommends a candidate for Director-General (DG) to the General Conference for appointment. The DG heads the UNIDO Secretariat.

As a global forum, UNIDO generates and disseminates knowledge relating to industrial matters and provides a platform for the various actors in the public and private sectors, civil society organisations and the policy-making community in general to enhance cooperation, establish dialogue and develop partnerships in order to address the challenges ahead.

As a technical cooperation agency, UNIDO designs and implements programmes to support the industrial development efforts of its clients. It also offers tailor-made specialized support for programme development. The two core functions are both complementary and mutually supportive. On the one hand, experience gained in the technical cooperation work of UNIDO can be shared with policy makers; on the other, the Organisation's analytical work shows where technical cooperation will have the greatest impact by helping to define priorities.

The broad programmatic objectives and priorities of UNIDO are given in the Business Plan on the Future Role and Functions of UNIDO endorsed by the seventh session of the General Conference in 1997, in its resolution GC.7/Res.1.

This Business Plan grouped the activities of UNIDO into two areas of concentration: (a) Strengthening industrial capacities, including programmes in support of the global forum function and policy advice; and (b) Cleaner and sustainable industrial development. In addition, while maintaining the universal character and vocation of UNIDO, the Business Plan provided for the Organisation's activities to be focused geographically on least developed countries, in particular in Africa; sectorally on agro-based industries; and thematically on small and medium enterprises (SMEs).

UNIDO achieves these objectives through: (a) Integrated programmes (IPs) or country service frameworks (CSFs), based on combinations of its eight service modules or in (b) Stand-alone projects involving only one or two service modules.

UNIDO's eight Service Modules are:

(1) Industrial governance and statistics;

(2) Investment and technology promotion;

(3) Quality and productivity;

(4) Small business development;

(5) Agro-industries;

(6) Industrial energy and Kyoto Protocol;

(7) Montreal Protocol;

(8) Environment management.

"Integration" within an IP is not just at the level of the Service Modules selected for the programme, it also has to be achieved at the level of donor mechanisms, national counterparts and other development activities in the country or region.

With regard to the methods of delivery of its technical cooperation services, UNIDO is in the process of developing a set of thematic initiatives to supplement the existing modalities of integrated programmes, country service frameworks and stand-alone projects. These initiatives are intended to provide specialized assistance to developing countries and countries with economies in transition in meeting particularly pressing development needs in line with the international development agenda and UNIDO's comparative advantages in the field of industrial development.

So far, two such initiatives have been launched: The Market Access Initiative, launched at the International Conference of Financing for Development (Monterrey, Mexico, March 2002) and the Rural Energy for Productive Use Initiative, launched a the World Summit for Sustainable Development (Johannesburg, September 2002).

UNITED NATIONS INTERNATIONAL DRUG CONTROL PROGRAMME (IDCP)

Established in 1991 as the United Nations International Drug Control Programme, the Drug Programme works to educate the world about the dangers of drug abuse. The Programme aims to strengthen international action against drug production, trafficking and drug-related crime through alternative development projects, crop monitoring and anti-money laundering programmes.

The United Nations Office on Drugs and Crime (UNODC) is a global leader in the fight against illicit drugs and international crime. Established in 1997, UNODC consists of the Drug Programme and the Crime Programme. UNODC has approximately 500 staff members worldwide. Its headquarters are in Vienna and it has 21 field offices as well as a liaison offices in New York. UNODC relies on voluntary contributions, mainly from governments, for 90 per cent of its budget.

UNODC is continuing its efforts to implement its operational priorities through an integrated approach to counter drugs, crime and terrorism.

UNODC provides trend and policy analyses and publicizes and disseminates data and information, raising governments' awareness of their position and role in the global drug and crime scene.

UNODC works in cooperation with the United Nations Interregional Crime and Justice Research Institute (UNICRI) in the collection and analysis of statistics on crime trends and the operations of criminal justice systems, as well as to promote crime surveys and research and studies on new and emerging forms of crime.

UNODC's Scientific Support Section sets and develops international standards required for drug testing, monitors the application of standards and their impact on national drug control efforts and assists national laboratories and law enforcement services in countries with limited resources.

As part of UNODC's crop monitoring programme, the Section is working to better assess the yield of opium poppy and coca leaf. In addition, the Section is developing methods to characterize and profile major drugs and their precursors, and as a resource for national drug testing laboratories in their support of law enforcement activities.

The UNODC Illicit Crop Monitoring Programme (ICMP) assists Member States in producing internationally comparable data on the illicit cultivation of drug crops in the context of the elimination strategy adopted at the General Assembly Special Session on Drugs in June 1998.

UNITED NATIONS POPULATION FUND (UNFPA)

UNFPA, the United Nations Population Fund, is the world's largest international source of funding for population and reproductive health programmes. Since it began operations in 1969, the Fund has provided nearly $6 billion in assistance to developing countries.

UNFPA works with governments and non-governmental organisations in over 140 countries, at their request, and with the support of the international community. It supports programmes that help women, men and young people:

- plan their families and avoid unwanted pregnancies.
- undergo pregnancy and childbirth safely.
- avoid sexually transmitted diseases (STDs)—including HIV/AIDS.
- combat violence against women.

Together, these elements promote reproductive health-a state of complete physical, mental and social well being in all matters related to the reproductive system. Reproductive health is recognized as a human right, part of the right to health.

UNFPA also helps governments in the world's poorest countries, and in other countries in need, to formulate population policies and strategies in support of sustainable development. All UNFPA-funded programmes promote women's equality.

UNFPA works to raise awareness of these needs among people everywhere. It advocates for close attention to population problems and help to mobilize resources to solve them.

Since 1969, access to voluntary family planning programmes in developing countries has increased and fertility has fallen by half, from six children per woman to three. Nearly 60 per cent of married women in developing countries have chosen to practise contraception, compared with 10-15 per cent when we started our work.

UNFPA's work is guided by the Programme of Action adopted by 179 governments at the International Conference on Population and Development in 1994. The conference agreed that meeting people's needs for education and health, including reproductive health, is a prerequisite of sustainable development.

The main goals of the Programme of Action are:

- Universal access to reproductive health services by 2015.
- Universal primary education and closing the gender gap in education by 2015.
- Reducing maternal mortality by 75 per cent by 2015.
- Reducing infant mortality.
- Increasing life expectancy.

These goals were refined and amplified in 1999. One of the most important additions concerned HIV/AIDS:HIV infection rates in persons 15-24 years of age should be reduced by 25 per cent in the most-affected countries by 2005 and by 25 per cent globally by 2010.

Reaching the goals of the Programme of Action will be critical for reaching the Millennium Development Goals-global targets set by world leaders in 2000 to halve extreme poverty by 2015.

Improving Reproductive Health

Reproductive health is a means to sustainable development as well as a human right. Some 350 million couples lack adequate means to plan their families or space their children. Each year, half a million women in developing countries die during pregnancy or in childbirth. Investments in reproductive health save and improve lives, slow the spread of HIV/AIDS and encourage gender equality. These in turn help to stabilize population growth and reduce poverty. Investments in reproductive health extend from the individual to the family, and from the family to the world.

UNFPA promotes a holistic approach to reproductive health care that includes: access to a range of safe and affordable contraceptive methods and to sensitive counselling; prenatal care, attended deliveries, emergency obstetric care and post-natal care; and prevention of sexually transmitted diseases including HIV/AIDS.

Supporting Adolescents and Youth

Today the world has the largest youth generation ever—the first generation of young people to grow up with HIV/AIDS. There are more than a billion people between 15 and 24. UNFPA works to ensure that adolescents and young people have accurate information as well as non-judgmental counselling, and comprehensive and affordable services to prevent unwanted pregnancy and sexually-transmitted infections including the HIV infection that leads to AIDS.

Preventing HIV/AIDS

Each day 14,000 people-half of them aged 15 to 24-are newly infected, and add to the epidemic's staggering impact on health and on the social and economic stability of nations. In some parts of sub-Saharan Africa, young women are now up to six times more likely than young men to be infected with HIV.

Prevention, the centre-piece of UNFPA's fight against the disease, is being integrated into reproductive health programming around the world. Prevention includes promoting safer sexual behaviour among young people, making sure condoms are readily available and widely and correctly used, empowering women to protect themselves and their children, and encouraging men to make a difference.

Promoting Gender Equality

Women can and must play a powerful role in sustainable development and poverty eradication. When women are educated and healthy, their families, communities and nations benefit. Yet gender-based discrimination and violence pervade almost every aspect of life, undermining women's opportunities and denying them the ability to fully exercise their basic human rights.

For more than 30 years, UNFPA has been in the forefront of bringing gender issues to wider attention, promoting legal and policy reforms and gender-sensitive data collection, and supporting projects that empower women economically. The Fund aims to improve the status of women at every stage of their lives.

Securing Reproductive Health Supplies

Without the essential commodities-from contraceptives to testing kits to equipment for emergency obstetric care-the right to reproductive health cannot be fully exercised. In many places, condoms are urgently needed to prevent the further spread of the deadly HIV virus.

The mandate of UNFPA in this area is to provide the right quantities of the right products in the right condition in the right place at the right time for the right price. This complex logistical process involves many actors, including the public and private sectors. UNFPA takes a lead role in reproductive health commodity security, coordinating the process, forecasting needs, mobilizing support and building logistical capacity at the country level.

Assisting in Emergencies

Humanitarian crises are reproductive health disasters. Complications of pregnancy and childbirth are the leading causes of death for displaced women of childbearing age. In conflicts, the risk of sexual violence and sexually transmitted infections, including HIV, increases dramatically.

Within the framework of coordinated, interagency responses to disasters, UNFPA takes the lead in providing supplies and services to protect reproductive health. Priority areas for emergency response include safe motherhood, prevention of sexually transmitted infections including HIV, adolescent health, and sexual and gender-based violence.

Advancing Sustainable Development

Changes in the structure, distribution, and size of populations are interlinked with all facets of sustainable development. Tracking these changes and analysing population trends helps governments and international agencies generate the political will to appropriately address current and future needs.

UNFPA helps developing countries collect and analyse population data and to integrate population and development strategies into national, regional and global planning.

Building Support

UNFPA is the world's leading advocate for reproductive health and rights, including the right to choose the number and spacing of one's children. The Fund also promotes the inclusion of population issues in national planning processes. Advocacy-at the individual, community, national, regional and global levels-is a powerful tool by which UNFPA is able to increase its impact.

Alliances-with other United Nations agencies, governments, NGOs, foundations and the private sector-enable the Fund to raise awareness of and mobilize support for the goals set forth in the International Conference on Population and Development and the UN Millennium Summit.

UNFPA supports programmes in four developing regions: Arab States and Europe, Asia and the Pacific, Latin America and the Caribbean, and sub-Saharan Africa. It works in 142 countries, areas and territories through nine Country Technical Services Teams and 112 country offices.

UNITED NATIONS RELIEF AND WORKS AGENCY FOR PALESTINE REFUGEES (UNRWA)

UNRWA provides education, health, relief and social services to eligible refugees among the 4.1 million registered Palestine refugees in its five fields of operations: Jordan, Lebanon, the Syrian Arab Republic, the West Bank and Gaza Strip. Some 1.3 million refugees, around one third of the total, live in 59 recognized camps, and UNRWA's services are located in or near these camps where there are large concentrations of refugees.

Unlike other United Nations organisations which work through local authorities or executing agencies, UNRWA provides its services directly to Palestine refugees. It plans and carries out its own activities and projects, and builds and administers facilities such as schools and clinics. The Agency currently operates or sponsors over 900 installations with some 24,215 staff throughout its area of operations. Because UNRWA services such as education and health care are the type of services normally provided within the public sector, the Agency cooperates closely with governmental authorities in the area of operations, who also provide some services to Palestine refugees.

Education

- Education is UNRWA's largest area of activity accounting for half its regular budget and two-thirds of its staff.
- In the 2002/2003 school year, UNRWA is providing basic, free education to 490,949 young Palestine refugees in 656 elementary and preparatory schools throughout its area of operations and in five secondary schools in Lebanon.
- The curriculum used is the same as that of the host governments/authorities. However the Agency also creates educational enrichment materials to supplement the local curriculum. One of UNRWA's key programmes is aimed at the promotion of non-violent conflict resolution and human rights. These systematic efforts, which have included translations into Arabic of relevant textbooks, the creation of special manuals and the

involvement of UNRWA pupils in cross-community summer camps, have reached every UNRWA school in the West Bank and Gaza and are to be expanded into other fields. The Agency's work in this area has been praised by, among others, the Israeli delegation to the United Nations.

- 50 per cent of the pupils are female.
- Eight vocational and technical training centres with 5,101 places equip young refugees with marketable skills and a teacher training programme ensures sufficient qualified teachers for Agency schools.
- The university-level teacher training programme in Jordan, Lebanon and the West Bank has 1,075 in-service and pre-service trainees in 2002/2003 with additional in-service training being offered to 921 UNRWA teachers.

To enhance opportunities for higher education for refugee youth, UNRWA continues to provide university scholarships to some 56 students annually. However, due to financial constraints, the Agency is no longer able to award new scholarships.

Health

- UNRWA offers primary health care to registered refugees through a network of 122 outpatient facilities which handled over 9 million patient visits in 2002.
- Services provided include outpatient medical care, disease prevention and control, mother-and-child health, family planning advice and health education.
- UNRWA also offers help with secondary care, especially emergency and life-saving treatment through contractual agreements with non-governmental and private hospitals or through partial reimbursement of treatment costs.
- The Agency operates a 43-bed hospital in Qalqilia in the West Bank. Environmental health services for the 1.3 million refugee camp residents include sewage disposal, management of storm water runoff, provision

of safe drinking water, collection and disposal of refuse, and control of insects and rodents.

Independent assessments have repeatedly confirmed that UNRWA's health care system is one of the most cost-effective in the region.

Relief & Social Services

- UNRWA supports Palestine refugee families unable to meet their own basic needs and helps promote the self-reliance of the refugee community through community social development.
- Direct material and financial assistance including food is given to families in special hardship. These are families without a male adult medically fit to earn an income and without other identifiable means of financial support sufficient to cover food, shelter and other basic needs. Some 233,044 persons, or 5.7 per cent of all Palestine refugees registered with the Agency are receiving assistance under this programme.
- UNRWA provides technical and financial support to 108 locally-managed women's programmes and community rehabilitation centres, which provide a range of social services to the refugee community.

This department also registers refugees and carries out assessments of eligibility for UNRWA services on an ongoing basis.

UNRWA's Micro-finance and Micro-enterprise Programme aims to:

- create employment and income generating opportunities to both Palestinian refugees and residents by promoting the development of small-scale and micro-enterprises through the provision of loans for working capital and investment funds at commercial interest rates;
- make credit available to enterprises in both the formal and informal sectors of the economy;
- encourage export-oriented manufacturing with foreign income-earning capacity;

- encourage import substitution in order to improve the balance of trade;
- increase the volume of lending and extend the programme's outreach to those who do not have access to credit because of a lack of collateral;
- encourage the participation of women in the economy;
- be self-sustaining with funds from its credit operations.

Emergency Aid

- UNRWA has provided emergency assistance to Palestine refugees and to their neighbours many times in its nearly 50 years of activity.
- During the prolonged civil conflict in Lebanon and the 1982 invasion of Lebanon by Israel, UNRWA repeatedly provided emergency housing, medical care and food to thousands of homeless, fleeing refugees.
- During the first *intifadah* (1987-1993) in the West Bank and Gaza Strip, the Agency provided emergency medical care to the injured and food rations for both refugees and other residents of the two areas.
- The Agency also regularly provides tents, blankets and food to refugees in the harsh winter weather which often affects the region.

Since September 2000, UNRWA has been providing emergency assistance to the thousands of refugees affected by the ongoing conflict in the West Bank and Gaza.

Special Programmes

UNRWA also undertakes special projects and programme activities in response to identified needs or to support broader political and socio-economic developments.

These include:

Projects—UNRWA carries out, on an ongoing basis, special projects to improve Agency and refugee camp infrastructure or special activities within the framework of UNRWA's regular programmes. These include the new Neirab Rehabilitation project in Syria and the recent relocation of refugees from Canada camp to the new housing project in Tel Es-Sultan in Rafah, south Gaza. Between October 1993 and December 1999, many projects were carried out under the Peace Implementation Programme, which was introduced following the signing of the Israeli-Palestinian Declaration of Principles in 1993. The Agency has received over US$310.9 million in contributions and pledges for 654 projects.

The European Gaza Hospital was an initiative of UNRWA and the European Union to contribute to the Palestinian health infrastructure. Construction of the 232-bed hospital near the city of Khan Younis in the Gaza Strip was completed in 1996, and it was handed over to the Palestinian Authority in 1999. New out-patient facilities were opened in July 2000. Funds were contributed by the European Union and its member states.

UNRWA has long-standing technical assistance agreements with the United Nations Educational, Scientific and Cultural Organisation (UNESCO) and the World Health Organisation (WHO), which provide the Agency with senior staff for its education and health programmes, respectively. In addition most of the Agency's international staff are paid directly from the United Nations headquarters in New York. UNRWA also receives medical supplies from the United Nations Children's Fund (UNICEF) and the United Nations Population Fund (UNFPA).

UNRWA and the United Nations High Commissioner for Refugees (UNHCR) are the two United Nations agencies with responsibility for refugees. In practice, Palestine refugees within UNRWA's area of operations are the responsibility of UNRWA, while those outside the area fall under UNHCR's mandate. There is a long tradition of cooperation between UNRWA and UNHCR in helping to resolve problems faced by Palestine refugees living outside UNRWA's area of operations.

UNIVERSAL POSTAL UNION (UPU)

The postal service forms part of the daily life of people all over the world. Even in the digital age, the Post remains, for millions of people, the most accessible means of communication and message delivery available.

The postal services of the Universal Postal Union's 189 member countries form the largest physical distribution network in the world. More than six million postal employees work in over 700000 postal outlets to ensure that some 430 billion mail items are processed and delivered each year to all corners of the world.

Keeping pace with the changing communications market, Posts are increasingly using new communication and information technologies to move beyond what is traditionally regarded as their core postal business They are meeting higher customer expectations with an expanded range of products and value-added services.

Established in 1874, the Universal Postal Union (UPU) with its Headquarters in the Swiss capital Bern, is the second oldest international organisation after the International Telecommunications Union.

The mission of the Universal Postal Union is to foster the sustainable development of quality universal, efficient accessible postal services in order to facilitate communication among the people of the world by:

- guaranteeing the free circulation of postal items through an interconnected single postal territory;
- promoting the adoption of fair and common standards and the application of technology;
- cooperation and interaction among stakeholders;
- facilitating the effective provision of technical cooperation;
- ensuring that the changing needs of customers are addressed.

With 189 member countries, the UPU is the primary forum for cooperation between postal services and helps to ensure a truly universal network of up-to-date products and services. In this way, the organisation fulfils an advisory, mediating and liaison role, and renders technical assistance where needed. It sets the rules for international mail exchanges and makes recommendations to stimulate growth in mail volumes and to improve the quality of service for customers.

However, as a non-political organisation, it does not interfere in matters that fall within the domestic domain of national postal services. For example, Posts set their own postage rates, decide which and how many postage stamps to issue, and how to manage their postal operations and staff.

By virtue of its mission to develop social, cultural and commercial communication between people through the efficient operation of the postal service, the UPU is called upon to play an important leadership role in promoting the continued revitalisation of postal services.

The same forces affecting the world's Posts—globalization, growing customer expectations, increased competition and progress in communications technologies—have also caused the UPU to review its own mission and role. Although its fundamental mission of developing social, cultural and commercial communication among the people of the world has remained remarkably constant throughout its history, the UPU has seen the need to reshape its structures in order to better meet the needs and expectations of its members.

The UPU will continue to work toward the goal of ensuring that all people have affordable and reliable access to postal services. One of its future roles will be to develop and monitor standards for the provision of universal postal service, including such features as access to service, efficiency, customer satisfaction, security and reasonable pricing.

The UPU will also continue to provide technical assistance, training and consultant services in order to improve the quality of the postal service and help implement new systems in developing countries.

The future role of the UPU will be one that is more inclusive of external stakeholders, ensuring that the changing needs of postal customers are addressed effectively. The UPU will therefore increasingly provide a global forum for its members and external partners. In this way, it will remain a vital force in the continued development of postal services.

THE WORLD BANK GROUP

The World Bank Group consists of five closely associated institutions, all owned by member countries that carry ultimate decision-making power. Each institution plays a distinct role in the mission to fight poverty and improve living standards for people in the developing world. The term "World Bank Group" encompasses the following five institutions:

- International Bank for Reconstruction and Development (IBRD).
- International Development Association (IDA).
- International Finance Corporation (IFC).
- Multilateral Investment Guarantee Agency (MIGA).
- International Centre for Settlement of Investment Disputes (ICSID).

The "World Bank" is the name that has come to be used for the International Bank for Reconstruction and Development (IBRD) and the International Development Association (IDA). Together these organisations provide low-interest loans, interest-free credit, and grants to developing countries. The International Finance Corporation (IFC) promotes private sector investment by supporting high-risk sectors and countries. The Multilateral Investment Guarantee Agency (MIGA) provides political risk insurance (guarantees) to investors in and lenders to developing countries. And the International Centre for Settlement of Investment Disputes (ICSID) settles investment disputes between foreign investors and their host countries.

The World Bank works to bridge the divide and turn rich country resources into poor country growth. One of the world's largest sources of development assistance, the World Bank supports the efforts of developing country governments to build schools and health centers, provide water and electricity, fight disease, and protect the environment. The World Bank is not a "bank" in the common sense. It is one of the United Nations' specialized agencies, and is made up of 184 member countries. These countries are jointly responsible for how the institution is financed and how its money is spent. Along with the rest of the development community, the World Bank centers its efforts on the reaching the Millennium Development Goals, agreed to by UN members in 2000 and aimed at sustainable poverty reduction.

The world's low-income countries generally cannot borrow money in international markets or can only do so at high interest rates. In addition to direct contributions and loans from developed countries, these countries receive grants, interest-free loans, and technical assistance from the World Bank to enable them to provide basic services. In the case of the loans, countries have 35-40 years to repay, with a 10-year grace period.

Interest-free credit and grant financing comes from IDA, the world's largest source of concessional assistance. Some 40 rich countries provide the money for this funding by making contributions every four years. The fund was replenished most recently in 2002, with nearly $9 billion from donors and another $6.6 billion from the Bank's resources. At that time, donors agreed on increased use of IDA grants—up to 21 per cent of resources—to help address the special difficulties, such as the HIV/AIDS epidemic, faced by the poorest and most vulnerable countries. IDA credits make up about one-quarter of the Bank's financial assistance. Aside from IDA funds, very little of the Bank's income is provided by its member countries.

Higher-income developing countries—some of which can borrow from commercial sources, but generally only at very high interest rates—receive loans from the IBRD. Countries that borrow from the IBRD have more time to repay than if they borrowed from a commercial bank—15 to 20 years with a three-to-five-year grace period before the repayment of principal begins. Developing country governments borrow money for specific programs, including poverty reduction efforts, delivery of social services, protection of the environment, and promotion of economic growth that will improve living standards. In fiscal 2002 IBRD provided loans totaling $11.5 billion in support of 96 projects in 40 countries.

The IBRD raises almost all its money in the world's financial markets—$23 billion in fiscal 2002. With a AAA credit rating, it issues bonds to raise money and then passes on the low interest rates to its borrowers.

Over the past few years, the World Bank has put significant resources into activities meant to have global impact. One is debt relief, and under the enhanced Heavily Indebted Poor Countries (HIPC) Initiative, 26 poor countries have received debt relief which will save them $41 billion over time. The money these countries save in debt repayments will instead be put into housing, education, health, and welfare programs for the poor.

The World Bank, along with 189 countries and numerous organisations, has committed to an unprecedented global partnership to fight poverty. The Millennium Development Goals define specific targets in terms of school enrolments, child mortality, maternal health, disease, and access to water to be met by 2015.

Among numerous other global partnerships, the World Bank has put supporting the fight against HIV/AIDS at the top of its agenda. It is the world's largest long-term financer of HIV/AIDS programs. Current Bank commitments for HIV/AIDS amount to more than $1.3 billion, with half of that for sub-Saharan Africa.

The World Bank works with countries in their anti-corruption efforts and has as well a number of mechanisms in place to prevent corruption and fraud in bank-financed projects. The Department of Institutional Integrity has a 24-hour Fraud and Corruption Hotline.

The Bank is currently involved in more than 1,800 projects in virtually every sector and developing country. These are as diverse as providing micro credit in Bosnia Herzegovina and raising AIDS awareness in communities in Guinea, supporting education of girls in Bangladesh and improving health care delivery in Mexico, helping East Timor rebuild upon independence or India to rebuild Gujarat after a devastating earthquake.

The World Bank is run like a cooperative, with its member countries as shareholders. The number of shares a country has is based roughly on the size of its economy. The United States is the largest single shareholder, with 16.41 per cent of votes, followed by Japan (7.87 per cent), Germany (4.49 per cent), the United Kingdom (4.31 per cent), and France (4.31 per cent). The rest of the shares are divided among the other member countries.

The World Bank's government shareholders are represented by a Board of Governors. Generally, these governors are ministers, such as Ministers of Finance or Ministers of

Development. The governors are the ultimate policy makers in the World Bank. They meet once a year at the Bank's Annual Meetings. Because these ministers meet only once a year, they delegate specific duties to their Executive Directors, who work onsite at the Bank. Every member government of the World Bank Group is represented by an Executive Director. The five largest shareholders-France, Germany, Japan, the United Kingdom, and the United States—appoint an Executive Director, while other member countries are represented by 19 Executive Directors.

The Bank's president is, by tradition, a national of the largest shareholder, the United States. Elected for a five-year renewable term, the president of the World Bank chairs meetings of the Board of Directors and is responsible for overall management of the Bank.

The Bank employs approximately 10,000 people, including economists, educators, environmental scientists, financial analysts, anthropologists, engineers, and many others. Employees come from about 160 different countries, and over 3,000 staff work in country offices.

IBRD—The International Bank for Reconstruction and Development

Established 1944, 184 Members
Cumulative lending: $383 billion
Fiscal 2003 lending: $11.2 billion for 99 new operations in 37 countries

IBRD aims to reduce poverty in middle-income and creditworthy poorer countries by promoting sustainable development, through loans, guarantees, and nonlending—including analytical and advisory—services. IBRD does not maximize profit but has earned a net income each year since 1948. Its profits fund several developmental activities and ensure financial strength, which enables low-cost borrowings in capital markets, and good terms for borrowing clients. Owned by member countries, IBRD links voting power to members' capital subscriptions—in turn based on a country's relative economic strength.

IDA—The International Development Association

Established 1960, 164 Members
Cumulative, lending: $142 billion
Fiscal 2003 lending: $7.3 billion for 141 new operations in 55 countries

Contributions to IDA enable the World Bank to provide $7 billion per year in interest-free credits to the world's 81 poorest countries, home to 2.5 billion people. This support is vital because these countries have little or no capacity to borrow on market terms. In most of these countries incomes average under just $500 a year per person, and many people survive on much less. IDA helps provide access to better basic services (such as education, health care, and clean water and sanitation) and supports reforms and investments aimed at productivity growth and employment creation.

IFC—The International Finance Corporation

Established 1956, 175 Members
Committed, portfolio: $23.4 billion (includes $6.6 billion in syndicated loans)
Fiscal 2003 commitments: $3.9 billion (includes syndications, $3.9 billion for own account) in 204 companies for 64 countries

IFC's mandate is to further economic development through the private sector. Working with business partners, it invests in sustainable private enterprises in developing countries and provides long-term loans, guarantees, and risk management and advisory services to its clients. IFC invests in projects in regions and sectors underserved by private investment and finds new ways to develop promising opportunities in markets deemed too risky by commercial investors in the absence of IFC participation.

MIGA—The Multilateral Investment Guarantee Agency

Established 1988, 163 Members
Cumulative guarantees issued: $12.4 billion
Fiscal 2003 guarantees issued: $1.4 billion (Includes $136 million leveraged through the Cooperative Underwriting Program.)

MIGA helps encourage foreign investment in developing countries by providing guarantees to foreign investors against losses caused by noncommercial risks, such as expropriation, currency inconvertibility and transfer restrictions, and war and civil disturbances. Furthermore, MIGA provides technical assistance to help countries disseminate information on investment opportunities. The agency also offers investment dispute mediation on request.

ICSID—The International Centre for Settlement of Investment Disputes

Established 1966, 139 Members
Total cases registered: 129
Fiscal 2003 cases registered: 26

ICSID helps to encourage foreign investment by providing international facilities for conciliation and arbitration of investment disputes, in this way helping to foster an atmosphere of mutual confidence between states and foreign investors. Many international agreements concerning investment refer to ICSID's arbitration facilities. ICSID also has research and publishing activities in the areas of arbitration law and foreign investment law.

WORLD FOOD PROGRAMME (WFP)

WFP's vision is a world in which everyone has access at all times to the nourishment they need for a full-life. It believes that the issue of hunger belongs at the top of the international agenda.

In November / December 1961, the Food and Agriculture Organisation (FAO) and the UN General Assembly adopted parallel resolutions establishing WFP.

The three-year experimental programme was not due to enter into operation until January 1963. In reality it was up and running several months early as an earthquake hit Iran, a hurricane swept through Thailand and newly independent Algeria was overwhelmed by 5 million returning refugees. Food aid was urgently needed and WFP was tasked to supply it.

Since it was set-up in 1963, the Rome-based organisation has invested US$27.8 billion and more than 43 million metric tonnes of food to combat hunger, promote economic and social development and provide relief assistance in emergencies throughout the world.

Since 1996, WFP has been governed by the WFP Executive Board, which consists of 36 Member States. The Executive Director, appointed jointly by the UN Secretary General and the Director-General of the FAO for fixed five-year terms, sits at the head of the Secretariat of WFP.

As the food aid arm of the UN, WFP uses its food to:

- meet emergency needs,
- support economic & social development.

The Agency also provides the logistics support necessary to get food aid to the right people at the right time and in the right place.

WFP works to put hunger at the centre of the international agenda, promoting policies, strategies and operations that directly benefit the hungry and the poor.

The frontline in the battle against hunger runs from sub-Saharan Africa and the Middle East to Latin America and Asia. Here, WFP food aid reaches the world's poorest nations as:

- **Food-for-Life.** In emergencies, WFP provides fast, efficient, life-sustaining relief to millions of people who are the victims of the ever rising number of natural or man-made disasters. This includes refugees and internally displaced persons. A decade ago, two out of three tonnes of the food aid provided by WFP was used for development projects. Today, 80 percent of WFP resources are used for relief activities.
- **Food-for-Growth.** These projects target needy people at the most critical times of their lives. Babies, school children, pregnant and breast-feeding women and the elderly. In these projects, WFP tries to use food aid as a preventive medicine. Each day, WFP school feeding projects use food aid to encourage millions of hungry children to school. In countries like Haiti, Pakistan, Morocco and Mozambique, WFP food also draws vulnerable mothers to health clinics as well as literacy and nutrition classes.
- **Food-for-Work.** Where people are chronically hungry, WFP promotes self-reliance through food-for-work projects. Workers are paid with food aid to allow communities to devote more time to development.

WFP pays workers with food to build roads or ports in Ghana and Lesotho, repair dykes in Bangladesh, terrace hillsides in China or Guatemala, replant forests in Ethiopia or repair irrigation canals in Somalia.

WORLD HEALTH ORGANISATION (WHO)

The World Health Organisation, the United Nations specialized agency for health, was established on 7 April 1948. WHO's objective, as set out in its Constitution, is the attainment by all peoples of the highest possible level of health. Health is defined in WHO's Constitution as a state of complete physical, mental and social well-being and not merely the absence of disease or infirmity.

WHO is governed by 192 Member States through the World Health Assembly. The Health Assembly is composed of representatives from WHO's Member States. The main tasks of the World Health Assembly are to approve the WHO programme and the budget for the following biennium and to decide major policy questions.

The World Health Assembly is the supreme decision-making body for WHO. It generally meets in Geneva in May each year, and is attended by delegations from all 192 Member States. Its main function is to determine the policies of the Organisation. The Health Assembly appoints the Director-General, supervises the financial policies of the Organisation, and reviews and approves the Proposed programme budget. It similarly considers reports of the Executive Board, which it instructs in regard to matters upon which further action, study, investigation or report may be required.

The Executive Board is composed of 32 members technically qualified in the field of health. Members are elected for three-year terms. The main Board meeting, at which the agenda for the forthcoming Health Assembly is agreed upon and resolutions for forwarding to the Health Assembly are adopted, is held in January, with a second shorter meeting in May, immediately after the Health Assembly, for more administrative matters. The main functions of the Board are to give effect to the decisions and policies of the Health Assembly, to advise it and generally to facilitate its work.

The Secretariat of WHO is staffed by some 3500 health and other experts and support staff on fixed-term appointments, working at headquarters, in the six regional offices, and in countries.

The Secretariat is headed by the Director-General, who is nominated by the Executive Board and elected by Member States for a period of five years

WHO's Secretariat is staffed by health professionals, other experts and support staff working at headquarters in Geneva, in the six regional offices and in countries. WHO's regional offices are:

- Regional Office for Africa - located in Brazzaville, Republic of Congo.
- Regional Office for Europe - located in Copenhagen, Denmark.
- Regional Office for South-East Asia - located in New Delhi, India.
- Regional Office for the Americas/Pan-American Health Organisation - located in Washington D.C., USA.
- Regional Office for the Eastern Mediterranean - located in Cairo, Egypt.
- Regional Office for the Western Pacific - located in Manila, Philippines.

In carrying out its activities, WHO's secretariat focuses its work on the following six core functions:

- Articulating consistent, ethical and evidence-based policy and advocacy positions.
- Managing information by assessing trends and comparing performance; setting the agenda for, and stimulating research and development.
- Catalysing change through technical and policy support, in ways that stimulate cooperation and action and help to build sustainable national and inter-country capacity.
- Negotiating and sustaining national and global partnerships.

- Setting, validating, monitoring and pursuing the proper implementation of norms and standards.

Stimulating the development and testing of new technologies, tools and guidelines for disease control, risk reduction, health care management, and service delivery.

WORLD INTELLECTUAL PROPERTY ORGANISATION (WIPO)

The World Intellectual Property Organisation (WIPO) is an international organisation dedicated to promoting the use and protection of works of the human spirit. These works—intellectual property—are expanding the bounds of science and technology and enriching the world of the arts. Through its work, WIPO plays an important role in enhancing the quality and enjoyment of life, as well as creating real wealth for nations.

With headquarters in Geneva, Switzerland, WIPO is one of the 16 specialized agencies of the United Nations system of organisations. It administers 23 international treaties dealing with different aspects of intellectual property protection. The Organisation counts 179 nations as member states.

WIPO carries out a wide variety of activities and services in its work. These include establishing international standards for intellectual property laws and practices and providing registration services that allow patents, trademarks and designs to be protected in many countries. WIPO also extends technical and legal assistance to developing countries, facilitates resolution of intellectual property disputes, and explores new issues arising in the global intellectual property arena. In all these activities, the latest information technologies are employed to promote efficiency and facilitate the electronic exchange of information on intellectual property.

In transforming WIPO's vision into reality, strategic goals are set out as follows:

- Promotion of an IP (Intellectual Property) culture; on the one hand, to encourage creators and innovators to obtain, use and license IP rights and assets, and, on the other hand, to seek greater respect by the public for IP rights and assets. This will include making resources and expertise available to assist Member

States in their own efforts to develop an IP culture through cooperation with governments, intergovernmental organisations and partners in private sectors.

- Development of balanced international IP laws which are: responsive to emerging needs; effective in encouraging innovation and creation; and sufficiently flexible to accommodate national policy objectives.
- Provision of consistent and customized assistance to Member States in developing national/regional IP systems, including legal infrastructure, institutional framework and human resources.
- Enhancement of global protection systems to make them more easily accessible and affordable to all stakeholders, in particular.
- Further streamlining of the management and administrative processes within WIPO to intensify efforts to achieve greater efficiency as well as the initiation of improved monitoring and evaluation systems to examine the achievement of expected results.

WIPO's activities are grouped into five areas, each with specific deliverables, as indicated below:

- Modernization of Management;

  - Enhancement of program and budget process and efficient implementation of program activities;

  - Consolidation and leveraging of IT-based tools;

  - Enhanced efficiency in PCT (Patent Cooperation Treaty), Madrid and Hague systems operations.

- IP Outreach and Support

  - Better understanding of the cultural and social dimension of IP-related issues;

  - Development of tools/guidelines to assist in building greater public awareness and understanding of IP and its role and more wide-spread respect for IPRs;

  - Enhanced use of IP by SMEs (Small and Medium Enterprises).

- Cooperation for Development

- Strengthening of IP's role in the development of national policy (supported with analyses of the economic impact of IP);

- Strengthening of national human resource capabilities, including training of IP professionals (e.g., training of trainers);

- Deployment of online tools for small IP Offices via WIPONET;

- Further development of customized regional/national action plans;

- Continuing assistance in IP Office automation.

• IP Issues and Progressive Development and Codification of International IP Law

- Better accessibility to the patent system through the WIPO Patent Agenda, including ongoing work on the draft Substantive Patent Law Treaty;

- Further development of harmonized principles and procedural and substantive aspects of the law of trademarks and industrial designs;

- Responses to new technologies, particularly the implementation of the WIPO Copyright Treaty (WCT) and the WIPO Performances and Phonograms Treaty (WPPT);

- Continuation of consultations on broadcasting rights and of negotiations to establish an international instrument for the protection of audiovisual performers;

- Continuation of the Intergovernmental Committee on Intellectual Property and Genetic Resources, Traditional Knowledge and Folklore with a view to strengthening the framework of protection;

- Use, where necessary, of "soft law" solutions for certain issues.

• Global IP Protection Systems and Services

- Progressive reform of the PCT and implementation of the results;

- Expansion of the Madrid and Hague systems;

- Expansion of the WIPO Arbitration and Mediation Center's services to include a wider range of IP disputes.

Under Madrid and the Hague System a trademark or industrial design owner in one of the member states can obtain protection of his mark or design in some or all of the other members by filling a single international application with WIPO. The resulting international registration is published by WIPO and notified to all the designated countries.

WORLD METEOROLOGICAL ORGANISATION (WMO)

The World Meteorological Organisation is an inter-governmental organisation with a membership of 187 Member States and Territories. It originated from the International Meteorological Organisation (IMO), which was founded in 1873. Established in 1950, WMO became the specialized agency of the United Nations for meteorology (weather and climate), operational hydrology and related geophysical sciences.

Since its establishment, WMO has played a unique and powerful role in contributing to the welfare of humanity. Under WMO leadership and within the framework of WMO programmes, National Meteorological and Hydrological Services (NMHS) have contributed substantially to the protection of life and property against natural disasters, to safeguarding the environment and to enhancing the economic and social well-being of all sectors of society in areas such as food security, water resources and transport. It has a unique role within the UN system it facilitates the free and unrestricted exchange of data and information, products and services in real- or near-real time on matters relating to safety and security of society, economic well being and the prevention of the environment.

As weather and climate know no national boundaries, international cooperation at a global scale is essential for the development of meteorology and operational hydrology as well as to reap the benefits from their applications. WMO provides the framework for such international cooperation. WMO is playing a leading role in international efforts to monitor and protect the environment through its Programmes, such as the World Weather Watch Programme, World Climate

Programme, the Atmospheric Research and Environment Programme, and the Hydrology and Water Resources Programme. For instance, in collaboration with the UN agencies and the NMHSs of Members, WMO continues to support the implementation of relevant conventions such as the UN Framework Convention on Climate Change, the International Convention to Combat Desertification, and the Vienna Convention on the Protection of Ozone Layer and its Protocols and Amendments. WMO is instrumental in providing advice and assessments to governments on matters relating to the above Conventions. These activities contribute towards ensuring the sustainable development and well-being of nations.

In the specific case of weather natural disasters which account for nearly three-quarters of all are such events, WMO's programmes provide the vital information for the advance warnings that save many lives and reduce damage to property and the environment. Human induced disasters chemistry, nuclear and forest fire . Numerous studies have shown that, apart from the incalculable benefit to human well-being, every dollar invested in meteorological and hydrological services produces an economic return many times greater, often ten times or more.

The vision of the WMO for the Sixth Long-term Plan (2004-2011) is to provide world leadership in expertise and international cooperation in weather, climate, hydrology and water resources, and related environmental issues, and thereby to contribute to the safety and well being of people throughout the world and to the economic benefit of all nations.

Purposes

- To facilitate world-wide cooperation in the establishment of networks of stations for the making of meteorological as well as hydrological and other geophysical observations related to meteorology, and to promote the establishment and maintenance of centres charged with the provision of meteorological and related services;
- To promote the establishment and maintenance of systems for the rapid exchange of meteorological and related information;

- To promote the standardization of meteorological and related observations and to ensure the uniform publication of observations and statistics;
- To further the application of meteorology to aviation, shipping, water problems, agriculture and other human activities;
- To promote activities in operational hydrology and to further close co-operation between Meteorological and Hydrological Services;
- To encourage research and training in meteorology and, as appropriate, in related fields and to assist in coordinating the international aspects of such research and training.

Structure

The World Meteorological Congress, the supreme body of the Organisation, brings together the delegates of Members once every four years to determine general policies for the fulfilment of the purposes of the Organisation, to approve long-term plans, to authorize maximum expenditures for the following financial period, to adopt Technical Regulations relating to international meteorological and operational hydrological practice, to elect the President and Vice-Presidents of the Organisation and members of the Executive Council and to appoint the Secretary-General.

The Executive Council, the executive body of the Organisation and is responsible to Congress for the coordination of the programmes of the organisation and of the utilization of its budgetary resources in accordance with the decision of Congress. composed of 37 directors of National Meteorological or Hydrometeorological Services, meets at least once a year to review the activities of the Organisation and to implement the programmes approved by Congress.

The six regional associations (Africa, Asia, South America, North America, Central America and the Caribbean, South-West Pacific and Europe), composed of Members, coordinate meteorological and related activities within their respective Regions.

The eight technical commissions, composed of experts designated by Members, study matters within their specific areas of competence (technical commissions have been established for basic systems, instruments and methods of observation, atmospheric sciences, aeronautical meteorology, agricultural meteorology, oceanography and marine meteorology, hydrology, and climatology).

The Secretariat, headed by the Secretary-General, serves as the administrative, documentation and information centre of the Organisation. It prepares, edits, produces and distributes the publications of the Organisation, carries out the duties specified in the Convention and other Basic Documents and provides secretariat support to the work of the constituent bodies of WMO described above.

In addition to its Headquarters in Geneva, the Secretariat includes Regional Office for Africa (Burundi), Regional Office for Asia and the South-West Pacific (Switzerland) and Regional Office for Americas (Paraguay); and Subregional Offices are West Africa (Nigeria), Eastern and Southern Africa (Kenya), South-West Pacific (Samoa) and for North and Central America and the Caribbean (Costa Rica).

Programmes

WMO carries out its work through ten major scientific and technical programmes. The scientific and technical programmes of WMO are designed to assist all Members to provide, and benefit from, a wide range of meteorological and hydrological services and to address present and emerging problems. The programmes are based on the concept and experience that mutual benefits are gained from cooperative use of the pool of knowledge that has been, and is still being, created by worldwide sharing of meteorological, hydrological and related information among Members. The programmes of WMO make possible the provision of meteorological and related services in all countries at costs far below those that would be incurred if each Member acted alone.

The World Weather Watch Programme (WWWP) is the backbone of the overall programme of WMO. It combines data-processing centres, observing systems and telecommunication facilities—operated by Members—to make available meteorological and related geophysical information that is needed in order to provide efficient meteorological and hydrological services within the countries. It also includes a Tropical Cyclone Programme, in which more than 60 countries are involved, an Instruments and Methods of Observation Programme to promote standardization and development of meteorological and related observations.

The World Climate Programme (WCP) promotes the improvement of the understanding of climate processes through internationally coordinated research and the monitoring of climate variations or changes. It also promotes the application of climate information and services to assist in economic and social planning and development. The research component of the Programme is the joint responsibility of WMO, the International Council for Science and the Intergovernmental Oceanographic Commission (IOC) of UNESCO. The Climate Impact Assessment and Response Strategies component is coordinated by the United Nations Environment Programme.

The Atmospheric Research and Environment Programme (AREP) promotes atmospheric research, in particular through the Global Atmosphere Watch (GAW), which integrates monitoring and research activities carried out under the Global Ozone Observing System and the Background Air Pollution Monitoring Network and serves as a system to detect changes in the composition of the atmosphere. The programme also includes weather-prediction research; a Tropical Meteorology Research Programme relating to studies of monsoons, tropical cyclones, rain-producing tropical weather systems and droughts; and a programme on physics and chemistry of clouds and weather modification.

The Applications of Meteorology Programme (AMP) comprises four vital areas of application of meteorological services and information: public weather services, agricultural meteorology, aeronautical meteorology and marine meteorology, and promotes the development of infrastructures and services which are required in those areas for the benefit of Member countries.

The Hydrology and Water Resources Programme (HWRP) is concerned with the assessment of the quantity and quality of water resources in order to meet the needs of society, to permit mitigation of water-related hazards, and to maintain or enhance the condition of the global environment. It includes standardization of all aspects of hydrological observations and the organized transfer of hydrological techniques and methods. The Programme is closely coordinated with UNESCO's International Hydrological Programme.

The Natural Disaster Prevention and Mitigation Programme (NSPMP) is a cross-cutting programme that ensures integration of relevant activities being carried out under the various WMO Programmes in the area of disaster prevention and mitigation. It provides for the effective coordination of the pertinent WMO activities with related activities of international, regional and national organisations including civil defence organisations. The Programme also provides scientific and technical support to WMO's actions in response to disaster situations.

The Space Programme (SP) is to make increasing contribution to the development of the Global Observing System (GOS) of WWWP, as well as to the other WMO-supported Programmes and associated observing systems. It will provide improved data, products and services continuously, from both operational and R&D satellites, and facilitate and promote their wider availability and meaningful utilization around the globe.

The Education and Training Programme (ETRP) holds the key to future development by promoting all efforts in Member countries to ensure that the necessary body of trained meteorologists, hydrologists, engineers and technicians is available. It is closely interrelated with all other major scientific and technical Programmes.

The Technical Cooperation Programme (TCP) comprises the mainstream of organized transfer of meteorological and hydrological knowledge and proven methodology among the Members of the Organisation. Particular emphasis is laid upon the development of a wide range of services (related to weather prediction, climatology and hydrology); on the development and operation of key World Weather Watch infrastructures; and on supporting the Education and Training Programme of WMO. The Programme is funded mainly by UNDP, by WMO's own Voluntary Cooperation Programme, trust funds and the WMO regular budget.

The Regional Programme (RP) cuts across the other major WMO Programmes of relevance to the Regions and addresses meteorological, hydrological and other geophysical issues which are unique to and of common concern to a Region or group of Regions. It provides a framework for the formulation of most of the global WMO Programmes and serves as a mechanism for their implementation at the national, subregional and regional levels.

WORLD TRADE ORGANISATION (WTO)

The World Trade Organisation (WTO) is the only global international organisation dealing with the rules of trade between nations. At its heart are the WTO agreements, negotiated and signed by the bulk of the world's trading nations and ratified in their parliaments. The goal is to help producers of goods and services, exporters, and importers conduct their business.

The World Trade Organisation came into being in 1995. One of the youngest of the international organisations, the WTO is the successor to the General Agreement on Tariffs and Trade (GATT) established in the wake of the Second World War. So while the WTO is still young, the multilateral trading system that was originally set up under GATT is well over 50 years old.

The past 50 years have seen an exceptional growth in world trade. Merchandise exports grew on average by 6% annually. Total trade in 1997 was 14-times the level of 1950. GATT and the WTO have helped to create a strong and prosperous trading system contributing to unprecedented growth.

The system was developed through a series of trade negotiations, or rounds, held under GATT. The first rounds dealt mainly with tariff reductions but later negotiations included other areas such as anti-dumping and non-tariff measures. The last round—the 1986-94 Uruguay Round—led to the WTO's creation. The negotiations did not end there. Some continued after the end of the Uruguay Round.In February 1997 agreement was reached on telecommunications services, with 69 governments agreeing to wide-ranging liberalization measures that went beyond those agreed in the Uruguay Round. In the same year 40 governments successfully concluded negotiations for tariff-free trade in information technology products, and 70 members concluded a financial services deal covering more than 95% of trade in banking, insurance, securities and financial information.

In 2000, new talks started on agriculture and services. These have now been incorporated into a broader work programme, the Doha Development Agenda (DDA), launched at the fourth WTO Ministerial Conference in Doha, Qatar, in November 2001. The agenda adds negotiations and other work on non-agricultural tariffs, trade and environment, WTO rules such as anti-dumping and subsidies, investment, competition policy, trade facilitation, transparency in government procurement, intellectual property, and a range of issues raised by developing countries as difficulties they face in implementing the present WTO agreements. The deadline for the negotiations is 1 January 2005.

The WTO's rules—the agreements—are the result of negotiations between the members. The current set were the outcome of the 1986-94 Uruguay Round negotiations which included a major revision of the original General Agreement on Tariffs and Trade (GATT). GATT is now the WTO's principal rule-book for trade in goods. The Uruguay Round also created new rules for dealing with trade in services, relevant aspects of intellectual property, dispute settlement, and trade policy reviews. The complete set runs to some 30,000 pages consisting of about 60 agreements and separate commitments (called schedules) made by individual members in specific areas such as lower customs duty rates and services market-opening.

Through these agreements, WTO members operate a non-discriminatory trading system that spells out their rights and their obligations. Each country receives guarantees that its exports will be treated fairly and consistently in other countries' markets. Each promises to do the same for imports into its own market. The system also gives developing countries some flexibility in implementing their commitments.

Goods

It all began with trade in goods. From 1947 to 1994, GATT was the forum for negotiating lower customs duty rates and other trade barriers; the text of the General Agreement spelt out important rules, particularly non-discrimination.

Since 1995, the updated GATT has become the WTO's umbrella agreement for trade in goods. It has annexes dealing with specific sectors such as agriculture and textiles, and with specific issues such as state trading, product standards, subsidies and actions taken against dumping.

Services

Banks, insurance firms, telecommunications companies, tour operators, hotel chains and transport companies looking to do business abroad can now enjoy the same principles of freer and fairer trade that originally only applied to trade in goods.

These principles appear in the new General Agreement on Trade in Services (GATS). WTO members have also made individual commitments under GATS stating which of their services sectors they are willing to open to foreign competition, and how open those markets are.

Intellectual Property

The WTO's intellectual property agreement amounts to rules for trade and investment in ideas and creativity. The rules state how copyrights, patents, trademarks, geographical names used to identify products, industrial designs, integrated circuit layout-designs and undisclosed information such as trade secrets—"intellectual property"—should be protected when trade is involved.

Dispute Settlement

The WTO's procedure for resolving trade quarrels under the Dispute Settlement Understanding is vital for enforcing the rules and therefore for ensuring that trade flows smoothly. Countries bring disputes to the WTO if they think their rights under the agreements are being infringed. Judgements by specially-appointed independent experts are based on interpretations of the agreements and individual countries' commitments.

The system encourages countries to settle their differences through consultation. Failing that, they can follow a carefully mapped out, stage-by-stage procedure that includes the possibility of a ruling by a panel of experts, and the chance to appeal the ruling on legal grounds. Confidence in the system is borne out by the number of cases brought to the WTO—around 300 cases in eight years compared to the 300 disputes dealt with during the entire life of GATT (1947-94).

The WTO's overriding objective is to help trade flow smoothly, freely, fairly and predictably. It does this by:

- administering trade agreements,
- acting as a forum for trade negotiations,
- settling trade disputes,
- reviewing national trade policies.

Structure

The WTO has nearly 150 members, accounting for over 97% of world trade. Around 30 others are negotiating membership. Decisions are made by the entire membership. This is typically by consensus. A majority vote is also possible but it has never been used in the WTO, and was extremely rare under the WTO's predecessor, GATT. The WTO's agreements have been ratified in all members' parliaments.

The WTO's top level decision-making body is the Ministerial Conference which meets at least once every two years. The Fifth WTO Ministerial Conference was held in Cancún, Mexico from 10 to 14 September 2003.

Below this is the General Council (normally ambassadors and heads of delegation in Geneva, but sometimes officials sent from members' capitals) which meets several times a year in the Geneva headquarters. The General Council also meets as the Trade Policy Review Body and the Dispute Settlement Body.

At the next level, the Goods Council, Services Council and Intellectual Property (TRIPS) Council report to the General Council.

Numerous specialized committees, working groups and working parties deal with the individual agreements and other areas such as the environment, development, membership applications and regional trade agreements.

The WTO Secretariat, based in Geneva, has around 560 staff and is headed by a director general. It does not have branch offices outside Geneva. Since decisions are taken by the members themselves, the Secretariat does not have the decision-making role that other international bureaucracies are given.

The Secretariat's main duties are to supply technical support for the various councils and committees and the ministerial conferences, to provide technical assistance for developing countries, to analyze world trade, and to explain WTO affairs to the public and media. The Secretariat also provides some forms of legal assistance in the dispute settlement process and advises governments wishing to become members of the WTO. The annual budget is roughly 155 million Swiss francs.

2.4 UN: ITS MAJOR ACHIEVEMENTS

The United Nations was established in the aftermath of a devastating war to help stabilize international relations and give peace a more secure foundation.

Amid the threat of nuclear war and seemingly endless regional conflicts, peace-keeping has become an overriding concern of the United Nations. In the process, the activities of blue-helmeted peace-keepers have emerged as the most visible role associated with the world organisation.

The United Nations, however, is much more than a peace-keeper and forum for conflict resolution. Often without attracting attention, the United Nations and its family of agencies are engaged in a vast array of work that touches every aspect of people's lives around the world. Child survival and development; Environmental protection; Human rights; Health and medical research; Alleviation of poverty and economic development; Agricultural development and fisheries; Education; Family planning; Emergency and disaster relief; Air and sea travel; Peaceful uses of atomic energy; Labour and workers' rights. The list goes on. Here, in brief, is a sampling of what the United Nations organisations have accomplished since 1945 when the world organisation was founded.

Maintaining peace and security. By having deployed a total of 54 peace-keeping forces and observer missions as of September 2001, the United Nations has been able to restore calm to allow the negotiating process to go forward while saving millions of people from becoming casualties of conflicts. There are presently 15 active peace-keeping forces in operation.

Making peace. Since 1945, the United Nations has been credited with negotiating many peaceful settlements that have ended regional conflicts. Recent cases include an end to the Iran-Iraq war, the withdrawal of Soviet troops from Afghanistan, and an end to the civil war in El Salvador. The United Nations has used quiet diplomacy to avert imminent wars.

Promoting democracy. The United Nations has enabled people in many countries to participate in free and fair elections, including those held in Cambodia, Namibia, El Salvador, Eritrea, Mozambique, Nicaragua, South Africa, Kosovo and East Timor. It has provided electoral advice, assistance, and monitoring of results.

Promoting development. The UN system has devoted more attention and resources to the promotion of the development of human skills and potentials than any other external assistance effort. The system's annual disbursements, including loans and grants, amount to more than $10 billion. The UN Development Programme (UNDP), in close cooperation with over 170 Member States and other UN agencies, designs and implements projects for agriculture, industry, education, and the environment. It supports more than 5,000 projects with a budget of $1.3 billion. It is the largest multilateral source of grant development assistance. The World Bank, at the forefront in mobilizing support for developing countries worldwide, has alone loaned $333 billion for development projects since 1946. In addition, UNICEF spends more than $800 million a year, primarily on immunization, health care, nutrition and basic education in 138 countries.

Promoting human rights. Since adopting the Universal Declaration of Human Rights in 1948, the United Nations has helped enact dozens of comprehensive agreements on political, civil, economic, social and cultural rights. By investigating individual complaints of human rights abuses, the UN Human

Rights Commission has focused world attention on cases of torture, disappearance, and arbitrary detention and has generated international pressure to be brought on governments to improve their human rights records.

Protecting the environment. The United Nations has played a vital role in fashioning a global programme designed to protect the environment. The "Earth Summit," the UN Conference on Environment and Development held in Rio de Janeiro in 1992, resulted in treaties on biodiversity and climate change, and all countries adopted "Agenda 21"—a blueprint to promote sustainable development or the concept of economic growth while protecting natural resources. The UN World Summit on Sustainable Development held in 2002 is remarkable in this regard and was considered as a follow-up to the first Earth Summit of 1992.

Preventing nuclear proliferation. The United Nations, through the International Atomic Energy Agency, has helped minimize the threat of a nuclear war by inspecting nuclear reactors in 90 countries to ensure that nuclear materials are not diverted for military purposes.

Promoting self determination and independence. The United Nations has played a role in bringing about independence in countries that are now among its Member States.

Strengthening international law. Over 300 international treaties, on topics as varied as human rights conventions to agreements on the use of outer space and seabed, have been enacted through the efforts of the United Nations.

Handing down judicial settlements of major international disputes. By giving judgments and advisory opinions, the International Court of Justice has helped settle international disputes involving territorial issues, non-interference in the internal affairs of States, diplomatic relations, hostage-taking, the right of asylum, rights of passage and economic rights.

Ending apartheid in South Africa. By imposing measures ranging from an arms embargo to a convention against segregated sporting events, the United Nations was a major factor in bringing about the downfall of the apartheid system, which the General Assembly called "a crime against humanity."

Elections were held in April 1994 in which all South Africans were allowed to participate on an equal basis, followed by the establishment of a majority government.

Providing humanitarian aid to victims of conflict. More than 30 million refugees fleeing war, famine or persecution have received aid from the UN High Commissioner for Refugees since 1951 in a continuing effort coordinated by the United Nations that often involves other agencies. There are more than 19 million refugees, mostly women and children, who are receiving food, shelter, medical aid, education and repatriation assistance.

Aiding Palestinian refugees. Since 1950, the United Nations Relief and Works Agency (UNRWA) has sustained four generations of Palestinians with free schooling, essential health care, relief assistance and key social services virtually without interruption. There are 2.9 million refugees in the Middle East served by UNRWA.

Alleviating chronic hunger and rural poverty in developing countries. The International Fund for Agricultural Development (IFAD) has developed a system of providing credit, often in very small amounts, for the poorest and most marginalised groups that has benefited over 230 million people in nearly 100 developing countries.

Focusing on African development. For the United Nations, Africa continues to be the highest priority. In 1986, the United Nations convened a special session to drum up international support for African economic recovery and development. The United Nations also has instituted a system-wide task force to ensure that commitments made by the international community are honoured and challenges met. The Africa Project Development Facility has helped entrepreneurs in 25 countries to find financing for new enterprises. The Facility has completed 130 projects which represent investments of $233 million and the creation of 13,000 new jobs. It is expected that these new enterprises will either earn or save some $131 million in foreign exchange annually.

Promoting women's rights. A long term objective of the United Nations has been to improve the lives of women and to empower women to have greater control over their lives.

Several conferences during the UN-sponsored International Women's Decade set an agenda for the advancement of women and women's rights for the rest of the century. The UN Development Fund for Women (UNIFEM) and the International Research and Training Institute for the Advancement of Women (INSTRAW) have supported programmes and projects to improve the quality of life for women in over 100 countries. They include credit and training, access to new food-production technologies and marketing opportunities, and other means of promoting women's work.

Providing safe drinking water. UN agencies have worked to make safe drinking water available to 1.3 billion people in rural areas during the last decade.

Eradicating smallpox. A 13-year effort by the World Health Organisation resulted in the complete eradication of smallpox from the planet in 1980. The eradication has saved an estimated $1 billion a year in vaccination and monitoring, almost three times the cost of eliminating the scourge itself. WHO also helped wipe out polio from the Western hemisphere, with global eradication expected by the year 2000.

Pressing for universal immunization. Polio, tetanus, measles, whooping cough, diphtheria and tuberculosis still kill more than eight million children each year. In 1974, only 5 per cent of children in developing countries were immunized against these diseases. Today, as a result of the efforts of UNICEF and WHO, there is an 80 per cent immunization rate, saving the lives of more than 3 million children each year.

Reducing child mortality rates. Through oral rehydration therapy, water and sanitation and other health and nutrition measures undertaken by UN agencies, child mortality rates in the developing countries have been halved since 1960, increasing the life expectancy from 37 to 67 years.

Fighting parasitic diseases. Efforts by UN agencies in North Africa to eliminate the dreaded screw worm, a parasite that feeds on human and animal flesh, prevented the spread of the parasite, which is carried by flies, to Egypt, Tunisia, sub-Saharan Africa and Europe. A WHO programme also has saved the lives of 7 million children from going blind from the river blindness and rescued many others from guinea worm and other tropical diseases.

Promoting investment in developing countries. The United Nations, through the efforts of the UN Industrial Development Organisation (UNIDO), has served as a "match-maker" for North-South, South-South and East-West investment, promoting entrepreneurship and self-reliance, industrial cooperation and technology transfer and cost-effective, ecologically-sensitive industry.

Orienting economic policy toward social need. Many UN agencies have emphasized the need to take account of human needs in determining economic adjustment and restructuring policies and programmes, including measures to safeguard the poor, especially in areas of health and education, and "debt swaps for children."

Reducing the effects of natural disasters. The World Meteorological Organisation (WMO) has spared millions of people from the calamitous effects of both natural and man-made disasters. Its early warning system, which utilizes thousands of surface monitors as well as satellites, has provided information for the dispersal of oil spills and has predicted long-term droughts. The system has allowed for the efficient distribution of food aid to drought regions, such as southern Africa in 1992.

Providing food to victims of emergencies. Nearly 815 million people are currently suffering from chronic malnutrition, including 300 million children. In 2001, the World Food Programme (WFP) distributed 4.2 million tons of food to 77 million people in 82 countries for a total operational expenditure of $ 1.74 billion. 20 million people received, through development projects, aid in food-for-work projects to promote agriculture, improve the environment, and in school feeding, health, and nutrition projects, and 57 million people were offered assistance through short- and long-term operations. These beneficiaries include internally displaced people, refugees, and victims of natural disasters such as floods and drought.

Clearing land mines. The United Nations is leading an international effort to clear land mines from former battlefields in Afghanistan, Angola, Cambodia, El Salvador, Mozambique, Rwanda and Somalia that still kill and maim thousands of innocent people every year.

Protecting the ozone layer. The UN Environment Programme (UNEP) and the World Meteorological Organisation (WMO) have been instrumental in highlighting the damage caused to the earth's ozone layer. As a result of a treaty, known as the Montreal Protocol, there has been a global effort to reduce chemical emissions of substances that have caused the depletion of the ozone layer. The effort will spare millions of people from the increased risk of contracting cancer due to additional exposure to ultraviolet radiation.

Curbing global warming. Through the Global Environment Facility, countries have contributed substantial resources to curb conditions that cause global warming. Increasing emissions from burning fossil fuels and changes in land use patterns have led to a build-up of gases in the atmosphere, which experts believe can lead to a warming of the Earth's temperature.

Preventing over-fishing. The Food and Agriculture Organisation (FAO) monitors marine fishery production and issues alerts to prevent damage due to over-fishing.

Limiting deforestation and promoting sustainable forestry development. FAO, UNDP and the World Bank, through a Tropical Forests Action Programme, have formulated and carried out forestry action plans in 90 countries.

Cleaning up pollution. UNEP led a major effort to clean up the Mediterranean Sea. It encouraged adversaries such as Syria and Israel, Turkey and Greece to work together to clean up beaches. As a result, more than 50 per cent of the previously polluted beaches are now usable.

Protecting consumers' health. To ensure the safety of food sold in the market place, UN agencies have established standards for over 200 food commodities and safety limits for more than 3,000 food containers.

Reducing fertility rates. The UN Population Fund (UNFPA), through its family planning programmes, has enabled people to make informed choices, and consequently given families, and especially women, greater control over their lives. As a result, women in developing countries are having fewer children—from six births per woman in the 1960s to 3.5 today. In the 1960s, only 10 per cent of the world's families were using effective methods of family planning. The number now stands at 55 per cent.

Fighting drug abuse. The UN International Drug Control Programme (UNDCP) has worked to reduce demand for illicit drugs, suppress drug trafficking, and has helped farmers to reduce their economic reliance on growing narcotic crops by shifting farm production toward other dependable sources of income.

Improving global trade relations. The UN Conference on Trade and Development (UNCTAD) has worked to obtain special trade preferences for developing countries to export their products to developed countries. It has also negotiated international commodities agreements to ensure fair prices for developing countries. And through the General Agreement on Tariffs and Trade (GATT), which has now been supplanted by the World Trade Organisation (WTO), the United Nations has supported trade liberalization, that will increase economic development opportunities in developing countries.

Promoting economic reform. Together with the World Bank and the International Monetary Fund, the United Nations has helped many countries improve their economic management, offered training for government finance officials, and provided financial assistance to countries experiencing temporary balance of payment difficulties.

Promoting worker rights. The International Labour Organisation (ILO) has worked to guarantee freedom of the right to association, the right to organize, collective bargaining, the rights of indigenous and tribal peoples, promote employment and equal remuneration and has sought to eliminate discrimination and child labour. And by setting safety standards, ILO has helped reduce the toll of work-related accidents.

Introducing improved agricultural techniques and reducing costs. With assistance from the Food and Agricultural Organisation (FAO) that has resulted in improved crop yields, Asian rice farmers have saved $12 million on pesticides and governments over $150 million a year in pesticide subsidies.

Promoting stability and order in the world's oceans. Through three international conferences, the third lasting more than nine years, the United Nations has spearheaded an international effort to promote a comprehensive global agreement for the protection, preservation and peaceful development of the oceans. The UN Convention on the Law of the Sea, which came into force in 1994, lays down rules for the determination of national maritime jurisdiction, navigation on the high seas, rights and duties of coastal and other states, obligation to protect and preserve the marine environment, cooperation in the conduct of marine scientific research and preservation of living resources.

Improving air and sea travel. UN agencies have been responsible for setting safety standards for sea and air travel. The efforts of the International Civil Aviation Organisation (ICAO) have contributed to making air travel the safest mode of transportation. To wit: In 1947, when nine million travelled, 590 were killed in aircraft accidents; in 1993 the number of deaths was 936 out of the 1.2 billion airline passengers. Over the last two decades, pollution from tankers has been reduced by as much as 60 per cent thanks to the work of the International Maritime Organisation (IMO).

Protecting intellectual property. The World Intellectual Property Organisation (WIPO) provides protection for new inventions and maintains a register of nearly 3 million national trademarks. Through treaties, it also protects the works of artists, composers and authors world-wide. WIPO's work makes it easier and less costly for individuals and enterprises to enforce their property rights. It also broadens the opportunity to distribute new ideas and products without relinquishing control over the property rights.

Promoting the free flow of information. To allow all people to obtain information that is free of censorship and culturally unbiased, UNESCO has provided aid to develop and strengthen communication systems, established news agencies and supported an independent press.

Improving global communications. The Universal Postal Union (UPU) has maintained and regulated international mail delivery. The International Telecommunications Union (ITU) has coordinated use of the radio spectrum, promoted cooperation in assigning positions for stationary satellites, and established international standards for communications, thereby ensuring the unfettered flow of information around the globe.

Empowering the voiceless. UN-sponsored international years and conferences have caused governments to recognize the needs and contributions of groups usually excluded from decision-making, such as the aging, children, youth, homeless, indigenous and disabled people.

Establishing "children as a zone of peace". From El Salvador to Lebanon, Sudan to former Yugoslavia, UNICEF pioneered the establishment of "Days of Tranquillity" and the opening of "Corridors of Peace" to provide vaccines and other assistance desperately needed by children caught in armed conflict.

Generating worldwide commitment in support of the needs of children. Through UNICEF's efforts, the Convention on the Rights of the Child entered into force as international law in 1990 and has become law in 166 countries by the end of September 1994; following the 1990 World Summit for Children convened by UNICEF, more than 150 governments have committed to reaching over 20 specific measurable goals to radically improve children's lives by the year 2000.

Improving education in developing countries. As a direct result of the efforts of UN agencies, over 60 per cent of adults in developing countries can now read and write, and 90 per cent of children in these countries attend school.

Improving literacy for women. Programmes aimed at promoting education and advancement for women helped raise steadily the female literacy rate in developing countries from 36 per cent in 1970 to 56 per cent in 1990 and to 72 per cent in 2000.

Safeguarding and preserving historic cultural and architectural sites. Ancient monuments in 81 countries including Greece, Egypt, Italy, Indonesia and Cambodia, have been protected through the efforts of UNESCO, and international conventions have been adopted to preserve cultural property.

Facilitating academic and cultural exchanges. The United Nations, through UNESCO and the United Nations University

(UNU), have encouraged scholarly and scientific cooperation, networking of institutions and promotion of cultural expressions, including those of minorities and indigenous people.

The UN has been, over the years, delivering laudable humanitarian assistance to the needy people. In response to the crises in Afghanistan, the UN through its World Food Programme (WFP) launched one of its largest relief operations ever to feed more than six million people. It also extended food relief operations to the civil war hit countries of Africa such as Angola and Sierra Leone. In natural disaster management, the UN role has been equally laudable. Whether it is volcanic eruption in Congo or an earthquake in Afghanistan or drought in Southern Africa and Central Asia or floods in Central Europe, China, Iran, Jamaica, Kenya, Phillipinnes and Russia, the UN or its agencies have been among the first to assist the concerned government in the rescue or the rehabilitation measures.

The United Nations Conference on Trade and Development (UNCTAD) continues to help developing countries participate in international trading system. The UNCTAD programmes are aimed at expanding the trading opportunities of developing countries by building up their capacities through advisory services and access to information and training. Addressing the needs of the developing countries has always remained a key concern of the UN agenda.

The UN has set Millennium Development Goal to mobilize domestic and international financial resources for development; enhancing foreign direct investment and other private flows; expanding international trade as an engine for development; increasing international financial and technical cooperation for development; making external debt sustainable; and addressing systematic issues.

2.5 UN: RELEVANCE IN THE EMERGING GLOBAL SCENARIO

The prevailing mood at the time of the inception of the UN was of hope and satisfaction for a peaceful and orderly international order. Soon the hope turned into despair. Simmering differences and discontents between the two erstwhile superpowers while pursuing the ideological and so called enlightened national interests via resource and territorial pursuits gave a stammering blow to the World Body. UN platform was sharply divided into two power blocs with their respective camp followers. It turned UN into an ideological battleground. International peace, security and order were at great risk on many occasions. Issues of vital concerned bypassed serious deliberations and clear cut solutions.

The rise of parallel bodies was another blow to the authority of the UN during the Cold War. The birth of several political and security related organisations, economics and social set-ups diverted the actual role of UN. These parallel bodies played their part in creating wide fissures within the UN on vital international issues and thus eluded any solutions for long. One serious implications of such a development was nuclear and missile race and proliferations worldwide.

Post Cold War World Order

The collapse of bi-polarity and the sudden demise of the Cold War ignited hopes in many quarters of the newly reshaped and refurbished World Body taking the reins of the world affairs in its legitimate way. The hope was that there would be no more violation of the international law in dealing with issues so vital for international relations and politics.

The transition of the Cold War saga of uneasines, sidelining and disregard of the UN and its authority was also seen in the post- Cold war era. It all started with the Gulf War-I when the World Body had no specific and clearly defined role to execute. Though the war was necessitated to liberate Kuwait from Iraqi aggression, yet the execution of War had no full-fledged approval of the UN. Since then the World Body entered a new quagmire of helplessness due to the style of the functioning of its own strongest member. UN continued to be the victim of negligence, apathy and lackadaisical attitude and this time due to unbridled authority of the Super Power exercising the self-appointed role of the Global Policeman in every domain of global affairs seeking justification of its action in the UN authority. UN's role in world peace and stability continued to be hijacked by the Super Power and the bodies like the Trans- Atlantic alliance in the form of NATO that has been strengthened and reshaped with the changing contours of the global political map. In this regard unilateralism demonstrated by the US defying the UN and taking the law in its own hand is what that deserves attention.

Gulf–War II

The US second war against Iraq (this time mainly along with the UK), without the UN security council approval has many grave implications. It is clear that this blatant violation of the UN approval to initiate a war against Iraq, is both a violation of the charter and a defiant violation of the political norms of international relations since the Second World War. The US-UK role can only be describe as twenty first century capitalism ending in (US) imperialism—a repetition of what other old colonial rulers of the seventeenth—nineteenth century resorted to for protecting their capitalism. The war espoused Unilateralism and exposed Multilateralism.

Now since the war is over, that the US war against Iraq was an unjust war need no elaboration. All the excuses and rationales put forward by the US to support its war have fallen flat. No weapons of mass destruction have been found. No links with international terrorism have been brought to light, and no credible threats to the US have been established. The war, in all respect , violated the UN principals of ensuring the sovereignty of member states, world peace and stability and peaceful resolutions of disputes.

Relevance and Prospects

The UN has suffered massive erosion of its values in recent years. The American doctrine of pre-emptive military intervention poses a fundamental challenge to world peace and stability on which the UN has rested since the last 58 years. The Gulf-War II has raised the doubts about the relevance and the creditability of the World Body.

A constant refrain has been that the recent events have rendered UN “irrelevant”. This blatantly exposed the delicate nature of UN arrangement. However, it was not for the first time that the open violation of the UN charter was discernible. Throughout the Cold War period, the collective security system remained virtually paralysed for want of unanimity among the P-5 (permanent members). US is not the only power that has defied the UN. The UN was nowhere in the picture when NATO bombed former Yugoslavia. Decades earlier, the Vietnam war was also kept out of the UN as if by the tacit consent of all concerned. The Soviet Union ignored UN opinion on Hungary and Czechoslovakia. Israel has chosen for many decades to take unilateral action, notwithstanding the UN resolutions. Apartheid South Africa also did the same. Thus, unilateralism is not something very new. Many states have practiced it at sometime or the other, even though the magnitude of actions have varied in terms of its global importance. The big difference, however, is that the US has engaged in such action rationalization that seems to defy logic, accompanied by threatening extension of that same rationalisation to yet other countries and situations.

In this background, the latest instance of the use of force in Iraq without the authorization of the Security Council cannot be said to have rendered the UN irrelevant. As a matter of fact, the UN deserves to be congratulated because this time it did not allow itself to be stampeded into legitimizing an unjust and illegal war.

Besides, the UN does not consist only of its collective security system. Over the years, the UN has put in place a comprehensive international system consisting of a number of sub-systems—the world aviation, postal, telecommunications; the human rights system; and the whole corpus of norms, standards, codes and guidelines in practically all spheres of international life. To these should be added the world trading, financial and monetary system which being a part of UN system, functions outside it. These sub-systems are indispensable for the world community, including the US. Without them, there would be utter chaos. Besides, some of these regimes, particularly the international trading, monetary and financial system, are designed to promote and accelerate the process of globalization. These have by no means rendered the UN irrelevant.

The future of the World Body can be estimated from its role in Iraq's reconstruction. Regardless of the past differences, it is essential for the every one to work towards a stable and democratic Iraq. A united stand would in all possibility curtail the self appointed role of the Global policeman. The support for the UN role is increasing. The Arab League supports for a strong UN role. The European Union is for the UN to step in for a viable multilateral effort. Even the UK and Australia has shown such preference. In the post-Iraq war, US is talking about problems such as rebuilding Iraq, Afghanistan, and fight proliferation of heinous weapons, AIDS and sex trafficking. The reason for American quiescence is apparently the lesson it has learnt in Iraq. Its continuing problem in that country has shown that even a hyper power needs help. The reluctance of countries like India to send troops to Iraq without a UN mandate has highlighted the relevance of the World Body in the matter of conferring legitimacy to a war. The US-UK have won a war but have failed to gain legitimacy for it so far. The UN as an organisation to bestow legitimacy, has greater credibility than any single power. The UN, therefore, has come through a difficult period in its history with its reputation intact, perhaps even enhanced.

Unipolarity and unilateralism—the commonly perceived enemies of the UN and the present international situation would not disappear. The UN represents the concept of multipolarity but it cannot by itself change the power structure or the system. Attitudes and mindsets have to change. This has not happened in last five decades and may take as many, if not more, years to do so. A more positive and healthier way of looking at things has to be developed. The UN should be nurtured as an institution which can serve the common interests of all. It must be based on the conviction that the post 1945 world represents a definite and distinct break from the past. The UN signifies a new paradigm for the ordering of international relations and it is the best road map for the future.

EXTRACTS FROM THE UN CHARTER

The Objectives

- to save succeeding generations from the scourge of war, which twice in our lifetime has brought untold sorrow to mankind,
- to reaffirm faith in fundamental human rights, in the dignity and worth of the human person, in the equal

rights of men and women and of nations large and small,

- to establish conditions under which justice and respect for the obligations arising from treaties and other sources of international law can be maintained,
- to promote social progress and better standards of life in larger freedom.

And for these Ends

- to practice tolerance and live together in peace with one another as good neighbours,
- to unite our strength to maintain international peace and security,
- to ensure, by the acceptance of principles and the institution of methods, that armed force shall not be used, save in the common interest,
- to employ international machinery for the promotion of the economic and social advancement of all peoples.

The **Purposes** of the United Nations are:

- To maintain international peace and security, and to that end: to take effective collective measures for the prevention and removal of threats to the peace; for the suppression of acts of aggression or other breaches of the peace, and to bring about by peaceful means, and in conformity with the principles of justice and international law, adjustment or settlement of international disputes or situations which might lead to a breach of the peace;
- To develop friendly relations among nations based on respect for the principle of equal rights and self-determination of peoples, and to take other appropriate measures to strengthen universal peace;
- To achieve international co-operation in solving international problems of an economic, social, cultural, or humanitarian character, and in promoting and encouraging respect for human rights and for fundamental freedoms for all without distinction as to race, sex, language, or religion;

- To be a centre for harmonizing the actions of nations in the attainment of these common ends.

The Organisation and its Members, in pursuit of the Purposes stated in Article 1, shall act in accordance with the following Principles:

- The Organisation is based on the principle of the sovereign equality of all its Members.
- All Members, in order to ensure to all of them the rights and benefits resulting from membership, shall fulfill in good faith the obligations assumed by them in accordance with the present Charter.
- All Members shall settle their international disputes by peaceful means in such a manner that international peace and security, and justice, are not endangered.
- All Members shall refrain in their international relations from the threat or use of force against the territorial integrity or political independence of any state, or in any other manner inconsistent with the Purposes of the United Nations.
- All Members shall give the United Nations every assistance in any action it takes in accordance with the present Charter, and shall refrain from giving assistance to any state against which the United Nations is taking preventive or enforcement action.
- The Organisation shall ensure that states which are not Members of the United Nations act in accordance with these Principles so far as may be necessary for the maintenance of international peace and security.
- Nothing contained in the present Charter shall authorize the United Nations to intervene in matters which are essentially within the domestic jurisdiction of any state or shall require the Members to submit such matters to settlement under the present Charter; but this principle shall not prejudice the application of enforcement measures under Chapter Vll.

Following is the list of the 191 Member States of the United Nations with dates on which they joined the Organisation:

Member — (Date of Admission)
Afghanistan — (19 Nov. 1946)
Albania — (14 Dec. 1955)
Algeria — (8 Oct. 1962)
Andorra — (28 July 1993)
Angola — (1 Dec. 1976)
Antigua and Barbuda — (11 Nov. 1981)
Argentina — (24 Oct. 1945)
Armenia — (2 Mar. 1992)
Australia — (1 Nov. 1945)
Austria— (14 Dec. 1955)
Azerbaijan — (2 Mar. 1992)
Bahamas — (18 Sep. 1973)
Bahrain — (21 Sep. 1971)
Bangladesh — (17 Sep. 1974)
Barbados — (9 Dec. 1966)
Belarus — (24 Oct. 1945)

On 19 September 1991, Byelorussia informed the United Nations that it had changed its name to Belarus.

Belgium — (27 Dec. 1945)
Belize — (25 Sep. 1981)
Benin — (20 Sep. 1960)
Bhutan — (21 Sep. 1971)
Bolivia — (14 Nov. 1945)
Bosnia and Herzegovina — (22 May 1992)

The Socialist Federal Republic of Yugoslavia was an original Member of the United Nations, the Charter having been signed on its behalf on 26 June 1945 and ratified 19 October 1945, until its dissolution following the establishment and subsequent admission as new members of Bosnia and Herzegovina, the Republic of Croatia, the Republic of Slovenia, The former Yugoslav Republic of Macedonia, and the Federal Republic of Yugoslavia.

The Republic of Bosnia and Herzegovina was admitted as a Member of the United Nations by General Assembly resolution A/RES/46/237 of 22 May 1992.

Botswana — (17 Oct. 1966)
Brazil — (24 Oct. 1945)

Brunei Darussalam — (21 Sep. 1984)
Bulgaria — (14 Dec. 1955)
Burkina Faso — (20 Sep. 1960)
Burundi — (18 Sep. 1962)
Cambodia — (14 Dec. 1955)
Cameroon — (20 Sep. 1960)
Canada — (9 Nov. 1945)
Cape Verde — (16 Sep. 1975)
Central African Republic — (20 Sep. 1960)
Chad — (20 Sep. 1960)
Chile — (24 Oct. 1945)
China — (24 Oct. 1945)
Colombia — (5 Nov. 1945)
Comoros — (12 Nov. 1975)
Congo — (20 Sep. 1960)
Costa Rica — (2 Nov. 1945)
Côte d'Ivoire — (20 Sep. 1960)
Croatia — (22 May 1992)

The Socialist Federal Republic of Yugoslavia was an original Member of the United Nations, the Charter having been signed on its behalf on 26 June 1945 and ratified 19 October 1945, until its dissolution following the establishment and subsequent admission as new members of Bosnia and Herzegovina, the Republic of Croatia, the Republic of Slovenia, The former Yugoslav Republic of Macedonia, and the Federal Republic of Yugoslavia.

The Republic of Croatia was admitted as a Member of the United Nations by General Assembly resolution A/RES/46/238 of 22 May 1992.

Cuba — (24 Oct. 1945)
Cyprus — (20 Sep. 1960)
Czech Republic — (19 Jan. 1993)

Czechoslovakia was an original Member of the United Nations from 24 October 1945. In a letter dated 10 December 1992, its Permanent Representative informed the Secretary-General that the Czech and Slovak Federal Republic would cease to exist on 31 December 1992 and that the Czech Republic and the Slovak Republic, as successor States, would apply for membership in the United Nations. Following the receipt of its application, the Security Council, on 8 January 1993, recommended to the General Assembly that the Czech Republic be admitted to United Nations membership. The Czech Republic was thus admitted on 19 January of that year as a Member State.

Democratic People's Republic of Korea — (17 Sep. 1991)
Democratic Republic of the Congo — (20 Sep. 1960)
Denmark — (24 Oct. 1945)
Djibouti — (20 Sep. 1977)
Dominica — (18 Dec. 1978)
Dominican Republic — (24 Oct. 1945)
Ecuador — (21 Dec. 1945)
Egypt — (24 Oct. 1945)

Egypt and Syria were original Members of the United Nations from 24 October 1945. Following a plebiscite on 21 February 1958, the United Arab Republic was established by a union of Egypt and Syria and continued as a single Member. On 13 October 1961, Syria, having resumed its status as an independent State, resumed its separate membership in the United Nations. On 2 September 1971, the United Arab Republic changed its name to the Arab Republic of Egypt.

El Salvador — (24 Oct. 1945)
Equatorial Guinea — (12 Nov. 1968)
Eritrea — (28 May 1993)
Estonia — (17 Sep. 1991)
Ethiopia — (13 Nov. 1945)
Fiji — (13 Oct. 1970)
Finland — (14 Dec. 1955)
France— (24 Oct. 1945)
Gabon — (20 Sep. 1960)
Gambia — (21 Sep. 1965)
Georgia — (31 July 1992)
Germany — (18 Sep. 1973)

The Federal Republic of Germany and the German Democratic Republic were admitted to membership in the United Nations on 18 September 1973. Through the accession of the German Democratic Republic to the Federal Republic of Germany, effective from 3 October 1990, the two German States have united to form one sovereign State.

Ghana — (8 Mar. 1957)
Greece — (25 Oct. 1945)
Grenada — (17 Sep. 1974)
Guatemala — (21 Nov. 1945)
Guinea — (12 Dec. 1958)
Guinea-Bissau — (17 Sep. 1974)

Guyana — (20 Sep. 1966)
Haiti — (24 Oct. 1945)
Honduras — (17 Dec. 1945)
Hungary — (14 Dec. 1955)
Iceland — (19 Nov. 1946)
India — (30 Oct. 1945)
Indonesia — (28 Sep. 1950)

By letter of 20 January 1965, Indonesia announced its decision to withdraw from the United Nations "at this stage and under the present circumstances". By telegram of 19 September 1966, it announced its decision "to resume full cooperation with the United Nations and to resume participation in its activities". On 28 September 1966, the General Assembly took note of this decision and the President invited representatives of Indonesia to take seats in the Assembly.

Iran (Islamic Republic of) — (24 Oct. 1945)
Iraq — (21 Dec. 1945)
Ireland — (14 Dec. 1955)
Israel — (11 May 1949)
Italy — (14 Dec. 1955)
Jamaica — (18 Sep. 1962)
Japan — (18 Dec. 1956)
Jordan — (14 Dec. 1955)
Kazakhstan — (2 Mar. 1992)
Kenya — (16 Dec. 1963)
Kiribati — (14 Sept. 1999)
Kuwait — (14 May 1963)
Kyrgyzstan — (2 Mar. 1992)
Lao People's Democratic Republic — (14 Dec. 1955)
Latvia — (17 Sep. 1991)
Lebanon — (24 Oct. 1945)
Lesotho — (17 Oct. 1966)
Liberia — (2 Nov. 1945)
Libyan Arab Jamahiriya — (14 Dec. 1955)
Liechtenstein— (18 Sep. 1990)
Lithuania — (17 Sep. 1991)
Luxembourg— (24 Oct. 1945)
Madagascar — (20 Sep. 1960)
Malawi — (1 Dec. 1964)
Malaysia— (17 Sep. 1957)

The Federation of Malaya joined the United Nations on 17 September 1957. On 16 September 1963, its name was changed to Malaysia, following the admission to the new federation of Singapore, Sabah (North Borneo) and Sarawak. Singapore became an independent State on 9 August 1965 and a Member of the United Nations on 21 September 1965.

Maldives— (21 Sep. 1965)
Mali — (28 Sep. 1960)
Malta — (1 Dec. 1964)
Marshall Islands — (17 Sep. 1991)
Mauritania — (27 Oct. 1961)
Mauritius — (24 Apr. 1968)
Mexico — (7 Nov. 1945)
Micronesia (Federated States of) — (17 Sep. 1991)
Monaco — (28 May 1993)
Mongolia — (27 Oct. 1961)
Morocco — (12 Nov. 1956)
Mozambique — (16 Sep. 1975)
Myanmar — (19 Apr. 1948)
Namibia — (23 Apr. 1990)
Nauru — (14 Sept. 1999)
Nepal — (14 Dec. 1955)
Netherlands — (10 Dec. 1945)
New Zealand — (24 Oct. 1945)
Nicaragua — (24 Oct. 1945)
Niger — (20 Sep. 1960)
Nigeria — (7 Oct. 1960)
Norway — (27 Nov. 1945)
Oman — (7 Oct. 1971)
Pakistan — (30 Sep. 1947)
Palau — (15 Dec. 1994)
Panama — (13 Nov. 1945)
Papua New Guinea — (10 Oct. 1975)
Paraguay — (24 Oct. 1945)
Peru — (31 Oct. 1945)
Philippines — (24 Oct. 1945)
Poland — (24 Oct. 1945)
Portugal — (14 Dec. 1955)
Qatar — (21 Sep. 1971)
Republic of Korea — (17 Sep. 1991)
Republic of Moldova — (2 Mar. 1992)

Romania — (14 Dec. 1955)
Russian Federation — (24 Oct. 1945)

> The Union of Soviet Socialist Republics was an original Member of the United Nations from 24 October 1945. In a letter dated 24 December 1991, Boris Yeltsin, the President of the Russian Federation, informed the Secretary-General that the membership of the Soviet Union in the Security Council and all other United Nations organs was being continued by the Russian Federation with the support of the 11 member countries of the Commonwealth of Independent States.

Rwanda — (18 Sep. 1962)
Saint Kitts and Nevis — (23 Sep. 1983)
Saint Lucia — (18 Sep. 1979)
Saint Vincent and the Grenadines — (16 Sep. 1980)
Samoa — (15 Dec. 1976)
San Marino — (2 Mar. 1992)
Sao Tome and Principe — (16 Sep. 1975)
Saudi Arabia — (24 Oct. 1945)
Senegal — (28 Sep. 1960)
Serbia and Montenegro — (1 Nov. 2000)

> The Socialist Federal Republic of Yugoslavia was an original Member of the United Nations, the Charter having been signed on its behalf on 26 June 1945 and ratified 19 October 1945, until its dissolution following the establishment and subsequent admission as new members of Bosnia and Herzegovina, the Republic of Croatia, the Republic of Slovenia, The former Yugoslav Republic of Macedonia, and the Federal Republic of Yugoslavia.
>
> The Federal Republic of Yugoslavia was admitted as a Member of the United Nations by General Assembly resolution A/RES/55/12 of 1 November 2000.
>
> Following the adoption and the promulgation of the Constitutional Charter of Serbia and Montenegro by the Assembly of the Federal Republic of Yugoslavia on 4 February 2003, the name of the State of the Federal Republic of Yugoslavia was changed to Serbia and Montenegro.

Seychelles — (21 Sep. 1976)
Sierra Leone — (27 Sep. 1961)
Singapore — (21 Sep. 1965)
Slovakia — (19 Jan. 1993)

Czechoslovakia was an original Member of the United Nations from 24 October 1945. In a letter dated 10 December 1992, its Permanent Representative informed the Secretary-General that the Czech and Slovak Federal Republic would cease to exist on 31 December 1992 and that the Czech Republic and the Slovak Republic, as successor States, would apply for membership in the United Nations. Following the receipt of its application, the Security Council, on 8 January 1993, recommended to the General Assembly that the Slovak Republic be admitted to United Nations membership. The Slovak Republic was thus admitted on 19 January of that year as a Member State.

Slovenia — (22 May 1992)

The Socialist Federal Republic of Yugoslavia was an original Member of the United Nations, the Charter having been signed on its behalf on 26 June 1945 and ratified 19 October 1945, until its dissolution following the establishment and subsequent admission as new members of Bosnia and Herzegovina, the Republic of Croatia, the Republic of Slovenia, The former Yugoslav Republic of Macedonia, and the Federal Republic of Yugoslavia.

The Republic of Slovenia was admitted as a Member of the United Nations by General Assembly resolution A/RES/46/236 of 22 May 1992.

Solomon Islands — (19 Sep. 1978)
Somalia — (20 Sep. 1960)
South Africa — (7 Nov. 1945)
Spain — (14 Dec. 1955)
Sri Lanka — (14 Dec. 1955)
Sudan — (12 Nov. 1956)
Suriname — (4 Dec. 1975)
Swaziland — (24 Sep. 1968)
Sweden — (19 Nov. 1946)
Switzerland — (10 Sep. 2002)
Syrian Arab Republic — (24 Oct. 1945)

Egypt and Syria were original Members of the United Nations from 24 October 1945. Following a plebiscite on 21 February 1958, the United Arab Republic was established by a union of Egypt and Syria and continued as a single Member. On 13 October 1961, Syria, having resumed its status as an independent State, resumed its separate membership in the United Nations.

Tajikistan — (2 Mar. 1992)
Thailand — (16 Dec. 1946)
The former Yugoslav Republic of Macedonia — (8 Apr. 1993)

The Socialist Federal Republic of Yugoslavia was an original Member of the United Nations, the Charter having been signed on its behalf on 26 June 1945 and ratified 19 October 1945, until its dissolution following the establishment and subsequent admission as new members of Bosnia and Herzegovina, the Republic of Croatia, the Republic of Slovenia, The former Yugoslav Republic of Macedonia, and the Federal Republic of Yugoslavia.

By resolution A/RES/47/225 of 8 April 1993, the General Assembly decided to admit as a Member of the United Nations the State being provisionally referred to for all purposes within the United Nations as "The former Yugoslav Republic of Macedonia" pending settlement of the difference that had arisen over its name.

Timor-Leste — (27 Sep. 2002)
Togo — (20 Sep. 1960)
Tonga — (14 Sep. 1999)
Trinidad and Tobago — (18 Sep. 1962)
Tunisia — (12 Nov. 1956)
Turkey — (24 Oct. 1945)
Turkmenistan — (2 Mar. 1992)
Tuvalu — (5 Sept. 2000)
Uganda — (25 Oct. 1962)
Ukraine — (24 Oct. 1945)
United Arab Emirates — (9 Dec. 1971)
United Kingdom of Great Britain and Northern Ireland — (24 Oct. 1945)
United Republic of Tanzania — (1 Nov. 1964)

Tanganyika was a Member of the United Nations from 14 December 1961 and Zanzibar was a Member from 16 December 1963. Following the ratification on 26 April 1964 of Articles of Union between Tanganyika and Zanzibar, the United Republic of Tanganyika and Zanzibar continued as a single Member, changing its name to the United Republic of Tanzania on 1 November 1964.

United States of America — (24 Oct. 1945)
Uruguay — (18 Dec. 1945)
Uzbekistan — (2 Mar. 1992)

Vanuatu — (15 Sep. 1981)
Venezuela — (15 Nov. 1945)
Viet Nam — (20 Sep. 1977)
Yemen — (30 Sep. 1947)

> Yemen was admitted to membership in the United Nations on 30 September 1947 and Democratic Yemen on 14 December 1967. On 22 May 1990, the two countries merged and have since been represented as one Member with the name “Yemen”.

Zambia — (1 Dec. 1964)
Zimbabwe — (25 Aug. 1980)

GLOBAL ISSUES ON THE UN AGENDA

Africa	Energy	The Millennium UN General Assembly - The Goals
Ageing	Environment	Question of Palestine
Agriculture	Family	Peace & Security
AIDS	Food	Population
Atomic Energy	Governance	Refugees
Children	Health	Social Development
Climate Change	Human Rights	Outer Space
Culture	Human Settlements	Statistics
Decolonization	Humanitarian Affairs	Sustainable Development
Demining	Indigenous People	Terrorism
Development Cooperation	Information Communications Technology	Trade & Development
Persons with Disabilities	Intellectual Property	Volunteerism
Disarmament	International Finance	Water
Drugs & Crime	Iraq	Women
Education	Labour	Youth
Elections	International Law	
	Law of the Sea & Antartica	
	Least Developed Countries	

SECRETARY GENERALS OF UN

KOFI ANAN (Ghana)
• Term of Office
1996- Till date

Boutros Boutros-Ghali (Egypt)
• Term of Office
1992-1996

Javier de Perez de Cuellar (Peru)
• Term of Office
1982-1991

Kurt Waldheim (Austria)
• Term of Office
1972-1981

U Thant (Myanmar)
• Term of Office
1961-1971

Dag Hammarskjöld (Sweden)
• Term of Office
1953-1961

Trygve Lie (Norway)
• Term of Office
1946-1952

2.6 UN: REFORMS AND RESTRUCTURING

The United Nations has ceased to be "a centre for harmonizing the actions of nations." The economically advanced countries have long succeeded in putting themselves outside the pale of UN's scrutiny and surveillance. They no longer allow it to direct its searchlight on their macro-economic policies. Hardcore economic issues relating even to the developing countries, such as financial flows, interest rates and exchange rate fluctuations, inflation, external indebtedness etc., are no longer allowed to be discussed within the forums of the UN. This is in contrast to the position till the beginnings of the 1970s when ideas such as trade preferences for developing countries, commodity price stabilization, various compensatory financing facilities under the IMF, issue of Special Drawing Rights by the IMF, target for the flow of financial resources, debt amelioration or forgiveness were all advanced and agreed upon within the UN.

Today, discussions in the UN are confined to the domestic, economic and social issues of developing countries. Among these, there is almost an exclusive concentration of how these countries can give greater play to free market forces and liberalise the external sectors of their economies. A great deal of emphasis is placed on technical assistance, almost as a diversion from real issues.

The major economic powers have succeeded in eroding the role and functions of the UN mainly by keeping it on the brink of financial bankruptcy by illegally withholding the payment of their contributions. For the same reason, they have spurned all suggestions for providing to the UN, access to the automatic and predictable sources of financing, such as through taxation on global commons. They have also forced upon all the organizations of the UN system for the last 20 years or so, a zero nominal growth in their budgets. This means a decline in real terms of 3 to 5 per cent per annum in their budgets.

The death and destruction brought about in the context of Iraq war has all the more questioned the relevance of the world body. The Iraq war represents the failure to resolve an international problem through multilateral channels. In fact, UN has been buried many times by critics, but it has survived. It has survived because the world does need a multilateral forum and a framework of international rules to create order and assist security.

While the U.N. may have been sidelined by the countries opting for unilateral action against Iraq, it is somewhat ironic that it has been called upon to pick up the pieces after the conflict. A range of UN agencies—the World Food Programme, UNICEF, the U.N. High Commission for Refugees, the UNDP and the Mine Action Service—sprang into action to alleviate hardship and suffering of the civilian population. The UN is also active to re-establish post-conflict governance and civil functions in Iraq.

Those challenging the relevance of the UN, also ignore the critical role it plays in wider areas of development, human rights, refugees and the environment. No other organization is able to confront the plethora of cross—border challenges:

global diseases including HIV/AIDS, malaria and TB, climate change, environmental degradation, refugee issues, people smuggling, human rights, poverty and hunger. If anything stands as a test to the United Nations, it is how it responds to these cross—border challenges. The U.N. system continues to set the international norms by which every member state should abide. In today's globalizing world, no member state, no matter how powerful it is, can disengage from multilateralism entirely.

The U.N. remains a relevant organization and will continue to have a central role to play in the 21st century. Notwithstanding media criticism of the United Nations, what seems to be forgotten is that the organization is only as strong as the will of its member states. The United Nations system relies on the collective will of all its members. It is these member states that set its priorities. The UN cannot act without their consent. It falls, therefore, upon us all to make the U.N. relevant in today's world.

For the U.N. to meet its potential it needs to reform. It needs to better prioritise its work to meet the needs of the member states. This was the essence of the Secretary General's second term reform initiative, which seeks to strengthen the organization to better respond to the priorities established in the Millennium Declaration and to meet the needs of Member States.

What is needed is to resurrect and update the UN. This will call for restoring to it Charter functions it has lost and introducing in it changes which reflect the transformations that have taken place in the world and which are in keeping with the core human values of liberty, justice, equity and respect for life.

The vast array of proposals on UN reforms contained in the reports of various commissions, working groups and individuals, submitted in the first half of the 1990s have to be taken into consideration. These included the report of the "Commission on Global Governance," "Our Global Neighbourhood ," that of the Independent Working Group on the future of the UN and that prepared on behalf of the Dag Hammarskjold Foundation by Erskine Childers and Brian

Urquhardt entitled, "Renewing the United Nations System." The last mentioned report made extensive suggestions on restructuring the Secretariat and the administrative and financial management of the U.N. It also cited elaborate facts and figures to convincingly explore the myths regarding the U.N.'s 'vast sprawling bureaucracy,' its 'large extravagant budgets' and its 'inefficiency and corruption,' deliberately perpetrated by the extra-conservative think—tanks in the West and exploited by their Government for whittling down the role and functions of the world body.

We need today to revisit the recommendations made in the 1990s and select those clamouring for urgent action and priority attention. Our effort should focus on the following areas:

First, the decision-making process in the Security Council on the issues of war and peace, i.e. on matters coming under chapter VII of the Charter, must reflect the vastly enhanced membership of the United Nations. This means expediting the process of expansion of both the permanent and non permanent membership of the Security Council. A crucial aspect of the reform of the Council should be to reach an agreement on phasing out within a specified time—frame, say, 10 to 15 years, to veto power of the permanent members of the council, and, in the interim, limiting this power strictly to issues relating to preventive action under Chapter VII.

Second, the U.N.'s capacity to mount speedily and effectively peacekeeping operations mainly under Chapter VI must be enhanced. This calls for the acceptance of the proposal made by the former Secretary General, Boutros Ghali, in his report "Agenda for peace,"to create a revolving fund so that peacekeeping operations can be mounted before assessed contributions star coming in. An alternative suggestion made in the report is the creation of a UN peace Endowment Fund of $1 billion, the returns from which could be used for initiating peacekeeping operations before contributions are received.

Third, there can be no peace without disarmament. The international community, therefore, must not allow the U.N. agenda of disarmament to remain suspended any longer. There are compelling reasons for reviving the agenda in which the highest priority must be attached to the elimination of nuclear and other weapons of mass destruction. There is no inconsistency between India pursuing the goal of nuclear disarmament and, at the same time, trying to build a nuclear deterrent. For, India is committed to put its entire nuclear arsenal on the negotiating table for arriving at a universal agreement for eliminating nuclear weapons. One of the suggestions intended to enable the U.N. to address the disarmament issue in an effective manner is to create a joint committee of the General Assembly and the Security Council, tasked to promote progress towards global disarmament.

Fourth, it is essential to bring global economic issues back on the UN agenda. The world body should be able to assess on a continuing basis the over-all state of the world economy, to provide a long-term strategy and policy frame work in order to promote stable, balanced and sustainable development; and to give political leadership and promote consensus on international economics issues. More specifically, it should once again be the venue for discussing harmonization of financial, monetary and trade policies pursued by the major governments transfer of resources and technology for development, functioning of the commodity markets, external indebtedness, stable international financial markets, etc.

Appropriate institutional changes within the U.N. have been suggested to enable it to resume these Charter functions. One of the suggestions is to convert the Economic and Social Council into an Economic Security Council with a much more limited membership. The other suggestion is to create two separate but smaller bodies namely, the Economic Council and the Social Council, to do full justice to the entire gamut of issues under these categories. Yet another suggestion is to streamline the functioning of the ECOSOC and devote one of its session specifically to discuss global economic issues and macro-economic policies of developed countries, insofar as they affect the development prospects of the world as a whole, particularly, those of the developing countries.

Fifth, the UN must have a close look at the emerging international financial architecture which is going to be more and more discretionary and fewer rule-based. The IMF and the World Bank will be left with no effective powers to intervene or play any intermediary role in the international financial and monetary systems. They will not be endowed with additional resources or liquidity to be able to play even a modest regulatory role. Bailing out operations will now be left to the discretion of the creditor countries which are likely to go mainly by political considerations in deciding to intervene.

Sixth, it is time to call off the prolonged financial blackmail against the UN. The organization must be allowed to breathe freely by lifting the embargo on increase in the budgets of the UN organizations, and considering their programmes on merit rather than within the straightjacket of the budgetary embargo. The UN must also be given access ot new and predictably recurring sources of financing. It should be allowed to impose levies on the exploitation and development of global commons and charges on the use of global resources such as ocean routes, airspace etc.

Finally, the U.N. mustaccommodate within its decision-making structure what has come to be known as the other superpower i.e. the peoples' power. It must find the means of ensuring that the voice of this superpower is heard in the U.N. and that its opinion is brought to bear on the organization's decision-making process. Among the suggestions made in this regard is the creation of a separate organ called the UN parliamentary assembly or an annual forum of civil society organizations to be convened at the UN headquarters just before the annual session of the General Assembly.

These suggestions cannot be pushed through the UN without the consent of the major powers of the world. What is important is to build a worldwide movement for UN reforms with the support of almost all the countries of the developing world, as many major powers as possible and the almost unanimous support of civil society organizations from all over the world. The process itself will be of great importance for enhancing the stature of the UN and, in the long run, it may very well culminate in a consensus on placing the UN on the highest pedestal of the international system.

3

OTHER MAJOR INTERNATIONAL ORGANISATIONS

AMNESTY INTERNATIONAL (AI)

Amnesty International is a world wide movement of people who campaign for internationally recognized human rights and is independent of any government, political ideology, economic interest or religion. Amnesty International mobilizes volunteer activists—people who give freely their time and energy in solidarity with those whose rights have been abused. It has more than one million members, supporters and subscribers in over 140 countries from all walks of life with widely different political and religious views, united with a determination to work for a world where everyone enjoys human rights.

The vision of Amnesty International is of a world in which every person enjoys all of the human rights enshrined in the Universal Declaration of Human Rights and other international human rights standards.

In pursuit of this vision, AI's mission is to undertake research and action focused on preventing and ending grave abuses of the rights to physical and mental integrity, freedom of conscience and expression, and freedom from discrimination, within the context of its work to promote all human rights.

Amnesty International works independently and impartially to promote respect for all the human rights set out in the Universal Declaration of Human Rights. It believes that the human rights are independent and indivisible—all human rights should be enjoyed by all people at all times, and no one set of rights should be enjoyed at the expense of the other rights. It concentrates on ending grave abuses of the rights to physical and mental integrity, freedom of conscience and expression, and freedom from discrimination.

Historically, the main focus of Amnesty International has been:

- to free all prisoners of conscience;
- to ensure a fair and prompt trial of all political prisoners;
- to abolish the death penalty, torture and other cruel, inhuman or degrading punishment;
- to end extra-judicial executions and "disappearances" and
- to fight impunity by working to ensure perpetrators of such abuses are brought to justice in accordance with international standards.

Over the years, the Amnesty International has expanded this mandate to encompass human rights abuses committed by non-governmental bodies and private individuals (non-state actors). It opposes abuses by armed political groups such as hostage taking, torture and unlawful killings. Amnesty International is opposed to human rights abuses against civilians and non-combatants by both sides during armed conflict. It has also targeted abuses in the home or community where governments have been complicit or have failed to take effective action. Amnesty International also assists asylum seekers who are at risk of being returned to a country where they will be at risk of violations of basic fundamental rights. It cooperates with other non-governmental organisations (NGOs), with the United Nations and with regional inter-governmental organisations and campaigns for increasing accountability in international military, security and police relations. Besides these, Amnesty International organizes human rights education and awareness raising programmes.

Organisation

Amnesty International is an organisation based on world wide voluntary membership and it shall consist of sections, structures international networks, affiliated groups and international members.

International Council. The ultimate authority of the conduct of the affairs of the Amnesty International is vested in the International Council.

International Executive Committee. The primary role of the committee is to provide leadership and stewardship for the whole of Amnesty International worldwide.

International Secretariat. The day-to-day affairs of the Amnesty International shall be conducted by the International Secretariat headed by the International Secretary General under the direction of the International Executive Committee.

Sections. A section of Amnesty International shall be established in any country, state or territory or region with the consent of International Executive Committee. These Sections should act in accordance with the core values and methods of Amnesty International as well as Integrated Strategic Plans, working rules and guidelines that are adopted from time-to-time by the International Council.

Structures. Structure of Amnesty International is any national or regional body established by the International Executive Committee, to promote and implement the movement's mission and vision. The purpose of a structure is to coordinate a sustained programme of human rights activities and consolidate its national and regional organisations.

International Networks. They exist to promote and implement the movement's vision and mission, primarily on the basis of a specific theme or identity.

The Amnesty International consists of more than 7,800 local, youth, specialists and professional groups in over 100 countries and territories. There are nationally organized sections in 58 countries, and pre-section coordinating structures in another 22 countries and territories worldwide.

ASIA-PACIFIC ECONOMIC COOPERATION (APEC)

Asia-Pacific Economic Cooperation, or APEC, is the premier forum for facilitating economic growth, cooperation, trade and investment in the Asia-Pacific region. APEC is the only inter governmental grouping in the world operating on the basis of non-binding commitments, open dialogue and equal respect for the views of all participants. Unlike the WTO or other multilateral trade bodies, APEC has no treaty obligations required of its participants. Decisions made within APEC are reached by consensus and commitments are undertaken on a voluntary basis.

APEC has 21 members—referred to as "Member Economies"—which account for more than a third of the world's population (2.6 billion people), over 50% of world GDP (US$ 19, 254 billion) and in excess of 41% of world trade. It also proudly represents the most economically dynamic region in the world having generated nearly 70% of global economic growth in its first 10 years.

APEC's 21 Member Economies are Australia; Brunei Darussalam; Canada; Chile; People's Republic of China; Hong Kong, China; Indonesia; Japan; Republic of Korea; Malaysia; Mexico; New Zealand; Papua New Guinea; Peru; The Republic of the Philippines; The Russian Federation; Singapore; Chinese Taipei; Thailand; United States of America; Viet Nam.

Purpose and Goals

APEC was established in 1989 to further enhance economic growth and prosperity for the region and to strengthen the Asia-Pacific community. Since its inception, APEC has worked to reduce tariffs and other trade barriers across the Asia-Pacific region, creating efficient domestic economies and dramatically increasing exports. Key to achieving APEC's vision are what are referred to as the 'Bogor Goals' of free and open trade and investment in the Asia-Pacific by 2010 for industrialised economies and 2020 for developing economies. These goals were adopted by Leaders at their 1994 meeting in Bogor, Indonesia.

Free and open trade and investment helps economies to grow, creates jobs and provides greater opportunities for international trade and investment. In contrast, protectionism keeps prices high and fosters inefficiencies in certain industries. Free and open trade helps to lower the costs of production and thus reduces the prices of goods and services—a direct benefit to all.

APEC also works to create an environment for the safe and efficient movement of goods, services and people across borders in the region through policy alignment and economic and technical cooperation.

Asia-Pacific Economic Cooperation (APEC) operates as a cooperative, multilateral economic and trade forum. It is unique in that it represents the only intergovernmental grouping in the world committed to reducing trade barriers and increasing investments without requiring its members to enter into legally binding obligations. The forum succeeds by promoting dialogue and equal respect for the views of all participants and making decisions based on consensus to achieve its free and open trade and investment goals.

APEC Member Economies take individual and collective actions to open their markets and promote economic growth.

Every year one of the 21 APEC Member Economies plays host to APEC meetings and serves as the APEC Chair. The APEC host economy is responsible for chairing the annual Economic Leaders' Meeting, selected Ministerial Meetings, Senior Officials Meetings, the APEC Business Advisory Council and the APEC Study Centres Consortium and also fills the Executive Director position at the APEC Secretariat. The Deputy Executive Director position is filled by a senior diplomat from the economy which will host in the next year.

Funding

APEC is not a donor organisation. Instead, APEC activities are centrally funded by small annual contributions from APEC Member Economies—since 1999 these have totalled US$3.38 million each year. These contributions are used to fund a small Secretariat in Singapore and various projects which support APEC's economic and trade goals. Since 1997 Japan has provided additional funds for projects (between US$2.7 and 4.2 million annually, depending on amount and exchange rates) which support APEC's trade and investment liberalisation and facilitation goals. Projects generally:

- Relate to the priorities of APEC Economic Leaders and APEC Ministers.
- Cover the interest of at least several APEC Member Economies.
- Build capacity.

- Improve economic efficiency.
- Encourage the participation of the business sector, non-governmental institutions and women.

APEC's Project Database contains information about all APEC projects.

APEC Member Economies also provide considerable resources to assist in the operations of APEC. These include the secondment of professional staff to the Secretariat; the hosting of meetings; and partial (or full) funding of some projects.

GROUP-7/8 (G-8)

Origins of the G-7 Summit

Four events in the early 1970s had a profound effect on the world economic system:

- "the collapse of the Bretton Woods monetary system" based on fixed exchange rates and on the United States dollar being convertible into gold. The two Bretton Woods institutions, the IMF and the World Bank, tried to set up the necessary reforms, but were not successful in this effort;
- the first enlargement of the European Community, with Britain, Denmark and Ireland joining the original six members;
- the first oil crisis that took place following the October 1973 Yom Kippur war, when OPEC placed an embargo on oil supplies. Western countries disagreed about how to respond to the embargo and to the sharp price increases;
- the 1974 economic recession in OECD countries, with inflation and unemployment rates up sharply.

With all these problems, "the traditional organs of international co-operation were no longer able to reconcile the differences among the leading Western powers or to give them a sense of common purpose."

It was in this context that the finance ministers of the United States, Germany, Britain and France met in April 1973 in the White House library, becoming known as the "Library

Group". Later joined by Japan, the group had met periodically for a number of years and had come to be known as the Group of Five finance ministers. The governors of the central banks of the Five sometimes joined the finance ministers at these meetings.

Two years after the initial get-together of the "Library Group", thirty-five heads of state and government gathered in Helsinki to sign the Final Act of the Conference on Security and Co-operation in Europe. The leaders of the four Western powers met for lunch at the British Embassy in Helsinki on 31 July, together with their foreign ministers. They discussed President Giscard's proposal that they should meet later that year, together with Japan, to address economic and monetary problems. This was the genesis of the summits.

Since 1975, the heads of state or government of the major industrial democracies have been meeting annually to deal with the major economic and political issues facing their domestic societies and the international community as a whole. The six countries at the first summit, held at Rambouillet, France in November 1975, were France, the United States, Britain, Germany, Japan and Italy. They were joined by Canada at the San Juan Summit of 1976 in Puerto Rico, and by the European Community at the London Summit of 1977. From then on, membership in the G7 was fixed, although 15 developing countries' leaders met with the G7 leaders on the eve of the 1989 Paris Summit, and the USSR and then Russia participated in a post-summit dialogue with the G7 since 1991. Starting with the 1994 Naples Summit, the G7 met with Russia at each summit (referred to as the P8 or Political 8). The Denver Summit of the Eight was a milestone, marking full Russian participation in all but financial and certain economic discussions; and the 1998 Birmingham Summit saw full Russian participation, giving birth to the G8 (although the G7 continued to function along side the formal summits). At the Kananaskis Summit in Canada in 2002, it was announced that Russia would host the G8 Summit in 2006, thus completing its process of becoming a full member.

The G7/8 Summit has consistently dealt with macro-economic management, international trade, and relations with developing countries. Questions of East-West economic relations, energy, and terrorism have also been of recurrent concern. From this initial foundation the summit agenda has broadened considerably to include microeconomic issues such as employment and the information highway, transnational issues such as the environment, crime and drugs, and a host of political-security issues ranging from human rights through regional security to arms control.

The responsibility of host rotates throughout the summit cycle at the end of the calendar year, as follows: France, United States, United Kingdom, Russia (as of 2006), Germany, Japan, Italy and Canada. Throughout the year, the leaders' personal representatives—known as sherpas—meet regularly to discuss the agenda and monitor progress.

In addition, the G7/8 has developed a network of supporting ministerial meetings, which allow ministers to meet regularly throughout the year in order to continue the work set out at each summit; these include the meetings of the finance ministers, foreign ministers and environment ministers, among others. G7/8 ministers and officials also meet on an ad hoc basis to deal with pressing issues, such a terrorism, energy, and development; from time to time the leaders also create task forces or working groups to focus intensively on certain issues of concern, such as a drug-related money laundering, nuclear safety, and transnational organized crime.

The G7/8 provides an important occasion for busy leaders to discuss major, often complex international issues, and to the develop the personal relations that help them respond in effective collective fashion to sudden crises or shocks. The summit also gives direction to the international community by setting priorities, defining new issues and providing guidance to established international organisations. At times it arrives at decisions that address pressing problems or shape international order more generally.

The summit members comply modestly with the decisions and consensus generated by and codified at their annual meeting. Compliance is particularly high in regard to agreements on international trade and energy, and on the part of Britain, Canada, and Germany. Summit decisions often create and build international regimes to deal with new international challenges, and catalyze, revitalize and reform existing international institutions.

In recognition of its centrality in the process of global governance, the summit has always attracted the attention of thousands of journalists at each leaders' meeting, and of a number of countries seeking admittance to this exclusive and powerful club. It has also become a prime occasion for non-governmental and civil society organisations to advocate on behalf of their concerns. The annual meeting has been an opportunity for anti-globalization demonstrations since the Birmingham Summit in 1998; the protests turned violent in 2001 at the Genoa Summit, resulting in the death of a protestor.

The 30th summit of the G-8 countries was held at sea Island in Georgia in June 2004. The main issues that dominated the summit were related to increase in oil prices, membership of India and China to G-8 and other economic, political, environmental and health related issues. Since 1998, this was for the first time that anti-globalisation protests were not held in this summit.

GROUP-15 (G-15)

G-15, a Summit level Group of 15 developing countries for consultation and cooperation, was an initiative taken at the Non-Aligned Summit at Belgrade in September, 1989. The rationale for setting up the G-15 was that there is considerable scope for cooperation among the developing countries consistent with mutuality of commercial and economic benefits especially over the medium and long term horizon. The mandate of the G-15 adopted at its inception in 1989 is:

- To identify new specific and concrete ideas or schemes to foster South-South Cooperation, commit their governments to them and mobilise wider support and
- To hold a review of the world economic situation and the state of international relations affecting developing countries with a view to developing common perceptions on them and suggest common strategies including initiatives to be proposed in North-South fora.

The membership of the G-15 includes both non-aligned and other developing countries. It comprises: Algeria, Argentina, Brazil, Chile, Egypt, India, Indonesia, Jamaica, Malaysia, Mexico, Nigeria, Peru, Senegal, Venezuela and Zimbabwe. A decision regarding admission of Kenya was taken at the Sixth G-15 Summit in Harare in November 1996.

A Technical Support Facility (TSF) functions as the G-15 Secretariat located in Geneva to assist in coordinating the work of the G-15. It is a small set-up having two or three professionals.

The Summits have provided useful opportunities to the participating Heads of States/Governments to exchange perceptions on major international issues, challenges faced by the developing countries in political, economic, environmental and social fields and to share their experiences in meeting these challenges. The Summits have helped the G-15 countries in developing better and common understanding on the evolving international situation and its implications for developing countries. The common perceptions and positions of the G-15 countries are reflected in the Joint Communiqué and the Summary Conclusions of the Summit.

The G-15 took an initiative to establish a dialogue with the G-7 on international economic issues. In messages sent to the G-7 Chairman, the G-15 has pointed out that radical changes in the international situation required a new world partnership based on shared global economic management and regular consultations. These could be instituted between the two groups to address structural problems in the global economy, issues relating to debt, money and finance, early and balanced implementation of results of the Uruguay Round, protection of environment and sustainable development and revitalisation of the UN. The G-7 Chairmen have acknowledged that the issues raised in the G-15 messages have relevance and are taken into account by G-7.

The G-15's mandate for South-South Cooperation has been implemented through well-conceived cooperative projects in diverse sectoral areas such as food production, population and family planning, geological and mineral research, telecommunications, energy, gene banks of medicinal and aromatic plants, solar energy applications, training in computers, business forum, small scale industries, etc. Another dimension has been added to this since the New Delhi Summit of March 1994 which decided to "broaden the scope of intra-G-15 economic cooperation" through the setting up of a Committee on Investment, Trade and Technology (CITT) which will work towards evolution of trans-regional arrangements, key elements of which would be "liberalisation, facilitation and promotion of trade to demonstrably increase economic interaction within the Group". The CITT was launched at the Buenos Aires Summit.

The G-15 mechanism has also intensified contacts and interaction among the businessmen of member countries to make use of new opportunities for cooperation in trade, investment, technology, improvement of infrastructure and other fields. The meetings among businessmen are also held at the time of the Summits as part of the Business Forum.

GROUP-20 (G-20)

On September 25, 1999 in Washington, D.C., the Finance Ministers of the Group of Seven (G-7) leading industrialized nations announced the creation of the Group of Twenty (G-20). This international forum of Finance Ministers and Central Bank Governors represents 19 countries, the European Union and the Bretton Woods Institutions (the International Monetary Fund—IMF—and the World Bank).

The creation of the G-20 fulfilled the commitment by G-7 leaders at the June 1999 Summit at Köln "...to establish an informal mechanism for dialogue among systemically important countries within the framework of the Bretton Woods institutional system."

The G-20 promotes discussion, and studies and reviews policy issues among industrialized countries and emerging markets with a view to promoting international financial stability.

Member countries include: Argentina, Australia, Brazil, Canada, China, France, Germany, India, Indonesia, Italy, Japan, México, Russia, Saudi Arabia, South Africa, Korea, Turkey, the United Kingdom, the United States and the European Union.

The Managing Director of the IMF and the President of the World Bank, as well as the Chairpersons of the International Monetary and Financial Committee and Development Committee of the IMF and World Bank, participate fully in the discussions.

Through broad participation by industrialized countries and key emerging markets, the G-20 represents a range of viewpoints essential for promoting consensus on the major international financial issues.

Like the G-7, but unlike larger international organisations such as the United Nations, the World Bank and the IMF, the G-20 has no permanent Secretariat. The size and structure of the G-20 is designed to encourage the informal exchange of views and the formation of consensus on international economic and financial issues. Each year, a temporary Secretariat is established by the chairing country with the objective of coordinating the work of the Group and organizing the meetings.

The G-20 complements the activities of other international organisations:

- The inclusion of the President of the World Bank, the Managing Director of the IMF and the Chairpersons of the International Monetary and Financial Committee and the Development Committee ensures that the G-20 process is well integrated with the activities of these institutions.
- The G-20 helps co-ordinate the activities of other international groups and organisations, such as the Financial Stability Forum.
- It also facilitates the deliberations of more formal bodies such as the International Monetary and Financial Committee.
- The potential for the development of common positions on complex issues among G-20 members provides a mechanism to expedite decision-making in other fora.
- Due to the broad focus of the policy discussions that take place in the context of the G-20 meetings, the Group invites institutional experts to join the dialogue

on selected subjects, thus increasing synergies between different bodies and institutions.

Meetings of Finance Ministers and Central Bank Governors are held every year. The most recent meeting of G-20 Ministers and Governors was held in New Delhi, India on November 23, 2002. Ministers' and Governors' Deputies meet for technical discussions on substantive matters and to prepare the content of the Ministers and Governors dialogue.

Ministerial meetings of the G-20 include the Finance Ministers and Deputies, and Central Bank Governors and Deputies of the member countries. As well, the Finance Minister of the country holding the Presidency of the European Union and the President of the European Central Bank participate.

The Managing Director of the IMF, the President of the World Bank, and the Finance Ministers of the countries chairing the International Monetary and Financial Committee and the Development Committee of the IMF and World Bank are also included as full members of the group.

Rationale of G-20

Since 1986, the G-7 Finance Ministers' grouping has proven to be an effective forum for informal and substantive discussion of important international economic issues, leading to greater understanding and co-ordination among policy makers in the G-7 countries.

The lack of emerging-market representation in the G-7 limits its ability to deal with some issues related to developments in the international economy and financial system. In today's economy, broader representation in policy discussions is crucial. The G-20 is designed to fulfill this need for representation from emerging markets.

In his April 27, 1999 remarks to the Interim Committee of the IMF, Minister Martin highlighted the need for more representative institutional arrangements. This need was further reflected in the June 1999 Report of G-7 Finance Ministers to the Köln Summit on Strengthening the International Financial Architecture.

Prior to the creation of the G-20, ad hoc groupings known as the G-22 and G-33 were convened to help address specific issues related to the emerging-markets financial crisis of the late 1990s but were not integrated with the governance structures of the IMF or the World Bank.

- The G-22 met in Washington in April and October 1998. The purpose of the G-22 was to involve non-G-7 countries in the resolution of the global aspects of the emerging-markets financial crisis.
- At two subsequent "outreach" meetings in March and April 1999, the G-33 discussed issues related to reform of the global economy and international financial system.

The useful suggestions for enhancing global economic security that emanated from the G-22 and G-33 processes demonstrated the potential value of a regular international consultative forum with a broader membership than the G-7.

The creation of the G-20 represents the next stage in the evolution of informal consultation among industrialized countries and emerging markets, necessary to bridge positions and promote mutual understandings, thus enhancing consensus.

GROUP-77 (G-77)

The Group of 77 (G-77) was established on 15 June 1964 by seventy-seven developing countries signatories of the "Joint Declaration of the Seventy-Seven Countries" issued at the end of the first session of the United Nations Conference on Trade and Development (UNCTAD) in Geneva. Beginning with the first Ministerial Meeting of the Group of 77 in Algiers in 1967 which adopted the Charter of Algiers, a permanent institutional structure gradually developed which led to the creation of Chapters of the Group of 77 in Rome (FAO), Vienna (UNIDO), Paris (UNESCO), Nairobi (UNEP) and the Group of 24 in Washington, D.C. (IMF and World Bank). Although the membership of the G-77 has increased to 135 countries, the original name was retained because of its historic significance.

As the largest Third World coalition in the United Nations, the Group of 77 provides the means for the developing world to articulate and promote its collective economic interests and enhance its joint negotiating capacity on all major international economic issues in the United Nations system, and promote economic and technical cooperation among developing countries (ECDC/TCDC).

The organisation and modalities of work of the G-77 in the various Chapters have certain minimal features in common such as a similarity in membership, decision-making and certain operating methods. The Group's work in each Chapter is coordinated by a chairman who acts as its spokesman. The chairmanship rotates on a regional basis (between Africa, Asia, and Latin America and the Caribbean) and is held for one year in all the Chapters. Currently the State of Qatar holds the Chairmanship of the Group of 77 in New York for the year 2004.

The Ministerial Meeting is the supreme decision-making body of the Group of 77. They are convened annually at the beginning of the regular sessions of the General Assembly of the United Nations in New York and periodically in preparation for UNCTAD sessions and the General Conferences of UNIDO and UNESCO. Special Ministerial Meetings are also called as needed such as on the occasion of the Group's 25th anniversary (Caracas, June 1989) and 30th anniversary (New York, June 1994). In April 2000 the Group of 77 met for the first time at the level of heads of state or government which therefore elevated decision-making within the Group of 77 to the highest political level. The Chairmanship is the highest political institution within the organisational structure of the Group of 77.

The Intergovernmental Follow-up and Coordination Committee on Economic Cooperation among Developing Countries (IFCC) is a plenary body consisting of senior officials which meets once every two years to review the state of implementation of the Caracas Programme of Action (CPA) adopted by the Group of 77 in 1981. The IFCC was last convened in Tehran, Islamic Republic of Iran, in August 2001. Subsidiary structures created to support the CPA include, among others, the Core of Assistants to the Chairman of the Group of 77, the Committee of Experts of the Perez-Guerrero Trust Fund (PGTF) for ECDC/TCDC, the General Conference and

Steering Committee of Chambers of Commerce and Industry of the Group of 77, Action Committees, and National Focal Points for ECDC.

The activities of the Group of 77 are financed through contributions by Member States and other developing countries.

Activities

1. It produces joint declarations, action programmes and agreements on specific topic such as Algiers Charter in 1967; Lima Declaration in 1971; Manila Declaration in 1976; Arusha Programme for Self-Reliance and Framework for Negotiations in 1979; Caracas Programme of Action on ECDC in 1981; Cairo Declaration on ECDC in 1986; Havana Declaration in 1987; Agreement on a Global System of Trade Preferences among Developing Countries (GSTP) in 1988; Caracas Declaration in 1989; Tehran Declaration in 1991; 30th Anniversary Ministerial Declaration in 1994; Ministerial Statement on "An Agenda for Development" in 1994; San Jose Declaration and Plan of Action on South-South Trade, Investment and Finance in 1997; Bali Declaration and Plan of Action on Regional and Subregional Economic Cooperation of the Developing Countries in 1998; Havana Programme of Action adopted by the South Summit in 2000; and Tehran Consensus adopted by IFCC-X in 2001.
2. Makes statements, sponsors and negotiates resolutions and decisions at global conferences and other meetings held under the aegis of the United Nations dealing with international economic cooperation and development.
3. Sponsors projects on ECDC/TCDC in developing countries through funding from the Perez-Guerrero Trust Fund.

In its first two decades, it was the dominant force shaping the agenda of economic and social issues at the UN. Political and security issues were left off the G-77 agenda; they were the primary focus of the Non-Aligned Movement because most Latin American countries sided with the West during the Cold War. G-77 influence peaked in the 1970s. Energized by the rising power of the Organisation of Petroleum Exporting States (OPEC), it tried unsuccessfully to negotiate a "new international economic order." Since then, due to internal and external reasons, its influence has waned.

Internal factors. Perhaps the most obvious of these is that the G-77 has no permanent structure. Its leadership changes annually. The Chairman is supported only by a small, seconded staff that changes every few years. Institutional memory resides disproportionately in its documentation, which has traditionally been negotiated issue by issue at regional levels, with substantive input from national sources and parts of the UN system (UNCTAD and the Regional Commissions, mostly). Regional positions are then merged into a G-77 paper or negotiating text. The process allows all interests within the Group to be reflected in the documentation, but does little for coherence. Lack of coherence has been further accentuated by the strengthening identities of a variety of subgroups of developing countries within the UN membership. A number of new groups such as the Least Developed Countries (LDCs), the Small Island Developing States, and the Landlocked Countries reflect special needs. Others, to mention only a few, are based on such factors as language (French, Spanish and Portuguese), religion (Islam), history (Commonwealth), and subregion (Andean, Arab, Southeast Asia, Caribbean, and South Pacific). All these groups deal with economic and social issues. There are arguments that this is desirable because it improves the focus on special needs and interests within the G-77, which it does. But the net result has been to weaken allegiance to the larger group and sap its ability to set effective overall strategy. Increasingly, the G-77 has become an umbrella for subgroup positions.

External factors. Outside forces that had a weakening impact on the G-77 include some of the broad political developments of our time. The end of apartheid and the beginning of the Middle East peace process both had the effect of reducing African-Arab dynamism and synergy within the G-77. The rise of OPEC opened up a large gap between its suddenly wealthy members and the rest of the G-77. The emergence of the Asian "Tigers" and the graduation of Mexico to the North American Free Trade Association (NAFTA) further underlined the differences between economically successful members of the G-77 and those at the opposite extreme. The end of the Cold War and the demise of the Eastern European Group at the UN (it survives only for electioneering) accentuated differences between democratic and totalitarian states in the G-77. In sum, these developments fundamentally altered the political underpinnings of the G-77 and had the effect of obscuring the overall rationale for the existence of the Group. Increasingly, the work of the Group became pro forma in nature.

All this is not to say that the basic rationale of the G-77 has weakened However, it is certainly still relevant in a world where industrialized countries have enjoyed swift progress, and most developing countries continue to exist in circumstances of deprivation, vulnerability and weakness. As a group, developing countries, have slipped further behind developed countries in income, and the technological gap is widening at an alarming rate. Even developing countries that have prospered over the last four decades remain vulnerable to international economic volatilities over which they have little control. With four-fifths of the world's population, developing countries continue to have little voice or influence in the arrangements that shape international political and economic realities.

INTERNATIONAL CRIMINAL COURT (ICC)

Based in The Hague, Netherlands, the International Criminal Court (ICC) is the first permanent court capable of trying individuals accused of the most serious violations of international humanitarian and human rights law, namely genocide, crimes against humanity and war crimes.

On July 17, 1998 the Rome Statute of the ICC was adopted. Governments convened regularly on the subject of the ICC through bi- or tri-annual meetings of the United Nations Preparatory Commission for the ICC. Through the efforts of the Preparatory Commission, a large volume of work was produced, including a complementary set of rules of procedure and evidence for investigating and prosecuting genocide, crimes against humanity and war crimes.

Following the Statute's entry into force on July 1, 2002, countries that have ratified and acceded to the Statute have convened in the Assembly of States Parties—the ICC's governing body responsible for the political, legislative, financial and management oversight of the ICC.

At the national level, much work remains in the campaign for universal ratification and effective implementation of the Rome Statute. While every region of the world is represented amongst ratifying countries, further support is needed from key regions, including Asia and the Middle East. Countries that ratify or accede to the Rome Statute must also adopt complementary national legislation to enable full cooperation with the ICC and to allow for national-level prosecutions of the same crimes.

Furthermore, like the UN and other independent international institutions, the ICC relies on a separate agreement known as the Agreement on Privileges and Immunities to protect the Court and its personnel. Both States Parties and non-States Parties must ratify this agreement to ensure the safe access of ICC staff to their territory and the unimpeded transfer of evidence, witnesses and other information to and from the Court.

In the late 80s and early 90s, only a handful of non-governmental organisations (NGOs) had active programs supporting the establishment of an International Criminal Court (ICC). Since that time, the Coalition has grown to include over 2,000 NGOs from all regions of the world and many sectors of global civil society, including human rights, the rights of women and children, peace, international law, humanitarian assistance, the rights of victims, and religion. These groups are united in their support for a fair and effective permanent International Criminal Court (ICC) and have made a significant contribution at all stages of the process, from the Preparatory Committee to the Rome Conference to the UN Preparatory Commission for the ICC.

With entry into force of the Rome Statute for the ICC on July 1, 2002, the Coalition has developed the following goals for its work in this phase:

- Obtaining worldwide ratification of the Rome Statute;

- Ensuring the development of strong implementing legislation in all ratifying countries;
- Ensuring that the appropriate mechanisms are in place for the Court to begin functioning effectively as early as possible;
- Monitoring and supporting the work of the Assembly of States Parties;
- Generating international public support for the Court;
- Providing information to key stakeholders at the national and international level about the Court, the Rome Statute & supporting documents;
- Monitoring and supporting the work of the functioning Court;
- Building the Coalition and its networks.

The role of the Coalition Secretariat is to coordinate, facilitate and support the work of its global membership in working towards these goals. This is done through regional coordinators around the world, and through a dedicated staff in New York and now the Hague, including information services coordinators for English, French and Spanish, a media liaison, a legal team, technical staff and others.

The creation of the International Criminal Court (ICC) is a historic victory for human rights and international justice. It is the first permanent international judicial institution with jurisdiction over individuals who commit the most egregious violations of human rights and humanitarian law. The ICC has often been described as the "missing link" in international human rights enforcement. Despite the existence of domestic legislation and several multilateral treaties dealing with some of the crimes included in the Rome Statute of the ICC (genocide, war crimes and crimes against humanity), no permanent enforcement mechanism with jurisdiction over individuals who commit these crimes, regardless of their official position, has ever existed at the international level.

While the creation of the ICC is of tremendous relevance to human rights advocates, it impacts those who work on a wide variety of causes, such as women's issues, children's rights, the non-proliferation of weapons, environmental issues and many others.

In the latter part of the 19th century and first decades of the 20th, international agreements on the laws of war raised the hope that when conflict broke out, there would be certain standards of conduct which would be respected by all parties, and which would reduce the horror and the devastating impact of war on the individuals, communities and nations involved. Yet despite this codification of laws to govern war, the 20th century was the most war-ravaged century in history. While wars became more frequent and more brutal, the majority of the horrific crimes perpetrated against innocent people were committed with impunity. What has been missing is the means to enforce legal standards, a commitment from states and organisations to participate in ensuring that these standards are met, and a clear indication that no nation and no individual may be above the law.

The International Criminal Court will make international standards of conduct more specific, provide an important mechanism for implementation of these standards and ensure that the perpetrators are brought to justice before the ICC when national Courts are unable or unwilling to do so. Equally important could be the impact on national laws as ratifying nations fulfill their obligation to ensure that these crimes can be tried within their own borders. While the Court's jurisdiction will not be retroactive, the future Hitlers, Pinochets, Pol Pots, and Idi Amins will have little opportunity to escape justice.

The ICC also represents one of the most significant opportunities the world has had to prevent or drastically reduce the deaths and devastation caused by conflict through deterrence and as a result of its ability to begin investigations and prosecutions at an early stage, thus contributing to the earlier cessation of violence and more expedient resolutions of conflicts. The establishment of the Court must also be understood in a broader context, in terms of its ability to affect some of the most critical issues of our time. These include the recruitment and use of child soldiers, the widespread incidence of crimes of sexual violence, the commission of crimes motivated by racism, the proliferation and widespread use of small arms, and many others.

INTERNATIONAL CRIMINAL POLICE ORGANISATION (INTERPOL)

International Criminal Police Organisation, is a worldwide clearinghouse for police information. Conceived in 1914, Interpol was formally established in 1923 with headquarters at Vienna. In 1938, it was effectively disbanded by Hitler's *Anschluss* of Austria. After World War II, the agency was reconstituted (1946) with headquarters in Paris.

Its principal services are to provide member nations with information on the whereabouts of international criminals, to organize seminars on scientific crime detection, and to facilitate the apprehension of criminals, although it does not apprehend criminals directly. The organisation claims to avoid those crimes that deal with political, military, religious, or racial matters. Interpol has been most successful with regard to counterfeiting, forgery, smuggling, and the narcotics trade. The United States became a member in 1938.

Interpol is the largest international police organisation in the world. It was set up in to facilitate cross-border criminal police cooperation and today has 181 member countries spread over five continents. It supports and assists all organisations, authorities and services whose mission is to prevent or combat international crime.

Interpol's General Secretariat in Lyon, France, provides a fast and reliable communication system that links police around the globe. Its priority activities concern public safety and terrorism, criminal organisations, drug-related crimes, financial and high-tech crime, trafficking in human beings, and fugitive investigation support. But Interpol's staff, many of them police officers seconded to Lyon from police forces around the world, also provide a range of crucial services in other areas of criminal investigation and crime prevention.

One of Interpol's most important tasks is to place member countries on alert about people who are being sought by police forces worldwide but it is a member country's domestic police who request that they be placed on the Interpol wanted list and it is domestic police who, for the most part, must track and arrest them.

Interpol is the sum of its constituent parts, but the General Secretariat in Lyon is the essential co-ordinating mechanism that gives its members access to international databases of criminal information as well as a global view on specific crimes, patterns and trends.

Organisational Strúcture

The General Assembly is composed of delegates appointed by the governments of Member States. As Interpol's supreme governing body, it meets once a year and takes all the major decisions affecting general policy, the resources needed for international co-operation, working methods, finances and programmes of activities. It also elects the Organisation's Executive Committee. Generally speaking, the Assembly takes decisions by a simple majority in the form of resolutions. Each Member State represented has one vote.

The Executive Committee is Interpol's select deliberative organ which meets three times a year, usually in March, July and immediately before the General Assembly. Its role, in accordance with Article 22 of the Constitution, is to supervise the execution of the decisions of the General Assembly prepare the agenda for sessions of the General Assembly submit to the General Assembly any programme of work or project which it considers useful supervise the administration and work of the Secretary General. The Executive Committee may propose amendments to the organisation's constitution, revises the Staff Rules and the Rules on the Deletion of Police Information and proposes their adoption to the General Assembly.

In accordance with Article 15 of the Constitution, the Executive Committee has 13 members comprising the president of the organisation, 3 vice-presidents and 9 delegates. These members are elected by the General Assembly and should belong to different countries, in addition, the president and the 3 vice-presidents must come from different regions. The president is elected for 4 years, and vice-presidents for 3. They are not immediately eligible for re-election either to the same posts, or as delegates to the Executive Committee. Voting is by secret ballot. A two-thirds majority is required for the election of the president. If this majority is not obtained after the second ballot, a simple majority is then sufficient. Vice-Presidents and delegates are elected on a simple majority.

Each member state has one vote; those member states attending the General Assembly are eligible to take part in the election, providing they are not prevented from doing so under Article 52 of the General Regulations.

The General Secretariat is headed by the Secretary General of the Organisation, who is appointed by the General Assembly for a period of 5 years. He may be re-elected. The Secretary General is effectively the Organisation's chief full-time official. He is responsible for seeing that the day-to-day work of international police co-operation is carried out, and the implementation of the decisions of the General Assembly and Executive Committee. The role is defined in the Constitution, in particular, Articles 28, 29 and 30. The General Regulations stipulate the broad framework for the election of the Secretary General in Articles 42, 43 and 44.

INTERNATIONAL FEDERATION OF THE RED CROSS (IFRC)

The International Federation was founded in 1919 in Paris in the aftermath of World War I. The war had shown a need for close cooperation between Red Cross Societies, which, through their humanitarian activities on behalf of prisoners of war and combatants, had attracted millions of volunteers and built a large body of expertise. A devastated Europe could not afford to lose such a resource.

It was Henry Davison, president of the American Red Cross War Committee, who proposed forming a federation of these National Societies. An international medical conference initiated by Davison resulted in the birth of the League of Red Cross Societies, which was renamed in October 1983 to the League of Red Cross and Red Crescent Societies, and then in November 1991 to become the International Federation of Red Cross and Red Crescent Societies.

The first objective of the Federation was to improve the health of people in countries that had suffered greatly during the four years of war. Its goals were "to strengthen and unite, for health activities, already-existing Red Cross Societies and to promote the creation of new Societies"

There were five founding member Societies: Britain, France, Italy, Japan and the United States. This number has grown over the years and there are now 178 recognized National Societies—one in almost every country in the world. Its first mission was to assist typhoid and famine victims in Poland; today it runs more than 80 relief operations a year.

The Red Cross idea was born in 1859, when Henry Dunant, a young Swiss man, came upon the scene of a bloody battle in Solferino, Italy, between the armies of imperial Austria and the Franco-Sardinian alliance. Some 40,000 men lay dead or dying on the battlefield and the wounded were lacking medical attention.

Dunant organized local people to bind the soldiers' wounds and to feed and comfort them. On his return, he called for the creation of national relief societies to assist those wounded in war, and pointed the way to the future Geneva Conventions.

The Red Cross was born in 1863 when five Geneva men, including Dunant, set up the International Committee for Relief to the Wounded, later to become the International Committee of the Red Cross. Its emblem was a red cross on a white background: the inverse of the Swiss flag. The following year, 12 governments adopted the first Geneva Convention; a milestone in the history of humanity, offering care for the wounded, and defining medical services as "neutral" on the battlefield.

The International Federation of Red Cross and Red Crescent Societies is the world's largest humanitarian organisation, providing assistance without discrimination as to nationality, race, religious beliefs, class or political opinions.

Founded in 1919, the International Federation comprises 181 member Red Cross and Red Crescent societies, a Secretariat in Geneva and more than 60 delegations strategically located to support activities around the world. There are more societies in formation. The Red Crescent is used in place of the Red Cross in many Islamic countries.

The Federation's mission is to improve the lives of vulnerable people by mobilizing the power of humanity. Vulnerable people are those who are at greatest risk from situations that threaten their survival, or their capacity to live with an acceptable level of social and economic security and human dignity. Often, these are victims of natural disasters, poverty brought about by socio-economic crises, refugees, and victims of health emergencies.

The Federation carries out relief operations to assist victims of disasters, and combines this with development work to strengthen the capacities of its member National Societies. The Federation's work focuses on four core areas: promoting humanitarian values, disaster response, disaster preparedness, and health and community care.

The unique network of National Societies - which cover almost every country in the world - is the Federation's principal strength. Cooperation between National Societies gives the Federation greater potential to develop capacities and assist those most in need. At a local level, the network enables the Federation to reach individual communities.

The role of the Secretariat in Geneva is to coordinate and mobilize relief assistance for international emergencies, promote cooperation between National Societies and represent these National Societies in the international field.

The role of the field delegations is to assist and advise National Societies with relief operations and development programmes, and encourage regional cooperation.

The Federation, together with National Societies and the International Committee of the Red Cross, make up the International Red Cross and Red Crescent Movement.

While the Secretariat is responsible for the day-to-day running of the Federation, the decisions on its direction and policy are made by the governing bodies. These bodies define a framework of purpose, policies, goals and programmes, and provide a mechanism for accountability and compliance.

The General Assembly is the highest decision-making body of the Federation. It meets every two years and comprises representatives from all member National Societies. It met in Geneva in November 2003.

A Governing Board acts between general assemblies, meeting twice a year with the authority to make certain decisions. The board comprises the Federation's president and vice presidents, representatives from elected member Societies and the chairman of the Finance Commission. Four other commissions cover health and community services, youth, disaster relief and development.

The General Assembly is responsible for appointing the secretary general, who is the chief executive officer of the Federation, directing the Secretariat and its delegations.

The International Federation's programmes are grouped into four main core areas: promoting humanitarian principles and values; disaster response; disaster preparedness; and health and care in the community. These activities are those which are carried out by most National Societies.

Red Cross Red Crescent promotes individual and community humanitarian values which encourage respect for other human beings and a willingness to work together to find solutions to problems. Disaster response continues to represent the largest portion of the work, with assistance to around 30 million people annually from refugees to victims of natural disasters. The sharp increase in the number of natural disasters worldwide in recent years has prompted the Federation to devote more attention to disaster preparedness activities. These aim to make National Societies and communities more aware of the risks they face, how to reduce their vulnerability, and how to cope when disaster strikes.

Too many people die as a result of no access to even the most basic health services and elementary health education. Health and community care has become a cornerstone of humanitarian assistance, and accounts for a large part of Red Cross Red Crescent spending. Through these programmes, the Federation aims to enable communities to reduce their vulnerability to disease, and prepare for and respond to public health crises.

Guiding and supporting the development of its member National Societies is one of the Federation's fundamental tasks, and runs through these four core areas and other programmes. Capacity building programmes include management and volunteer training, branch structures, planning, fund-raising and gender equality. Creating the opportunity for National Societies to network and work together is one of the Federation's key roles.

In a world with increasing isolation, tension and recourse to violence, it is clear that the Red Cross Red Crescent must champion the individual and community values which encourage respect for other human beings and a willingness to work together to find solutions to community problems.

The International Federation has embarked on a consistent and inspirational approach to promoting humanitarian values and the seven Fundamental Principles of the Red Cross and Red Crescent. This has been identified as one of the four core areas of activity for each National Society and for the International Federation under Strategy 2010. The seven Fundamental Principles are; humanity, impartiality, neutrality, independence, voluntary service, unity and universality.

The aim is to influence the behaviour of the people it works with, through a better understanding of Fundamental Principles and humanitarian values. The three main target groups are those working within Red Cross Red Crescent societies, public and private authorities, and members of the communities where it works.

The main priorities are:

Developing a better understanding internally. New initiatives will be developed to ensure that Red Cross Red Crescent volunteers and staff understand and act on the basis of the Fundamental Principles in their work with vulnerable people in times of peace, disaster or armed conflict. Training will include: the legal and ideological basis of the Red Cross Red Crescent, decision-making processes and mandates as well as communications and relations with others.

Raising awareness of public and private authorities. Ensuring that partner authorities understand how Red Cross Red Crescent works will facilitate better cooperation. Informing these groups about operational procedures, National Societies' law and status, and the need to respect the emblem, for example, are all important elements in building good working partnerships.

Influencing behaviour in the community. By applying these principles and values in our work with communities and vulnerable groups, we can show their importance. Based on experience and operational capacity, Red Cross Red Crescent can be a catalyst for change and can make a difference in the way people behave towards each other.

The following are values that the Movement has formally stated it believes to be of importance for external promotion:

- the protection of life, health and human dignity;
- respect for the human being;
- non-discrimination on the basis of nationality, race, gender, religious beliefs, class or political opinions;
- mutual understanding, friendship, cooperation and lasting peace among people;
- service by volunteers.

INTERNATIONAL ORGANISATION FOR MIGRATION (IOM)

IOM is committed to the principle that humane and orderly migration benefits migrants and society. As the leading international organisation for migration, IOM acts with its partners in the international community to:

- Assist in meeting the growing operational challenges of migration management,
- Advance understanding of migration issues,
- Encourage social and economic development through migration and
- Uphold the human dignity and well-being of migrants.

After half a century of worldwide operational experience, IOM has become the leading international organisation working with migrants and governments to provide humane responses to migration challenges.

Established in 1951 as an intergovernmental organisation to resettle European displaced persons, refugees and migrants, IOM has now grown to encompass a variety of migration management activities throughout the world. With offices and operations on every continent, IOM helps governments and civil society through:

- rapid humanitarian responses to sudden migration flows,

- post-emergency return and reintegration programmes,
- assistance to migrants on their way to new homes and lives,
- facilitation of labour migration,
- assisted voluntary return for irregular migrants,
- recruitment of highly qualified nationals for return to their countries of origin,
- aid to migrants in distress,
- training and capacity-building of officials,
- measures to counter trafficking in persons,
- migration medical and public health programmes,
- mass information and education on migration,
- research related to migration management and other services for migrants.

While not part of the United Nations system, IOM maintains close working relations with UN bodies and operational agencies. IOM has as partners a wide range of international and non-governmental organisations.

INTER-PARLIAMENTARY UNION (IPU)

Created in 1889 on the initiative of two parliamentarians and men of peace, William Randal Cremer (United Kingdom) and Frédéric Passy (France), the Inter-Parliamentary Union was the first permanent forum for political multilateral negotiations.

Promoting the concepts of peace and international arbitration, the IPU provided the origins for today's form of institutionalized multilateral co-operation and advocated the establishment of corresponding institutions at the inter-governmental level—which eventually came into being as the United Nations. The IPU was also instrumental in setting up what is now the Permanent Court of Arbitration in The Hague.

The IPU has transformed itself from an association of individual parliamentarians into the international organisation of the Parliaments of sovereign States (Article 1 of the Statutes of the Inter-Parliamentary Union). It is a centre for dialogue and parliamentary diplomacy among legislators representing every political system and all the main political leanings in the world—constituting a unique platform for observing political opinions and trends around the world. IPU statutory Assemblies and specialized meetings serve as a testing ground for new ideas and initiatives leading to important breakthroughs in the search for peace and advancing international co-operation.

The Union is the focal point for world-wide parliamentary dialogue and works for peace and co-operation among peoples and for the firm establishment of representative democracy.

To that end, it:

- Fosters contacts, co-ordination, and the exchange of experience among parliaments and parliamentarians of all countries;
- Considers questions of international interest and concern and expresses its views on such issues in order to bring about action by parliaments and parliamentarians;
- Contributes to the defence and promotion of human rights—an essential factor of parliamentary democracy and development;
- Contributes to better knowledge of the working of representative institutions and to the strengthening and development of their means of action.

Over a hundred-thirty national parliaments are currently members of the IPU. Five regional parliamentary assemblies are Associate Members.

The IPU is financed by its members out of public funds. Its budget for 2004 totals 9.91 million Swiss Francs.

The site of the Union's Headquarters is Geneva (Switzerland).

The main areas of activity of IPU are as follows:

- **Promotion of Representative Democracy.** This includes:
  Promotion of knowledge of Parliaments
  Parliamentary elections
  Support to parliamentary institutions
- **International peace and security**. This includes:
  Disarmament

Peace situations
Security and cooperation in Mediterranean

- **Sustainable Development**
  Social and Economic Development
  Environment
- **Human Rights and Humanitarian Law**
  Defence of human rights of parliamentarians
  General issues of human rights
  International humanitarian law
- **Education science and Culture**

The IPU supports the efforts of the United Nations, whose objectives it shares, and works in close co-operation with it. It also co-operates with regional inter-parliamentary organisations, as well as with international intergovernmental and non-governmental organisations which are motivated by the same ideals.

INTERNATIONAL SEABED AUTHORITY (ISA)

The International Seabed Authority is an autonomous international organisation established under the 1982 United Nations Convention on the Law of the Sea and the 1994 Agreement relating to the Implementation of Part XI of the United Nations Convention on the Law of the Sea. The Authority is the organisation through which States Parties to the Convention shall, in accordance with the regime for the seabed and ocean floor and subsoil thereof beyond the limits of national jurisdiction (the Area) established in Part XI and the Agreement, organize and control activities in the Area, particularly with a view to administering the resources of the Area.

The Authority, which has its headquarters in Kingston, Jamaica, came into existence on 16 November 1994, upon the entry into force of the 1982 Convention. The first Secretary-General of the Authority was elected in March 1996, and the Authority became fully operational as an autonomous international organisation in June 1996, when it took over the premises and facilities in Kingston, Jamaica previously used by the United Nations Kingston Office for the Law of the Sea. Meetings of the Authority are held at the Jamaica Conference Centre in downtown Kingston.

The International Seabed Authority consists of the following organs:

The Assembly, Council, Legal and Technical Commission, and the Secretariat.

INTERNATIONAL ORGANISATION FOR STANDARDISATION (ISO)

ISO is a network of the national standards institutes of 148 countries, on the basis of one member per country, with a Central Secretariat in Geneva, Switzerland, that coordinates the system.

ISO occupies a special position between the public and private sectors. This is because, on the one hand, many of its member institutes are part of the governmental structure of their countries, or are mandated by their government. On the other hand, other members have their roots uniquely in the private sector, having been set up by national partnerships of industry associations.

Therefore, ISO is able to act as a bridging organisation in which a consensus can be reached on solutions that meet both the requirements of business and the broader needs of society, such as the needs of stakeholder groups like consumers and users.

ISO standards are developed according to the following principles:

- Consensus
  The views of all interests are taken into account: manufacturers, vendors and users, consumer groups, testing laboratories, governments, engineering professions and research organisations.
- Industry-wide
  Global solutions to satisfy industries and customers worldwide.
- Voluntary
  International standardization is market-driven and therefore based on voluntary involvement of all interests in the market-place.

ISO standards are developed by technical committees comprising experts on loan from the industrial, technical and business sectors which have asked for the standards, and which subsequently put them to use. These experts may be joined by others with relevant knowledge, such as representatives of government agencies, testing laboratories, consumer associations, environmentalists, and so on. The experts participate as national delegations, chosen by the ISO national member institute for the country concerned. These delegations are required to represent not just the views of the organisations in which their participating experts work, but of other stakeholders too. According to ISO rules, the member institute is expected to take account of the views of the range of parties interested in the standard under development and to present a consolidated, national consensus position to the technical committee.

ISO's national members pay subscriptions that meet the operational cost of ISO's Central Secretariat. The subscription paid by each member is in proportion to the country's Gross National Product and trade figures. Another source of revenue is the sale of standards. However, the operations of ISO Central Secretariat represent only about one fifth of the cost of the system's operation. The main costs are borne by the member bodies which manage the specific standards' development projects and the business organisations which loan experts to participate in the technical work. These organisations are, in effect, subsidizing the technical work by paying the travel costs of the experts and allowing them time to work on their ISO assignments

All strategic decisions are referred to the ISO members, who meet for an annual General Assembly. The proposals put to the members are developed by the ISO Council, drawn from the membership as a whole, which resembles the board of directors of a business organisation. ISO Council meets three times a year and its membership is rotated to ensure that it is representative of ISO's membership. Operations are managed by a Secretary-General, which is a permanent appointment. The Secretary-General reports to a President who is a prominent figure in standardization or in business, elected for two years. The Secretary-General is based at ISO Central Secretariat in Geneva, Switzerland, with a compact staff which provides administrative and technical support to the ISO members, coordinates the decentralized standards' development programme, and publishes the output.

The ISO 9000 and ISO 14000 families are among ISO's most widely known standards ever. ISO 9000 and ISO 14000 standards are implemented by some 610 000 organisations in 160 countries. ISO 9000 has become an international reference for quality management requirements in business-to-business dealings, and ISO 14000 is well on the way to achieving as much, if not more, in enabling organisations to meet their environmental challenges.

The ISO 9000 family is primarily concerned with "quality management". This means what the organisation does to fulfil:

- the customer's quality requirements,
- applicable regulatory requirements, while aiming to
- enhance customer satisfaction,
- achieve continual improvement of its performance in pursuit of these objectives.

The ISO 14000 family is primarily concerned with "environmental management". This means what the organisation does to:

- minimize harmful effects on the environment caused by its activities,
- achieve continual improvement of its environmental performance.

The vast majority of ISO standards are highly specific to a particular product, material, or process. However, the standards that have earned the ISO 9000 and ISO 14000 families a worldwide reputation are known as "generic management system standards".

"Generic" means that the same standards can be applied:

- to any organisation, large or small, whatever its product,
- including whether its "product" is actually a service,
- in any sector of activity and
- whether it is a business enterprise, a public administration, or a government department.

"Generic" also signifies that no matter what the organisation's scope of activity, if it wants to establish a quality management system or an environmental management system, then such a system has a number of essential features for which the relevant standards of the ISO 9000 or ISO 14000 families provide the requirements.

"Management system" refers to the organisation's structure for managing its processes—or activities—that transform inputs of resources into a product or service which meet the organisation's objectives, such as satisfying the customer's quality requirements, complying to regulations, or meeting environmental objectives.

NON-ALIGNED MOVEMENT (NAM)

The Non-Aligned Movement is a Movement of 115 members representing the interests and priorities of developing countries. The Movement has its origin in the Asia-Africa Conference held in Bandung, Indonesia in 1955. The meeting was convened upon the invitation of the Prime Ministers of Burma, Ceylon, India, Indonesia and Pakistan and brought together leaders of 29 states, mostly former colonies, from the two continents of Africa and Asia, to discuss common concerns and to develop joint policies in international relations. Prime Minister Nehru, the acknowledged senior statesman, along with Prime Ministers Soekarno (Indonesia) and Nasser (Egypt), led the conference. At the meeting Third World leaders shared their similar problems of resisting the pressures of the major powers, maintaining their independence and opposing colonialism and neo-colonialism, specially western domination.

Following this meeting a preparatory meeting for the First NAM Summit Conference was held in Cairo, from 5-12 June 1961. Where the invitations for Bandung were on a regional basis, the invitations for the first Summit were based on each invited country's commitment to a set of shared principles. At the Cairo preparatory meeting the participants discussed in detail the principal aims and objectives of a policy of non-alignment. These were adopted as criteria for membership as well as for the invitations to the First Summit Conference.

The criteria are the following:

- The country should have adopted an independent policy based on the coexistence of States with different political and social systems and on non-alignment or should be showing a trend in favour of such a policy.

- The country concerned should be consistently supporting the Movements for National Independence.
- The country should not be a member of a multilateral military alliance concluded in the context of Great Power conflicts.
- If a country has a bilateral military agreement with a Great Power, or is a member of a regional defence pact, the agreement or pact should not be one deliberately concluded in the context of Great Power conflicts.
- If it has conceded military bases to a Foreign Power the concession should not have been made in the context of Great Power conflicts.

The above criteria and principles of NAM, adopted at the Cairo preparatory meeting, have been reaffirmed by the Heads of State or Government during the XI Summit in Cartagena.

The first Conference of Non-Aligned Heads of State, at which 25 countries were represented, was convened at Belgrade in September 1961, largely through the initiative of Yugoslavian President Tito. He had expressed concern that an accelerating arms race might result in war between the Soviet Union and the USA.

Subsequent conferences involved ever-increasing participation by developing countries. The 1964 Conference in Cairo, with 47 countries represented, featured widespread condemnation of Western colonialism and the retention of foreign military installations. Thereafter, the focus shifted away from essentially political issues, to the advocacy of solutions to global economic and other problems.

NAM Summits

- First Conference - Belgrade, September 1-6, 1961
- Second Conference - Cairo, October 5-10, 1964
- Third Conference - Lusaka, September 8-10, 1970
- Fourth Conference - Algiers, September 5-9, 1973
- Fifth Conference - Colombo, August 16-19, 1976

- Sixth Conference - Havana, September 3-9, 1979
- Seventh Conference - New Delhi, March 7-12, 1983
- Eighth Conference - Harare, September 1-6, 1986
- Ninth Conference - Belgrade, September 4-7, 1989
- Tenth Conference - Jakarta, September 1-7, 1992
- Eleventh Conference - Cartagena de Indias, October 18-20, 1995
- Twelfth Conference - Durban, September 2-3, 1998
- Thirteenth Conference - Kuala Lumpur, February 20-25, 2003

The founders of the Non-Aligned Movement and their successors recognised that the Movement would probably be destroyed if they created such formal structures for the Movement as a constitution and internal secretariat. A multilateral trans-national organisation made up of states with differing ideologies and purposes could never create a rational administrative structure to implement its policies that all could accept.

The Non-Aligned Movement has created a unique form of administrative style. Non-Aligned administration is non-hierarchical, rotational and inclusive, providing all member states, regardless of size and importance, with an opportunity to participate in global decision-making and world politics. The Summit is the occasion when the Movement formally rotates its Chair to the Head of State of the host country of the Summit, who then holds office until the next Summit. The Chair is at the same time also delegated certain responsibilities for promoting the principles and activities of the Movement.

By creating the practice of a rotating chair, Non-Aligned countries therefore place the onus of an administrative structure on the country assuming the Chair. When a country assumes the Chair of the Movement, it creates or designates an entire section of the Foreign Ministry to deal specifically with Non-Aligned issues. Secondly, since Non-Aligned countries meet regularly at the UN and conduct much of their work there, the Chairs' Ambassador at the United Nations essentially functions as the "Minister of Non-Aligned Affairs". The work of the non-aligned often consumes the activities of the Chairs' Permanent Mission in New York.

To facilitate the Chairs' responsibilities a number of structures aimed at improving the coordination and functioning of the existing Working Groups, Contact Groups, Task Forces and Committees of NAM were created. The structures also exist in order to promote the process of achieving a commonality of positions and interests and to see to it that Non-Aligned countries speak with one voice in international meetings and negotiations.

The Coordinating Bureau is the vocal point for coordination. The Bureau reviews and facilitates the harmonisation of the work of the NAM Working Groups, Contact Groups, Task Forces and Committees.

The Heads of State or Government entrusted the Coordinating Bureau with the task of intensifying its actions to further strengthen coordination and mutual cooperation among Non-Aligned countries, including unified action in the United Nations and other international fora on issues of common concern.

The Chair has the responsibility of leading and coordinating the activities of NAM within the United Nations and, as appropriate, in other international fora. Besides the Coordinating Bureau, the Chair may therefore also preside over NAM mechanisms as necessary. Working Groups could be presided over by other members.

All NAM Working Groups, Contact Groups, Task Forces and Committees meet as often as necessary. In the fulfilment of their mandates due regard is paid to coordination, efficiency and preparedness.

At a meeting of Foreign Ministers of NAM, representing past, present and future Chairs, in New Delhi on 6 April 1997, the concept of a Troika (of the past, present and future Chairs) started to emerge. The Chair, the Colombian Foreign Minister, at the meeting announced that the first meeting of the Troika would take place at the 52nd UN General Assembly. The Troika subsequently formally met for the first time in New York in September 1997.

The high level meetings of the Movement are: Summit Conferences, Ministerial Conferences, Ministerial Meetings in New York during the regular Session of the UN General Assembly, Extraordinary Ministerial Meetings, Ministerial Meetings of the Coordinating Bureau, meetings of the Ministerial Committee on Methodology, meetings of the Standing Ministerial Committee on Economic Cooperation and Ministerial Meetings in various fields of International Cooperation. There are other meetings of NAM such as the meetings of the Coordinating Bureau in New York and the meetings of the Working Groups, Task Forces, Contact Groups and Committees that are held at different levels.

The Summit Conference of Heads of State or Government is the highest decision-making authority of the Movement. The existing practice is to hold the Summit Conference every three years. The Summit should be held at least one month before the regular Session of the UN General Assembly. The programme of the Summit includes a formal ceremony for the handing over of the Chair.

The decisions of a Summit should be action-orientated. Senior Officials and Ministerial meetings, which are preparatory to the Summit Conference, precede the Summit of the Heads of State or Government. The Summit has two committees, one for political issues and another for economic and social issues. In order to facilitate finalising the Drafts of the main documents, the committees begin their work informally during the Senior Officials meeting.

The Ministerial Conference is held with the purpose of reviewing the developments and implementation of decisions of the preceding Summit, to prepare for the following Summit, and to discuss matters of urgency. These conferences are convened eighteen months after the Summit Conference

The practice of the Movement is to make all decisions by consensus. Consensus has enhanced the solidarity and unity of the Movement. This concept presupposes understanding of and respect for different points of view, including disagreement and implies mutual accommodation on the basis of which agreement can emerge by a sincere process of adjustment among member nations in the true spirit of Non-Alignment.

NORTH ATLANTIC TREATY ORGANISATION (NATO)

The North Atlantic Treaty Organisation (NATO) is an alliance of 26 countries from North America and Europe committed to fulfilling the goals of the North Atlantic Treaty signed on 4 April 1949. In accordance with the Treaty, the fundamental role of NATO is to safeguard the freedom and security of its member countries by political and military means. During the last fifteen years, NATO has also played an increasingly important role in crisis management and peacekeeping. Recently seven more members have been added to NATO. The expansion increases the alliances membership from the current 10 to 26. The new members are: Bulgaria, Estonia, Latvia, Lithuania, Romania, Slovakia and Slovaenia, which were all communist-ruled countries and within the orbit of the Soviet Union and in the shadow of the Soviet dominated Warsaw Pact Alliance, which was a counter-balance against NATO during the Cold War. The expansion of the NATO is rated as the Juljilmeat of the European Quest to create a continent united in democratic values and consolidated by its bond with the United States.

NATO's essential purpose is to safeguard the freedom and security of all its members by political and military means in accordance with the North Atlantic Treaty and the principles of the United Nations Charter. The Alliance has worked since its inception for the establishment of a just and lasting peaceful order in Europe based on common values of democracy, human rights and the rule of law. This central Alliance objective has taken on renewed significance since the end of the Cold War because, for the first time in the post-war history of Europe, the prospect of its achievement has become a reality.

NATO embodies the trans-atlantic link by which the security of North America is permanently tied to the security of Europe. It is the practical expression of effective collective effort among its members in support of their common security interests.

The fundamental principle underpinning the Alliance is a common commitment to mutual cooperation among the member states, based on the indivisibility of their security. Solidarity and cohesion within the Alliance ensure that no member country is forced to rely upon its own national efforts alone in dealing with basic security challenges. Without depriving member states of their right and duty to assume their sovereign responsibilities in the field of defence, the Alliance enables them to realise their essential national security objectives through collective effort. In short, the Alliance is an association of free states united in their determination to preserve their security through mutual guarantees and stable relations with other countries.

The North Atlantic Treaty of April 1949—which is the legal and contractual basis for the Alliance—was established within the framework of Article 51 of the United Nations Charter, which reaffirms the inherent right of independent states to individual or collective defence. As the preamble to the Treaty states, the aim of the Allies is to "promote peaceful and friendly relations in the North Atlantic Area." However, at the time of the Treaty's signature, the immediate purpose of NATO was to defend its members against a potential threat resulting from the policies and growing military capacity of the former Soviet Union.

The North Atlantic Treaty Organisation (NATO) provides the structure which enables the goals of the Alliance to be implemented. It is an inter-governmental organisation in which member countries retain their full sovereignty and independence. The Organisation provides the forum in which they consult together on any issues they may choose to raise and take decisions on political and military matters affecting their security. It provides the structures needed to facilitate consultation and cooperation between them, in political, military and economic as well as scientific and other non-military fields.

The resulting sense of equal security among the members of the Alliance, regardless of differences in their circumstances or in their national military capabilities, contributes to stability in the Euro-Atlantic area. It creates conditions which favour increased cooperation among Alliance members as well as between members of the Alliance and other countries.

The means by which the Alliance carries out its security policies include the maintenance of a sufficient military capability to prevent war and to provide for effective defence;

an overall capability to manage crises affecting the security of its members; and active promotion of dialogue with other nations and of a cooperative approach to European security, including measures to bring about further progress in the field of arms control and disarmament.

To achieve its essential purpose, as an Alliance of nations committed to the Washington Treaty and the United Nations Charter, the Alliance performs the following fundamental security tasks:

Security: To provide one of the indispensable foundations for a stable Euro-Atlantic security environment, based on the growth of democratic institutions and commitment to the peaceful resolution of disputes, in which no country would be able to intimidate or coerce any other through the threat or use of force.

Consultation: To serve as an essential transatlantic forum for Allied consultations on any issues that affect their vital interests, including possible developments posing risks for members' security, and for appropriate coordination of their efforts in fields of common concern.

Deterrence and Defence: To deter and defend against any threat of aggression against any NATO member state.

And in order to enhance the security and stability of the Euro-Atlantic area:

- *Crisis Management: To stand ready, case-by-case and by consensus, to contribute to effective conflict prevention and to engage actively in crisis management, including crisis response operations.*
- *Partnership: To promote wide-ranging partnership, cooperation, and dialogue with other countries in the Euro-Atlantic area, with the aim of increasing transparency, mutual confidence and the capacity for joint action with the Alliance.*

The structures created within NATO enable member countries to coordinate their policies in order to fulfil these fundamental tasks. They provide for continuous consultation and cooperation in political, economic and other non-military fields as well as the formulation of joint plans for the common defence; the establishment of the infrastructure and basic installations and facilities needed to enable military forces to operate; and arrangements for joint training programmes and exercises. Underpinning these activities is a complex civilian and military structure involving administrative, budgetary and planning staffs, as well as agencies which have been established by the member countries of the Alliance in order to coordinate work in specialised fields.

ORGANISATION FOR ECONOMIC COOPERATION AND DEVELOPMENT (OECD)

The OECD groups 30 member countries sharing a commitment to democratic government and the market economy. With active relationships with some 70 other countries, NGOs and civil society, it has a global reach. Best known for its publications and its statistics, its work covers economic and social issues from macroeconomics, to trade, education, development and science and innovation.

The OECD plays a prominent role in fostering good governance in the public service and in corporate activity. It helps governments to ensure the responsiveness of key economic areas with sectoral monitoring. By deciphering emerging issues and identifying policies that work, it helps policy-makers adopt strategic orientations. It is well known for its individual country surveys and reviews.

The OECD produces internationally agreed instruments, decisions and recommendations to promote rules of the game in areas where multilateral agreement is necessary for individual countries to make progress in a globalised economy. Sharing the benefits of growth is also crucial as shown in activities such as emerging economies, sustainable development, territorial economy and aid.

Dialogue, consensus, peer review and pressure are at the very heart of OECD. Its governing body, the Council, is made up of representatives of member countries. It provides guidance on the work of OECD committees and decides on the annual budget.

The OECD Member States discusses, develop and refine economic and social policies. They compare experiences, seek answers to common problems and work to co-ordinate domestic and international policies to help members and non-members deal with an increasingly globalised world. Their exchanges may lead to agreements to act in a formal way—for example by establishing legally binding agreements to crack down on bribery, or codes for free flow of capital and services. The OECD is also known for 'soft law'—non-binding instruments on difficult issues such as its Guidelines for multinational enterprises. Beyond agreements, the discussions at the OECD make for better-informed work within member countries' own governments across the broad spectrum of public policy and help clarify the impact of national policies on the international community.

The OECD is a group of like-minded countries. The core of original European and North American members has expanded to include Japan, Australia, New Zealand, Finland, Mexico, Korea and four former communist states in Europe: the Czech Republic, Hungary, Poland and the Slovak Republic. Non-members are invited to subscribe to OECD agreements and treaties, and the organisation now involves in its work some 70 non-member countries from Brazil, China and Russia to least developed countries in Africa and elsewhere.

Exchanges between OECD governments flow from information and analysis provided by a Secretariat in Paris. The organisation is one of the world's largest and most reliable sources of comparable statistical, economic and social data. Parts of the Secretariat collect data, monitor trends, analyse and forecast economic developments, while others research social changes or evolving patterns in trade, environment, agriculture, technology, taxation and more.

The OECD is at the forefront of efforts to understand and help governments respond to new challenges such as sustainable development, electronic commerce and biotechnology. This work underpins discussion by member countries when they meet in specialised committees of the OECD. Much of the research and analysis is published, on paper or online.

In recent years the OECD has moved beyond a focus on its member countries to offer its analytical expertise and accumulated experience to developing and emerging market economies.

The emergence of globalisation has seen the scope of the OECD's work move from examination of each policy area within each member country to analysis of how various policy areas interact with each other, between countries and beyond the OECD area. This is reflected in work on issues such as sustainable development, bringing together environmental, economic and social concerns across national frontiers for better understanding of the problems and the best way to tackle them together.

The Organisation is also expanding its relationship with civil society. Initially focused on relations with business and labour, these have broadened to include a wide range of non-government organisations. The OECD also increasingly invites public comment on various aspects of its work.

As it opens to many new contacts around the world, the OECD will broaden its scope, looking ahead to a post-industrial age in which it aims to weave OECD economies into a yet more prosperous and increasingly knowledge-based world economy.

Member countries meet and exchange information in committees. They bring together representatives of member countries, either from national administrations or from their permanent delegations to the OECD, located in Paris. The most powerful body is the Council, which has the decision-making power. It is composed of one representative of each member country, as well as a representative of the European Commission. The Council meets regularly at the level of ambassadors to the OECD to give general guidance to the Organisation and its work. The Council meets at ministerial level once a year, when foreign, finance and other ministers from member countries discuss important issues and set priorities for OECD work over the coming year.

Specialised committees meet to advance ideas and review progress in more tightly defined areas of policy, such as economic policy, trade, science and technology, development assistance or financial markets. There are about 200 committees, working groups and expert groups in all. Some 40000 senior officials from national administrations come to OECD committee meetings each year to request, review and contribute to work undertaken by the OECD Secretariat. And even from home they have access to OECD documents and can exchange information through the OECD OLIS data network.

The 2300 staff of the OECD Secretariat in Paris work directly or indirectly to support the activities of committees. Some 700 economists, lawyers, scientists and other professional staff, mainly based in a dozen substantive directorates, provide research and analysis. The Secretariat is directed by a Secretary-General, assisted by four Deputy Secretaries-General. The Secretary-General also chairs the Council, providing the crucial link between national delegations and the Secretariat.

The OECD works in two official languages: English and French. Staff members are citizens of OECD member countries but serve as international civil servants with no national affiliation during their OECD posting. There is no quota system for national representation; there is simply an equal opportunity policy of employing highly qualified men and women with a cross-section of experience and nationalities.

The OECD is funded by the member countries. National contributions to the annual budget are based on a formula related to the size of each member's economy. The largest contributor is the United States, which provides 25% of the budget, followed by Japan. With the approval of the Council, countries may also make separate contributions to particular programmes or projects.

The size of the annual budget, currently about US$ 200 million per year, as well as the programme of work to be undertaken, is decided by member countries in the Council.

Activities

The OECD provides a setting for reflection and discussion, based on policy research and analysis that helps governments shape policy that may lead to a formal agreement among member governments or be acted on in domestic or other international fora. Unlike the World Bank or the International Monetary Fund, the OECD does not dispense money.

The OECD's way of working consists of a highly effective process that begins with data collection and analysis and moves on to collective discussion of policy. Mutual examination by governments, multilateral surveillance and peer pressure to conform or reform are at the heart of OECD effectiveness. It was the behind the scenes work at the OECD that evaluated the cost of agricultural subsidies, key material in agreements negotiated later to lower farm subsidies. OECD analysis of the contribution of the information technology revolution to economic growth helps governments craft economic policy, while work on the causes and cures for unemployment helps give political impetus to policies to reduce it. Crucial analytical work and consensus building on trade in services fed into the successful conclusion of the Uruguay Round.

Sometimes the discussions evolve into negotiations at the OECD and countries agree on rules of the game for international co-operation. They can culminate in formal agreements, for example on combating bribery, on export credits, or on capital movements; or they may produce standards and models for international taxation or recommendations and guidelines covering environmental practices or electronic commerce.

Much of the material collected and analysed at the OECD is published; from press releases and regular compilations of data and projections to one-time publications or monographs on particular issues; from surveys of the economy of each member country to regular reviews of education systems, science and technology policies or environmental performance.

Over time the OECD's focus has broadened to include extensive contacts with non-member economies and it now maintains co-operative relations with some 70 of them. These contacts aim to further economic integration by making the OECD's experience available to other countries and enabling the OECD to profit from the insights and perspectives of non-members. Following the collapse of the Soviet bloc in 1989, the OECD launched a programme of assistance to the countries of Central and Eastern Europe, which led to the Czech Republic, Hungary, Poland and the Slovak Republic, joining the Organisation. At roughly the same time a programme of organised contacts was initiated with the most dynamic economies outside Europe. In Asia, regular dialogue was begun with Hong Kong-China, Malaysia, Singapore, Chinese Taipei and Thailand. In Latin America, links were established with Argentina, Brazil and Chile. In 1998 a new Centre for Co-operation with Non-Members was created to co-ordinate charge of all activities concerning non-members. The Centre has two types of programme. One is based on policy themes such as sustainable development, trade, investment, taxation and agriculture, while the other is country or region-based. Prominent among the latter type are programmes with Russia, China and Brazil.

As an intergovernmental organisation, the OECD is committed to communicating with transparency and openness with a broad range of stakeholders, whether policy-makers, academics, business, labour, civil society organisations or the media. An increasing amount of information is being made available on the OECD website, which has also been used to invite public comment on certain projects. The OECD publishes books in print and is also a pioneer in electronic publishing.

The OECD has undertaken close consultations and dialogue with civil society since its creation in 1961. For many years this was primarily with the business and labour sectors through the Business and Industry Advisory Committee to the OECD and the Trade Union Advisory Committee to the OECD. But over the past decade the OECD has undertaken increasingly extensive dialogue and consultations with other civil society organisations in areas such as the environment , development co-operation, electronic commerce and social policy. The OECD also places a high priority on relations with the parliamentary/legislative branch of government, notably through its close and long-standing links with the Council of Europe and its Parliamentary Assembly, and the Economic Committee of the NATO Parliamentary Assembly.

As part of its relations with other international organisations and bodies, the OECD has official relations with the International Labour Organisation, Food and Agriculture Organisation, International Monetary Fund, World Bank, International Atomic Energy Agency, and many other United Nations bodies. The OECD also co-ordinates with the European Conference of Ministers of Transport , a separate body attached to the OECD Secretariat that deals with issues of improvement of all forms of transportation.

ORGANISATION OF PETROLEUM EXPORTING COUNTRIES (OPEC)

OPEC is an international Organisation of eleven developing countries which are heavily reliant on oil revenues as their main source of income. Membership is open to any country which is a substantial net exporter of oil and which shares the ideals of the Organisation. The current Members are Algeria, Indonesia, Iran, Iraq, Kuwait, Libya, Nigeria, Qatar, Saudi Arabia, the United Arab Emirates and Venezuela.

Since oil revenues are so vital for the economic development of these nations, they aim to bring stability and harmony to the oil market by adjusting their oil output to help ensure a balance between supply and demand. Twice a year, or more frequently if required, the Oil and Energy Ministers of the OPEC Members meet to decide on the Organisation's output level, and consider whether any action to adjust output is necessary in the light of recent and anticipated oil market developments.

OPEC's eleven Members collectively supply about 40 per cent of the world's oil output, and possess more than three-quarters of the world's total proven crude oil reserves.

OPEC's objective is to co-ordinate and unify petroleum policies among Member Countries, in order to secure fair and stable prices for petroleum producers; an efficient, economic and regular supply of petroleum to consuming nations; and a fair return on capital to those investing in the industry.

In the formative years, the Organisation, started life as a group of five oil-producing, developing countries, seeking to assert its Member Countries' legitimate rights in an international oil market. Activities were generally of a low-profile nature, as OPEC set out its objectives, established its Secretariat, which moved from Geneva to Vienna in 1965, adopted resolutions and engaged in negotiations with the companies. Membership grew to ten during the decade.

OPEC rose to international prominence during this decade, as its Member Countries took control of their domestic petroleum industries and acquired a major say in the pricing of crude oil on world markets. There were two oil pricing crises, triggered by the Arab oil embargo in 1973 and the outbreak of the Iranian Revolution in 1979, but fed by fundamental imbalances in the market; both resulted in oil prices rising steeply. The first Summit of OPEC Sovereigns and Heads of State was held in Algiers in March 1975. OPEC acquired its 11th and final current Member, Nigeria, in 1971.

Prices peaked at the beginning of the decade, before beginning a dramatic decline, which culminated in a collapse in 1986—the third oil pricing crisis. Prices rallied in the final years of the decade, without approaching the high levels of the early-1980s, as awareness grew of the need for joint action among oil producers if market stability with reasonable prices was to be achieved in the future. Environmental issues began to appear on the international agenda.

A fourth pricing crisis was averted at the beginning of the decade, on the outbreak of hostilities in the Middle East, when a sudden steep rise in prices on panic-stricken markets was moderated by output increases from OPEC Members. Prices then remained relatively stable until 1998, when there was a collapse, in the wake of the economic downturn in South-East Asia. Collective action by OPEC and some leading non-OPEC producers brought about a recovery. As the decade ended, there was a spate of mega-mergers among the major international oil companies in an industry that was experiencing major technological advances. For most of the 1990s, the ongoing international climate change negotiations threatened heavy decreases in future oil demand.

Representatives of OPEC Member Countries (Heads of Delegation) meet at the OPEC Conference to co-ordinate and unify their petroleum policies in order to promote stability and harmony in the oil market. They are supported in this by the OPEC Secretariat, directed by the Board of Governors and run by the Secretary General, and by various bodies including the Economic Commission and the Ministerial Monitoring Committee.

The Member Countries consider the current situation and forecasts of market fundamentals, such as economic growth rates and petroleum demand and supply scenarios. They then consider what, if any, changes they might make in their petroleum policies. For example, in previous Conferences the Member Countries have decided variously to raise or lower their collective oil production in order to maintain stable prices and steady supplies to consumers in the short, medium and longer term.

The Conference is the supreme authority of the Organisation, and consists of delegations normally headed by Their Excellencies the Ministers of Oil, Mines and Energy of Member Countries. The Conference generally meets twice a year, in March and September, and in extraordinary sessions whenever required. It operates on the principle of unanimity and one Member, one vote. It is responsible for the formulation of the general policy of the Organisation and the determination of the appropriate ways and means of its implementation.

The Conference also decides upon applications for membership of the Organisation, and on reports and recommendations submitted by the Board of Governors on the affairs of the Organisation. It approves the appointment of Governors from each Member Country and elects the Chairman of the Board. Moreover, the Conference directs the Board to submit reports or make recommendations on any matter of interest to the Organisation, and considers and decides upon the Organisation's budget, as submitted to it by the Board.

The OPEC Secretariat functions as the Headquarters of OPEC. It is responsible for carrying out the executive functions of the Organisation, in accordance with the provisions of the Statute and under the direction of the Board.

The Secretariat consists of the Secretary General, and the Research Division headed by the Director of Research, and comprising the Petroleum Market Analysis, Energy Studies and Data Services Departments. Other functions include the PR & Information Department, the Administration & Human Resources Department, and the Office of the Secretary General.

The Secretariat was originally established in Geneva, Switzerland, in 1961 but it was moved to Vienna, Austria, in

1965. The 8th (Extraordinary) OPEC Conference approved the Host Agreement with the Austrian Government in April 1965, prior to the opening of the OPEC Secretariat in Vienna on September 1, 1965.

The OPEC Member Countries established the OPEC Fund For International Development in 1976 in order to assist non-OPEC developing countries to improve their economies, including their trade. The OPEC Fund has so far committed itself to loans or grants totalling more than $4 billion. The OPEC Fund has been active in many regions, including Asia, Africa, Latin America, the Middle East and the Caribbean. The OPEC Fund has supported a range of different types of projects, from providing clean water and energy to remote communities, to building houses, schools, hospitals and roads and developing industry, farming and trade opportunities.

OPEC also assists in other ways: by supporting developing countries' efforts to help themselves; by helping to remove trade barriers in individual countries and on an international level, for instance through the World Trade Organisation; and by helping the world to maintain a strong economic system, based on steady supplies of oil at a reasonable price. OPEC cannot do this alone. It has been working hard to encourage other oil producers to co-operate in the oil market, and therefore to help preserve the balance of the world economy.

TECHNO-ECONOMIC APPROACH FOR AFRICA INDIA MOVEMENT (TEAM-9)

The TEAM-9 was formally inaugurated on March 1, 2004 by External Affairs Minister Yashwant Sinha and his counterparts from Burkina Faso, Chad, Coted'Ivoire, Equatorial Guinea, Ghana, Guinea Bissau, Mali and Senegal.

The two sides have signed a Memorandum of Understanding (MoU) which, among other things, calls for accelerating economic growth, social progress and cultural development in the region, promoting and developing scientific and technological advancement and strengthening mutual cooperation in international fora on matters of common interest.

India would provide concessional credit facilities for financial assistance for various projects and schemes identified for implementation under the TEAM-9 cooperation, access to training resources in India and facilitate deputation of Indian scientists, technologists and other experts to the eight African countries.

India, which had the appropriate technology that Africa required, could focus on eight suitably chosen African countries including Senegal for promoting greater economic interaction with West Africa. The basic premise is that India's scientific and technological capabilities could be utilised for assisting these eight countries in select sectors and simultaneously accessing business opportunities and obtaining political support from them for causes closer to New Delhi's diplomatic endeavours in the wider world.

The new concept—TEAM-9, envisages close cooperation between Governments and private sector, wherein the Government will play the facilitating role. The Government would provide appropriate policy framework and make available necessary resources while leaving it to the private sector to ensure that these projects succeed. In fact, Team-9 visualises the private sector as the engine leading the cooperation effort, while Government would assist by creating the proper environment.

The essential logic is that countries in West Africa and India, which have evolved from similar environment and backgrounds, and can, therefore, usefully share these experiences. The cooperation identifies key areas that India and West Africa can share experiences in the field of small scale industries as also in large projects, in infrastructure, in building, roads, pipelines, railways etc. It actually relates to technology at the grass root levels, technology, which is human friendly and is based on utilisation of local resources and technology, which generates employment.

THE COMMONWEALTH

The Commonwealth is a voluntary association of 53 sovereign states, which work together to achieve international goals. Spread over every continent and ocean, the Commonwealth's 1.7 billion people make up 30% of the world's population.

Emphasising equality, trust and understanding, the Commonwealth facilitates the advancement of democracy, human rights and sustainable economic and social development within its member countries and beyond.

With a common working language and similar systems of law, public administration and education, the Commonwealth has built on its shared history to become a vibrant and growing association of states in tune with the modern world.

Today's Commonwealth is a world away from the handful of British Dominions which were the first Commonwealth members. From Africa to Asia, from Pacific shores to the Caribbean, the Commonwealth's 1.7 billion people make up 30% of the world's population.

The modern Commonwealth gradually evolved out of United Kingdom's imperial past, mainly through decolonisation, the effects of two world wars and changing patterns of international relations. Today it helps to advance democracy, human rights, sustainable economic and social development within its member countries and beyond. Armed with a common working language and similar systems of law, public administration and education, the Commonwealth has built on its shared history to become a vibrant and growing association of states in tune with the modern world.

The Commonwealth is active in a number of diverse areas from providing models for good health practices for women to observing elections, from advising member countries on debt management to helping them negotiate better trade arrangements.

The Commonwealth Secretariat provides policy advise and technical assistance to member countries through its programmes. These Programmes are implemented through its Divisions.

The main areas covered by the Commonwealth Secretariat are as follows:

- CHOGM
  Commonwealth Heads of Government Meetings
- Human Rights
  Promoting and protecting fundamental human rights
- Democracy
  The Secretariat is committed to democratic principles
- Law
  Facilitating Commonwealth legal co-operation
- Education
  The Commonwealth believes that everyone has a right to education
- Environment
  Integrating environmental considerations in economic development
- Gender
  A leading international voice on the promotion of gender equality
- Globalisation
  Helping members strengthen their ability to benefit from globalization
- Health
  Providing capacity building and other health sector related assistance
- Youth Empowerment
  Working for a world where young people can reach their full potential
- Sustainable Development
  Sustainable development stands at the heart of the Commonwealth's work
- Strategic Planning and Evaluation
  Managing the strategic planning, monitoring the work programmes and promoting internal co-ordination
- Small States
  The Secretariat is devoted to the unique needs of its 32 Small State members

- Publications
  The Publications Unit publishes a wide range of material on the Commonwealth

WORLD CUSTOMS ORGANISATION (WCO)

The World Customs Organisation (WCO) aids the national economic wealth and social protection of its Members by promoting an honest, transparent and predictable Customs environment. This permits legitimate international trade to flourish and effective action to be taken against illegal activity.

Established in 1952 as the Customs Co-operation Council, the WCO is an independent intergovernmental body whose mission is to enhance the effectiveness and efficiency of Customs administrations. With 162 Member Governments, it is the only intergovernmental worldwide organisation competent in Customs matters. In order to fulfil this mission, the World Customs Organisation:

- Establishes, maintains, supports and promotes international instruments for the harmonization and uniform application of simplified and effective Customs systems and procedures governing the movement of commodities, people and conveyances across Customs frontiers;
- Reinforces Members' efforts to secure compliance with their legislation, by endeavouring to maximize the level of effectiveness of Members' co-operation with each other and with international organisations in order to combat Customs and other transnational offences;
- Assists Members in their efforts to meet the challenges of the modern business environment and adapt to changing circumstances, by promoting communication and co-operation among Members and with other international organisations, and by fostering integrity, human resource development, transparency, improvements in the management and working methods of Customs administrations and the sharing of best practices.

The history of the WCO began in 1947 when the thirteen European Governments represented in the Committee for European Economic Co-operation agreed to set up a Study Group. This Group examined the possibility of establishing one or more inter-European Customs Unions based on the principles of the General Agreement on Tariffs and Trade (GATT). In 1948, the Study Group set up two committees—an Economic Committee and a Customs Committee. The Economic Committee was the predecessor of the Organisation for Economic Co-operation and Development (OECD), the Customs Committee became the Customs Co-operation Council (CCC). In 1952, the Convention formally establishing the CCC came into force. The Council is the governing body of the CCC and the inaugural Session of the Council was held in Brussels on 26 January 1953. Representatives of seventeen European countries attended the first Council Session of the CCC.

After years of membership growth, in 1994 the Council adopted the working name World Customs Organisation, to more clearly reflect its transition to a truly global intergovernmental institution. It is now the voice of 159 Customs administrations which operate on all continents and represent all stages of economic development. Today, WCO Members are responsible for processing more than 95% of all international trade.

The WCO is a forum where delegates representing a wide variety of Members can tackle Customs issues on an equal footing. Each Member has one representative and one vote. It offers its Members a wide range of Conventions and other international instruments. WCO Members can also take advantage of the technical assistance and training services delivered either directly by the Secretariat or provided with its involvement. The WCO is directed by the full Council and the Policy Commission (24 Members), with financial advice from the Finance Committee (17 Members). The WCO works through its Committees and its Secretariat to complete the work set forth in the key activities of the WCO Strategic Plan, which is approved annually by the Council.

The principal Committees of the WCO are the:

- PERMANENT TECHNICAL COMMITTEE, including the Information Management Sub- Committee

- ENFORCEMENT COMMITTEE
- HARMONIZED SYSTEM COMMITTEE, including the Harmonized System Review Sub-Committee and the Scientific Sub-Committee
- TECHNICAL COMMITTEE ON CUSTOMS VALUATION
- TECHNICAL COMMITTEE ON RULES OF ORIGIN.

For many years, the WCO has been making progress on the harmonization of international Customs procedures. These efforts have met with considerable success. The WCO developed and introduced the Harmonized Commodity Description and Coding System, which is used world-wide as the basis for classifying goods and for the collection of Customs revenue. In June 1999, a revised International Convention on the Simplification and Harmonization of Customs Procedures (the Kyoto Convention) was approved by the Council. The revised Convention is a response to the growth in international cargo, the incredible developments in information technology and a highly competitive international business environment based on quality service and customer satisfaction, all of which have created a conflict with traditional Customs methods and procedures.

The WCO also administers the WTO Valuation Agreement and has recently developed Harmonized Rules of Origin which have been forwarded for consideration by the WTO in Geneva for eventual use by its Members. Working closely together, the WCO, WTO and UNCTAD are co-ordinating their efforts to remove the remaining barriers to trade by simplifying and harmonizing Customs procedures and processes throughout the world. Combining the influence of the WTO, UNCTAD and the WCO will make a significant contribution to both trade facilitation and trade compliance.

This commitment to partnership is further reflected in the close working relationship that the WCO enjoys with the International Chamber of Commerce (ICC). A Co-operation Agreement between the two organisations seeks to further standardize and improve the level of Customs capabilities world-wide.

Although significant progress has been made, efficient and effective performance is not spread evenly among all

Customs administrations, or in all regions of the world. In fact, many Customs administrations are still suffering the ill-effects of inefficiency and corruption. To address this issue, the WCO provides extensive technical assistance to Members and has developed a Customs Reform and Modernization Programme (CRM) which is designed to assist Member administrations which seek to become more self-reliant through better use of resources, strengthening of management capabilities, and designing appropriate and efficient Customs processes and procedures.

WORLD ECONOMIC FORUM (WEF)

The World Economic Forum is the foremost global community of business, political, intellectual and other leaders of society committed to improving the state of the world. The Forum is an independent international organisation incorporated as a Swiss not-for-profit foundation and has NGO consultative status with the Economic and Social Council of the United Nations.

In 1970 Klaus Schwab brought together Europe's chief executives for an informal gathering in the Swiss mountain town of Davos. A year later, the meeting became known as the "Davos Symposium" and it had the patronage of the Commission of the European Communities, as well as the encouragement of Europe's industry associations. Each year since the Forum's Annual Meeting's participant-base has grown and its agenda has developed to encompass all the challenges to global economic, social and environmental improvement. It is now the most important meeting of its kind in the world.

Over the course of more than 30 years the people of Davos have witnessed the growth and international impact of the meeting. In 1987, the Foundation changed its name to the World Economic Forum, reflecting the engagement of its membership and widening scope of its goals. Now more than 2,000 people participate in the Annual Meeting. The event provides the opportunity to interact with some of the most knowledgeable, dynamic and influential people in the world. Davos is the world's foremost summit for global leaders. Although more than half the participants come from business, they are drawn from every part of society. Of the 2,000 participants at an Annual Meeting, one in 100 will be a head of state, one in 30 will be from an NGO, one in 15 will be an academic and one in 10 will be an editor. This diversity and the informal and collaborative 'spirit of Davos' mean that, as well as engaging with familiar faces, participants get the chance to connect with people they don't know, who challenge the way they think and act: from Nobel Prize-winning scientists and editorial cartoonists to activists and young business gurus destined to shape the future. Such opportunities also exist at our regional and country summits, which bring hundreds of leaders together to define, discuss and advance key local issues.

For over 30 years WEF has been bringing together global leaders, from all walks of life, to pursue economic and social activity that will improve the state of the world. The vision for the World Economic Forum is threefold.

It aims to be:

- the foremost organisation which builds and energizes leading global communities;
- the creative force shaping global, regional and industry strategies;
- the catalyst of choice for its communities when undertaking global initiatives to improve the state the world.

WEF enjoy a unique global standing by recognizing and responding to two new developments:

- The world's key challenges cannot be met by governments, business or civil society alone,
- In a world characterized by complexity, fragility and ever greater synchronicity, strategic insights cannot be passively acquired. They are best developed through continuous interaction with peers and with the most knowledgeable people in the field.

To carry out its mission, the World Economic Forum has developed an integrated value chain by involving world leaders in communities, inspiring them with strategic insights and enabling them through initiatives.

The members represent the world's 1,000 leading companies, along with 200 smaller businesses, many from the developing world, that play a potent role in their industry or region. However, members are more than just influential, talented and powerful people. Many are also innovative and inspiring individuals who challenge conventional thinking and are committed to making the world a better place. It also works closely with communities of leaders from academia, government, religion, the media, non-governmental organisations and the arts.

Partners are select member companies who strongly support, contribute to and benefit from the World Economic Forum's commitment to improving the state of the world. They are actively involved in the organisation's activities and contribute their expertise and resources.

WEF is striving towards a world-class corporate governance system where values are as important a basis as rules. The motto is 'entrepreneurship in the global public interest'. It believes that economic progress without social development is not sustainable, while social development without economic progress is not feasible.

WORLD WIDE FUND FOR NATURE (WWF)

Since its inception in 1961, WWF has worked to conserve nature and ecological processes through a combination of action on the ground, national and international advocacy work to establish appropriate policies, and international campaigns to highlight and demonstrate solutions to crucial environmental problems.

Indeed, over the course of its 41 year history, WWF has contributed significantly to the development and impact of the world conservation movement and to sustainable development in a period of great pressure on the world's natural resources. In just over four decades, WWF (formerly known as the World Wildlife Fund) has become one of the world's largest and most respected independent conservation organisations.

WWF originally stood for "World Wildlife Fund". However, in 1986, WWF had come to realize that its name no longer reflected the scope of its activities. WWF changed its name from World Wildlife Fund to the "World Wide Fund for Nature". The United States and Canada, however, retained the old name.

The resulting confusion caused by the name change in 1986, together with its translation into more than 15 languages, led the WWF Network in 2001 to agree on using the original acronym as its one, global name—the acronym that it had always been known by since its inception way back in 1961: "WWF".

WWF's Purpose, as laid down in its Statutes, first established in 1961 and slightly modified in 1993, is "to conserve the natural environment and ecological processes worldwide". This is taken to include fauna and flora, the landscape, water, soils, air and other natural resources, with particular emphasis on the maintenance of essential ecological processes and life support systems, and on the preservation of genetic, species and ecosystem diversity, and on ensuring that the utilization of wild plant and animal species and natural ecosystems is sustainable.

WWF's mission is to stop the degradation of the planet's natural environment and to build a future in which humans live in harmony with nature, by:

- conserving the world's biological diversity,
- ensuring that the use of renewable natural resources is sustainable,
- promoting the reduction of pollution and wasteful consumption.

To guide WWF in its task of achieving the mission goals, the following principles have been adopted. WWF will:

- be global, independent, multicultural and non party political;
- use the best available scientific information to address issues and critically evaluate all its endeavours;
- seek dialogue and avoid unnecessary confrontation;

- build concrete conservation solutions through a combination of field based projects, policy initiatives, capacity building and education work;
- involve local communities and indigenous peoples in the planning and execution of its field programmes, respecting their cultural as well as economic needs;
- strive to build partnerships with other organisations, governments, business and local communities to enhance WWF's effectiveness;
- run its operations in a cost effective manner and apply donors' funds according to the highest standards of accountability.

The various WWF offices around the world come under two categories:

- those that can raise funds and carry out work independently and
- those that must work under the direction of one of the independent WWF offices.

In all cases, WWF's offices carry out local conservation work, within national boundaries, such as practical field projects, scientific research, advising local and national governments on environmental policy, promoting environmental education, and raising awareness of environmental issues. Each office that can work independently (type 1) also contributes funding to WWF's global conservation programme, while all offices help contribute to an enormous pool of environmental expertise and knowledge.

A specialist WWF office in Brussels works to influence the policies and activities of the European Union, while a second WWF Office in Washington DC works to influence global institutions involved in international economic issues, such as the World Bank.

WWF's five Associate Organisations are non-governmental organisations that work closely with WWF in countries where WWF has no independent office (type 1). The Associates promote shared conservation objectives, but do not contribute financially to the WWF Network.

In all, WWF has primary offices and associates in over 40 countries around the world, working as a team towards an overall goal: to halt and reverse the destruction of our natural environment.

Part II
Regional Organisations

4

REGIONALISM: EVOLUTION AND GROWTH

Regionalism by now is a fairly established part of the lexicon of international relations both as a concept and as an experiment. It would, therefore, be useful to have a comprehensive idea of this concept in all its dimensions so that one can understand the principles on which various regional organisations stand, their potentialities and limits and their contribution to the further growth of regionalism.

Regionalism is defined, as 'the creation by governments of international economic links between adjacent countries'; it also makes possible an increase in the bargaining powers of the member countries vis-à-vis third countries.

The emergence of regional cooperation and organisations after the second World War were initially the consequence of fear & security but latter on, particularly after the demise of the Soviet Union, these organisations were based on economic cooperation and mutual prosperity. The rapid spread of regionalism is surely the most important recent development in the global trade system.[1] More generally, the phenomenon of globalisation has been matched by the rise of regionalisation.

Regional cooperation as an antithesis of autarky and global cooperation has become an inevitable intermediate link in the system of international cooperation and interdependence. The epoch of global One-worldism appears to be premature, given the as yet utopian nature of attempts to consolidate the world's highly unequal sovereign nation-states into a single world system. At the present time, the balanced progress towards greater regional focus motivated by considerations

1. Baldwin, R., "The causes of Regionalism", World Economy, 20(7), 1997.

of economic and social benefits and requirements, offers the best alternative.

The basis for regional cooperation lies in common national interests deriving from propinquity, similarity of socio-political systems, comparable levels of development and complementarity of economies and affinities of language, culture, historical tradition and religion. The smallness of most of the Third World countries' individual markets compels them to join forces to develop their industries and reap the benefits of economies of scale, attract foreign investors by organizing a frontier-less market with a critical mass of potential consumers and create the jobs that their constantly expanding populations demand.

However, on the whole, the majority of the attempts made in the developing world have been plagued by serious difficulties. Some of these have stemmed from the unequal level of development of the member states, others from inequalities in resources and labor forces and the economic and political ideals, and still others from the insufficiently developed linkages between the nascent regional units and the rest of the world economy. Unequal distribution of the costs and benefits of regional cooperation has often led to resentment and resistance, which sacrificed long-term benefits to be achieved through more equitable cooperation to the short-term advantages of a return to bilateral economic relationships. Success among the attempts at regional cooperation have been achieved mainly in regions with a relatively developed economic, educational, technological, and scientific infrastructure, and with the capability and the will to provide a significant and dependable level of investment in programmes of economic cooperation.

Regional economic arrangements of the variety, more generally recognised now, emerged and were continually refined under colonial rule between 1870 – 1950 in various parts of developing world such as in South Asia, East Asia and the Middle East as well as in various sub-regions of Africa and the Caribbean. The most successful form of regional cooperation that evolved and culminated in full economic and political union on a more or less voluntary and democratically determined basis, was the progressive expansion and the formation of the USA during 1820-1920. This unique, experience, however is not usually seen as an example of regional cooperation among nations as such but as exemplifying the evolution and expansion of a federation welding together functions of semi–sovereign, constituent states.

Regionalism as a concept has evolved gradually. First cogent and articulate version of regionalism was laid down in the United Nations Charter. The chapter VIII of the UN Charter deals exclusively with the 'Regional Arrangement.[2] The charter confirms that its universal principles of maintenance of international peace can collaterally exist with regional arrangements based on their regional interests—political or economic. It implies that as per the charter of the UN, Universalism and regionalism are not contradictory but confirmatory to each other in that any regional arrangements which confirm to the principles of the UN may be helpful in sustenance of international peace and security.

The onset of the cold war marked a beginning of an entirely new world—order characterised by the formation of hosts of political & military regional arrangements. Two-power blocs led by two Supers—Powers (USA and USSR) created two major military regional alignments. NATO (led by USA) and WASAW Pact (led by USSR). In Asia, two other such arrangements were South East Asian Treaty Organisation (SEATO) and Central Treaty Organisation (CENTO). These military arrangements were regional as well as bloc—centric in the sense that they not only attempted to create a near balance of power in a particular region but also between two Super Powers.

The world witnessed simultaneous formation of political regional groupings. The European Economic Community (EEC), The European Free Trade Association (EFTA), and the European Coal and Steel Community (ECSC) achieved phenomenal success in regional integration in Europe. The Organisation of African States (OAS) vitalized Latin America's interest in regional cooperation. The formation of the Association of South East Asian Nations (ASEAN) reflects Asia's potential to the potentialities of regional cooperation. In the mid 1980s,

2. Refer to article 52 – 54 of the UN Charter.

regionalism eventually came into being in South Asia with the formation of South Asian Association for Regional Cooperation (SAARC). In Africa, we see the establishment of Organisation of African Unity (OAU) and recently the African Union (AU). The Arab world established the Arab League and later on the Gulf Cooperation Council (GCC).

The most successful case of economic regionalism is the European Union (EU), which replaced European Community after the Maastricht Treaty of 1994. It has established a very novel system of a common market, common currency, common minimum economic policy and completely free flow of goods and services to the extent of even partially demolishing the traditional wall of sovereign nation state system.

The most recent example of political and economic integration is the launching of the African Union (AU) in Durban, July 2002. The new 53 member AU is a political, economic and social project molded along the lines of the EU. It seeks a higher form of collaborative union for the continent—a single organisation with two dimensions—political and economic.

The most surprising aspect of this new face of economic regionalism or neo-regionalism in the 1990s is that none of the economic arrangements has banned member countries from any universal economic formation like the WTO or even participation in multilateral arrangements.

Regional integration agreements are contracts that restrict governments' ability to set policy unilaterally. There are two types of Regional Integration schemes:

(i) Deep Integration Scheme. European Union's single market programme and Maastricht Treaty are deep integration agreements. In theory they imply that member states cannot restrict imports of EU goods or services at the border, or by means of domestic health safety and environmental standards. Nor can they restrict intra-EU capital and labour movements, or inhibit establishment of firms from EU nations. Member states cannot choose their state aids policy, competition policy, or indirect taxation rates. All these restrictions are supervised by the supranational European Commission and can be enforced by supranational European Court of Justice. Finally, nations joining the Monetary Union will no longer control their monetary policy. This is the reason, why so few deep type regional arrangements exist.[3]

(ii) Shallow Integration Schemes. Such regional schemes are Free Trade Agreements (FTA), the US—Canada FTA (CUSTA), and US—Israel FTA, the North American FTA (NAFTA) and other regional schemes in Latin America, Africa and Asia. These involve shallow integration, often little more than tariff and quota liberalisation. The U.S. Canada FTA eliminates, all bilateral tariffs by 1998, and relaxes some restrictions on governments' procurement and cross border direct investments. Service trade is not substantially liberalised. The complex issues like—most notable subsidies, energy sector investment, transport services and intellectual property rights proved insurmountable in the bilateral talks and were dropped.

Factors in the Growth of Regionalism

Proximity is an important factor in the growth of regionalism in the world today. Generally it is found that countries lying in a particular geographical region enter into cooperative agreements amongst themselves. Most of the regional integration schemes are based on the basis of regional contiguity and aim at promoting the socio-economic and political interests of the region. The countries lying in close proximity are in a better position to utilize the potentials of the region for their own development. They formulate a common economic and monetary policy which could ultimately lead to the establishment of an Economic Union (like European Union).

Homogeneity: Regionalism can develop efficiently if there is similarity amongst the nations concerned. Social, political and economic homogeneity are the essential criteria for the growth of regional cooperation and integration. Social homogeneity is expressed in the similar attitudes, cultures and values of the people. Political homogeneity implies the similarity in the Governmental structures and functioning. It helps to develop understanding trust and confidence between neighbouring countries. Homogeneity in terms of economy is

3. Baldwin, "The causes of Regionalism", The World Economy, Vol. 20, No.7, 1997, p. 887.

also an important factor. It leads to economic cooperation and facilitates easy movement of men and materials. Regionalism can foster well if there is cooperation on these fronts.

Functional Interest. Functional interest is an integrative factor in international relations. It is based on the premise that at present the nation states are incapable of solving the cross border issues. Functionalism attempts to identify common international economic and social problems and helps in the creation of regional and global organisations. A number of regional organisations such as GCC, SAARC and UN specialized agencies such as the UNESCO, WHO, FAO etc. are based on the premise of functionalism.

Strategic Interest. The countries of a particular region come together due to a particular strategic interest. Even during the Cold War period the major Pacts such as the NATO and the Warsaw Pact were signed keeping in mind the strategic interest of the respective blocs. Common threat perception is a prime factor in the regional cooperation and integration arrangement. The SAARC, ASEAN, GCC are some of the organisations based on the security oriented effort.

Common foreign policy Orientation. Foreign policy behaviour in regional context is influenced by affinities and interdependence with neighbours' economic and military power. Common foreign policy orientation is a pre-requisite for the healthy growth of regionalism. European Union has established a common foreign and security policy for its Member States. The success of some of the regional organisations of the developing countries has been impeded due to dissimilar foreign policy orientations of the Member countries.

Peace and Harmony. Regional cooperation will never achieve its full potential unless disputes and tensions are resolved peacefully. The leaders of regional organisations should move towards solving the disputes boldly with the objective of seeking honourable solutions with mutual respect and in the spirit of accommodation. If we fail, cynicism will take over and the integration arrangement will lose its creditability and momentum. No meaningful cooperation in the region is possible unless strategic discord is smoothened and mutual security dilemmas are contained, if not resolved.

Dominance of a particular Nation. The countries of region must accept the dominance of a particular power in the region. If this is not accepted, there will be constant fear of hegemony creating hindrances to regionalism. In almost all the regional integration arrangements, a dominant nation has played the pivotal role, for example Saudi Arabia in GCC; Indonesia in ASEAN; South Africa in SADC; India in SAARC. These countries have played an important role in the establishment of their respective organisations and coordinating their activities. They also play an important role in making their voices heard at the other multilateral and international forums at the global level.

Regional Institutions. A regional institution can develop cohesiveness and solidarity between national societies and become more oriented towards integrative activities. Establishment of regional institutions to shape and implement regional policies is indispensable. A number of regional organisations in the world have played an important role in integrating the socio-economic and political diversities and putting forward the common demands of the region at the World Body such as the UN.

The recent resurgence of regionalism has been explained by a number of thinkers. The reasons why such blocs are infact, emerging are, as follows[4]:

(i) A large number of participants in multilateral trade negotiations contribute to non-cooperation and fosters greater rigidity in negotiations.

(ii) Modern trade barriers are more complex, more varied and less transparent than the tariffs and quotas considered in the early GATT Rounds. This causes multilateral bargaining, harder and renders monitoring of any eventual agreements more problematic.

---

4. Krugman, P., "Regionalism Vs Multi lateralism ; An Analytical Notes", in DeMelo and Panagariya (eds), *New Dimensions in Regional Cooperation*, Cambridge University Press 1994, p. 73.

(iii) According to theory of hegemonic stability, the reduced economic dominance of the US makes the world trade system harder to run.

(iv) Socio – political – economic differences between Atlantic economies and Asia make it much easier for Asia to get away with non-compliance, so Atlantic economies are reluctant to bargain on an unconditional Most Favored Nation (MFN) basis.

Thus, regionalism spread due to frustration with the GATT in general and Uruguay Round talks in particular.

There are other explanations for spreading regionalism. According to the Domino Theory of Regionalism,[5] regionalism triggered a multiplier effect that knocked down bilateral import barrier like a row of dominos. In the domino theory, the basic idea is simple, forming a preferential trade area, or deepening an existing one, produces trade and investment diversion which in turn generates new Political Economy forces in non participating nations or pressures for inclusion. With the size of the trade bloc, the pressure increases, but the size depends upon how many nations join. Thus, a simple incident of regionalism may trigger several round of membership requests from nations that were previously happy as non-members. Two situations may occur, firstly, when the trade bloc is open to expansion, regionalism may spread like wildfire and secondly, if the trade bloc is closed to expansion, the new political economy flames may find vent in preferential arrangements among included nations. Such regionalism could occur despite any progress being made in ongoing multilateral talks, unless these are promised to fully offset the discrimination.

Evolution

The urge for cooperative relations between states is as old as the beginning of civilized life, but the experimentation of this concept gained currency after the Second World War. A treaty of 1278 BC between the Pharos and the Hitties incorporate almost every stipulation that a treaty of regional cooperation might contain today. The Greek history reveals

5. Baldwin, *Op. cit.*

that their existed a number of regional organisations, viz. Amphictyomic League from the pre-historic period, Lacedaemonian League in the sixth century, the Peloponesian League and the Athenian League. Before the period of Waterloo, many alliances took place. In 1800, Baltic powers entered into an alliance among themselves to maintain the freedom of the seas against the monopoly of England. Following the Napoleanic wars, the European monarchs entered into the Holy Alliance and the Quadruple Alliances against France. Numerous regional arrangements came into existence in the inter-war period (1918-39) of which the Draft Treaty of Mutual Trust and Locarno Pact are significant. League Covenant also provided for regional understanding for securing peace.

The emergence of bipolarity after the Second World War led to the formation of a number of treaties, pacts and regional integration schemes in both the developed and the developing world. The nations of the Americas are working more closely together than ever before—strengthening democracy, advancing human rights, promoting peace and security, expanding trade and tackling complex problems caused by poverty, drugs and corruption. The Organisation of American States (OAS) is playing a central role in working toward many of the goals that are shared by the countries of North, Central and South America and the Caribbean.

The first specific and important manifestations of the Latin American economic integration process were the Central American Common Market (CACM, 1960) and the Latin American Free Trade Association (LAFTA, 1960). The former linked the five Central American countries and other economic areas in trade, in order to establish a unified market, and diverse institutions were created to promote its operations. The latter—comprising ten South American countries and Mexico—was a more flexible and less ambitious mechanism for drawing closer to a Free Trade Zone by the negotiation of trade preferences on the basis of product lists.

Subsequently, the signing of the Cartagena Agreement (1969) and the creation of the Andean Development Fund (CAF, 1969) would lead to the establishment of the Andean Group, a subregional scheme incorporating a number of intermediate and lesser developed countries among the LAFTA member countries, and that included accelerated and strict integration mechanisms, along with a common treatment for foreign investments and a Joint Industrial Development Program. Concomitantly, in 1968, five Caribbean English-speaking countries established the Caribbean Free Trade Area (CARIFTA) which in just a short time was transformed into the Caribbean Community (CARICOM). The establishment of the Caribbean Community and Common Market (CARICOM) was the result of a 15-year effort to fulfil the hope of regional integration which was born with the establishment of the British West Indies Federation in 1958. The West Indies Federation came to an end in 1962 but its end, in many ways must be regarded as the real beginning of what is now the Caribbean Community. The Community has concentrated on the promotion of functional cooperation, especially in relation to human and social development, and in integrating the economies of Member States.

The idea of European integration was conceived to prevent such killing and destruction from ever happening again. It was first proposed by the French Foreign Minister Robert Schuman in a speech on 9 May 1950. The EU is the result of a process of deep regional cooperation and integration that began in 1951 among Benalux Countries (Belgium, Netherlands & Luxembourg) and grew to include Germany, France and Italy. In 1952, Treaty of Paris was signed establishing the European Coal and Steel Community (ECSC). The logic behind this was that, if the two basic industries which had provided the where-withal to make war were placed under joint, rather than national, control, the inclination to resort to force to settle disputes would be thwarted. The power to take decisions about coal and steel industries, in those countries was placed in the hands of an independent, supranational body called the "High Authority". The ECSC was such a success that, within a few years, these same countries decided to go further and integrate other sectors of their economies. In 1957, they signed the Treaty of Rome which established the European Atomic Energy Community (EURATOM) and the European Economic Community (ECC). A preamble to this treaty defined the ultimate purpose of the great European enterprise as 'ever closer union among the people of Europe'. The member states set about removing trade barriers between them and forming a "common market".

In 1967, the institutions of the three European communities were merged. From this point on, there was a single Commission and a single Council of Ministers as well as the European Parliament. All the above three bodies collectively came to be known as European Community. Amendments were carried out to the earlier treaties by the Single European Act of Luxembourg in 1985. The collapse of the Soviet Union and the reunification of Germany in 1989 presented European leaders with provable challenges. They realised that the opportunities offered by the end of the cold war reinforced the need for further integration in the Western half of the continent. As a result of these development, Maastricht Treaty was signed in 1992. It introduced new forms of cooperation between the member state governments and led to the creation of European Union.

In Africa, demands for the Pan-African unity were especially noticeable in the early 1960s after most of the African States achieved independence. This was realized in the establishment of the Organisation of African Unity (OAU) in 1963. The end of the Cold War and emergence of a United Europe after the establishment of European Union (EU) confronted Africa and the rest of the developing world with enormous challenges. Consequently the OAU in June 1991, at its 27th annual summit in Abuja, Nigeria, adopted the Abuja Treaty to establish the African Economic Community (AEC) by the year 2025. This Treaty came into force in May 1994. Since then the idea of African unity and cooperation has assumed new dynamics and direction. The Abuja Treaty also recommended the establishment of an African Union (AU) and a Pan-African Parliament (PAP). The OAU endorsed the Abuja Treaty proposal for an African Union in 1999. The OAU summit in Lome in July 2000 declared the establishment of African Union by a unanimous decision. It came into existence on 26 May 2001. It was formally launched in Durban, South Africa on July, 9, 2002. The African Union which has replaced the OAU aims at "achieving greater unity and solidarity between the African countries and the people of Africa" and "accelerate the political and socio-economic integration of the continent".

The establishment of regionalism in Middle East was not a product of the moment but an institutional embodiment of a historical, social and cultural reality. Deep religious and cultural ties link these states, and strong kin relations prevail among their citizens. All these factors, enhanced by one geographical entity extending from sea to desert, have facilitated contacts and interaction among them, and created homogeneous values and characteristics. League of Arab States was formed in 1945 for strengthening ties among the member states, coordinate their policies, and promote their common interests. The Organisation of the Islamic Conference (OIC), set up by the Kings and Heads of State and Government of Islamic States, in 1969, was the concrete expression of a great awareness, on the part of the Ummah, of the necessity to establish an Organisation embodying its aspirations and capable of carrying out its just struggle against the various dangers which threatened it and still persist. GCC established in 1981 is a continuation, evolution and institutionalisation of old prevailing realities, it is, on the other, a practical answer to the challenges of security and economic development in the area. It is also a fulfilment of the aspirations of its citizens towards some sort of Arab regional unity.

The first ever attempt at regionalism in Asia was made at the 'Asian Relations Conference' in March 1947, but it largely focused on the de-colonisation movements taking place in Asia. The region witnessed a few efforts by mid 1950s. However, these efforts were either promoted by anti-colonial ethos or by the prodding of ex-colonial masters. Their scope and membership even included extra regional powers and invariably remained too diffused to have any lasting and visible impact. During the Cold War period, regional politics in South Asia emerged primarily to support and sustain military alliances and to rebuild, coordinate and integrate, markets and economies of allies. The South Asian nations could not do more than preoccupy themselves with quarrels and conflicts. In fact, the divisions and conflicts in South Asia were seen to serve the greater and better purpose in Cold War politics.

The first regional grouping in Asia emerged in East Asian region. It was the SEATO (South East Asian Treaty Organisation), a military alliance supported by the United States. From South

Asia, Pakistan became a member of SEATO, as well as CENTO (Central Treaty Organisation)—a military and economic alliance of Britain, Iran, Pakistan and Turkey. After the Bandung Conference of 1955, Non-Alignment as an international group emerged at the Belgrade Conference of 1961. Except Pakistan, all other South Asian countries became its member. India, due to its dominant position was a leading player in the region. Tensions between India and its neighbours were exploited to serve extra-regional interests. The dominant strategic interests associated with the Cold War did not allow any attempt to create regional groupings outside the Cold War context to succeed. South Asia was eventually divided in the Cold War rivalries. Thus, regionalism could neither be imposed from the global hegemonic forces, nor could it be evolved through autonomous initiatives from within the South Asian regions. Despite this situation, each South Asian country had bilateral relations with various regional economic groupings. These countries also remained members of international groupings such as UNCTAD and the Group of 77.

In the mid 1980s, regionalism eventually came into being in South Asia with the formation of SAARC. It sought to achieve the integrated package of greater cooperation in the following phases:

(a) the establishment SAARC Preferential Trading Arrangement (SAPTA). The agreement to this effect was signed in April 1993 and entered into force in December 1995;

(b) the establishment of a South Asian Free Trade Area (SAFTA) by the year 2010 by the least developed Member States and by 2008 by other Member States;

(c) the establishment of a South Asian Customs Union (SACU) by the year 2015 and

(d) the commencement of the process of implementing the remaining measures for moving towards a South Asian Economic Union by the year 2020.

Signing of the SAFTA Agreement at the 12th SAARC Summit in January, 2004 visualizes a graded reduction in import tariffs over the next decade. The first milestone will be in 2006 which will see a reduction of tariffs between the seven member nations to between 0-5% by the time the Agreement is fully implemented on December 31, 2015. The SAFTA accord also allows any contracting States to pull out of the treaty at any time, after it comes into force from January 1, 2006. Such withdrawal shall be effective on the expiry of the six months from the date on which a written notice thereof is received by the Secretary General of the SAARC.

Regional agreements mushroomed, prompted by the uncertain outcome of the GATT/Uruguay Round negotiations, and apprehensions about a possible transformation of the EU into 'fortress Europe'. The collapse of the Soviet Union and the removal of the Iron Curtain gave a renewed impulse to the tendency to emphasise economic interactions at the expense of political and strategic preoccupations.

In a number of cases, the revival of regionalism meant reforming the so-called 'first-generation' regional organisations, which were established in the 1960s to promote integration through import-substitution strategies and 'delinking' from the global market. More frequently, regionalisation involved the creation of new groupings, such as the North American Free Trade Area (NAFTA) and MERCOSUR in the Americas; the Asia-Pacific Economic Conference (APEC) and the Free Trade Agreement of the Association of South East Asian Nations (ASEAN) in Asia. In Europe, the expansion and deepening of European integration prompted the formation of the European Union (EU). In Africa, the member states of the Organisation of African Unity (OAU) joined the move and signed in 1991 the Treaty of Abuja towards the establishment of a transcontinental African Economic Community (AEC) and recently with the inauguration of the African Union in 2002, the integration of the continent has become a reality.

Far from implying the formation of mutually exclusive regional integration groupings, this process was strongly outward-oriented; regional cooperation & integration also meant the opening of discussions towards the enlargement of existing institutions and the conclusion of inter-regional agreements. This kaleidoscopic interplay between institutions, identities and socio-political factors accounts for the polymorphous nature of the so-called new regionalisation process. Closely tied to the advancement of globalisation, the regionalisation process often endorses already existing international economic links between neighbouring states. Regionalisation, as in Europe or North America, represented an opportunity to establish a more appropriate framework for absorbing the pressures of multilateralism and globalisation. Elsewhere, as in Asia or Africa, regionalisation was associated with the trade and investment strategies of private agents who operated in the absence of—or, as in Africa, in opposition to—institutionalised regional structures.

Old and New Regionalism

The recent integration initiatives are often referred to as 'new regionalism' to distinguish them from the 'old regionalism' practised in the 1960s and 1970s. The first wave may have faltered, but it seems that the second wave is here to stay. The lack of success, 'first time around' can be attributed mainly to three shortcomings: a misplaced focus on inward-looking economic policies, the absence of basic preconditions, and weaknesses in institutional design[6].

During the 1960s and 1970s, the key development strategy was import substituting industrialisation using high protective barriers. The main theoretical justification for tariff protection was the 'infant industry' argument. The view was that, in order to gain a manufacturing foothold, local companies should have protection from established foreign competitors. At the same time, people were over-optimistic about the capacity of governments to plan economic development. High tariffs were needed to support import substitution, but they also became a useful source of funds for the rapidly expanding public sector. This inward-looking trade policy was reinforced by restrictive foreign exchange policies which led to overvalued currencies.

Because most developing countries had small economies, it was felt that import substitution would have a better chance if pursued at a regional level and this led to various integration schemes. One element underpinning this approach was

6. Kennes, Walter, "Developing Countries and Regional Integration", *The Courier ACP-EU*, No.165, September-October 1997.

regional industrial planning. The idea was that industries would be shared out among participating countries, on the basis that they would then go on to supply the whole regional market.

The reasons for the failure of this strategy have been extensively documented elsewhere. In short, it led to massive underutilisation of production capacity and a lack of competitiveness. It did not encourage technical innovation and acted as a strong disincentive for export activities. This, however, only partly explains the failure of the first wave of integration. Even if inefficient, one might reasonably expect such a strategy to increase intra-regional trade, but there is little evidence that this actually occurred. There were clearly other problems as well.

Regional integration can only succeed if certain economic and non-economic preconditions are fulfilled. Important aspects here include structural stability (peace and security), the rule of law, good governance, and macroeconomic and monetary stability. In many of the countries that participated in the 'first wave' of regionalism, one or more of these preconditions were lacking. Two examples suffice to illustrate the problem. The absence of good governance can lead to a battery of irregular non-tariff barriers which restrict the flow of goods across national borders within a region. And if there is conflict or civil strife in one of the member states, it is hardly realistic to expect any meaningful progress towards economic integration.

Inadequate institutional design also contributed to the difficulties. Most literature on economic integration glosses over such matters. If countries say they want to form a customs union or free trade area, it is simply taken for granted that they can do it, provided only that they devise a workable scheme on paper. However, fixing the core part of the menu is similar to variable geometry, but with a thematic rather than a geographic orientation. However, the actual implementation is a delicate process covering the setting of realistic targets, negotiation, implementation, control and resolution of disputes. It is conditioned by the nature of the decision making process which can be intergovernmental, supranational or mixed. Since its origin, the EU has been following a supranational approach on economic integration (recently complemented by an intergovernmental approach for the two new 'pillars' introduced by the Maastricht Treaty: foreign and security policy, and justice and home affairs.

For various reasons, developing countries were not keen on supra-nationalism, which would have implied the sharing of sovereignty only recently acquired. The result, in almost all cases, was the creation of regional institutions with weak secretariats and little or no authority. These bodies were invariably hampered by lack of resources, and political interference in personnel management. They were not able to ensure adequate preparation, implementation and control of agreed integration policies. And in some cases they became over-dependent on donor funding, even for their day-to-day functioning. This is clearly not a sound basis for progress.

An important aspect of institutional design is to achieve an efficient distribution of labour between different regional organisations. In some cases there were overlaps in membership and contradictory objectives. Rivalry between regional organisations sometimes contributed to failures in the implementation of agreed policies. A number of approaches have now been developed to facilitate the coherence of regional organisations as well as to deal with the accession of new member states and the introduction of new policy areas. These include: variable speed, variable geometry, integration 'à la carte' and flexible integration.

Under the variable speed approach, common objectives are agreed, but some member states can move more rapidly towards implementation. Rather than let progress be determined by the slowest member, those who are ready to proceed can do so. Variable geometry accommodates a situation where a sub-group of member states moves towards deeper integration than the others. With 'à la carte' integration, each member can make its own selections from a menu of integration policies. Clearly, this is not very manageable in practice. Flexible integration involves defined core themes to which all state parties must subscribe and other areas where participation is voluntary. This last approach gives structure to 'à la carte' integration, by fixing the core part of the menu and is similar to variable geometry, but with a thematic rather than a geographic orientation.

Two other reasons are frequently cited to explain the relative failure of regional integration initiatives among developing countries. These are disparities between member states and lack of infrastructure. There are many types of disparity relating to income levels, development, economic size and the degree of industrialisation, as well as differences in political systems, culture, history and language. Such divergences clearly make the management of integration more complex and costly.

Having said this, the effect of divergent income levels on the distribution of the gains of integration is often exaggerated. In the long run, economic integration will tend to reduce disparities, though in the short-term (during the transition phase), the benefits may not be evenly spread. Divergences will decrease most rapidly if integration goes well beyond trade liberalisation to include free movement of capital and workers, the right of establishment, and common competition and fiscal policies.

Lack of adequate transport and communications infrastructure is a formidable constraint that makes trade between many developing countries difficult and costly. This applies particularly to landlocked nations. Improving transport facilities has long been a priority for EU regional development cooperation. But this is not really a reason for lack of progress in economic integration. The latter usually leads to better infrastructures rather than vice versa since successful integration will result in an increased rate of return from cross-border transport and communications investments.

Why should the new integration initiatives have any better chance of succeeding than those attempted in the past? The main reason is that the current initiatives are taking place in a very different political and economic context. The key political difference is that the Cold War is over. Certain rivalries that used to hamper conflict resolution no longer exist.

In addition, many developing countries have evolved from authoritarian to democratic regimes and the influence of civil society on economic decision-making has significantly increased. On the economic front, there has been a policy shift towards more openness and reliance on market forces. Macro-economic policies have become much more stable. Most developing countries have implemented Structural Adjustment Programmes (SAPs) in collaboration with the Bretton Woods Institutions and other cooperation agencies. And by and large, the economic shocks that so badly affected developing countries during the 1970s and 1980s (commodity price, interest rate and exchange rate movements) have diminished.

Recent integration initiatives no longer emphasize high protective barriers or regional import substitution, and they are more outward-oriented. Additionally, the concept of regionalism has been broadened to cover a variety of issues 'beyond the borders' such as: common technical standards, competition policy, investment regulations, the provision of services and government procurement.

Technological innovations especially in the areas of information management and communication, combined with increased capital mobility, have exposed the limitations of national economic policies, even in large industrial nations. A discussion on regionalism cannot ignore this globalisation process, which implies both opportunities and challenges. There is a legitimate fear in many developing countries that they will lose out unless they prepare themselves.

Regionalism as a Tool for Integrating into the World Economy

There is an underlying assumption that integration into the world economy will be good for economic development and social welfare. This assumption is much debated (and criticised) since a lot depends on the way in which the integration is actually achieved. An immediate question is whether developing countries should pursue this goal separately, or in a coordinated and structured way through regionalism.

Small economies and specialisation mean that most developing countries are extremely vulnerable to economic shocks. The opening up of such economies has often led to greatly increased interdependence. Countries have become 'stakeholders' in the economic policies of their neighbours.

In such circumstances, some form of regional policy coordination becomes imperative. So in reality, the question for developing countries is no longer whether they should take part in regionalism, but what kind of regionalism best suits them.

Recalling the preconditions mentioned above, successful regionalism should be based on general political principles including the rule of law, respect for human rights, and government accountability and transparency. In the economic sphere, the starting point should be the basic principles of orderly monetary and economic management. These principles underpin the multilateral system and are essential for membership of the IMF and WTO. But the global arrangements are not all-encompassing, and many economic policy options remain to be determined at national or regional level.

There has always been controversy over the extent to which the multilateral system actually benefits developing countries. The latter often sought to justify import substitution strategies on the grounds that the international system was 'unfair' to them. At the same time, they neglected the possibility of exerting influence on the direction of multilateral developments. The rapidly rising developing state membership of the WTO, and the fact that more and more of these countries are fulfilling the IMF requirements on current account convertibility, suggest an important shift in attitude. This is highly significant, because it means that developing countries should become much more influential in the global system.

The WTO has a system of rules that establish rights and obligations for member states. Developing countries enjoy 'special and differential treatment', mainly in the form of longer transition periods before obligations enter into force and sometimes involving less stringent treatment. They can receive technical help to meet their obligations or deal with disputes. The WTO has also responded to the specific concerns of the least developed countries who are likely to suffer more than most from certain effects of the Uruguay Round (for example the increase in world cereal prices).

But there are limits to what the multilateral system can do. One basic limitation is that most developing countries lack the capacity to participate effectively in the structure. Another is that in many areas, the international rules offer only the legal framework an outline which must be filled in by governments. If national resources are not up to the task, a solution may be found in adopting a regional approach, as a complement to multilateralism. Thus, regional organisations can ensure that the interests of their members are taken into account in the multilateral system, as well as dealing with issues not yet covered by the latter.

Unilateral liberalisation has often been recommended, especially by the Bretton Woods Institutions, as a key strategy for developing countries. If many countries open up their economies at the same time the result is a move towards overall free trade. Unilateral reform (whether or not in the context of a formal adjustment programme) may help to achieve macroeconomic and monetary stability, and to eliminate distortions, but it does not automatically improve market access. Inefficient industries producing import substitutes may disappear before new export-oriented industries can be established. Where this happens, the result can, in fact, be renewed macroeconomic instability, not to mention an increase in social problems.

So, rapid unilateral liberalisation can pose some big risks, especially for the least-developed countries. A diversified economy may be able to respond quickly to new market opportunities' but the same is not necessarily true of a country that depends on just a few commodities for its export earnings. There are significant adjustment costs that are difficult to handle in a vulnerable economy. Balance of payments support under a structural adjustment programme can contribute to the government budget and help maintain imports, but it does not directly increase the competitiveness of the private sector. It may, therefore, not lead to new investments and the desired supply response.

Another point that most developing countries must bear in mind is that unilateral liberalisation will require major fiscal adjustments, given governments' continuing heavy reliance on trade-related taxes. Regional liberalisation should help to ease this.

Similarly, speedier and more coordinated liberalisation at the level of the regional market (vis-à-vis the world market) will mitigate the adjustment costs for the private sector. Unlike the unilateral approach, it will improve access to the markets of regional partners. Thus, regional integration taken in conjunction with an orderly and gradual opening up of markets to the rest of the world will be superior to quick unilateral liberalisation (which may be reversed if adjustment costs become too high). One final point is that regionalism reduces the influence of pressure groups who would like to see protection restored and hence, may be more credible than unilateral liberalisation.

Support for Regional Economic Integration

The EU is keen to support realistic integration initiatives among developing countries that are consistent with national SAPs and with the multilateral system. Recent experience has led to a strategy comprising three interrelated areas:

- capacity building (including technical assistance, training and research) on the subject of regional economic integration at the level of regional institutions and national governments;
- assistance to the private sector to facilitate restructuring in the wider regional and world markets, including improvements in the financial sector;
- support to governments that are committed to implementing regional integration, to help them cope with the transitional effect on budgetary resources (balance of payments or budgetary support).

In more concrete terms, certain orientations might be envisaged. Under the heading of 'capacity building', adequate attention must be given to the institutional design and legal framework of regional integration. There is also a need to develop analytical capacities—for example in predicting the economic effects of trade liberalisation and regional integration. The approach could cover the training of personnel responsible for policy design and for handling WTO and regional obligations. An effort is needed to upgrade customs services to deal with issues such as verification of origin, and phytosanitary and sanitary regulations. There is also a need to simplify and harmonise rules of origin. The private sector should be involved in capacity building, for example, in areas such as standardisation, quality control and international payments procedures. Regional organisations should be strengthened so that they are able to provide real services to their member states in these areas. Customs unions (and other 'deeper' integration structures) should be mandated to represent their member states in the WTO thus both saving resources and ensuring a higher profile. Multilateral surveillance of monetary and trade policies could be more closely linked to economic policy surveillance at regional level. And if all of this is to work, capacity building is essential.

The benefits of unilateral liberalisation and regional integration will materialise through decisions by the private sector. Subsidies to enterprises that are no longer viable in the regional or global markets should be resisted. This will be easier at regional level because of the reduced influence of pressure groups. At the same time, it should be recognised that adjustment and restructuring costs are real. There needs to be a new industrial policy that facilitates adoption of and transition to improved technologies. Development cooperation can play a useful role here. Special attention should also be given to integrating developing countries more effectively into the global financial markets.

Trade liberalisation may diminish government revenue. The sharpest effects will be felt in the short term as it will take time for new private sector activities to generate higher revenue for governments. Particular care will therefore be needed in undertaking fiscal adjustments. However, it should be kept in mind that reforms to increase the efficiency of customs services will tend to diminish the decline in government revenue resulting from lower tariff rates. Furthermore, trade expansion will gradually increase tariff revenue.

The EU has recently been involved in some initiatives to support economic integration among developing countries along the lines of the above-mentioned principles. Together with the African Development Bank the IMF and the World Bank, the EU is helping to facilitate regional trade in goods and services and investments and payments in Eastern and

Southern Africa and the Indian Ocean (the Cross-Border Initiative). In collaboration with France, the IMF and the World Bank, it is also supporting the construction of the West African Economic and Monetary Union.

Despite the widespread view that the 'second wave' of regional integration is here to stay, it is too early to declare it a success. What is clear is that the circumstances are now very different from those that pertained during the 'first wave' and important lessons have been learnt in the meantime. In view of this, regionalism may well prove to be a gangplank for developing countries striving to get aboard the global economic vessel.

Lessons Learned

From the standpoint of the Integration Process the lessons learned are the following:

- First, sustained macroeconomic stability in member countries is essential for advancing regional integration.
- Second, regional integration and cooperation needs political commitment at the highest level and sustained benevolent leadership from the major market partner(s).
- Third, regarding sub-regional or extra-regional integration agreements, consolidating quickly and preserving secure preferential market access for trade is essential "glue" for deepening integration, or even pursuing parallel cooperation programs.
- A fourth major lesson for regional integration is the importance of maintaining forward momentum in the development of transparent and equitable rules-based systems (with formal contingent mechanisms) as well as functional regional institutions and national counterparts with a capacity to formulate, coordinate, and implement regional policy. Likewise, agenda setting must be accompanied by realistic roadmaps and calendars with fall-back positions that can help preserve forward momentum.
- Fifth, the effects of regional integration are highly conditioned by factors in the home market. Effective

domestic policies and rules-based democratic institutions are necessary to ensure equitable public access to the benefits of regional integration and to provide social protection and conditions for socially efficient adjustment in the face of increased competition and economic transformations which create losers as well as winners. Particular attention should be given to the poor so that they benefit from the integration process.

- Finally, for regional integration to be effective, both collectively and for the individual partner, there is a need for efficient national counterparts of regional policy.

There are clear positive synergies among various regional agreements and between them and gradual unilateral opening and development of the multilateral system. Hence policies on these fronts must work in tandem.

Good and sustainable trade and integration agreements demand: good negotiations (including channels of communication with civil society and its representatives in the legislative branch); effective implementation; and socially efficient adjustments. There are severe asymmetric capabilities on all three of these fronts in the emerging initiatives with North America, the EU, Asia and the WTO. Without capacity building these initiatives could be in jeopardy.

Broad-based functional cooperation initiatives—while not necessarily bearing the same level of political commitment as formal integration—nevertheless needs political backing from the participating countries at the highest national level and sectorally, a prioritisation of agendas, forward looking calendars with precise collective work programs, benchmark reviews, monitoring and follow-up. They also need adequate collective technical, financial and logistical support.

Despite numerous problems and obstacles, regional cooperation and integration has become a crucial element of the development process. In the light of the current developments in the rest of the world, it has become vitally important for the independent nations to map out a strategy of regionalism to face the challenges posed by powerful forces of globalisation and lay the foundation for sustainable development in the twenty-first century.

In order to give the dream of an Economic Union and common currency goal a touch of reality, it is necessary to transform the entire approach and policies of Member States towards these organisations. The biggest challenge is to make the mainstream process a dynamic exercise with a multiplicity of stakeholders and institutions. Our search for pragmatism, maturity and wisdom will have to involve both Government and civil society.

5

MAJOR REGIONAL ORGANISATIONS OF THE WORLD

5.1: AFRICAN REGIONAL ORGANISATIONS

AFRICAN DEVELOPMENT BANK GROUP

The African Development Bank Group is a multinational development bank supported by 77 nations (member countries) from Africa, North and South America, Europe and Asia. Headquartered in Abidjan, Cote d' Ivoire, the Bank Group consists of three institutions:

- The African Development Bank [ADB],
- The African Development Fund [ADF],
- The Nigeria Trust Fund [NTF].

Established in 1964, its mission is to promote economic and social development through loans, equity investments, and technical assistance.

The African Development Bank [ADB]

The African Development Bank is a regional multilateral development bank, engaged in promoting the economic development and social progress of its Regional Member Countries (RMCs) in Africa. The Bank, established in 1964, started functioning in 1966 with its Headquarters in Abidjan, Cote d' lvoire. Its shareholders are the 53 countries in Africa as well as 24 countries in the Americas, Europe, and Asia.

The Bank's principal functions are: (i) to make loans and equity investments for the economic and social advancement of the RMCs; (ii) to provide technical assistance for the preparation and execution of development projects and programs; (iii) to promote investment of public and private capital for development purposes and (iv) to respond to requests for assistance in coordinating development policies and plans of RMCs. In its operations, the Bank is also required to give special attention to national and multinational projects and programs which promote regional integration.

The financial resources of the Bank consist of ordinary capital resources, comprising subscribed capital, reserves, funds raised through borrowings, and accumulated net income. The ADB's capital is subscribed such that RMCs hold two-thirds of total subscribed capital, and non-regional members hold one-third. The Bank has borrowed funds for its ordinary operations from the international money and capital markets. The Bank's callable capital backs its borrowings in the capital markets.

The Bank's operations cover the major sectors, with particular emphasis on agriculture, public utilities, transport, industry, the social sectors of health and education, and concerns cutting across sectors, such as poverty reduction, environmental management, gender mainstreaming, and population activities. Most Bank financing is designed to support specific projects. However, the Bank also provides program, sector, and policy-based loans to enhance national economic management. The Bank also finances non-publicly guaranteed private sector operations. The Bank actively pursues co-financing activities with bilateral and multilateral institutions.

The Bank's highest policy-making body is its Board of Governors, which consists of one governor for each member country, and which issues general directives concerning the operational policies of the Bank. Amendments to the Bank's Agreement, the admittance of new members, and capital increases require the approval of the Bank's Governors. With the exception of certain powers specifically reserved to it under the Agreement, the Board of Governors has delegated its powers to the Board of Directors. In accordance with Article 32 of the Agreement Establishing the Bank, the Board of Directors is responsible for the conduct of the general operations of the Bank. It is composed of 18 Executive Directors who are elected every three years, 12 representing the RMCs and 6 representing non-regional members. The Board of Directors approves all loans, guarantees, equity investments, and borrowings; it also sets policy guidelines for Bank operations, including operational and financial policies, and borrowing programs.

The President of the Bank is elected by the Board of Governors for a term of five years, after which he may be re-elected for one other term only. The Bank's Agreement mandates that the President be a national of one of the regional members. The President is Chairman of the Board of Directors and, under its direction, conducts the business of the Bank. He is responsible for the management of the Institution in accordance with regulations adopted by the Board. In this, he is assisted by Vice Presidents, who are appointed by the Board of Directors on his recommendation. At the end of 1996, the Bank had 18 Departments and seven Units at Headquarters staffed by 446 professionals, and 456 staff of other categories.

The Bank lends at a variable lending rate calculated on the basis of the cost of borrowings. The rate is adjusted twice a year, on January 1st and July 1st, to reflect changes in the average cost of borrowings over the preceding six-month period. The other terms include a commitment charge of 1.00 per cent, maturities of up to 20 years, including a 5-year grace period.

The African Development Fund [ADF]

The African Development Fund provides development finance on concessional terms to low-income RMCs which are unable to borrow on the non-concessional terms of the Bank. In accordance with its lending policy, poverty reduction is the main aim of Fund development activities in borrowing countries. The Fund, which was established in 1972, commenced operations in 1974. Its current membership comprises 24 non-African State Participants and the African Development Bank. The Fund's Board of Governors meets annually, and the direction of general operations is conducted by a Board of Directors—six appointed by State Participants, and six designated by the African Development Bank from among the regional Executive Directors of the Bank.

Its sources of funds are mainly contributions and periodic replenishments by State Participants. The Fund is normally replenished on a three-year basis, unless State Participants decide otherwise. The total subscriptions, at the end of 1996, amounted to US$12.58 billion.

The Fund finances projects and technical assistance as well as studies. It lends at no interest rate, with a service charge of 0.75 per cent per annum, a commitment fee of 0.50 per cent, and a 50-year repayment period, including a 10-year grace period.

The Nigeria Trust Fund [NTF]

The Nigeria Trust Fund was established by the Government of Nigeria in 1976, with an initial capital of US$80 million which was subsequently replenished with US$71 million in 1981. The purpose of the NTF is to assist in the development efforts of the poorer ADB members.

The NTF is required by its Agreement to use its resources to provide financing for projects of national or regional importance which further the economic and social development of the low-income RMCs whose economic and social conditions and prospects require financing on non-conventional terms.

The NTF is under ADB management and, it lends at a 4 per cent interest rate, with a 25-year repayment period, including a five year grace period.

AFRICAN UNION (AU)

The AU is Africa's premier institution and principal organisation for the promotion of accelerated socio-economic integration of the continent, which will lead to greater unity and solidarity between African Countries and people.

The process of constituting the African Union was completed at an extra-ordinary summit in Sirte in March 2001, where the establishment of the AU was proclaimed. The Union was formally launched in Durban, South Africa on July 9, 2002.

The novel 53 member AU is a political, economic and social project molded along that of the European Union. It seeks a higher form of collaborative union for the continent and, unlike the OAU, it has the right and power to intervene in the internal affairs of its member states. The OAU was to evolved into the AU—an organisation that transcended the traditional institutional frameworks and integrated the OAU and the AEC. In other words, a single organisation with two dimensions—political and economic.

The AU is based on the common vision of a united and strong Africa and on the need to build a partnership between governments and all segments of civil society, in particular women, youth and the private sector, in order to strengthen solidarity and cohesion amongst the people of Africa.

As a continental organisation, it focuses on the promotion of peace, security and stability on the continent as a pre-requisite for the implementation of the development and integration agenda of the Union.

The AU has been conceived as an institution with a re-invigorated mandate and vision for the continent. It should be seen and understood as a developmental organisation, and not aversely as a traditional coordinating governmental body.

Aims of the AU

The new union aims not only at reflecting a common African identity but also at creating a contiguous democratic space across Africa, which will ensure good governance to the peoples of Africa and provide quicker mechanism for conflict resolution.

The aim is to create a set of core values such as constitutional rule in African States, peace, democracy and respect for human rights. It is envisaged that the AU should be as democratic as possible, moving as rapidly as possible towards establishing directly elected Pan African parliament, in accordance with the Constitutive Act.

The Objectives of the AU

- To achieve greater unity and solidarity between the African countries and the peoples of Africa;
- To defend the sovereignty, territorial integrity and independence of its Member States;
- To accelerate the political and socio-economic integration of the continent;

- To promote and defend African common positions on issues of interest to the continent and its peoples;
- To encourage international cooperation, taking due account of the Charter of the United Nations and the Universal Declaration of Human Rights;
- To promote peace, security, and stability on the continent;
- To promote democratic principles and institutions, popular participation and good governance;
- To promote and protect human and peoples' rights in accordance with the African Charter on Human and Peoples' Rights and other relevant human rights instruments;
- To establish the necessary conditions which enable the continent to play its rightful role in the global economy and in international negotiations;
- To promote sustainable development at the economic, social and cultural levels as well as the integration of African economies;
- To promote co-operation in all fields of human activity to raise the living standards of African peoples;
- To coordinate and harmonize the policies between the existing and future Regional Economic Communities for the gradual attainment of the objectives of the Union;
- To advance the development of the continent by promoting research in all fields, in particular in science and technology;
- To work with relevant international partners in the eradication of preventable diseases and the promotion of good health on the continent.

The Organs of the AU

In view of the long and varied experience of subregional and regional attempts at formation & operation of the regional organisation, the AU Constitutive Act provides for establishment of the following organs & institutes:

The Assembly. Composed of Heads of State and Government or their duly accredited representatives. The Assembly of Heads of State and Government is the supreme organ of the Union.

The Executive Council. Composed of Ministers or Authorities designated by the Governments of Members States. The Executive Council is responsible to the Assembly.

The Commission. Composed of the Chairperson, the Deputy Chairperson, eight Commissioners and Staff members; Each Commissioner shall be responsible for a portfolio.

The Permanent Representatives' Committee. Composed of Permanent Representatives of Member States accredited to the Union. The Permanent Representatives Committee is charged with the responsibility of preparing the work of the Executive Council.

Peace and Security Council (PSC). By decision AHG/Dec 160 (xxxvii) of the Summit of Lusaka, July 2001, a decision was made for the creation within the African Union of the Peace and Security Council. The Protocol establishing the PSC is in the process of ratification.

Pan-African Parliament. A Pan-African Parliament, and organ to ensure the full participation of African peoples in governance, development and economic integration of the Continent. The protocol relating to the composition, powers, functions and organisation of the Pan-African Parliament has been signed by Member States and is in the process of ratification.

ECOSOCC. The Economic, Social and Cultural Council, an advisory organ composed of different social and professional groups of the Member States of the Union.

The Court of Justice. A Court of Justice of the Union shall be established. The statutes defining the composition and functions of the Court of Justice have been prepared and was submitted to the Assembly in Maputo.

The Specialized Technical Committees. The following Specialized Technical Committees are meant to address sectoral issues and are at Ministerial Level:

- The Committee on Rural Economy and Agricultural Matters;

- The Committee on Monetary and Financial Affairs;
- The Committee on Trade, Customs and Immigration Matters;
- The Committee on Industry, Science and Technology, Energy, Natural Resources and Environment;
- The Committee on Transport, Communications and Tourism;
- The Committee on Health, Labour and Social Affairs and
- The Committee on Education, Culture and Human Resources.

The Financial Institutions

- The African Central bank
- The African Monetary Fund
- The African Investment Bank

Agenda for the effective take-off of the AU

The first agenda item is the crucial need to establish an effective AU Commission headed by a very competent, knowledge and strong personality. The Commission should be fully equipped with the necessary human and financial resources to enable it to develop and articulate its vision and programmes as well as monitor them.

The second item on the agenda is ensuring good governance in Africa. The success of the AU will generally depend on good governance, stakeholder participation, human right and democratisation at all levels. There is the need to deepen democracy and promote participation.

Third is the need to ensure the active role of national parliaments in AU programmes. Parliament and parliamentarians have a central role to play in mobilising and representing the people towards, the effective establishment of the A.U. National parliaments have the responsibility of passing the necessary legislation to realise integration objectives and providing the necessary oversight of their government's policies, budgetary appropriation and other measures relevant to regional and continental economic and political cooperation and integration.

The need to devise new mechanism for financing the Union is the fourth major, item on the agenda. The AU should investigate new mechanism for financing to avoid complete dependence on the dues of member states.

The fifth item on agenda is the need to make the private sector a driving force. For effective implementation of the AU programmes, the private sector should be brought into the structures of decision-making of the AU in a more meaningful manner. The Constitutive Act of the Union includes provision that gives status to the private sector and civil society organisations as two major components of the economic integration process, and mandates their participation in the specialized technical commissions.

On the whole, the need to broaden participation and deepen ownership is a sine qua non for the success of the AU. The process of regional and continental integration in the AU must be owned by the African peoples. The AU should be responsive to the needs of ordinary Africans rather than to the whims and caprices of African leaders.

ARAB MAGHREB UNION (AMU)

The Arab Maghreb Union (AMU) encompasses five North African countries that have strong historical, cultural, and language affinities. The first Conference of Maghreb Economic Ministers, which took place in Tunis in 1964, established the Conseil Permanent Cunsultatif du Maghreb (CPCM) between Algeria, Libya, Morocco, and Tunisia, to coordinate and harmonize the development plans of the four countries as well as intra-regional trade and relations with the EU. However, for a number of reasons, the plans never came to fruition. It was not until the late 1980s that new impetus began to bring the parties together again. The first Maghreb Summit of the five Heads of State, held at Zeralda (Algeria) in June 1988, resulted in a decision to set up the Maghreb High Commission and various specialized commissions. Finally, on February 17, 1989 in Marrakech, the Treaty establishing the AMU was signed by the Heads of State of the five countries.

The main objectives of the AMU Treaty are to strengthen all forms of ties among Member States (in order to ensure regional stability and enhance policy coordination), as well as to introduce gradually free circulation of goods, services, and factors of production among them. Common defense and non-interference in the domestic affairs of the partners are also key aspects of the Treaty. The Treaty highlights the broad economic strategy to be followed, namely, the development of agriculture, industry, commerce, food security, and the setting up of joint projects and general economic cooperation programs. The agreement does not view bilateral arrangements between the parties as an obstacle to the development of multilateral relations. Finally, the agreement provides the possibility for other Arab and African countries to join the Union at a later stage.

Since 1990, the five countries have signed more than 30 multilateral agreements covering diverse economic, social, and cultural areas. While member countries have ratified varying numbers of these agreements, only five have been ratified by all members of the union. These include agreements on trade and tariffs (covering all industrial products); trade in agricultural products, investment guarantees; avoidance of double taxation; and phyto-sanitary standards.

Since 1989, the Governors and technical staff of the five central banks of the AMU have been meeting regularly. In December 1991, the five banks signed a multilateral agreement to help facilitate inter-bank payments within the union. The agreement sets unified modalities of payments between the five central banks, and provides for monthly settlement of balances between any two countries without charge of interest on interim balances. The unit of account is the SDR and the settlement currency is chosen by the creditor country.

COMPOSITION AND STRUCTURE

5 member countries: Algeria, Libya, Mauritania, Morocco, Tunisia

The supreme institutional organ that has the authority to make decisions and to which all AMU institutions answer is the Council of Heads of State; its decisions require unanimity. Since the signing of the Treaty, the Council has met, as scheduled (in 1993 this was changed from twice a year to annually), to take decisions concerning regional issues.

A Council of Foreign Affairs Ministers also meets regularly to prepare for the sessions of the Council of Heads of State and to examine proposals formulated by subordinate committees and four specialized ministerial commissions (economy and finance, human resources, basic infrastructures and food security). Since 1989, several working groups have been created to address technical issues. The countries have agreed to set up a regional development bank to finance projects in the region.

A follow-up Committee, consisting of representatives from each Member State, follows the implementation of resolutions adopted by the Council of Heads of State.

A Consultative Assembly, consisting of 30 representatives from each Member State that can advise the Council of Heads of State, and a Court of Justice, composed of two judges from each Member State, have been set up in Algiers and Nouakchott respectively.

In 1992, the AMU's Secretariat General, was established permanently in Rabat. It has an annual operational budget of US$1.7 million, attained through equal contributions from each member.

A number of specialized committees have been working in such areas as food security, economic and financial affairs, basic infrastructure, and human resources.

COMMON MARKET FOR EASTERN AND SOUTHERN AFRICA (COMESA)

The origins of the COMESA can be traced as far back as the mid-sixties. Before the Lagos Plan of Action and the Final Act of Lagos were adopted, the countries of Eastern and Southern Africa had already initiated the process towards creating an Eastern and Southern African co-operation arrangement.

In October 1965, the ECA convened a ministerial meeting of the then politically independent states of eastern and southern Africa to consider proposals for the establishment of a mechanism for the promotion of sub-regional economic integration. The meeting, which was held in Lusaka, Zambia, recommended the creation of an Economic Community of

Eastern and Southern African states. To achieve this objective, the meeting also recommended that an Interim Council of Ministers, assisted by an Interim Economic Committee of officials, should be set up to negotiate the treaty and initiate programmes on economic co-operation, pending the completion of negotiations on the treaty.

At the first meeting of the interim Ministerial Council held in Addis Ababa, in May 1966, the Terms of Association to govern the interim arrangements before the signing of the formal Treaty were adopted and signed by Burundi, Ethiopia, Kenya, Madagascar, Malawi, Mauritius, Rwanda, Somalia, Tanzania, and Zambia. In November 1967, a meeting of the Interim Economic Committee of officials recommended an interim programme of action for implementation which would be integrated into the Treaty when approved. Parallel with these developments, two other organisations were established, the Pan-African Freedom Movement in East, Central and Southern Africa (PAFMECSA), and the conference of East and Central African states. Although these were mainly political in their orientation, their membership extended beyond the sub-region and they included in their activities programmes on economic co-operation.

In the 1970's, the need for a sub-regional economic arrangements became more urgent as a result of three major developments. First, the collapse of the federations in Eastern and Central Africa reduced political co-operation amongst States of the region and this needed to be addressed. Second, the destabilisation of the economies of the southern African States by apartheid South Africa made it necessary to create, as a matter urgency, a sub-regional organisation which would be an economic counterweight to South Africa. Third, despite the failure of earlier efforts to establish a sub-regional economic co-operation arrangement, the countries of Eastern and Southern Africa recognised that there was no alternative to reducing their traditional economic dependence on the industrialized countries of the north and that this could only be done through the adoption of self-sustaining development measures in all sectors.

In March 1978 the First Extra-ordinary meeting of Ministers of Trade, Finance and Planning met in Lusaka. The meeting recommended the creation of a sub-regional economic community, beginning with a sub-regional trade area which would be gradually upgraded over a ten-year period to a common market until the community had been established. To this end, the meeting adopted the "Lusaka Declaration of Intent and Commitment to the Establishment of a Preferential Trade Area for Eastern and Southern Africa" and created an Inter-governmental Negotiating Team on the Treaty for the establishment of the PTA. The meeting also agreed on an indicative time-table for the work of the Intergovernmental Negotiating Team.

After the preparatory work had been completed a meeting of Heads of State and Government was convened in Lusaka on 21st December 1981 at which the Treaty establishing the PTA was signed. The Treaty came into force on 30th September 1982 after it had been ratified by more than seven signatory states as provided for in Article 50 of the Treaty.

The PTA Treaty envisaged its transformation into a Common Market and, as such, the Treaty establishing COMESA was signed on 5th November 1993 in Kampala, Uganda and was ratified a year later in Lilongwe, Malawi on 8th December 1994. At present it consists of 20 members.

The process of economic integration in Eastern and Southern Africa has, therefore, not been episodic, but rather systematic, following a logical progression on a step by step basis. Firstly, a Preferential Trade Area was established and operated for over a decade, which was then transformed into a common market. The third phase will involve the eventual establishment of an Economic Community.

Objectives of COMESA

The aims and objectives of COMESA have been designed so as to remove the structural and institutional weaknesses in the member States by pooling their resources together in order to sustain their development efforts either individually or collectively. These are as follows:

- to attain sustainable growth and development of the member States by promoting a more balanced and harmonious development of its production and marketing structures;

- to promote joint development in all fields of economic activity and the joint adoption of macro -economic policies and programmes; to raise the standard of living of its peoples, and to foster closer relations among its member States;
- to co-operate in the creation of an enabling environment for foreign, cross-border and domestic investment, including the joint promotion of research and adaptation of science and technology for development;
- to co-operate in the promotion of peace, security and stability among the member States in order to enhance economic development in the region;
- to co-operate in strengthening the relations between the Common Market and the rest of the world and the adoption of common positions in international fora and
- to contribute towards the establishment, progress and the realisation of the objectives of the African Economic Community.

The COMESA agenda is to deepen and broaden the integration process among member States through the adoption of more comprehensive trade liberation measures such as the complete elimination of tariff and non-tariff barriers to trade and elimination of customs duties; through the free movement of capital, labour, goods and the right of establishment; by promoting standardised technical specifications, standardisation and quality control; through the elimination of controls on the movement of goods and individuals; by standardising taxation rates (including value added tax and excise duties), and conditions regarding industrial co-operation, particularly on company laws, intellectual property rights and investment laws; through the promotion of the adoption of a single currency and the establishment of a Monetary Union; and through the adoption of a Common External Tariff (CET).

By agreeing to the above, member States have agreed on the need to create and maintain:

- a full free trade area guaranteeing the free movement

of goods and services produced within COMESA and the removal of all tariffs and non-tariff barriers;

- a customs union under which goods and services imported from non-COMESA countries will attract an agreed single tariff all COMESA States;
- free movement of capital and investment supported by the adoption of common investment practices 50 as to create a more favourable investment climate for the entire COMESA region;
- a gradual establishment of a payments union based on the COMESA Clearing House and the eventual establishment of a common monetary union with a common currency;
- the adoption of a common visa arrangement, including the right of establishment leading eventually to free movement of bona fide persons.

Organs

There are four organs of COMESA which have the power to take decisions on behalf of COMESA, these being: the Authority of Heads of State and Government; the Council of Ministers; the Court of Justice; and the Committee of Governors of Central Banks. The Intergovernmental Committee, the Technical Committees, the Secretariat and the Consultative Committee make recommendations to the Council of Ministers, which in turn make recommendations to the Authority.

- The Authority
- The Council of Ministers
- The COMESA Court of Justice
- The Secretariat
- The Committee of Governors of Central Banks
- The Inter-governmental Committee
- The Consultative Committee of the Business Community and other Interest Groups
- There are 12 Technical Committees, namely, on Administrative and Budgetary Matters; on Agriculture; on Comprehensive Information Systems; on Energy; on Finance and Monetary Affairs; on Industry; on

Labour, Human Resources and Social Affairs; on Legal Affairs; on Natural Resources and Environment; on Tourism and Wildlife; on Trade and Customs; and on Transport and Communications. The Technical Committees are responsible for the preparation of comprehensive implementation programs and monitoring their implementation and then making recommendations to the Council.

Institutions Under COMESA

- Leather & Leather Products Institute
- Eastern And Southern African Development Bank
- Reinsurance Company (Zep-Re)
- Comesa Bankers' Association
- The Comesa Clearing House

COMESA offers very extensive benefits and advantages for its member States as well as the business community. Because of its focus on full private sector participation in integration, COMESA offers new opportunities for industrial, production, investment, development and trade opportunities not hitherto available under the previous regional arrangements. These advantages are briefly enumerated below:

- A wider, harmonized and more competitive market.
- Greater industrial productivity and competitiveness.
- Increased agricultural production and food security.
- A more rational exploitation of natural resources.
- More harmonized monetary, banking and financial policies.
- More reliable transport and communications infrastructure.

COMESA Agenda

Globalisation and economic liberalisation in particular, have continued to pose real challenges to all COMESA Member States. Worse still, the region has been further traumatized by regional conflicts that threaten to erode the gains already made and undermine investor confidence. Events taking place elsewhere such as the Asian economic crises, have their ripple effect felt in the sub-region such as depressed demand for exports, increased and often unfair competition. With increased integration in Europe under the European Union—the traditional market for exports from COMESA—and the end of preferences under the World Trade Organisation, entry into that market has become extremely competitive. The signals are clear. Only the most efficient economies will manage under the evolving global economic environment. COMESA Member States must therefore carefully develop and implement their strategies, their options and quickly take advantage of opportunities as soon as they present themselves.

Since the early 1990s, COMESA Member States have enjoyed renewed interest brought about by privatisation of State-owned enterprise (SOE) and the improved policy framework that encourages private capital flows into the region. Most of the erstwhile SOE have found it very difficult to operate in the changed environment without State protection or subsidies, thus rendering them uncompetitive. There is also the factor of changed behaviour - consumers; are now better informed and therefore demand products that are competitive in quality and price.

Unlike South East Asia, COMESA Member States have not benefited from massive currency depreciation that has taken place. This is because COMESA's exports outside the region comprise mainly of commodities that do not enjoy a high income elasticity of demand as is the case with manufactured products. Furthermore, the limited domestic demand does not facilitate exploitation of economies of scale.

The massive redundancies that ensued following privatisation of SOEs implied that effective demand was severely reduced as poverty increased. For example, the tourism sector suffered badly as a result of Western holiday makers switching to cheaper destinations in Asia to take advantage of currency devaluations.

Duplication in membership with other regional organisations remains problematic, though that between Southern African Development Community (SADC) and the Common Market for Eastern and Southern Africa (COMESA) has to an extent been resolved through the creation of joint

SADC-COMESA Task Force in May 2001. A number of different areas have been identified to co-ordinate regional strategy, including:

- Harmonisation of customs regulations and procedures.
- Elimination of non-tariff barriers and other obstacles to inter-regional trade.
- Exchange of trade information.
- Harmonisation of trade facilitation measures and standards.

EAST AFRICAN COMMUNITY (EAC)

The East African Community is the regional intergovernmental organisation of the Republics of Kenya, Uganda and Tanzania, with its Headquarters located in Arusha, Tanzania. The East African Heads of State signed the Treaty for the Establishment of the East African Community in Arusha on 30th November 1999.

The three East African countries cover an area of 1.8 million square kilometres and have a population of 82 million who share a common history, language, culture and infrastructure. These advantages provide the Partner States with a unique framework for regional co-operation and integration.

From Co-operation to Community

Prior to re-launching the East African Community in 1999, Kenya, Tanzania and Uganda had enjoyed a long history of co-operation under successive regional integration arrangements. These included the Customs Union between Kenya and Uganda in 1917, which the then Tanganyika later joined in 1927; the East African High Commission (1948-1961); the East African Common Services Organisation (1961-1967); the East African Community (1967-1977), and the East African Co-operation (1993-1999).

Development Strategy for EAC

The East African Community operates on the basis of a five-year Development Strategy. The Strategy document spells out the policy guidelines, priority programmes and implementation schedules.

The EAC strategy emphasises economic co-operation and development with a strong focus on the social dimension. The role of the private sector and civil society is considered as central and crucial to the regional integration and development in a veritable partnership with the public sector.

Areas of Co-operation

The regional co-operation and integration envisaged in the EAC is broad based, covering trade, investments and industrial development; monetary and fiscal affairs; infrastructure and services; human resources, science and technology; agriculture and food security; environment and natural resources management; tourism and wildlife management; and health, social and cultural activities.

Other areas of co-operation include free movement of factors of production; and co-operation in political matters, including defence, security, foreign affairs, legal and judicial affairs.

Partnerships

The EAC collaborates with other African organisations in the spirit of the Abuja Treaty for the establishment of the African Economic Community. Among these organisations are the African Union, Common Market for East and Southern Africa, Inter-governmental Authority on Development and the Southern African Development Community.

Funding

The core budget of the EAC's Secretariat is funded by equal contributions from the Partner States. Regional projects and programmes are funded through the mobilisation of resources from both within and outside the region.

Institutions

The Summit comprising of heads of government of partner states gives general direction towards the realisation of the goal and objectives of the Community.

The Council of Ministers is the main decision-making institution. It is made up of ministers from the partner states responsible for regional co-operation.

The Co-ordinating Committee consists of permanent secretaries and reports to the council. It is responsible for regional co-operation and co-ordinates the activities of the sectoral committees.

Sectoral Committees conceptualise programmes and monitor their implementation. Council establishes the committees on recommendation of the respective co-ordinating committee.

The East African Court of Justice ensures that Community law is interpreted and implemented in line with the Treaty.

The East African Legislative Assembly provides a democratic forum for debate. It has a watchdog function and also plays a part in the legislative process.

The Secretariat is the executive organ of the Community. As the guardian of the Treaty, it ensures that regulations and directives adopted by the Council are properly implemented.

Autonomous Institutions

The Council has authority to establish other autonomous institutions of the Community. Currently, other autonomous institutions of the Community include:

- Lake Victoria Development Programme,
- The East African Development Bank (EADB),
- Lake Victoria Fisheries Organisation (LVFO) and
- The Inter-University Council for East Africa (IUCEA).

ECONOMIC COMMUNITY OF WEST AFRICAN STATES (ECOWAS)

Plans for the Economic Community of West African States (ECOWAS) were first formally set out at the Monrovia Group meeting of April 1968. The Community was established by the Treaty of Lagos, which was signed by representatives of 15 West African States in Lagos on May 28, 1975. It entered into force in July 1975 when the necessary seven States ratified the Treaty. The first meetings of the Council of Ministers and the Authority of Heads of State and Government took place in Lomé, Togo, November 4-5, 1976 at which time additional protocols to the Treaty were signed. Cape Verde later acceded to the Treaty and thus became the sixteenth Member State of the Community.

A revised Treaty was signed by the sixteen West African Heads of State on July 24, 1993. The revised Treaty reflects West Africa's regional cooperation experiences over the preceding fifteen years and takes into account the exigencies of continental integration as envisaged in the Treaty of the African Economic Community.

The principal objectives of the Treaty, to be achieved in stages, is the creation of an economic and monetary union. To this end, a regional trade liberalisation scheme has been adopted for the creation of a free trade area by the end of 1999, and a common external tariff is being implemented in phases. The three-phase programme for the free movement of Community citizens has been completed. The Community has been pursuing the physical integration of its Member States through the development and modernisation of regional highway and telecommunication networks.

Member States have committed themselves to the coordination and harmonisation of national economic and financial policies in order to enhance the effectiveness of national structural adjustment and economic reform programs. This is also to facilitate the regional approach to economic development and the establishment of a monetary union. The monetary program adopted by the Community has the medium-term objectives of achieving regional convertibility of the nine national currencies and, in the longer term, the creation of a single monetary zone. Meanwhile, an ECOWAS travelers check was launched in October 1998 to facilitate regional travel and commercial transactions.

The West African Monetary Institute (WAMI), a fore-runner to the West African Central Bank, became operational in January, 2001. The two-year transitional body is based in Accra, Ghana. There is also a Committee of Governors of West African Central Banks which has been coordinating the implementation of the ECOWAS monetary program.

In addition, the Community has been implementing such sectoral programs as the inter-connection of national electricity grids and regional pipeline for the distribution of natural gas,

Community seed production and cattle breeding centers, agricultural research program, regional master plan for industrial development, coordination of desertification control programs, rural water supply schemes, cooperation in health matters, establishment of equivalence for degrees and diplomas, etc.

In the Treaty, particular emphasis has been placed on promoting the involvement and participation of the private sector and the general public in the development and integration of the economies of the region. Already, the Community has encouraged the establishment and functioning of a privately-owned regional commercial bank (ECOBANK), Federation of West African Manufacturers Associations, Federation of West African Chambers of Commerce, West African Journalists Association, West African Youth Union, West African Women's Association, West African Road Transporters Union, etc.

Composition and Structure

15 member countries: Benin, Burkina Faso, Cape Verde, Côte d'Ivoire, Gambia, Ghana, Guinea, Guinea-Bissau, Liberia, Mali, Niger, Nigeria, Senegal, Sierra Leone, Togo.

The Authority of Heads of State and Government is the supreme organ; it has a rotating chairmanship and meets at least once a year.

The Council of Ministers, comprising two representatives from each Member State and also having a rotating chairmanship, meets at least twice a year. Its decisions are made by a consensus.

The Executive Secretariat is headed by an Executive Secretary appointed for a four-year term. There are at present five specialized commissions dealing with different aspects of cooperation.

Also provided in the Treaty is a Court of Justice to ensure "the observance of law and justice, to interpret the provisions of the Treaty, and to settle disputes referred to it. Its decisions shall be final.

The Treaty also provides for a West African Parliament and an Economic and Social Council. The West African

Parliament, inaugurated in Bamako, Mali on November 16, 2000, held its maiden session in Abuja, Nigeria from January 21 to 27, 2001.

Additionally, ECOWAS leaders adopted two important defense protocols in 1978 and 1981. These protocols call for mutual respect and non-interference in internal affairs and the establishment of a regional mechanism for mutual assistance in defense matters. Uniquely, however, these protocols place equal emphasis on threats from without and within—domestic fissures and fission. It states in Article 4 that ECOWAS is compelled to intervene in "internal armed conflict within any Member State engineered and supported actively from outside likely to endanger the security and peace in the entire Community." The protocol allows for legitimate intervention in internal affairs of member states, unlike the non-intervention clauses in the UN and OAU charters.

These provisions have facilitated regional conflict resolution efforts initiated by ECOWAS. The ECOWAS Monitoring Group (ECOMOG) was established initially on an ad hoc basis as a multinational peacekeeping/peace enforcement force, and was the first such group to be established by a regional body. ECOMOG was principally responsible for the restoration of peace in Liberia. In addition, ECOMOG forces have been deployed to Guinea-Bissau and Sierra Leone as well to address conflicts in those states. These recent civil wars and other political unrest in some West African countries have forcefully revealed the need for social and political stability in the development process. Widespread political instability has also hindered progress in ECOWAS' primary mandate to promote economic integration and regional cooperation. In December of 1999, ECOWAS Heads of State signed a protocol establishing a Mechanism for Conflict Prevention, Management, Resolution, Peacekeeping and Security.

SOUTHERN AFRICAN DEVELOPMENT COMMUNITY (SADC)

The Southern African Development Co-ordination Conference, SADCC, the forerunner of the SADC, the Community, was established in April 1980 by Governments of the nine Southern African countries of Angola, Botswana, Lesotho, Malawi, Mozambique, Swaziland, Tanzania, Zambia and Zimbabwe.

The formation of SADC was the culmination of a long process of consultations by the leaders of Southern Africa. Towards the end of the 1970's, it became clear to the leaders of the region that just having a national flag and a national anthem would not meet the needs of the people for improved living standards. Secondly, the positive experiences gained in working together in the group of Frontline States, to advance the political struggle, had to be translated into broader co-operation in pursuit of economic and social development.

From 1977, active consultations were undertaken by representatives of the Frontline States, culminating in a meeting of Foreign Ministries of the Frontline States in Gaborone, in May 1979, which called for a meeting of ministers responsible for economic development. That meeting was subsequently convened in Arusha, Tanzania, in July 1979. The Arusha meeting led to the birth to the Southern African Development Co-ordination Conference a year later.

The SADCC or the conference, was formed with four principal objectives, namely:

- to reduce Member States dependence, particularly, but not only, on apartheid South Africa;
- to implement programmes and projects with national and regional impact;
- to mobilise Member States' resources, in the quest for collective self-reliance and
- to secure international understanding and support.

These objectives were pursued with determination and vigour. Through SADCC, the founding fathers sought first to demonstrate the tangible benefits of working together, and to cultivate a climate of confidence and trust among member States.

SADC has developed since then, to become an organisation that has a Programme of Action, covering several broad economic and social sectors, namely, Energy, Tourism, Environment and Land Management, Water, Mining, Employment and Labour, Culture, Information and Sport and Transport and Communications. Other sectors are Finance and Investment, Human Resource Development, Food,

Agriculture and Natural Resources, Legal Affairs and Health. Sectors are each co-ordinated by a Member State with some member states co-ordinating more than one sector.

Over the past two years SADC has undertaken an exercise to restructure its institutions and a report on this was adopted by an Extra-Ordinary Summit on March 9, 2001 in Windhoek, Namibia. This restructuring was necessitated by the number of difficulties and constraints encountered in the process of moving the organisation from a coordinating conference into a Community. These include:

- Inadequate institutional reforms to enable the effective transformation from SADCC (Coordinating Conference) to SADC (the Community). Furthermore, the resource provision and the management system were not adequately addressed.
- The need to put in place appropriate mechanisms capable of translating the high degree of political commitment to shape the scope and scale of community building through regional integration. This implies delegating authority and strengthening the capacity for decision-making to the relevant agencies responsible for implementing the SADC agenda.
- Lack of synergy between the objectives and strategies of the Treaty on one hand and the existing SADC Programme of Action (SPA) and the institutional framework on the other.
- Limited capacity to mobilize significant levels of the region's own resources for the implementation of its Programme.
- The external financial overdependence of the SADC Programme of Action (SPA) to the tune of more than 80 percent, which compromises the Programme's sustainability.

Transformation from Conference to Community

This transformation occurred in August 1992, when the Heads of State and Government of the Southern African Development Co-ordination Conference met in Windhoek,

Namibia, to sign a Declaration and Treaty establishing the new SADC—the Southern African Development Community.

The SADCC leaders had come to realise that although the co-ordination conference had served them well and had demonstrated the crucial need to cooperate in their development efforts, time had come to give the Organisation a legal and more formal status. There was also a need to shift the focus of the organisation from co-ordination of development projects to a more complex task of integrating the economies of member States. Hence the Treaty is the blueprint for building a Community of Southern African states.

SADC and its member States are expected to act according to the following principles:

- Sovereign equality of all member States;
- Solidarity, peace and security;
- Human rights, democracy, and the rule of law;
- Equity, balance and mutual benefit;
- Peaceful settlement of disputes.

Objectives

The Objectives of SADC remain relevant and valid as provided for under Article 5 of the Treaty. However, the Report on the Restructuring of SADC Institutions underscores the need to ensure that poverty alleviation is addressed in all SADC activities and programmes so that cross-cutting solutions are found for liberating the peoples of the SADC region from abject poverty. It was agreed that the ultimate objective should be it's eradication. HIV/AIDS has been singled out as a major threat to the attainment of the objectives of SADC and therefore it is being accorded priority in the health programme and other relevant sectors.

The Objectives of the Community as stated in the Treaty are to:

- Achieve development and economic growth, alleviate poverty. enhance the standard and quality of life of the peoples of Southern Africa and support the socially disadvantaged through regional integration.
- Evolve common political values, systems and institutions.

- Promote and defend peace and security.
- Promote self-sustaining development on the basis of collective self-reliance, and the inter-dependence of Member States.
- Achieve complementarity between national and regional strategies and programmes.
- Promote and maximise productive employment and utilisation of resources of the region.
- Achieve sustainable utilisation of natural resources and effective protection of the environment.
- Strengthen and consolidate the long-standing historical, social and cultural affinities and links among the peoples of the region.

However, Member States stressed the need to ensure that poverty alleviation is addressed in all SADC activities and programmes so that cross-cutting solutions are found for liberating the peoples of the SADC region from abject poverty. Emphasis was also placed on the need for Member States to adhere to commitments they have made at various international fora, including the Copenhagen Declaration of the Social Summit, on the issue of poverty eradication.

Accordingly, it was agreed that the ultimate objective in addressing the issue of poverty should be its eradication and that this ultimate objective shall be included in the Objectives, Priorities and Common Agenda of SADC.

Member States also recognized and appreciated that the HIV/AIDS pandemic represents a major threat to the attainment of the objectives of SADC and, as such, should be accorded priority in the health programme and other relevant sectors.

Member States therefore agreed that combating of HIV/AIDS and other deadly diseases should also be included in SADC priorities.

The SADC Common Agenda remains as reflected in Article 5 of the Treaty. However, it was observed that the SADC Common Agenda is not clearly articulated and effectively operationalised. Consequently, it was agreed that a more explicit common agenda be articulated—one that would clearly spell out common areas of focus taking into account the following principles:

- **Development Orientation.** That all programmes and activities of the Organisation undertaken in the Member States should have an impact on sustainable socio-economic development including poverty alleviation, reduction and its ultimate eradication.
- **Subsidiarity.** That all programmes and activities should be undertaken at levels where they can best be handled based on consultations between governments and relevant stakeholders. The involvement of institutions, authorities, and agencies outside SADC structures to initiate and implement regional programmes using their own generated resources should be promoted and encouraged.
- **Market Integration.** That all programmes and activities which directly integrate markets should be undertaken to facilitate free movement of factors of production, goods and services as well as the promotion of regional speciliasation based on comparative advantages.
- **Development, facilitation and promotion of trade and investment.** That all programmes and activities should facilitate the development, and/or promotion of national, intra and inter-regional and international trade and investment.
- **Dynamic and economy of scale gains.** That all programmes and activities should be undertaken which can be carried out through regionally coordinated investments or operations by means of which substantial cost-savings, investments and employment benefits could be realized.
- **Additionality.** That all programmes and activities should be undertaken only if they add value to regional integration, enhance capacity to achieve SADC objectives or bring additional resources.
- **Variable geometry.** That given the varying levels of development and patterns of relations between Member States, there should be flexibility to accommodate special circumstances and particular arrangements

between some Member States while aiming at greater harmonisation at a progressively higher level of integration within the community as a whole.

Based on the above principles, SADC's Common Agenda includes the following:

- The promotion of sustainable and equitable economic growth and socio-economic development that will ensure poverty alleviation with the ultimate objective of its eradication;
- The promotion of common political values, systems and other shared values which are transmitted through institutions which are democratic, legitimate and effective; and;
- The consolidation and maintenance of democracy, peace and security.

The ultimate objective of SADC, the Community is, therefore, to build a Region in which there will be a high degree of harmonisation and rationalisation to enable the pooling of resources to achieve collective self-reliance in order to improve the living standards of the people of the region.

Institutional Framework

In deciding on the Conference's institutions, the Founding Fathers were particularly sensitive to the lessons and experiences of past attempts at regional co-operation in Africa, some of which had ended in dismal failure and bitter disappointment. Such failures were largely because sensitive issues of how best to equitably share the costs and benefits of regional co-operation had not been sufficiently addressed and agreed upon at both national and regional levels.

To avoid similar pitfalls, SADC from the very beginning placed particular emphasis on a decentralised institutional arrangement that would ensure that member States are the principal actors in the formulation and implementation of policy decisions.

However, under the new restructuring exercise, it has become clear that there are a number of problems that inhibit the efficient and effective performance of the current structure and these include:

- Inadequate provision of resources and staffing by member States which has led to inequitable distribution of responsibilities and obligations.
- Different management and administrative procedures and rules, varying standards, qualifications and performance criteria for staff involved in the management of the Regional Programme.
- Rapid increase of Sectors and therefore a plethora of priorities and activities dependent on limited resources which has led to a proliferation of meetings and an increase in associated costs.
- Under the current structure and circumstances, the Secretariat has been unable to execute its mandate as provided for in the Treaty, especially that of undertaking strategic planning and management.
- Lack of an institutional framework in which Ministers responsible for Foreign Affairs in the SADC region could discuss and adopt common positions on matters pertaining to the organisation in various international fora.

The principal institutions of SADC following the adoption by the extra-ordinary Summit of the Report on the Restructuring of SADC Institutions are as follows:

Summit. Made up of Heads of State and/or Government, the Summit is the ultimate policy-making institution of SADC. It is responsible for the overall policy direction and control of functions of the Community. The Summit usually meets once a year around August/September in a member State at which a new Chairperson and Deputy are elected. Under the new structure, it is recommended that Summit meets twice a year.

The Troika. The Extra-Ordinary Summit decided to formalise the practice of a Troika system consisting of the Chair, Incoming Chair and the Outgoing Chair of SADC which has been effective since it was established by Summit at its meeting in Maputo, Mozambique in August 1999. Other member States may be co-opted into the Troika as and when necessary. This system has enabled the Organisation to execute tasks and implement decisions expeditiously as well as provide policy direction to SADC Institutions in period between regular SADC meetings. The Troika system will operate at the level of the Summit, the Organ on Politics, Defence and Security, Council and Standing Committee of Senior Officials.

Organ on Politics, Defence and Security. The Extra-Ordinary Summit adopted the Report of the Ministerial Committee on Foreign Affairs, Defence and Security which met on November 23, 2000 in Harare, Zimbabwe and addressed the following issues, pertaining to the Organ, in particular that:

(a) The Organ should be coordinated at the level of Summit on a Troika basis and reporting to the Chairperson of SADC.

(b) The Chairperson of the Organ shall be on a rotation basis for a period of one year.

(c) The Member State holding the Chairpersonship of the Organ shall provide the Secretariat services.

(d) The Chairperson of the Organ shall not simultaneously hold the Chair of the Summit.

(e) The structure, operations and functions of the Organ shall be regulated by the Protocol on Politics, Defence and Security Cooperation which shall be submitted to Summit in Blantyre in August 2001 for approval and signature.

Council of Ministers. The functions of Council should remain as provided for under Article 11 of the Treaty. The Council of Ministers consists of Ministers from each member State, usually from the Ministries of Foreign Affairs and Economic Planning or Finance. The Council is responsible for overseeing the functioning and development of SADC and ensuring that policies are properly implemented. Council usually meets twice a year in January and just before summit in August or September. Under the new structure it is recommended that Council should meet four times a year.

Integrated Committee of Ministers. This is a new institution aimed at ensuring proper policy guidance, coordination and harmonisation of cross-sectoral activities. The Integrated Committee of Ministers will perform the following functions:

(a) To oversee the activities of the four core areas of integration notably: Trade, Industry, Finance and Investment; Infrastructure and Services; Food, Agriculture and Natural Resources (FANR); Social and Human Development and Special Programmes, including the implementation of the Strategic Plan in their areas of competence.

(b) Be constituted by least two Ministers from each Member State and should be responsible to Council.

(c) Provide policy guidance to the Secretariat and make decisions on matters pertaining to the Directorates as well as monitor and evaluate their work.

(d) Should have decision-making powers ad referendum to ensure rapid implementation of the programmes that otherwise would wait for a formal meeting of the Council.

(e) Should monitor and control the implementation of the Regional Indicative Development Plan once approved by Council.

(f) Take the role of Sectoral Committee of Ministers that has been abolished.

Tribunal. The Treaty also makes provision for a yet to be established Tribunal. A protocol to establish the Tribunal was signed in Windhoek, Namibia during the 2000 Ordinary Summit. Once established, the Tribunal will ensure adherence to, and proper interpretation of the provisions of the SADC Treaty and subsidiary instruments, and to adjudicate upon disputes, referred to it.

SADC National Committees. These Committees shall be composed of key stakeholders notably government, private sector and civil society in member States. Their main functions will be to provide inputs at the national level in the formulation of regional policies, strategies, SPA as well as coordinate and oversee the implementation of the these programmes at the national level. The Committees shall also be responsible for the initiation of projects and issue papers as an input to the preparation of the Regional Indicative Development Plan.

Standing Committee of Senior Officials. The functions of this Committee shall remain as provided for under Article 13 of the Treaty. The Standing Committee of Officials consists of one Permanent/Principal Secretary or an official of equivalent rank from each Member State, preferably from a ministry responsible for economic planning or finance. This Committee is a technical advisory committee to the Council. The Chairperson and Vice-Chairperson of the Standing Committee shall be appointed from the member States holding the Chairperson-ship and Vice-Chairperson-ship, respectively, of the Council.

Secretariat. This is the principal executive institution of SADC responsible for strategic planning, co-ordination and management of SADC programmes. It is headed by an Executive Secretary and has its headquarters in Gaborone, Botswana. The Extra-Ordinary Summit agreed that the Secretariat should be strengthened in terms of both its mandate and the provision of adequate resources for it to be able to perform its functions effectively as provided for under Article 14 of the Treaty and consistent with the Abuja Treaty, as follows:

- Strategic planning and management of the programme of SADC;
- Implementation of the decisions of the Summit and Council;
- Organisation and management of the SADC meetings;
- Financial and general administration;
- Representation and promotion of SADC and
- Promotion and harmonisation of policies and strategies of Member States.

In addition, the Secretariat should perform the following functions:

- Gender mainstreaming in all SADC programmes and activities;
- Organisation and servicing of the meetings of the Troika and any other committees established by the Summit, Council and the Troika on an ad-hoc basis;
- Submission of harmonized policies and programmes to the Council for consideration and approval;
- Monitoring and evaluating the implementation of regional policies and programmes;

- Collation and dissemination of information on the community and maintenance of a reliable database;
- Development of capacity, infrastructure and maintenance of intra-regional Information Communication Technology (ICT);
- Mobilisation of resources, co-ordination and harmonisation of the programmes and projects with co-operating partners;
- Devising appropriate strategies for self-financing and income generating activities and investment;
- Management of special programmes and projects;
- Undertaking of research on Community Building and the integration process.

The Structure of Secretariat shall comprise the following:

Office of the Executive Secretary:

- Deputy Executive Secretary;
- Department of Strategic Planning, Gender and Development and Policy Harmonisation;
- Legal Affairs;
- Internal Audit;
- Information, Communication and Technology including statistics and library services;
- Administration and
- Finance.

The Department of Strategic Planning, Gender and Development and Policy Harmonisation has been established in order to strengthen the Secretariat in executing its functions, particularly strategic planning, gender mainstreaming, management and harmonisation of policies, and to address problems arising from the current parallel and independent structure of the Sector Coordinating Units.

This department shall be composed of the following four Directorates under which the current 20-odd sectors will be clustered:

- Trade, Industry, Finance and Investment (TIFI);
- Infrastructure and Services;

- Food, Agriculture and Natural Resources (FANR);
- Social and Human Development and Special Programmes.

Commissions and Sector Coordinating Units (SCUs). The Extra-Ordinary Summit agreed that SCUs and Commissions should be phased out within a period not exceeding two years. The process of phasing out should be accelerated for specific priority areas.

THE SADC PROGRAMME OF ACTION-SPA

The SPA is a totality of Sectoral Programmes, with their policy objectives, strategies and projects designed to realise the overall goals and objectives of SADC. The SPA has evolved over time in line with the priorities and challenges facing the organisation.

The number of projects under the SPA now stands at 407 with an estimated cost of US$8.09 billion. Approximately 90 per cent of this amount is from external sources and close to 50 per cent has already been secured.

Under the SPA, several protocols have been developed and signed in the areas of Shared Water Course Systems, Energy, Combating Illicit Drug Trafficking, Transport, Communication and Meteorology, Trade, Education and Training, Mining, Immunities and Privileges, Health, Wildlife Conservation and Law Enforcement, Tribunal and Legal Affairs. Most of these have been ratified and are at various stages of implementation.

The Trade Protocol is critical for SADC's integration process and entered into force on the 25th of January, 2000 following its ratification by the required number of member States. The implementation of this protocol was launched on 1st September 2000.

In addition to these protocols, the Summit has signed a Declaration on Gender and Development. This declaration calls for the equal representation of women and men in the decision making of member states and SADC Structures at all levels, and the achievement of at least 30 per cent target of women in political and decision-making structures by the year 2005. In addition, a Declaration on Productivity which commits member States to increase productivity in order to meet global competitiveness challenges was signed in August 2000.

5.2: ASIAN AND PACIFIC REGIONAL ARRANGEMENTS

ANZUS PACT

Anzus Treaty defense agreement was signed in 1951 by Australia, New Zealand, and the United States. The name Anzus is derived from the initials of the three signatory nations. As a result of the re-establishment of peace between Japan and the United States in 1951, Australia and New Zealand asked for a treaty making it clear that an attack on any of the three signatory countries would be considered an attack upon all. The pact became effective in 1952. New Zealand's 1985 refusal to allow U.S. nuclear-powered or nuclear-armed ships to enter its ports caused the United States to abrogate its ANZUS responsibilities toward New Zealand in 1986; however, New Zealand has not formally withdrawn from the alliance. From Australia and New Zealand's point of view at the time, ANZUS offered a protection against a possible future threat of Soviet or Chinese aggression.

For the US, ANZUS represented a secure stake in the Pacific, as it sought to strengthen its alliances around the world, in its efforts to contain communist powers. ANZUS did not guarantee military support from the US, but provided for consultation in the event of an attack on any of the three countries. The treaty was also significant in that Australia joined the US in a regional security alliance that did not include its traditional ally, Britain.

In 1986, New Zealand banned the entry of US Navy ships into their ports in the belief that they were carrying nuclear weapons or were nuclear-powered. The US responded by suspending relations with New Zealand as a member of ANZUS. For Australia, this alliance with the US has continued to be a foundation of its defence policy.

ASIAN DEVELOPMENT BANK (ADB)

ADB is a multilateral development finance institution dedicated to reducing poverty in Asia and the Pacific. Established in 1966, it has 63 members, mostly from the region.

Its headquarters is in Manila and has 24 other offices around the world:

- 16 resident missions in Asia
- a regional mission for the Pacific in Vanuatu
- a country office in the Philippines
- representative offices in Frankfurt for Europe, Tokyo for Japan, and Washington, DC for North America
- a special office in Timor-Leste
- extended missions in Gujarat, India and Papua New Guinea.

It has over 2,000 employees from nearly 50 countries.

ADB is managed by a Board of Governors, a Board of Directors, a President, four Vice-Presidents, and the Heads of departments and offices. Each member country nominates one Governor and an Alternate Governor to vote on its behalf.

The Board of Governors elects the 12 Directors (each with an alternate)—eight representing countries within the Asia-Pacific region and four representing countries outside the region. The Board of Governors also elects the President for a term of five years, with the possibility of re-election. The President chairs the Board of Directors and follows its directions in conducting the business of ADB.

Strategic Development Objectives

The adoption of poverty reduction as a strategy gave primacy to ADB's fight against poverty. ADB continues to carry out activities to promote economic growth, develop human resources, improve the status of women, and protect the environment, but these strategic development objectives now serve its poverty reduction agenda. Its other key development objectives, such as law and policy reform, regional cooperation, private-sector development, and social development, also contribute significantly to this main goal.

Poverty Reduction, the New Over-arching Goal of ADB

A new social policy agenda is emerging in Asia and the Pacific. Economic growth and investment in human development are in themselves not sufficient to eradicate poverty in the region. In response to this agenda, ADB's President announced that reducing poverty would become ADB's main goal; and in November 1999, ADB's new poverty reduction strategy was adopted.

The new strategy rests on three pillars:

- pro-poor, sustainable economic growth based on policies and programs that facilitate employment and income generation for the poor;
- social development, which can enable the poor to make full use of opportunities to improve their living standard, and programs that directly address the severity of poverty and
- good governance to ensure that the poor have better access to basic services and greater voice and participation in the decisions affecting them. The strategy requires that all ADB operations-lending, technical assistance, capacity building, economic and sector work, donor coordination, and policy dialogue-contribute to reducing poverty in each DMC.

Promoting Pro-poor, Sustainable Economic Growth

Growth is neither automatically pro-poor, nor by itself broad-based and inclusive. It must be made so. This requires that:

- equity in access to and use of production factors, such as land, capital, knowledge, labor, and other factor markets be addressed;
- economic development that generates income and employment for the poor be promoted;
- macro-economic constraints that penalize the poor, such as inflation, tariffs, and prices, and national and external terms of trade policies, be tackled;
- market-driven, effective private sector development that benefits the poor and free public resources for

improving social development and reducing poverty be promoted;

- socio-economic development through regional and sub-regional cooperation be accelerated;
- infra-structure projects be located in poor areas or that they incorporate specific components to ensure that the poor have increased access to project facilities and services and
- economic growth be sustained by enhancing quality and productivity of the environment and natural resources.

Other goals of ADB includes:

- Supporting social development
- Protecting the Environment
- Facilitating good governance
- Promoting Economic Growth
- Supporting Agriculture and Natural Resources
- Supporting Human Development
- Supporting Education
- Supporting Primary Health Care
- Supporting Water Supply and Sanitation
- Supporting Urban Development
- Improving the Status of Women

ASSOCIATION OF SOUTH-EAST ASIAN NATIONS (ASEAN)

The Association of South-east Asian Nations or ASEAN was established on 8 August 1967 in Bangkok by the five original Member Countries, namely, Indonesia, Malaysia, Philippines, Singapore, and Thailand. Brunei Darussalam joined on 8 January 1984, Vietnam on 28 July 1995, Laos and Myanmar on 23 July 1997, and Cambodia on 30 April 1999.

The ASEAN region has a population of about 500 million, a total area of 4.5 million square kilometers, a combined gross domestic product of US$737 billion, and a total trade of US$ 720 billion.

Objectives

The ASEAN Declaration states that the aims and purposes of the Association are:

- to accelerate the economic growth, social progress and cultural development in the region through joint endeavours in the spirit of equality and partnership in order to strengthen the foundation for a prosperous and peaceful community of Southeast Asian nations and
- to promote regional peace and stability through abiding respect for justice and the rule of law in the relationship among countries in the region and adherence to the principles of the United Nations Charter.

In 1995, the ASEAN Heads of States and Government re-affirmed that "Cooperative peace and shared prosperity shall be the fundamental goals of ASEAN."

Fundamental Principles

The Treaty of Amity and Cooperation (TAC) in Southeast Asia, signed at the First ASEAN Summit on 24 February 1976, declared that in their relations with one another, the High Contracting Parties should be guided by the following fundamental principles:

- Mutual respect for the independence, sovereignty, equality, territorial integrity, and national identity of all nations;
- The right of every State to lead its national existence free from external interference, subversion or coercion;
- Non-interference in the internal affairs of one another;
- Settlement of differences or disputes by peaceful manner;
- Renunciation of the threat or use of force and
- Effective cooperation among themselves.

Political Cooperation

The TAC stated that ASEAN political and security dialogue and cooperation should aim to promote regional peace and stability by enhancing regional resilience. Regional resilience shall be achieved by cooperating in all fields based on the principles of self-confidence, self-reliance, mutual respect, cooperation, and solidarity, which shall constitute the foundation for a strong and viable community of nations in Southeast Asia.

Some of the major political accords of ASEAN are as follows:

- ASEAN Declaration, Bangkok, 8 August 1967;
- Zone of Peace, Freedom and Neutrality Declaration, Kuala Lumpur, 27 November 1971;
- Declaration of ASEAN Concord, Bali, 24 February 1976;
- Treaty of Amity and Cooperation in Southeast Asia, Bali, 24 February 1976;
- ASEAN Declaration on the South China Sea, Manila, 22 July 1992;
- Treaty on the Southeast Asia Nuclear Weapon-Free Zone, Bangkok, 15 December 1997;
- ASEAN Vision 2020, Kuala Lumpur, 15 December 1997;
- Declaration of ASEAN Concord II, Bali, 7 October 2003

The ASEAN Security Community is envisaged to bring ASEAN's political and security cooperation to a higher plane to ensure that countries in the region live at peace with one another and with the world at large in a just, democratic and harmonious environment.

In 1992, the ASEAN Heads of State and Government declared that ASEAN should intensify its external dialogues in political and security matters as a means of building cooperative ties with states in the Asia-Pacific region. Two years later, the ASEAN Regional Forum or ARF was established. The inception of the ARF began with its inaugural meeting in Bangkok in July 1994. At this session it brought together the Foreign Ministers of 18 Asia-Pacific countries for a multi-lateral dialogue on the various security issues that posed a problem to the region.

The ARF aims to promote confidence-building, preventive diplomacy and conflict resolution in the region. The present participants in the ARF include: Australia, Brunei Darussalam, Cambodia, Canada, China, European Union, India, Indonesia,

Japan, Republic of Korea, Laos, Malaysia, Myanmar, Mongolia, New Zealand, Papua New Guinea, Philippines, the Russian Federation, Singapore, Thailand, the United States, Vietnam. Pakistan joined as a full fledged "participating country" in ARF in July 2004. The forum now consists of 24 members. While the 10 ASEAN members form the core group, the other are participants.

Through political dialogue and confidence building, no tension has escalated into armed confrontation among ASEAN members since its establishment more than four decades ago.

Economic and Functional Cooperation

When ASEAN was established, trade among the Member Countries was insignificant. Estimates between 1967 and the early 1970s showed that the share of intra-ASEAN trade from the total trade of the Member Countries was between 12 and 15 percent. Thus, some of the earliest economic cooperation schemes of ASEAN were aimed at addressing this situation. One of these was the Preferential Trading Arrangement of 1977, which accorded tariff preferences for trade among ASEAN economies. Ten years later, an Enhanced PTA Programme was adopted at the Third ASEAN Summit in Manila further increasing intra-ASEAN trade.

The Framework Agreement on Enhancing Economic Cooperation was adopted at the Fourth ASEAN Summit in Singapore in 1992, which included the launching of a scheme toward an ASEAN Free Trade Area or AFTA. The strategic objective of AFTA is to increase the ASEAN region's competitive advantage as a single production unit. The elimination of tariff and non-tariff barriers among the member countries is expected to promote greater economic efficiency, productivity, and competitiveness. The Fifth ASEAN Summit held in Bangkok in 1995 adopted the Agenda for Greater Economic Integration, which included the acceleration of the timetable for the realisation of AFTA from the original 15-year timeframe to 10 years.

In 1997, the ASEAN leaders adopted the ASEAN Vision 2020, which called for ASEAN Partnership in Dynamic Development aimed at forging closer economic integration within the region. The vision statement also resolved to create a stable, prosperous and highly competitive ASEAN Economic Region, in which there is a free flow of goods, services, investments, capital, and equitable economic development and reduced poverty and socio-economic disparities. The Hanoi Plan of Action, adopted in 1998, serves as the first in a series of plans of action leading up to the realisation of the ASEAN vision.

In addition to trade and investment liberalisation, regional economic integration is being pursued through the development of Trans-ASEAN transportation network consisting of major inter-state highway and railway networks, principal ports and sea lanes for maritime traffic, inland waterway transport, and major civil aviation links. ASEAN is promoting the inter-operability and inter-connectivity of the national telecommunications equipment and services. Building of Trans-ASEAN energy networks, which consist of the ASEAN Power Grid and the Trans-ASEAN Gas Pipeline Projects are also being developed.

ASEAN cooperation has resulted in greater regional integration. Within three years from the launching of AFTA, exports among ASEAN countries grew from US$43.26 billion in 1993 to almost US$80 billion in 1996, an average yearly growth rate of 28.3 percent. In the process, the share of intra-regional trade from ASEAN's total trade rose from 20 percent to almost 25 percent. Tourists from ASEAN countries themselves have been representing an increasingly important share of tourism in the region. In 1996, of the 28.6 million tourist arrivals in ASEAN, 11.2 million or almost 40 percent, came from within ASEAN itself.

Today, ASEAN economic cooperation covers the following areas: trade, investment, industry, services, finance, agriculture, forestry, energy, transportation and communication, intellectual property, small and medium enterprises, and tourism.

Desiring to build a community of caring societies, the ASEAN leaders resolved in 1995 to elevate functional cooperation to a higher plane to bring shared prosperity to all its members. The Framework for Elevating Functional Cooperation to a Higher Plane was adopted in 1996 with a theme: "Shared prosperity through human development, technological competitiveness, and social cohesiveness." Functional cooperation is guided by the following plans:

- ASEAN Plan of Action on Social Development;
- ASEAN Plan of Action on Culture and Information;
- ASEAN Plan of Action on Science and Technology;
- ASEAN Strategic Plan of Action on the Environment;
- ASEAN Plan of Action on Drug Abuse Control and
- ASEAN Plan of Action in Combating Transnational Crime

External Relations

The ASEAN Vision 2020 affirmed an outward-looking ASEAN playing a pivotal role in the international community and advancing ASEAN's common interests.

ASEAN has made major strides in building cooperative ties with states in the Asia-Pacific region and shall continue to accord them a high priority. Cooperation with other East Asian countries has accelerated with the holding of an annual dialogue among the leaders of ASEAN, China, Japan, and the Republic of Korea. In 1997, a joint statement between ASEAN and each of them was signed providing for framework for cooperation towards the 21st century. In November 1999, the leaders of ASEAN, China, Japan and the Republic of Korea issued a Joint Statement on East Asia Cooperation outlining the areas of cooperation among them.

The ASEAN Summit of 1992 mandated that "ASEAN, as part of an increasingly interdependent world, should intensify cooperative relationships with its Dialogue Partners." Consultations between ASEAN and its Dialogue Partners are held at the Foreign Ministers' level on an annual basis. ASEAN's Dialogue Partners include Australia, Canada, China, the European Union, India, Japan, the Republic of Korea, New Zealand, the Russian Federation, the United States of America, and the United Nations Development Programme. ASEAN also promotes cooperation with Pakistan on certain sectors.

Consistent with its resolve to enhance cooperation with other developing regions, ASEAN maintains contact with other inter-governmental organisations, namely, the Economic Cooperation Organisation, the Gulf Cooperation Council, the Rio Group, the South Asian Association for Regional Cooperation, and the South Pacific Forum.

Most ASEAN Member Countries also participate actively in the activities of the Asia-Pacific Economic Cooperation (APEC), the Asia-Europe Meeting (ASEM), the East Asia-Latin America Forum (EALAF).

Structures and Mechanisms

The highest decision-making organ of ASEAN is the Meeting of the ASEAN Heads of State and Government. The ASEAN Ministerial Meeting (Foreign Ministers) is held on an annual basis. Ministerial meetings on several other sectors are also held: agriculture and forestry, economics, energy, environment, finance, information, investment, labour, law, regional haze, rural development and poverty alleviation, science and technology, social welfare, transnational crime, transportation, tourism, youth, the AIA Council and, the AFTA Council. Supporting these ministerial bodies are 29 committees of senior officials and 122 technical working groups.

To support the conduct of ASEAN's external relations, ASEAN has established committees composed of heads of diplomatic missions in the following capitals: Brussels, London, Paris, Washington D.C., Tokyo, Canberra, Ottawa, Wellington, Geneva, Seoul, New Delhi, New York, Beijing, Moscow, and Islamabad.

The Secretary-General of ASEAN is appointed on merit and accorded ministerial status. The Secretary-General of ASEAN, who has a five-year term, is mandated to initiate, advise, coordinate, and implement ASEAN activities. The members of the professional staff of the ASEAN Secretariat are appointed on the principle of open recruitment and region-wide competition.

ASEAN has several specialized bodies and arrangements promoting inter-governmental cooperation in various fields: ASEAN University Network, ASEAN-EC Management Centre, ASEAN Centre for Energy, ASEAN Agricultural Development Planning Centre, ASEAN Earthquake Information Centre, ASEAN Poultry Research and Training Centre, ASEAN Regional Centre for Biodiversity Conservation, ASEAN Rural Youth Development Centre, ASEAN Specialized Meteorological Center, ASEAN Tourism Information Centre, and ASEAN Timber Technology Centre.

In addition, ASEAN promotes cooperative activities with organisations with related aims and purposes: ASEAN-Chambers of Commerce and Industry, ASEAN Business Forum, ASEAN Tourism Association, ASEAN Council on Petroleum, ASEAN Ports Association, ASEAN Vegetable Oils Club, and the ASEAN-Institutes for Strategic and International Studies. Furthermore, there are 53 Non-Governmental Organisations (NGOs), which have formal affiliations with ASEAN.

During the first few years of its existence the ASEAN made little progress towards any substantial regional co-operation beyond laying down the framework for the five member countries to work out their consensus through periodic consultation. However, after 1975, ASEAN underwent transformation and it really began to move. It not only enlarged its administrative machinery by increasing the membership to 10 in 1999, but also made serious proposals in respect of economic co-operation and took unified stand on extra regional affairs. The significance of ASEAN in international affairs lies in the fact that it represents an effort to develop Asian solution to the Asian problem in cooperative arrangement consisting wholly of nations in the region.

BANGLADESH-INDIA-MYANMAR-SRI LANKA-THAILAND ECONOMIC COOPERATION (BIMST-EC)

In recognition of the enormous economic potentials offered by countries to the west of Thailand, and Thailand's need to establish closer links with these regions in order to realize these potentials, Thailand's Look West Policy emerged. The main focus of this policy is to strengthen relations with countries in South Asia, the Middle East, and Africa. During H.E. Pitak Indravitayannana the former Deputy Foreign Minister of Thailand's official visit to the South Asian States, including Sri Lanka, Bangladesh and India, Thailand took the initiative to form a new economic cooperation. Consequently, BIST-EC (Bangladesh, India, Sri Lanka and Thailand Economic Cooperation) was formed during a meeting of Ministers in

Bangkok in June 1996 with the aim of encouraging and promoting economic cooperation among member countries to bring about regional development. Myanmar attended the June Meeting as observer. Eventually, Myanmar joined the organisation as a full member during a Special Ministerial Meeting held in Bangkok in December 1997, upon which the name of the grouping was changed to BIMST-EC to accommodate Myanmar's presence. Later, Bhutan and Nepal joined to take the membership to seven. At the first ever Summit level BIMSTEC meet held on July 31, 2004, the name was transformed to Bay of Bengal Initiative for Multi-Sectoral Technical and Economic Cooperation. However, BIMST-EC retained its original acronym.

The concept of BIMST-EC cooperation is to pursue cooperation which encourages the member countries to fully utilize their economic potentials. The five nations-Bangladesh, India; Myanmar, Sri Lanka and Thailand-all possess substantial resources and economic growth. It is believed that this growth may be better realized through a combined collaborative effort than by individual unilateral approach, that underlines the initiative to propose a degree of across-border cooperation.

The aims and purposes of BIST-EC/BIMST-EC, according to the Bangkok Declaration on the Establishment of BIST-EC, are:

- to create an enabling environment for rapid economic development through identification and implementation of specific cooperation projects;
- to accelerate the economic growth and social progress in the sub-region through joint endeavours in a spirit of equality and partnership;
- to promote active collaboration and mutual assistance on the matters of common interest in the economic, social, technical and scientific field;
- to provide assistance to each other in the form of training and research facilities in the education, professional and technical spheres;
- to cooperate more effectively in joint efforts that are supportive of a complementary to national development plans of Member States which result in tangible benefits

to the people in raising their living standards and generating employment as well as improving transportation and communication infrastructure;

- to maintain close and beneficial cooperation with existing international and regional organisations with similar aims and purposes;
- and to cooperate in projects that can be dealt with most productively on a sub-regional basis among the BIMST-EC countries and that make best use of available synergies.

Although BIMST-EC is a young grouping, the peoples of the BIMST-EC region have had close cultural and commercial ties throughout history. Close proximity meant that the business communities maintained active contacts with each other, in addition to cultural & social interaction and people-to-people contacts.

BIMST-EC is seen as an attempt to creatively tap the synergies of land & maritime contiguity in yet another geo-economic setting. BIMST-EC represents the reinforcement of India's relations with two of its South-Asian neighbors (Bangladesh and Sri Lanka), and of its link with ASEAN (Myanmar and Thailand). It is significant that with all these countries India has had deep and abiding cultural ties. They are also among our contemporary partners with whom our trade and investment relations in recent years have shown great dynamism because of inherent and emerging complementarities. Through its participation in BIMST-EC India seeks to strengthen its bilateral trade, investment and technology links with Bangladesh, Myanmar, Sri Lanka and Thailand.

BIMST-EC summit of July 2004 was significant in the sense that it was the first time that leaders of the respective governments got together. The earlier engagements were at the working level among trade ministers and officials of the various countries. Involvement of the top leaders is expected to provide impetus to regional trade that was missing till now.

One of the major achievements of this summit was the Indo-Thai Free Trade Agreement signed by Thai Prime Minister

Mr Thaksin Shinawatra and the Indian Prime Minister Dr Manmohan Singh. According to the agreement 82 items have been identified on which import duties would be halved from September 1, 2004. Duties would be further halved the next year and reduced to zero from September 2006.

INDIAN OCEAN RIM ASSOCIATION FOR REGIONAL COOPERATION (IOR-ARC)

The last a half century has been characterized by a tremendous increase in regional organisations all over the world promoting regional integration. It is now widely accepted that the path to economic prosperity can no longer be anomaly, traveled alone. Globalisation has further enhanced the need for regional groupings.

It is in the context that the Indian Ocean Rim-Association for Regional Cooperation (IOR-ARC), initially known as the Indian Ocean Rim Initiative, was established in Mauritius in March 1995 by six countries bordering the Indian Ocean and further extended to 14 member countries in March 1997. The pioneers were Australia, India, Kenya, Mauritius, Singapore, and South Africa.

At present, IOR-ARC consists of 19 member states: Australia, Bangladesh, India, Indonesia, Iran, Kenya, Madagascar, Malaysia, Mauritius, Mozambique, Oman, Seychelles, Singapore, South Africa, Sri Lanka, Tanzania, Thailand, United Arab Emirates and Yemen. The five new members, Bangladesh, Iran, Seychelles, Thailand and UAE were admitted at the Council of Ministers Meeting in Maputo, Mozambique, on 30-31 March 1999. There are also five dialogue partners of IOR-ARC; namely, France, Japan, United Kingdom, Egypt and China. At present, only the Indian Ocean Tourism Organisation (IOTO) has the observer status. All decisions including granting of Dialogue Partner status and admission of new members are taken by consensus.

The objectives of IOR-ARC are:

- To promote sustainable growth and balanced development of the region and Member States;
- To focus on those areas of economic cooperation which provide maximum opportunities to develop shared interests and reap mutual benefits and

- To promote liberalisation, remove impediments and lower barriers towards a freer and enhanced flow of goods, services, investment, and technology within the Indian Ocean rim.

The IOR-ARC is based on the principles of open regionalism, which is a flexible arrangement that is more member-friendly than other neo-liberal regional arrangements such as preferential trading arrangements, free trade areas, customs unions, common markets, etc. Decisions are made by consensus, and compliance remains without any rigid institutional structure to specify any rules and regulations. IOR-ARC is a unique (tripartite) Association in that it combines officials, business and academics as an integral part of its functioning. The businessmen also meet in parallel in the Indian Ocean rim Business Forum (IORBF). Similarly, the academicians meet in their Indian Ocean Rim Academic Group (IORAG). Both academicians and businessmen have been actively involved in the consideration, formulation and implementation of the projects in the work programmes of IOR-ARC and in the conceptualisation of the initiatives itself.

The Indian Ocean Rim defines a distinctive area in international politics consisting of coastal states bordering the Indian Ocean. It is a region of much diversity whether in culture, race, religion, economic development or strategic interests. The countries vary in the size of their population, economies, trade, technological development and in the composition of their Gross Domestic Product (GDP). A number of sub-regions are evident, for example Southern and Eastern Africa, the Horn of Africa and the Red Sea, South Asia, Southeast Asia, and Australasia. It also includes a number of regional organisations.

This is a group that consists of countries that are developed, newly developed, developing, least developed, oil based, agricultural based etc. Today, it encompasses around 1,700 million people and produces goods and services worth US $ 1,700 billion.

With significant complementarities among its members, the case for regional trade and other economic cooperation was clearly established in academic discussions. These studies broadly endorsed "open regionalism" as a right policy framework for the IOR-ARC. Due to the Vastness of the region, it was believed that this grouping had the potential to, become as important as the European Union (EU), ASEAN and APEC.

The main focus of IOR-ARC is on regional economic cooperation which aims at lessening discrimination in certain areas of common interest, rather than on economic integration which runs through stages like Preferential Trade Area (PTA), Free Trade Area (FTA), Customs Union (CU), Common Market and an Economic Union. It is primarily an outward looking forum for economic dialogue and cooperation.

IOR-ARC activities include several on-going topical projects and work programs conducted by member countries of shared interests, all of which under the umbrella of 3 separate working groups, namely:

- Working Group on Trade and Investment (WGTI),
- Indian Ocean Rim Business Forum (IORBF) and
- Indian Ocean Rim Academic Group (IORAG).

Open regionalism as is the case for the IOR-ARC has four components:

- trade liberalisation;
- trade and investment facilitation;
- economic and technical cooperation and
- trade and investment dialogue.

The Association holds a Council of Ministers meeting once every two years. A notable outcome of the Oman meetings was the endorsement of the report of the IOR-ARC High Level Task Force (HLTF). The HLTF had been established in 2001 by the IOR-ARC Council of Ministers to consider the future directions of the IOR-ARC and ways to improve its operations. The final HLTF report includes recommendations which seek to ensure that the Association's work program is reflective of its key objectives of trade and investment facilitation as well as guidelines on the size and management structure of the secretariat.

SOUTH ASIAN ASSOCIATION FOR REGIONAL COOPERATION (SAARC)

The South Asian Association for Regional Cooperation (SAARC) was established when its Charter was formally adopted on December 8, 1985 by the Heads of State of Bangladesh, Bhutan, India, Maldives, Nepal, Pakistan and Sri Lanka. It is an Association based on the consciousness that in an increasingly interdependent world, the objectives of peace, freedom, social justice and economic prosperity are best achieved in the South Asian region by fostering mutual understanding, good neighbourly relations and meaningful cooperation among the Member States which are bound by ties of history and culture.

The spirit of the SAARC is reflected in its objectives and the principles, which provides a platform for the people of South Asia to work together in a spirit of friendship, trust and understanding. It aims to accelerate the process of economic and social development in the Member States. Cooperation in SAARC is based on the respect for the principles of sovereign equality; territorial integrity; political independence; non-interference in the internal affairs of Member States; and mutual benefits. Regional cooperation is, in fact, seen as a complement to the bilateral and multilateral relations of its Member States.

Objectives

- To promote the welfare of the peoples of South Asia and to improve their quality of life;
- To accelerate economic growth, social progress and cultural development in the region and to provide all individuals the opportunity to live in dignity and to realize their full potential;
- To promote and strengthen collective self-reliance among the countries of South Asia;
- To contribute to mutual trust, understanding and appreciation of one another's problems;
- To promote active collaboration and mutual assistance in the economic, social, cultural, technical and scientific fields;

- To strengthen cooperation with other developing countries;
- To strengthen cooperation among themselves in international forums on matters of common interests and
- To cooperate with international and regional organisations with similar aims and purposes.

Principles

- Cooperation within the framework of the Association is based on respect for the principles of sovereign equality, territorial integrity, political independence, non-interference in the internal affairs of other States and mutual benefit;
- Such cooperation is to complement and not to substitute bilateral or multilateral cooperation and
- Such cooperation should be consistent with bilateral and multilateral obligations of Member States.

Decisions at all levels in SAARC are to be taken on the basis of unanimity; and bilateral and contentious issues are to be excluded from the deliberations of the Association. The Charter of the Association provides for the following:

The Summit. It is the highest authority of the Association consists of the Heads of State or Government, who meet annually at the Summit level. To date, twelve Summits have been held: Dhaka (1985), Bangalore (1986), Kathmandu (1987), Islamabad (1988), Malé (1990), Colombo (1991), Dhaka (1993), New Delhi (1995), Malé (1997), Colombo (1998) and Kathmandu (2002). The Twelfth SAARC Summit was held in Islamabad (2004). Thirteenth Summit is scheduled to be held in Dhaka, Bangladesh.

The Council of Ministers. It comprises of the Foreign Ministers of Member States. The Council is responsible for formulating policies; reviewing progress; deciding on new areas of cooperation; establishing additional mechanisms as deemed necessary; and deciding on other matters of general interest to the Association.

The Standing Committee. The Standing Committee comprising the Foreign Secretaries of Member States is entrusted with the task of overall monitoring and coordination of programmes; approving of projects and programmes, and modalities of financing; determining inter-sectoral priorities; mobilising regional and external resources; and identifying new areas of cooperation. The Standing Committee is assisted by a Programming Committee (which is not a SAARC Charter body) comprising senior officials to scrutinize the Secretariat Budget, finalize the Calendar of Activities and take up any other matter assigned to it by the Standing Committee. The Programming Committee has also been entrusted to consider and submit to the Standing Committee recommendations for action on the Reports of the Technical Committees, SAARC Regional Centres and the SAARC Audio Visual Exchange (SAVE) Committee.

The Technical Committees. At present, there are seven Technical Committees functioning in various fields under the agreed areas of cooperation. The Technical Committees formulate specialized programmes and projects in their respective fields under the SAARC Integrated Programme of Action (SIPA). They are also responsible for monitoring the implementation of such activities and submit their reports to the Standing Committee through the Programming Committee. These committees initiate cooperation in important areas such as trade, manufactures and services; basic needs; human resources development; database on socio-economic indicators; energy modeling techniques; plan modeling techniques; and poverty alleviation strategies.

Specialised Ministerial Meetings. Since the establishment of the Association, a number of SAARC ministerial meetings have been held to focus attention on specific areas of common concern, such as international economic issues, environment, housing, tourism, women, youth, health etc. and these have now become an integral part of the consultative structure.

SAARC Secretariat. It is based in Kathmandu. It coordinates and monitors implementation of SAARC activities, prepares for SAARC meetings and serves as a channel of communication between the association and other regional organisations and inter-governmental institutions.

A SAARC Preferential Trading Arrangement (SAPTA). It has been established and negotiations are continuing on the reduction of tariffs and other impediments to a more free flow of trade within the region. The agreement on SAPTA was signed on 11 April 1993. It entered into force on 7 December 1995. The basic principles underlying SAPTA are:

(a) overall reciprocity and mutuality of advantages so as to benefit equitably all Contracting States, taking into account their respective level of economic and industrial development, the pattern of their external trade, and trade and tariff policies and systems;

(b) negotiation of tariff reform step by step, improved and extended in successive stages through periodic reviews;

(c) recognition of the special needs of the Least Developed Contracting States and agreement on concrete preferential measures in their favour and

(d) inclusion of all products, manufactures and commodities in their raw, semi-processed and processed forms.

The initiation of SAPTA and the move towards establishment of SAFTA are the steps to avail itself of the vast opportunities for deeper regional integration that lie ahead.

One of the core principles of the SAPTA Agreement is that there should be special treatment for Least Developed Countries through the consideration of additional measures. It was accordingly decided in 1999 to reduce the domestic content requirement further under the SAPTA Rules of Origin to enable the smaller and Least Developed Countries to benefit equitably from economic liberalisation. This reduction would apply to all products covered so far in the trade negotiations. SAPTA was envisaged primarily as the first step towards the transition to a South Asian Free Trade Area (SAFTA) leading subsequently, towards a Customs Union, Common Market and Economic Union.

SAFTA: Towards a Reality

Recognizing the need to address asymmetries in development and other complexities that may stand in the way of such a tight schedule, the Tenth SAARC Summit in Colombo directed that the text of the regulatory framework for creating a Free Trade Area in the Region should be finalized by 2001. The Eleventh SAARC Summit held in Kathmandu on 4-6 January 2002 provided further impetus to the regional economic cooperation. To give effect to the shared aspirations for a more prosperous South Asia, the Leaders agreed to the vision of a phased and planned process eventually leading to a South Asian Economic Union and agreed to accelerate cooperation in the core areas of trade, finance and investment to realize the goal of an integrated South Asian economy in a step-by-step manner. They expressed their determination to make full use of regional synergy to maximize the benefits of globalisation and liberalisation and to minimize their negative impacts on the region. While recognizing that trade and economic expansion is closely inter-linked, the Leaders made a commitment to widen and deepen the scope of regional networks of activities in trade and financial matters.

Signing of the SAFTA Agreement at the 12th SAARC Summit in January, 2004 visualizes a graded reduction in import tariffs over the next decade. The first milestone will be in 2006 which will see a reduction of tariffs between the seven member nations to between 0-5% by the time the Agreement is fully implemented on December 31, 2015. The SAFTA accord also allows any contracting States to pull out of the treaty at any time, after it comes into force from January 1, 2006. Such withdrawal shall be effective on the expiry of the six months from the date on which a written notice thereof is received by the Secretary General of the SAARC.

In the period between now and the implementation of the Agreement, member countries will complete four procedural formalities: formation of sensitive lists, outlining the products whose tariffs will not be reduced; rules of origin; revenue loss compensation mechanism for the lesser developed countries and; an arbitration council or dispute settlement body. Under the agreement, India and Pakistan get seven years to achieve the 0-5% goal, Sri lanka gets eight years and lesser developed Bangladesh, Nepal, Maldives and Bhutan get ten years. Under the treaty, each of the countries will create two sensitive lists, one for the more and the other for the less developed countries.

A SAFTA Ministerial Council comprising Commerce/Trade Ministers and a Committee of Experts have been envisaged in SAFTA for the administration and implementation of the Agreement. It will be guided by this ministerial council of Commerce Ministers of all States and this will be its highest decision making body.

Any dispute that may arise among the contracting States regarding the interpretation and the application of the provisions of this (SAFTA) Agreement or any instrument adopted within its framework concerning the rights and obligations of the States will be amicably settled through a process initiated by a request for bilateral consultations.

SAFTA Agreement also suggests a number of measures that a member may adopt, including the removal of barriers to the intra-SAARC investment, harmonisation of customs facilities, transit facilities for efficient intra-SAARC trade and simplification of procedures for business visas. The Agreement has been described as a major 'milestone' towards further broadening of economic cooperation and to ensure equitable distribution of benefits of trade.

SAFTA is as much about bilateral economic ties as it is a regional trading arrangement. The establishment of SAFTA, will over the next decade sharply boost economic cooperation between countries of the region primarily, India and Pakistan. For long, Pakistan had denied India, the status of a Most Favoured Nation. It now wants to use SAFTA for a liberalized trading arrangement with India. This in turn would lead to closer people to people ties and create a network of friendly relationships in which the Kashmir issue can be meaningfully addressed. This will catalyse cross border affinities that would integrate two vast nations.

But, SAFTA is not enough, the vision is to achieve a much wider goal of regional integration: A South Asian Union, modeled on European Union that would abolish trade and travel restrictions, launch a common currency and elect a Supra-national parliament.

There are a number of daunting challenges that must be met, if the new effort at promoting trade in South Asia is not to fail again. The first is to maintain the momentum in improving the bilateral political relations between India and Pakistan. The second is to address economic insecurity among the smaller countries of South Asia. This necessitates making unilateral trade concessions of some substance. The third challenge is to create the basic economic infrastructure required to handle higher volumes of trade. Finally, the fears of specific sectors in each country—for example, tea in India, textile in Bangladesh, and light engineering in Pakistan—that they have more to lose than to gain from SAFTA can be assuaged only with a more gradual reduction of tariffs on "sensitive" products.

It is hoped that the recent Indo-Pakistan peace initiative will achieve positive results and that it will create a favourable climate to operationalise SAFTA at the earliest and to achieve the ultimate objective of a South Asian Union.

5.3: CENTRAL AND LATIN AMERICAN REGIONAL ORGANISATIONS

ANDEAN GROUP

The desire to advance toward a more accelerated integration led a group of Latin American Free Trade Area (LAFTA) member countries to establish a broader-scope scheme with stricter commitments. This was the forerunner of the Andean sub-regional group which achieved legal status through the Cartagena Agreement signed by Bolivia, Colombia, Chile, Ecuador and Peru in 1969, with Venezuela, a country that had participated in the initial negotiations, joining later.

The aim of the members of the Andean Group was to cover the deficiencies they perceived in LAFTA as an instrument of progress toward a common market. But their agreement was forged within the framework of a regional mechanism which accepted the existence of sub-regional groups for which the Most Favored Nation clause would not be in effect. All the signatories of the Cartagena Agreement were considered, within LAFTA, as countries with insufficient markets or of lesser relative development. The establishment of special preferences among them could, therefore, stand up to the critiques that had been formulated against the Free Trade Area, claiming that their mechanisms had preferentially benefited the participants with the greatest relative development.

In contrast with LAFTA, the Cartagena Agreement established mechanisms for automatic and linear tariff reduction, in order to quickly create a free trade zone. The adoption of a Common External Tariff (CET) was also envisaged that would be applied "at the latest by December 31, 1980." In the case of Bolivia and Ecuador, countries with a lesser relative development, the deadline would be December 31, 1985.

The most distinctive characteristic of the Andean Group was the commitment of its members to undertake a joint program for their industrial development. The objective of that program, among others, was to achieve a better expansion, specialisation and diversification of production and a more equitable distribution of benefits. With this aim, industrial sectors were reserved for joint programs, and products were assigned by countries.

As a complement, a system for the common treatment of foreign investments was established by Decision 24 of the Cartagena Agreement Commission. The purpose of the Decision was to strengthen the participation of national companies in the subregional market and to outline the rights and obligations of foreign investors. Under this system, sectors considered to be strategic or sufficiently covered by sub-regional investments could be reserved for national or "multinational Andean" companies.

In the institutional aspect, the Cartagena Agreement established a Board of three members as the principal executive body, independent of national governments. The supranational elements of the Board were an innovation in the Latin American sphere.

Prior to the signing of the Cartagena Agreement, its member countries—including Venezuela—had created the Andean Development Fund to act as the financial body of the Andean Group. One of the main objectives of the Fund was to finance joint industrial development programs, in addition to the necessary infrastructure to accelerate integration.

The Andean Reserve Fund (ARF) was created, in 1975, in the monetary area and in order to finance balance of payments problems, which was subsequently opened to members from outside the sub-region and renamed the Latin American Reserve Fund (LARF), while 1979 saw the creation of the Andean Court of Justice to interpret Andean legislation and resolve disputes.

The member countries of the Cartagena Agreement signed a number of cooperation agreements, noteworthy among which are the Andrés Bello Agreement in education, the Hipólito Unanue Agreement in Health and the Simón Rodríguez Agreement in social matters. Andean labor and business councils were created as auxiliary bodies followed later by the establishment of the Andean Parliament as a forum for national parliaments.

Despite its institutional development, the Andean Group encountered serious problems in advancing its accelerated integration program. Negotiations with regard to joint industrial development programs proved to be particularly difficult, among which only those involving the chemical and petrochemical industries were relatively successful. The interrelation of those programs with automatic tariff reduction under the originally agreed terms, was an additional element for infringement of the latter.

The withdrawal of Chile from the Cartagena Agreement in 1974 was a traumatic blow for the progress of the Andean Group. A partial reason why Chile took this step was because of the common system regarding foreign investments which had been strongly opposed in international circles.

Subsequently, the debt crisis and the balance of payments problems of the member countries during the eighties led to a generalized breach of their obligations within the framework of the Cartagena Agreement which were eased by the Quito Protocol in 1987. At the beginning of the nineties the Pact was revitalized and intra-subregional trade increased.

The implementation of the common external tariff in Colombia, Ecuador and Venezuela; the establishment of a price band system for certain agricultural products; and the setting up of a working group to study ways of reforming the institutional system of the Andean Group are some of the recent developments. A Common External Tariff has been in effect since February 1, 1995 for Colombian, Venezuelan and

Ecuadoran imports from non-Andean Group countries. The countries of the Andean Group have also been applying the Andean Price Band System since February 1, 1995. The purpose of this system is to stabilize the import costs of agricultural staples through adjustments to the tariffs on such products.

Colombia, Venezuela, and Mexico signed an agreement forming the "Group of Three" (G-3), that will gradually reduce tariffs across the board over a ten-year period, culminating in the establishment of a Free Trade Area (FTA) in 2005. The overlap between G-3 and the CET of the Andean Group has sparked protests from the private sector in Colombia and Venezuela, based on fears that duty-free access for intermediate inputs from the United States under NAFTA will give Mexican producers an unfair advantage over Colombian and Venezuelan manufacturers, who are subject to a tariff floor of 5 per cent under the aforementioned CET.

CENTRAL AMERICAN COMMON MARKET (CACM)

Central American Common Market (CACM), trade organisation started in 1960 by a treaty between Guatemala, Honduras, Nicaragua, El Salvador, and later Costa Rica. By the mid-1960s the group had made advances toward economic integration, and by 1970 trade between member nations had risen more than tenfold over 1960 levels. During the same period, imports doubled and a common tariff was established for 98% of the trade with non-member countries. In 1967, at the conference of American presidents at Punta del Este, Uruguay, it was decided that CACM, together with the Latin American Free Trade Association (see Latin American Integration Association), would be the basis for a comprehensive Latin American common market. However, by the early 1990s little progress toward a Latin American common market had been made, in part because of internal and internecine strife, in part because CACM economies were competitive, not complementary. Nonetheless, CACM has been judged more successful at lowering trade barriers than other Latin American groupings.

CARIBBEAN COMMUNITY (CARICOM)

Established as the Caribbean Community and Common Market by the Treaty of Chaguaramas signed on 4 July 1973. By Treaty revision, effective February 2002, the successor entity is now the Caribbean Community, including the CARICOM Single Market and Economy (CSME). Original signatories to the Treaty are Prime Ministers of: Barbados—Errol W. Barrow; Guyana—L.F.S. Burnham; Jamaica—Michael Manley; and Trinidad and Tobago—Eric Williams.

CARICOM Single Market is an arrangement which allows CARICOM goods, services, people and capital to move throughout the Caribbean Community without tariffs and without restrictions to achieve a single large economic space, and to provide for a common Economic and Trade Policy.

CARICOM Single Economy is an arrangement which further harmonises economic, monetary and fiscal policies and measures across all Member States of the Caribbean Community to underpin the sustainable development of the Region. This would mean the coordination of foreign exchange and interest rate policies, the harmonisation of tax regimes and of laws and the convergence of economic performance among other measures

Some benefits of the CARICOM Single Market and Economy are:

- Increased production and trade in goods and services in a combined market of over 6 million persons and for the world beyond.
- Competitive products of better quality and prices.
- Improved services provided by enterprises and individuals, including transportation and communication.
- Greater opportunity for travel.
- Opportunities for nationals to study and work in CARICOM countries of their choice.
- Increased employment and improved standards of living.

The CARICOM member states are: Antigua and Barbuda, The Bahamas, Barbados, Belize, Dominica, Grenada, Guyana,

Haiti, Jamaica, Montserrat, Saint Lucia, St. Kitts and Nevis, St. Vincent and the Grenadines, Suriname, and Trinidad and Tobago.

The Community has the following objectives:

- improved standards of living and work;
- full employment of labour and other factors of production;
- accelerated, co-ordinated and sustained economic development and convergence;
- expansion of trade and economic relations with third States;
- enhanced levels of international competitiveness;
- organisation for increased production and productivity;
- the achievement of a greater measure of economic leverage and effectiveness of Member States in dealing with third States, groups of States and entities of any description;
- enhanced co-ordination of Member States' foreign and [foreign] economic policies and
- enhanced functional co-operation, including—
- more efficient operation of common services and activities for the benefit of its peoples;
- accelerated promotion of greater understanding among its peoples and the advancement of their social, cultural and technological development;
- intensified activities in areas such as health, education, transportation, telecommunications.

The meetings of the Heads of Government and of the ministerial Councils, also known as institutions, represent the main means of achieving consensus on regional issues and policies.

The Conference of Heads of Government is the highest decision-making forum and the final authority of the Community. The primary responsibility of the Conference is to determine and to provide the policy direction for the Community. It is the final authority for the conclusion of Treaties on behalf of the Community and for entering into relationships between the Community and International Organisations and States. Conference is also responsible for making the financial arrangements to meet the expenses of the Community but has delegated this function to the Community Council. Decisions of the Conference are generally taken unanimously. It is made up of the Heads of Government of the Member States. Because of the increasing number of issues to be decided and implemented, a subset of the Conference, called the Bureau, was instituted in 1992. The Bureau meets as necessary and reports to the Conference.

The Community Council of Ministers is the second highest organ of CARICOM, and consists of Ministers responsible for Community Affairs and any other Minister designated by Member States in their absolute discretion. The Community Council has primary responsibility for the development of Community strategic planning and co-ordination in the areas of economic integration, functional co-operation and external relations. The Community Council also has the responsibility for establishing a system of regional/ national consultations in order to ensure the effectiveness of the decision-making and implementation processes in the Community.

The following Ministerial Councils were also established to streamline the functioning of the Community and increase the smooth functioning of the different sectors:

- The Council for Trade and Economic Development (COTED), which has been charged with the responsibility for the promotion of trade and economic development of the Community;
- The Council for Foreign and Community Relations (COFCOR), which has been charged with responsibility for determining relations between the Community, and international organisations and Third States;
- The Council for Finance and Planning (COFAP), which has been charged with primary responsibility for economic policy coordination and financial and monetary integration of Member States;
- The Council for Human and Social Development (COHSOD), which is responsible for human and social development in the Community especially in the areas

of health, education, labour and industrial relations, youth, women, and sports.

The following Subsidiary Bodies have also been established:

(a) the Legal Affairs Committee composed of Ministers responsible for Legal Affairs and/or Attorneys-General of Member States;

(b) the Committee of Central Bank Governors consisting of the Governors and Heads of Central Banks of Member States or their nominees;

(c) the Budget Committee consisting of senior officials of Member States.

LATIN AMERICAN FREE TRADE AREA (LAFTA)

The Latin American Free Trade Association (LAFTA) was established in 1960 with the signing of the Montevideo Treaty. Its original members were Argentina, Brazil, Chile, Mexico, Paraguay and Uruguay. They were later joined by Bolivia, Colombia, Ecuador, Peru and Venezuela and the Secretariat was set up in Uruguay.

LAFTA's aim was to create a free trade area among its members by the gradual freeing of trade, which would be accomplished through selective negotiations among them. This practical and flexible mechanism was adopted to take into account the different development levels among the participating countries and the difficulties in abandoning restrictive trade practices that characterized their national policies.

Selective negotiation made it possible to progress at a faster pace than a system of scheduled tariff reductions in freeing those products with regard to which there were no problems of competition. Also contemplated was a total liberation of traditional trade within a twelve-year term, and it was hoped that this would provide sufficient time for adapting national productions and to avoid the inconveniences of a very accelerated opening up of the markets.

The annual rounds of LAFTA negotiations made it possible, during the early years, to agree to more than eight thousand five hundred tariff reductions, added to those that each country gave to the rest of the group. Of these, one fifth implied the total elimination of tariff duties and other restrictions. These rounds of negotiations, however, were increasingly less fruitful. While at the first round 3,500 tariff concessions were made, by the fourth round that number dropped to 300, less than ten percent of the concessions made in the first round. The active role played by the private sector in these negotiations should be noted.

In the early years of LAFTA's existence, intra-zonal trade strengthened notably. Between 1961, the year prior to the entry in force of the first reductions, and 1963, the aforementioned trade increased by 44% to approximately one billion dollars. Its participation in total trade of the LAFTA members rose from 6% to 8.4% during those same years. Of this trade, more than three-quarters corresponded to products incorporated into the national lists of the integration scheme. By 1971, intra-zonal trade had reached about 1.5 billion dollars and represented 12% of total trade.

Particular mention should be made of the special treatment that was given to countries with lesser relative development, such as Ecuador, Bolivia, Uruguay and Paraguay, in the granting of preferences. Such preferences were not extended to other countries in the area and in their case the most favored nation clause was not in effect. Also, the situation of the intermediate size countries known as those with "insufficient markets", such as Colombia, Chile, Peru and Venezuela were also taken into account.

Starting up LAFTA required finding solutions to many technical problems to facilitate and make negotiations possible. Among these were the preparation of a Common Tariff Nomenclature, the reconciliation of customs procedures and the establishment of criteria for the certification of origin.

The Montevideo treaty also contemplated the possibility of establishing industrial complementation agreements in products and sectors. The coordination and adoption of such agreements was, however, scarce. On the other hand, in 1965, an agreement for reciprocal payments and credit by LAFTA countries was signed for the purpose of facilitating commercial transactions and the offsetting of balances (subsequently, with the incorporation of the Dominican Republic, this agreement was referred to as the Santo Domingo Agreement).

In 1967, annual negotiations could not take place and were postponed for a year. Then, in 1968, an attempt was made to introduce a system of automatic tariff reductions, but in light of the generalized infringement of this system, LAFTA began to lose its dynamism. Because of this situation, it was thought that a new treaty could be negotiated that would be more realistic and would salvage the progress that had already been made or the so-called "historical heritage." These negotiations ended with the signing of the Montevideo Treaty of 1980 and the creation of the Latin American Integration Association (ALADI) which replaced LAFTA.

LATIN AMERICAN INTEGRATION ASSOCIATION

Established in 1980 to replace the Latin American Free Trade Area (LAFTA), Asociación Latinoamericana de Integracion (ALADI)—or the Latin American Integration Association (LAIA)—was the dominant regional body dealing with Latin American trade prior to the development of Mercosur. It is a loose association of 11 Latin American countries with a flexible mandate to establish, in a gradual and progressive manner, a Latin American common market. In implementing this goal, ALADI has encouraged bilateral, sub-regional, and pan-regional trade and tariff agreements. This elastic manner of promoting economic integration reflects the vastly different political and economic climates of the member countries.

The members of ALADI are divided into three categories: most developed—Argentina, Brazil, and Mexico; intermediate-Chile, Columbia, Peru, Uruguay, and Venezuela; and least developed—Bolivia, Ecuador, and Paraguay—which enjoy a special preferential system. The differential benefits go to the less and least developed countries by application of the "principle of non-reciprocal treatment" when they sign their bilateral tariff arrangements with the more developed countries. The least developed countries receive MFN treatment, thereby receiving the same rights other ALADI countries obtain through their bilateral treaties. The Andean Common Market countries (Colombia, Peru, Venezuela, Bolivia, and Ecuador) function as a single trading nation and do not grant individual tariff concessions or tariff cuts on any item greater than those granted to other Andean Pact members. More than 23,000 tariff cuts have been implemented, although inter-ALADI trade still accounts for only about 11 per cent of the member countries' total exports.

ALADI provides for and encourages multilateral links or agreements with Latin American non-member countries or integration organisations, as well as with other developing countries or economic groups outside the continent. Indeed, most Central American countries, plus Cuba, Italy, Portugal, Russia, Spain, Switzerland, the EU, and the Organización de Estados Americanos (OEA)—the Organisation of American States (OAS)—all participate in ALADI as observers.

As the development of MERCOSUR has gained momentum, ALADI has made independent attempts to strengthen its own role in Latin American integration. It has sought to expand intra-ALADI trade, provide additional support for less developed members, expand and diversify fields of cooperation, and harmonize macroeconomic policies among its members. However, little progress has been made in this regard due to the primary focus of the more powerful members on MERCOSUR (or NAFTA) commitments. ALADI may yet serve a strategic role in the region as a bridge between MERCOSUR and the Andean Pact (AP), as well as among Mercosur, AP, and NAFTA.

MERCOSUR: MERCADO COMÚN DEL SUR (SOUTHERN COMMON MARKET)

In December 1994 Argentina, Brazil, Paraguay, and Uruguay signed the Protocol of Ouro Preto, implementing the Southern Common Market, known widely as MERCOSUR. Over the past year, Chile and Bolivia have entered into agreements with MERCOSUR as well.

MERCOSUR calls for a gradual elimination of all tariffs on goods originating in and traded among the member states and the formation of a Common External Tariff (CET). It operates within the context and terms of larger groupings, including ALADI and GATT, of which it is a part. During the transition period that begun in 1991 and ended December 31, 1994, tariffs were reduced automatically, with a sharp initial cut and periodic reductions until eventually all tariffs were eliminated. Mercosur has an average trade-weighted external tariff of 14 per cent. As of the inauguration of the customs union in January 1995, approximately 80 per cent of all products traded-about 8,000 categories of goods-began to be traded duty-free within the bloc. Exceptions include textiles, steel, automobiles, and petrochemicals, which will remain protected by domestic tariffs for a period until 1999. Sugar will be under a transitional regime until 2001.

MERCOSUR is still far from being a true common market, but the members have managed to achieve a customs union (although the CET has not covered all items), and they will continue negotiations aimed at full common market status by 2006. As a common market, MERCOSUR will be required to do more than reduce and harmonize tariffs. It must also coordinate the economic, legislative, environmental, infrastructure and technology policies of the various member countries. Members are eventually expected to harmonize their standards, establish a supra-national bureaucracy with considerable power to affect the policymaking decisions of each country's government, and implement fully a common external tariff structure. They have a way to go to achieve such goals. There is no final date for full to commitment to common market status among the members. Currently there are ambitious working groups, ad-hoc committees, and specialized meetings with the Common Market Council negotiating implementation. Nevertheless, trade among MERCOSUR countries has already increased fourfold-it exceeded US$20.8 billion in 1997-since the initial agreement was signed in anticipation of even greater cohesion. More importantly, MERCOSUR helped to lock in the changes already made by its members during the past few years. A momentum toward such change has been created that will be very difficult to halt or reverse.

Within Argentina, MERCOSUR has been especially important; intra-MERCOSUR trade with Argentina has increased fourfold in five years. The loss of import revenues from duties on goods originating within MERCOSUR countries has been more than compensated by the earnings generated by more competitive duty-free exports to these countries. Argentine export trade grew from US$13.1 billion in 1993 to US$26.2 billion in 1997; its export trade with MERCOSUR increased from US$3.7 billion in 1993 to almost US$9.5 billion in 1997. In 1993 MERCOSUR countries absorbed 28 per cent of Argentina's exports; this figure rose to 36 per cent of all exports in 1997. MERCOSUR has especially improved Argentina's trade status with Brazil, its largest neighbor, the recovering economy which now gobbles up more than 31 per cent of Argentina's total exports.

The effects of MERCOSUR are being felt beyond the Brazil-Argentina border. The combined population of the six member countries is 200 million (220 million with Chile and Bolivia)-more than two thirds of South America's population-with a total GDP of approximately US$1.1 trillion. MERCOSUR's territory covers nearly 12 million sq km (4.6 million sq mi), comprises 70 per cent of the total land mass of South America, stretches from the tropical jungles of northern Brazil to the sub-antarctic zone of Argentina, and includes some of the world's most important agricultural and mineral resources. This wide variety of topographies, climates, and resources provides substantial opportunities for expansion and complementation in production.

Administrative Structure

The governing body of MERCOSUR is the Common Market Council, consisting of the member states' ministers of foreign relations and economy. It is responsible for political leadership and decisionmaking to ensure compliance with the objectives and the time frames set within the agreement.

The executive body of MERCOSUR is the Common Market Group, which is composed of 16 members and represents the foreign relations offices, the economic ministries, and the central banks of the member states. The Common Market Group has established an administrative headquarters in Montevideo, Uruguay, and has already appointed 11 working groups to deal with policy matters.

A MERCOSUR Trade Commission will monitor trade regulations among members and be vested with the authority to review claims and mediate disputes. According to the terms of the Brasilia Protocol, final settlement of disputes among members will be through arbitration. This administrative body will also serve as MERCOSUR's negotiating unit with other nations and trade blocs.

Elimination of Tariffs and Other Trade Barriers All non-tariff restrictions and other limitations on trade between the member states were eliminated according to a gradual progressive automatic schedule, reaching zero duty and the removal of tariff restrictions of all kinds. These goals have already been achieved, leaving only a few sensitive products subject to limits based on national import policy.

Common External Tariff Member states further agreed to set common external tariffs toward third countries or groups of countries and to coordinate their individual positions in regional and international economic trade forums. Such a tariff is necessary to the creation of a customs union in that once a CET is implemented, importers of finished goods for which the importer has paid the CET may sell the finished goods in the territories of other member countries without paying a second tariff. Until then, unless a product qualifies for preferential treatment under the rules of origin established by MERCOSUR, a trader must either pay the applicable tariff each time the product crosses a border of a member state or establish independent distribution centers in each member state.

MERCOSUR members have had some difficulty establishing a CET. However, in August 1994, the MERCOSUR presidents ratified the formation of a CET structure-effective January 1, 1995-that sets CET rates of 0 to 20 per cent for more than 80 per cent of the tariff lines. In 1997 MERCOSUR members decided a 3 per cent increase in the CET, for a three year period beginning on January 1st, 1998 until the year 2001; during such period the CET ranges from 0 to 23 per cent. A CET of 14 per cent on capital goods will be introduced only in 2001; even then, Paraguay and Uruguay will be given an additional five years to bring their external tariffs into line. A common levy tentatively set at 16 per cent on informatics and telecommunications equipment will wait until 2006. The importation of chemicals has been partially resolved with a tentative agreement establishing a 0 to 16 per cent tariff, but this is subject to modification in the future.

Rules of Origin: Until a CET is fully implemented, member countries must apply rules of origin to determine whether some particular good qualify for the preferential tariff rate. Importers and exporters alike need to understand these rules of origin before attempting to do business in any MERCOSUR market. MERCOSUR's rules of origin are straightforward:

1. Goods produced (for example, extracted, harvested, gathered, or born) within a member territory qualify as originating.
2. All goods manufactured wholly within the territory of one or more members from originating materials qualify as originating. Thus, if an Argentine company manufactures a telephone from plastic produced in Paraguay and audio components produced in Brazil, assembling the product in Argentina, the phone would qualify as originating. The manufacturer could export it to any member of MERCOSUR at the prevailing preferential tariff rate.
3. Depending on the product in question, this rule requires that either all non-originating components shift their tariff headings pursuant to the tariff nomenclature established under MERCOSUR; or all non-originating components shift their tariff headings and the finished product meets a regional value test. The MERCOSUR regional value test specifies that the value of originating goods may not be less than 60 per cent of the free-on-board (FOB) value of the exported good.
4. A final rule applies if a particular product does not meet the requirements established by any of the other three rules, it permits a product to qualify as originating if the total value of non-originating materials incorporated into the finished product does not exceed 40 per cent of the final export value of the finished product.

Sensitive Products: Each country may maintain a list of sensitive products that enjoy extended protection from the complete elimination of tariffs on intrabloc trade. These products will be protected for an additional four years in Argentina and Brazil and five years in Paraguay and Uruguay.

Macroeconomic Policy Coordination: MERCOSUR aims to harmonize fiscal, monetary, capital, and external trade policies in all sectors to guarantee adequate competitive conditions among member states. However, the reconciliation of pertinent laws in the individual member countries to make regulation compatible has so far not been a high priority issue in the various member countries. In fact, there are several substantial points of contention. An underlying problem has been the huge disparity in economic policy development among the members. Argentina, Uruguay, and Paraguay have achieved some stability through stabilisation programs that seek to curb inflation, achieve fiscal balances, and open their economies. Brazil has anti-inflation and privatisation programs that have been put in force more recently, and it maintains some export subsidies as well as tariff protections for key industries.

There are other gaps in coordination. As yet there has been no sign of any deal to coordinate member nation's policies regarding labour or the service industries, and social policies and programms differ vastly. Some steps have been taken toward coordinating the free movement of capital and the protection of foreign investment, but huge problems remain. Frontier bureaucracy has been one of MERCOSUR's leading practical enemies. At the twin-city interface of Uruguaiana (Brazil) and Paso de los Libres (Argentina), where 70 per cent of MERCOSUR trade crosses the border, trucks in transit used to spend 12 to 24 hours awaiting customs clearance-excluding weekends, holidays, and frequent customs strikes. Train crews also used to lose a day clearing cargos at the border. This situation was changed as of January 1995, and Customs officials have agreed to make timely clearance a priority.

More mundane problems plague MERCOSUR's evolution into a full common market: for example, Uruguay's electrical system operates at 50 hertz while Brazil's is at 60; and transport companies have complained that the customs agents in the different countries had not yet learned to cooperate among themselves. These and many other issues will have to be resolved before true common market status can be achieved.

Expansion: The MERCOSUR agreement provides that its membership base may be expanded and individual countries or other regional trading blocs allowed to join, after an initial period of five years and with the unanimous consent of the existing member states.

NORTH AMERICAN FREE TRADE AGREEMENT (NAFTA)

The North American Free Trade Agreement (NAFTA) is a regional agreement between the Government of Canada, the Government of the United Mexican States and the Government of the United States of America to implement a free trade area. The NAFTA was signed at:

- Ottawa, on the 11th day and the 17th day of December 1992,
- Mexico, D.F., on the 14th day and the 17th day of December 1992,
- Washington, D.C., on the 8th day and the 17th day of December 1992.

The North American Free Trade Agreement (NAFTA) between Canada, the United States and Mexico entered into force on January 1, 1994.

Article 102 of the NAFTA states that:

"the objectives of this Agreement, as elaborated more specifically through its principles and rules, including national treatment, most-favoured-nation treatment and transparency, are to:

- eliminate barriers to trade in, and facilitate the cross-border movement of goods and services between the territories of the Parties;
- promote conditions of fair competition in the free trade area;
- increase substantially investment opportunities in the territories of the Parties;
- provide adequate and effective protection and enforcement of intellectual property rights in each Party's territory;
- create effective procedures for the implementation and application of this Agreement, for its joint administration and for the resolution of disputes and
- establish a framework for further trilateral, regional and multilateral cooperation to expand and enhance the benefits of this Agreement."

The Parties endeavour to fully implement these objectives by 2008.

The NAFTA Secretariat is an independent agency that is responsible for the impartial administration of the dispute settlement provisions of the North American Free Trade Agreement. It has a Canadian, a Mexican, and a United States Section, each headed by a national Secretary, and with offices in each national capital. The Secretariat is accountable to the NAFTA Free Trade Commission, which comprises the ministers responsible for international trade in the three NAFTA partner countries.

The national Sections, which are "mirror-images" of each other, are each headed by a Secretary appointed by their respective government. The Parties are responsible for the costs of operating their national section of the Secretariat.

NAFTA was primarily established to gain comparative advantage against the enlarged European Union and to outpace the European Economic Area. NAFTA has a provision by which other countries can also be admitted as members of NAFTA. The main objective of NAFTA is to eliminate all trade and investment restrictions among the member countries over a period of 15 years. The duty free arrangements under the Agreement are likely to benefit the three countries immensely.

ORGANISATION OF AMERICAN STATES (OAS)

On April 30, 1948, 21 nations of the hemisphere met in Bogota, Colombia, to adopt the Charter of the Organisation of American States (OAS), which affirmed their commitment to common goals and respect for each nation's sovereignty. Since then, the OAS has expanded to include the nations of the Caribbean, as well as Canada.

The principles that embody the OAS grew out of a history of regional cooperation dating back to the 19th century. In 1826, Simón Bolívar convened the Congress of Panama with the idea of creating an association of states in the hemisphere. In 1890, the First International Conference of American States, held in Washington, D.C., established the International Union of American Republics and its secretariat, the Commercial Bureau of the American Republics—the forerunner of the OAS.

In 1910, this organisation became the Pan American Union. In 1948, at the Ninth International American Conference, participants signed the OAS Charter and the American Declaration of the Rights and Duties of Man, the first international expression of human rights principles.

The transition from the Pan American Union to the OAS was smooth. The Director General of the former became the first Secretary General of the OAS.

35 independent countries of the Americas have ratified the OAS Charter and belong to the Organisation. Cuba remains a member, but its government has been excluded from participation in the OAS since 1962.

The Organisation of American States (OAS) is playing a central role in working toward many of the goals that are shared by the countries of North, Central and South America and the Caribbean. Through the Summit of the Americas process, the hemisphere's heads of state and government have given the OAS important responsibilities and mandates, including:

- Strengthening freedom of speech and thought as a basic human right.
- Promoting greater participation by civil society in decision-making at all levels of government.
- Improving cooperation to address the problem of illegal drugs.
- Supporting the process to create a Free Trade Area of the Americas.
- The OAS also brings together government leaders from member states to focus on education, justice, security and other issues that touch people's lives in tangible ways.

In the 1990s the region left behind the divisions of the Cold War and moved toward greater agreement and closer cooperation. The OAS Charter was reformed to reflect the hemisphere's strengthened commitment to representative democracy. In recent years the Organisation has adopted landmark conventions against corruption, illegal arms trafficking and violence against women.

Priorities of OAS

- Strengthening democracy
- Building on peace
- Defending human rights
- Fostering free trade
- Combating drugs
- Promoting sustainable development

Made up of 35 member states, the OAS is the region's premier political forum for multilateral dialogue and action. With four official languages — English, Spanish, French and Portuguese — the Organisation reflects the rich diversity of peoples and cultures across the Americas.

Each member state has one vote. Major policies and directions are established by the **General Assembly**, which once a year brings together the hemisphere's foreign ministers. The **Permanent Council**, which meets regularly at OAS headquarters in Washington, handles ongoing political and administrative issues. Each member country appoints an ambassador to sit on the Permanent Council. The **Inter-American Council for Integral Development** focuses on promoting economic development and combating poverty.

The OAS **General Secretariat** carries out the programs and policies set by the General Assembly and the councils. **Specialized units** focus on such areas as trade, sustainable development, education and promotion of democracy. The **Office of Summit Follow-Up** was created to coordinate tasks assigned to the Organisation by the hemisphere's leaders.

At OAS headquarters, the Art Museum of the Americas and the Columbus Memorial Library promote culture and education.

Also under the OAS umbrella are several specialized organisations:

- the Inter-American Children's Institute;
- the Inter-American Commission of Women;
- the Pan American Institute of Geography and History;
- the Inter-American Indian Institute;

- the Inter-American Institute for Cooperation on Agriculture and
- the Pan American Health Organisation.

5.4: EUROPEAN REGIONAL ORGANISATIONS

COMMONWEALTH OF INDEPENDENT STATES (CIS)

CIS is a community of independent nations established by a treaty signed at Minsk, Belarus, on Dec. 8, 1991, by the heads of state of Russia, Belarus, and Ukraine. Between Dec. 8 and Dec. 21, the three original signatories were joined by Armenia, Azerbaijan (its parliament, however, rejected ratifying its membership until 1993), Kazakhstan, Kyrgyzstan, Moldova, Tajikistan, Turkmenistan, and Uzbekistan. When Georgia joined in 1993 all of the former republics of the USSR except the Baltic States had become members of the CIS. Its headquarters are in Minsk.

The organisation was conceived as the successor to the USSR in its role of coordinating the foreign and economic policies of its member nations. The treaty recognized current borders and each republic's independence, sovereignty, and equality, and established a free-market ruble zone embracing the republics' interdependent economies and a joint defense force for participating republics. Strategic nuclear weapons, in Belarus, Kazakhstan, Russia, and Ukraine, were to be under the joint control of those republics, with day-to-day authority in the hands of the Russian president and defense minister; Belarus, Kazakhstan, and Ukraine, however, no longer possess such weapons. The CIS at first convened only a council of the heads of state of its members, but in 1992 it convened a council of heads of government and a council of foreign ministers.

The republics' level of receptivity to integration with Russia has varied. All CIS nations now have their own currency, and most members have had occasion to criticize Russia for slow implementation of CIS agreements. Ukraine (which had a prolonged disagreement with Russia over the disposition of the Black Sea and remains wary of Russian power), Turkmenistan (whose large gas reserves free it from dependence on Russia), Azerbaijan (whose oil reserves also allow for independence from Russia), and Moldova (which faced an insurgency in the Russian-dominated Trans-Dniester region) have been relatively inactive in the alliance. Armenia (surrounded by the Muslim nations of Azerbaijan, Iran, and Turkey), Georgia (with a separatist movement in the region of Abkhazia), Tajikistan (torn by a persistent civil war), and Uzbekistan (vulnerable because of its limited natural resources) accepted Russia's protection under a joint defense system, although Georgia is seeking the ultimate removal of Russian forces from its soil. In 1995 the CIS established a joint air-defense system; not all CIS nations are members.

In 1996, Belarus signed a treaty with Russia to coordinate their defense and foreign policy apparatus and to eliminate trade restrictions and eventually unite their currencies. Individual sovereignty is to be maintained, but they created supranational bodies to effect these changes. The two nations have since signed several follow-up agreements, but actual progress toward integration has been slow. They, Kazakhstan (which has a large Russian community), and Kyrgyzstan additionally agreed to pursue economic integration without customs restrictions; an eventual customs union including additional CIS nations is planned.

THE COUNCIL FOR MUTUAL ECONOMIC ASSISTANCE (COMECON)

The founding of the Council for Mutual Economic Assistance (also referred to as Comecon, CMEA, CEMA, or the Council) dates from a 1949 communiquÈ agreed upon by the Soviet Union, Bulgaria, Czechoslovakia, Hungary, Poland, and Romania. The stated purpose of the organisation was to enable member states "to exchange economic experiences, extend technical aid to one another, and to render mutual assistancc with respect to raw materials, foodstuffs, machines, equipment, etc."

Until the late 1960s, cooperation was the official term used to describe COMECON activities. In 1971, with the development and adoption of the Comprehensive Program for the Further Extension and Improvement of Cooperation and the Further Development of Socialist Economic Integration by COMECON Member Countries, COMECON activities were officially termed integration. In simplest terms, economic integration is defined as internationalizing the production of manufactured and semi-manufactured goods, resources, and services. More specifically, integration attempts to equalize "differences in relative scarcities of goods and services between states through the deliberate elimination of barriers to trade and other forms of interaction." Although such equalisation has not been a pivotal point in the formation and implementation of COMECON's economic policies, improved economic integration has always been COMECON's goal.

The primary documents governing the objectives, organisation, and functions of Comecon are the Charter of the Council for Mutual Economic Assistance (first adopted in 1959 and subsequently amended; all references herein are to the amended 1974 text); the Comprehensive Program for the Further Extension and Improvement of Cooperation and the Further Development of Socialist Economic Integration by the Comecon Member Countries, adopted in 1971; and the Comprehensive Program for Scientific and Technical Progress up to the Year 2000, adopted in December 1985. The 1985 Comprehensive Program for Scientific and Technical Progress and the rise to power of Soviet general secretary Mikhail S. Gorbachev increased Soviet influence in COMECON operations and have led to attempts to give COMECON some degree of supranational authority. The Comprehensive Program for Scientific and Technical Progress seeks to improve economic cooperation through the development of a more efficient and interconnected scientific and technical base.

Membership

In a January 1949 meeting in Moscow, representatives of Bulgaria, Czechoslovakia, Hungary, Poland, Romania, and the Soviet Union reached the formal decision to establish the Council for Mutual Economic Assistance. The communiquÈ announcing the event cited the refusal of these countries to "subordinate themselves to the dictates of the Marshall Plan" and their intention to resist the trade boycott imposed by "the United States, Britain and certain other countries of Western Europe" as the major factors contributing to the decision "to organize a more broadly based economic cooperation among the countries of the people's democracy and the USSR."

Albania joined the six original members in February 1949, and East Germany entered COMECON in 1950. (Albania, although it had not formally revoked its membership as of mid-1987, stopped participating in COMECON activities in 1961.) Mongolia acceded to membership in 1962, and in the 1970s COMECON expanded its membership to include Cuba (1972) and Vietnam (1978). As of 1987 there were ten full members: the Soviet Union, six East European countries, and three extraregional members

Official statements stress, however, that COMECON is an open international organisation. Its Charter (Article II, Paragraph 2) invites membership from "other countries which share the aims and principles of the Council and have expressed their willingness to assume the obligations contained in the . . . Charter." In the late 1950s, a number of other communist-ruled countries—China, the Democratic People's Republic of Korea (North Korea), Mongolia, Vietnam, and Yugoslavia—were invited to participate as observers in COMECON sessions. Although Mongolia and Vietnam later gained full membership, China stopped attending COMECON sessions after 1961. Yugoslavia negotiated a form of associate status in the organisation, specified in its 1964 agreement with COMECON.

Structure

Although not formally part of the organisation's hierarchy, the Conference of First Secretaries of Communist and Workers' Parties and of the Heads of Government of the COMECON Member Countries is COMECON'S most important organ. These party and government leaders gather for conference meetings regularly to discuss topics of mutual interest. Because of the rank of conference participants, decisions made here have considerable influence on the actions taken by COMECON and its organs.

The official hierarchy of COMECON consists of the Session of the Council for Mutual Economic Assistance, the Executive Committee of the Council, the Secretariat of the Council, four council committees, twenty-four standing commissions, six interstate conferences, two scientific institutes, and several associated organisations.

The Session, officially the highest COMECON organ, examines fundamental problems of socialist economic integration and directs the activities of the Secretariat and other subordinate organisations. Delegations from each COMECON member country attend these meetings. Prime ministers usually head the delegations, which meet during the second quarter of each year in a member country's capital (the location of the meeting is determined by a system of rotation based on the Cyrillic alphabet). All interested parties must consider recommendations handed down by the Session. A treaty or other kind of legal agreement implements adopted recommendations. Comecon itself may adopt decisions only on organisational and procedural matters pertaining to itself and its organs.

Each country appoints one permanent representative to maintain relations between members and COMECON between annual meetings. An extraordinary Session, such as the one in December 1985, may be held with the consent of at least one-third of the members. Such meetings usually take place in Moscow.

The highest executive organ in COMECON, the Executive Committee, is entrusted with elaborating policy recommendations and supervising their implementation between sessions. In addition, it supervises work on plan coordination and scientific- technical cooperation. Composed of one representative from each member country, usually a deputy chairman of the Council of Ministers, the Executive Committee meets quarterly, usually in Moscow. In 1971 and 1974, the Executive Committee acquired economic departments that rank above the standing commissions. These economic departments considerably strengthened the authority and importance of the Executive Committee.

There are four council committees: Council Committee for Cooperation in Planning, Council Committee for Scientific and Technical Cooperation, Council Committee for Cooperation in Material and Technical Supply, and Council Committee for Cooperation in Machine Building. Their mission is "to ensure the comprehensive examination and a multilateral settlement of the major problems of cooperation among member countries in the economy, science, and technology."

All committees are headquartered in Moscow and usually meet there. These committees advise the standing commissions, the Secretariat, the interstate conferences, and the scientific institutes in their areas of specialisation. Their jurisdiction is generally wider than that of the standing commissions because they have the right to make policy recommendations to other Comecon organisations.

The Council Committee for Cooperation in Planning is the most important of the four. It coordinates the national economic plans of COMECON members. As such, it ranks in importance only after the Session and the Executive Committee. Made up of the chairman of Comecon members' national central planning offices, the Council Committee for Cooperation in Planning draws up draft agreements for joint projects, adopts a resolution approving these projects, and recommends approval to the concerned parties. If its decisions were not subject to approval by national governments and parties, this committee would be considered Comecon's supranational planning body.

The international Secretariat, COMECON's only permanent body, is COMECON's primary economic research and administrative organ. The secretary, who has been a Soviet official since COMECON creation, is the official COMECON representative to COMECON member states and to other states and international organisations. Subordinate to the secretary are his deputy and the various departments of the Secretariat, which generally correspond to the standing commissions. The Secretariat's responsibilities include preparation and organisation of COMECON sessions and other meetings conducted under the auspices of COMECON; compilation of digests on COMECON activities; conduct of economic and other research for COMECON members; and preparation of recommendations on various issues concerning COMECON operations.

The commissions have been rearranged and renamed a number of times since the establishment of the first eight. In 1986 there were twenty-four standing commissions.

Each commission is headquartered in the capital of a member country and headed by one of that country's leading authorities in the field addressed by the commission. The Secretariat supervises the actual operations of the commissions. The standing commissions have authority only to make recommendations, which must then be approved by the Executive Committee, presented to the Session, and ratified by the interested member countries. Commissions usually meet twice a year in Moscow.

The six interstate conferences (on water management, internal trade, legal matters, inventions and patents, pricing, and labor affairs) serve as forums for discussing shared issues and experiences. They are purely consultative and generally act in an advisory capacity to the Executive Committee or its specialized committees.

The scientific institutes on standardisation and on economic problems of the world socialist system concern themselves with theoretical problems of international cooperation. Both are headquartered in Moscow and are staffed by experts from various member countries.

Several affiliated agencies, having a variety of relationships with COMECON, exist outside the official COMECON hierarchy. They serve to develop "direct links between appropriate bodies and organisations of COMECON member countries." These affiliated agencies are divided into two categories: intergovernmental economic organisations (which work on a higher level in the member countries and generally deal with a wider range of managerial and coordinative activities) and international economic organisations (which work closer to the operational level of research, production, or trade). A few examples of the former are the International Bank for Economic Cooperation (manages the transferable ruble system), the International Investment Bank (in charge of financing joint projects), and Intermetal (encourages cooperation in ferrous metallurgy). International economic organisations generally take the form of either joint enterprises, international economic associations or unions, or international economic partnerships. The latter includes Interatominstrument (nuclear machinery producers), Intertekstilmash (textile machinery producers), and Haldex (a Hungarian-Polish joint enterprise for reprocessing coal slag).

Nature of Operation

COMECON is an interstate organisation through which members attempt to coordinate economic activities of mutual interest and to develop multilateral economic, scientific, and technical cooperation. The Charter states that "the sovereign equality of all members" is fundamental to the organisation and procedures of COMECON. The Comprehensive Program further emphasizes that the processes of integration of members' economies are "completely voluntary and do not involve the creation of supranational bodies." Hence under the provisions of the Charter, each country has the right to equal representation and one vote in all organs of COMECON, regardless of the country's economic size or the size of its contribution to COMECON's budget.

The "interestedness" provisions of the Charter reinforce the principle of "sovereign equality." COMECON's recommendations and decisions can be adopted only upon agreement among the interested members, and each has the right to declare its "interest" in any matter under consideration. Furthermore, in the words of the Charter, "recommendations and decisions shall not apply to countries that have declared that they have no interest in a particular matter."

Although COMECON recognizes the principle of unanimity, disinterested parties do not have a veto but rather the right to abstain from participation. A declaration of disinterest cannot block a project unless the disinterested party's participation is vital. Otherwise, the Charter implies that the interested parties may proceed without the abstaining member, affirming that a country that has declared a lack of interest "may subsequently adhere to the recommendations and decisions adopted by the remaining members of the Council."

The descriptive term COMECON applies to all multilateral activities involving members of the organisation and is not restricted to the direct functions of COMECON and its organs. This usage may be extended as well to bilateral relations among members, because in the system of socialist international economic relations, multilateral accords—typically of a general nature—tend to be implemented through a set of more detailed, bilateral agreements.

COMECON joins together 450 million people in 10 countries and on 3 continents. The level of industrialisation from country to country differs greatly: the organisation links three underdeveloped countries—Cuba, Mongolia, and Vietnam—with some highly industrialized states. Likewise, a large national income difference exists between European and non-European members. The physical size, military power, and political and economic resource base of the Soviet Union make it the dominant member. In trade among COMECON members, the Soviet Union usually provides raw materials, and East European countries provide finished equipment and machinery. The three underdeveloped COMECON members have a special relationship with the other seven. COMECON realizes disproportionately more political than economic gains from its heavy contributions to these three countries' underdeveloped economies.

Socialist economic integration or "plan coordination" forms the basis of COMECON's activities. In this system, which mirrors the member countries' planned economies, the decisions handed down from above ignore the influences of market forces or private initiative. COMECON has no supranational authority to make decisions or to implement them. Its recommendations can only be adopted with the full concurrence of interested parties and do not affect those members who declare themselves disinterested parties.

COUNCIL OF EUROPE

Council of Europe was founded in 1949 to promote greater unity within Europe and to safeguard its political and cultural heritage by promoting human rights and democracy. The council is headquartered in Strasbourg, France. The conventions and treaties signed under the auspices of the Council of Europe deal with humanitarian, cultural, economic, and social problems. In 1959 the council established a European Court of Human Rights to protect the rights of individuals in member nations against arbitrary government action. The court has heard cases involving corporal punishment; the protection of minorities, immigrants, suspects, prisoners, and the mentally ill; and the infringement of rights of speech, the press, religion, privacy, and sexuality. Member countries have been censured and risk expulsion if they fail to abide by the rulings. Britain (one of the founders) has, for instance, been upbraided for actions involving the IRA and the jailing of minors, and British representatives have bridled at the court's intervention in Britain's justice system. In the years after the dissolution of the Soviet Union and the end of dictatorial Communist rule in Eastern Europe, most Eastern European nations joined the council, bringing the membership total to 45. Only Belarus, Monaco, and Vatican City are not members.

EUROPEAN COAL AND STEEL COMPANY (ECSC)

European Coal and Steel Community (ECSC) is the first treaty organisation of what has become the European Union; It was established by the Treaty of Paris (1952). It is also known as the Schuman Plan, after the French foreign minister, Robert Schuman, who proposed it in 1950. Member nations of ECSC pledged to pool their coal and steel resources by providing a unified market for their coal and steel products, lifting restrictions on imports and exports, and creating a unified labor market. Economically, the Coal and Steel Community achieved early success; between 1952 and 1960 iron and steel production rose by 75% in the ECSC nations, and industrial production rose 58%. When overproduction of coal became a problem after 1959, especially in Belgium, the ECSC demonstrated its flexibility by reducing Belgium's coal-producing capacity by 30% and by making available large sums of money to aid in retraining miners and developing new industries. The ECSC had, by 1970, granted about $150 million in aid to retrain over 400,000 coal miners. The executive machinery of the ECSC provided an important precedent for the future growth of a united Europe: the nine-member High Authority, which became a part of the European Commission in 1967, was chosen by the member governments and made independent of those governments. Its independence was guaranteed by providing the authority with its own source of income.

EUROPEAN ATOMIC ENERGY COMMUNITY (EURATOM)

European Atomic Energy Community (EURATOM or EAEC) is the economic organisation that came into being as the third treaty organisation of what has become the European

Union; established by the Treaty of Rome (1958). The members pledged themselves to the common development of Europe's nuclear energy resources by coordinating their nuclear research and development programs and by permitting the free movement of nuclear raw materials, equipment, investment capital, and specialists within the community. EURATOM is vested with wide powers, including the right to conclude contracts, obtain raw materials, and establish standards to protect workers and the general population against the dangers of radiation. It is administered by the European Commission, which is advised by the Scientific and Technical Committee and the Economic and Social Committee. It merged with European Community in 1967.

EUROPEAN UNION (EU)

The European Union is the largest and is frequently cited as the most successful regional economic integration scheme in the world. Its success in terms of institutional survival and growth both widening and deepening are indeed impressive, and it is also true that the period of its existence has witnessed very significant economic advances.

The European Union (EU) is a family of democratic European Countries, committed to working together for peace and prosperity. It is not a state intended to replace existing states. The EU is infact, unique. Its member states have set up common institutions to which they delegate some of their sovereignty so that decisions on specific matters of joint interest can be made democratically at European level.

The EU is the result of a process of deep regional cooperation and integration that began in 1951 among Benalux Countries (Belgium, Netherlands and Luxembourg) and grew to include Germany, France and Italy. In 1952, Treaty of Paris was signed establishing the European Coal and Steel Community (ECSC).

The ECSC was such a success that, within a few years, their same countries decided to go further and integrate other sectors of their economies. In 1957, these same countries signed the Treaty of Rome which established the European Atomic Energy Community (EURATOM) and the European Economic Community (ECC). A preamble to this treaty defined the ultimate purpose of the great European enterprise as 'ever closer union among the peoples by Europe'. The member states set about removing trade barriers between them and forming a "common market".

In 1967, the institutions of the three European communities were merged. From this point on, there was a single Commission and a single Council of Ministers as well as the European Parliament. All the above three bodies collectively came to be known as European Community. Amendments were carried out to the earlier treaties by the Single European Act of Luxembourg in 1985.

The collapse of the Soviet Union and the reunification of Germany in 1989 presented European leaders with provable challenges. They realised that the opportunities offered by the end of the cold war reinforced the need for further integration in the Western half of the continent. As a result of these development, Maastricht Treaty was signed in 1992. It introduced new forms of cooperation between the member state governments and led to the creation of European Union. The treaty was intended to be their response to the seismic developments in the continent. The most eye catching decision was the abandonment of the name 'Community' in favour of 'Union'.

During these 50 years of political, economic and social cooperation, the EU expanded to include 15 members (Austria, Belgium, Denmark, Finland, France, Germany, Greece, Ireland, Italy, Luxembourg, Netherlands, Portugal, Spain, Sweeden, United Kingdom). EU has grown in size with successive waves of accessions. Initially EU consisted of just six countries, Ireland and the United Kingdom joined in 1973 followed by Greece in 1981, Spain and Portugal in 1986 and Austria, Finland and Sweeden in 1995. The EU has further added 10 countries (Cypress, The Czech Republic, Estonia, Hungary, Latvia, Luthuania, Malta, Poland, Slovakia and Slovania) in Eastern and Southern Europe as its member. These countries have joined the EU in May 2004. Bulgaria, Romania and Turkey are expected to follow a few years later. To ensure that the EU can continue functioning efficiently with 25 or more members, its decision making system must be streamlined The treaty of Nice (December 2000) was a response to this enlargement. It lays down new rules governing the size of the EU institutions and the way they work. It came into force on February 1, 2003.

In 1992, the EU decided to go for Economic and Monetary Union (EMU), involving the introduction of a single European currency managed by European Central Bank. The single currency—the euro—became a reality on January 1, 2002, when euro notes and coins replaced national currencies in twelve[1] of the 15 countries of the EU. Having a single currency makes it easier to travel and to compare prices, and it provides a stable environment for European business stimulating Growth and competitiveness. EU single market, unified by a single currency, brings with it reduced trade barriers, reduced risk and a more competitive market environment.

After 50 years of integration, Europe is working on a Constitution. The European Union needs simpler treaty—a constitution clearly setting out the EU's aims and values, and saying who is responsible for doing what. To draft this document, a convention was set up in 2002, bringing together representatives of all the member states and candidate countries as well as the EU institutions. The convention will lead to an Inter-Governmental Conference, at which the leaders of the governments of the EU countries will sign the new Treaty.

The European Union's mission is to organise relations between the Members States and between their peoples in a coherent manner and on the basis of solidarity.

The main objectives are:

- To promote economic and social progress;
- To assert the identity of the European Union on the international scene;
- To introduce European citizenship;
- To develop an area of freedom, security and justice;
- To maintain and build on established EU law.

The European Union is built on an institutional set up which is the only one of its kind in the world. The Member States delegate sovereignty for certain matters to independent

1. U.K., Denmark and Sweedon have not yet adopted Euro.

institutions which represent the interests of the Union as a whole, its member countries and its citizens. The Commission traditionally upholds the interests of the union as a whole, while each national government is represented within the Council, and the European Parliament is directly elected by citizens. Democracy and the rule of law are therefore the cornerstones of the structure.

This "institutional triangle" of Commission, Council and Parliament is flanked by two more institutions—the Court of Justice and the Court of Auditors—and five other European bodies. In addition, thirteen specialised agencies have been set up to handle certain essentially technical, scientific or management tasks.

There are five EU institutions, each playing a specific role:

- European Parliament (elected by the peoples of the member states);
- Council of European Union (Representing the govts of the Members states);
- European Commission (driving force and executive body);
- Court of Justice (ensuring competence with the law);
- Court of Auditors (controlling sound and lawful management of the EU budget).

These are flanked by five other important bodies:

- European Economic and social committee (expresses the opinions of organized civil society on economic & social issues);
- European Central Bank (responsible for monetary policy and managing the euro);
- European Ombudsman (deals with citizens complaints about mal-administration by any EU institution or body);
- European Investment Banks (helps achieve EU objectives by financing investment projects);

A number of agencies and other bodies complete the system.

Priorities of EU

Freedom, security and justice. European countries are making a joint effort to tackle these problems. They include international terrorism, drug trafficking and abuse, trafficking in human beings and the illegal exploitation of foreign women for prostitution by adopting common rules and through co-operation between their police, customs and law courts. The EU also plays a role in asylum and migration policy. It guarantees respect for the right to seek asylum. At the same time, the EU countries are co-ordinating their policies for refugees and trying to tackle the problem at source by combating poverty and preventing conflict in the countries from which people might want to flee.

Keeping the peace. The EU is the biggest donor of financial assistance to troubled places in the world. It is active in peace keeping and peace making actions and it runs many projects that help to make human rights and democracy succeed in practical terms. The EU is now increasingly involved in preserving peace and creating stability in neighbouring countries. To enable its member states to speak and act in unison on the world stage, the EU is developing its Common Foreign and Security Policy and there are plans for more co-operation on defence questions.

Free mobility. EU provides for freedom of movement, in all the European Union Countries for EU citizens. The EU is working constantly to give its citizens greater freedom of movement as a fundamental right and to get rid of all discrimination based on nationality. In most of the EU you can travel without carrying a passport and without being stopped for checks at the borders. With very few exceptions, you may buy anything you want anywhere you want and take it all back home with you.

Fewer Frontiers: More jobs. Safeguarding employment in Europe and creating new jobs is one of the European Union's key tasks. By creating a frontier—free single market and a single currency, the euro, the EU has already given a significant boost to trade and employment in Europe. It has an agreed strategy for stimulating growth and generating more and better jobs. Tomorrow's jobs will be created through research, training and education, a spirit of entrepreneurship adaptability to new working methods and equal opportunities for everybody. One-third of the entire EU budget is taken up by the structural funds which promote growth and jobs in less well—off regions, in order to ensure that wealth in Europe is more evenly distributed.

Technological development. The EU is increasingly active in helping European research to achieve scientific excellence. In a variety of sectors covering the whole spectrum of modern technology, the EU finances projects undertaken by research centres, universities and industries. The emphasis is on putting research and innovation to work for precise socio-economic objectives, such as job creation and improved quality of life. The EU's research priorities include nano technology, life sciences, the space, food quality, sustainable development and the knowledge—based society.

Environmental Protection. The EU has a special role to play in environmental protection. Many environmental problems in Europe could not be tackled without joint action by all EU countries. The EU has adopted over 200 environmental protection directive that are applied in all member states. Most of the directives are designed to prevent air and water pollution and encourage waste disposal. Other major issues include nature conservation and the supervision of dangerous industrial processes. The main emphasis of EU is on sustainable development.

The Common Foreign and Security Policy. Global and regional crises and challenges, coupled with developments within the EU, have made new demands on the regions external activities. As a result, in 1993 the EU laid the groundwork for a common Foreign and Security Policy (CFSP), further building upon Europe's solidarity. A common Security and Defence policy has been added to the CFSP framework. Its objective are: preserving peace and strengthening international security in accordance with the principles of the UN charter, promoting international co-operation and developing democracy and the rule of law, as well as respect for human rights and fundamental freedoms.

NORDIC COUNCIL

The Nordic countries have many things in common: democracy, strong civil societies, respect for individual freedoms, protection of nature and the environment, taking care of the less-fortunate, equality. Mobility between the Nordic countries and unofficial interaction has been part of everyday reality for centuries. To facilitate official cooperation between them the Nordic countries have created two organisations: the Nordic Council for inter-parliamentary cooperation, and the Nordic Council of Ministers for inter-governmental cooperation.

Cooperation within the frameworks of the two councils has a close bearing on everyday practicalities. Its goal from the outset has been to make it easier for individuals, companies, goods and capital to move between the Nordic countries. Tangible obstacles to movement have been reduced by introducing passport-free travel, abolishing border formalities, and cross-border cooperation. To promote mobility, a range of scholarship and exchange programmes have been set up. Social welfare and educational systems have been closely aligned with the aim of lowering barriers to people moving from one Nordic country to another. In order to pursue its goals the Nordic Council can give recommendations to Nordic governments and the Council of Ministers.

The two councils deal with a great variety of matters. Cooperation in the fields of culture, education and research has always been important. More recently, consumer affairs, environmental cooperation as well as cooperation with neighbouring countries and regions have also assumed a prominent role. Since the 1990s, the Nordic countries' relations with the three Baltic States, Russia, the countries of the Baltic Sea Region and international organisations in adjacent geographical areas have become increasingly closer.

International cooperation has the goal of ensuring stability throughout the region: avoiding environmental catastrophes, maritime safety and preventing the spread of crime and infectious diseases. In addition, an important goal in especially the Baltic Sea Region is to open up energy markets and safeguard energy distribution in crisis situations. The Nordic countries are pioneers in having succeeded in creating the world's most open international energy market.

Treaties and Rules of Procedure

Cooperation between the Nordic countries is based on several agreements concluded in the course of the decades. The most important of these is the 1962 Helsinki Treaty, in which the goals and organisation are broadly defined. The Treaty has subsequently been amended on several occasions, such as in 1971 when the Nordic Council of Ministers was established. The best-known of the other treaties between the countries relate to the passport union (1954), social security (1955) and the common labour market (1954).

The work of the Nordic Council is regulated by the Rules of Procedure, the most recent version of which entered into force in October 2001.

Members

The members of the Nordic Council are the sovereign states of Denmark, Finland, Iceland, Norway and Sweden as well as the autonomous territories of Åland, the Faeroe Islands and Greenland. Countries are represented on the Council by legislators which their parliaments and those of the autonomous regions have chosen from among the own numbers. The 87 members of the Council represent: Denmark (incl. the Faeroe islands and Greenland) 20, Finland (incl. Åland) 20, Iceland 7, Norway 20, and Sweden 20. The Governments appoint the delegates who represent them at sessions of the Council. The representatives from each country form a national delegation, which has a secretariat in its own parliament.

Finnish Delegation

The Nordic Council has 18 Finnish delegates that represent the Eduskunta and 2 that are chosen by the Åland Lagting. The members of the delegation participate in the work of the Council all year round through committees and in the presidium. In addition, each national delegation holds a meeting of its own about once a month. The secretariat of the Finnish delegation works within the International Unit at the Eduskunta.

Sessions and Meetings

The Nordic Council's most important decision-making body is the Ordinary Annual Session, which takes place in autumn. Extraordinary sessions can also be arranged, such as the one held in Kungälv, Sweden in 2001 to deliberate a strategy for sustainable development in the Nordic region. The Annual Session is where parliamentarians meet government representatives. The politicians discuss topical themes and decide on proposals. The Nordic Council of Ministers reports on what it has done to implement recommendations made earlier by the Council or parliamentarians. In recent years, also the foreign and defence ministers have made their own reports. The Annual Sessions are unique, because at them parliamentarians have direct contact with not only their own government, but also those of the other Nordic countries. In recent years it has become customary to arrange, in addition to the Ordinary Annual Session, a limited number of special sessions devoted to particular themes. The theme chosen for the one in Reykjavik in April 2002 was Nordic democracy. The choice was in honour of the 50th anniversary of the Nordic Council.

Committees and Presidium

In the intervals between Ordinary Annual Sessions, the members of the Nordic Council meet in committees and the presidium. The five committees are: Culture and Education and Training, Citizens' and Consumer Rights, Environment and Natural Resources, Welfare, and Business and Industry.

The Presidium meets regularly and conducts the work of the Nordic Council between sessions. Questions of foreign and security policy as well as the Nordic Council's external relations are among its areas of responsibility. The Chair rotates on an annual basis.

International Relations

Since the 1990s, the Nordic Council and the Nordic Council of Ministers have been developing their relations with the countries of the so-called Adjacent Areas and organisations in them. Cooperation with the Baltic States and North-West Russia gained momentum when information offices were opened in the Estonian, Latvian and Lithuanian capitals as well as in St. Petersburg. Several branch offices have since been opened and there are plans to open the next office in Kaliningrad.

Since 1992 the Nordic Council has been cooperating with the Baltic Assembly through, for example, biennial joint sessions with this inter-parliamentary body and in joint committees. The Nordic Council of Ministers' cooperation partner is the Baltic Council. When the individual Baltic countries' bilateral cooperation with Estonia, Latvia and Lithuania is added to this, the scope and diversity of matters dealt with is truly broad.

When the Baltic States join the EU, the focus of the Nordic countries' Adjacent Areas cooperation will shift to Russia, and especially its north-western regions. In the work of the two councils, this is already reflected in lively contacts with Russian administrators and politicians. For example, the Nordic Council has regular meetings with representatives of the Duma, the Federal Council, the Parliamentary Assembly of the CIS and the St. Petersburg and Leningrad Oblast governments. Russian observers have likewise attended sessions of the Nordic Council.

Arctic regions have also been traditionally seen as belonging to the sphere of the Nordic countries' Adjacent Areas cooperation. The Nordic countries have had a separate Arctic cooperation programme since 2001. In 2000 the Nordic Council of Ministers obtained observer status in the Arctic Council, the permanent members of which are the Nordic countries, Canada, Russia and the USA. The Nordic Council participates as an observer in the work of the Committee of Parliamentarians of the Arctic Region.

The Baltic Sea is a major frame of reference for the Nordic countries. Inter-parliamentary cooperation in the region began in 1991, and the Nordic Council has had a central role in its development. In addition to members nominated by the Nordic Council and the Baltic Assembly, the organisation's permanent committee contains representatives of Germany, Poland and Russia. Inter-governmental work is done within the framework of the Council of Baltic Sea States. The central areas of cooperation are the environment, energy, maritime safety and combating infectious diseases and drugs.

In the European Union's Northern Dimension programme, both the individual Nordic countries and the Nordic Council and Nordic Council of Ministers have a central role. This includes implementing and financing in their own Adjacent Areas cooperation concrete projects that relate to Northern Dimension policy. The Nordic Investment Bank (NIB) is the biggest single financier of the South West Wastewater Treatment Plant in St. Petersburg. It also contributes a considerable share of the funding for Adjacent Areas cooperation and was the initiator of the Northern Dimension Environmental Partnership (NDEP).

The Nordic members of the European Union cooperate in many matters and EU affairs are regularly discussed at Nordic ministerial and other conferences. For Iceland and Norway, which are not EU members, but part of the European Economic Area (EEA), Nordic conferences provide an opportunity to obtain first-hand information about the Union.

In addition to those mentioned above, the cooperation partners of the two councils include the West Nordic Council, Sami organisations, the Benelux Parliament, the Parliamentary Assembly of the Council of Europe, and the European Parliament.

Secretariats

The secretariat of the Nordic Council shares premises with the secretariat of the Nordic Council of Ministers in Copenhagen. Each national delegation has its own secretariat. The Finnish secretariat works within the Eduskunta's International Unit.

The Nordic Council of Ministers

The names "Council" and "Council of Ministers" often cause confusion. The Nordic Council is a forum where parliamentarians and government representatives meet. By contrast, the Nordic Council of Ministers is a vehicle for co-operation between the governments of the Nordic countries. It was created through an amendment of the Helsinki Treaty in 1971, 19 years after the establishment of the Nordic Council. The designation Council of Ministers is actually misleading, because in practice the ministers meet in as many as 19 different compositions, depending on the matters under deliberation. Its work is coordinated by the Nordic cooperation ministers, but the ultimate responsibility resides with the countries' prime ministers, who work outside the actual structure of the Council of Ministers.

The range of matters deliberated by the Council of Ministers is as broad as in the case of the Nordic Council: from consumer policy to culture. The Council of Ministers gives reports about its actions and plans to the Nordic Council, which in turn issues recommendations to guide the work of the Council of Ministers.

Outside the framework of the Council of Ministers proper, the Nordic prime ministers and their cabinet colleagues responsible for foreign affairs, foreign trade, defence and development cooperation meet on a regular basis. The presidency of the Nordic Council of Ministers rotates annually.

THE ORGANISATION FOR SECURITY AND COOPERATION IN EUROPE (OSCE)

The Organisation for Security and Cooperation in Europe (OSCE) had its origin in the early 1950s when the Soviet Union first proposed the creation of an all-European security conference. In the mid-1960s the Warsaw Pact renewed calls for such a conference. In May 1969, the Government of Finland sent a memorandum to all European countries, the United States and Canada, offering Helsinki as a conference venue. Beginning in November 1972, representatives from the original 35 nations met for nearly three years to work out the arrangements and the framework for the conference, concluding their work in July 1975.

On August 1, 1975, the leaders of the original 35 participating States gathered in Helsinki and signed the Final Act of the Conference on Security and Cooperation in Europe. Also known as the Helsinki Accords, the Final Act is not a treaty, but rather a politically binding agreement consisting of three main sections informally known as "baskets," adopted on the basis of consensus. This comprehensive Act contains a broad range of measures designed to enhance security and cooperation in the region extending from Vancouver to Vladivostok.

Basket I contains a Declaration of Principles Guiding Relations between participating States, including the all-important Principle VII on human rights and fundamental freedoms. It also includes a section on confidence-building measures and other aspects of security and disarmament aimed at increasing military transparency.

Basket II covers economic, scientific, technological and environmental cooperation, as well as migrant labor, vocational training and the promotion of tourism.

Basket III is devoted to cooperation in humanitarian and other fields: freer movement of people; human contacts, including family reunification and visits; freedom of information, including working conditions for journalists; and cultural and educational exchanges. Principle VII and Basket III together have come to be known as "The Human Dimension."

Since 1975, the number of countries signing the Helsinki Accords has expanded to 55, reflecting changes such as the breakup of the Soviet Union, Czechoslovakia and Yugoslavia.

Institutionalisation of the Conference in the early 1990s led to its transformation to the Organisation for Security and Cooperation in Europe, effective January 1995.

The Commission on Security and Cooperation in Europe, also known as the Helsinki Commission, is an independent U.S. Government agency created in 1976 to monitor and encourage compliance with the Helsinki Final Act and other OSCE commitments.

The Commission consists of nine members from the United States Senate, nine members from the U.S. House of Representatives, and one member each from the Departments of State, Defense, and Commerce. The positions of Chair and Co-Chair are shared by the House and Senate and rotate every two years, when a new Congress convenes. A professional staff assists the Commissioners in their work.

The Commission contributes to the formulation of U.S. policy on the OSCE and takes part in its execution, including through Member and staff participation on U.S. Delegations to OSCE meetings and in certain OSCE bodies. Members of the Commission have regular contact with parliamentarians, government officials, NGOs, and private individuals from other OSCE participating States.

The Commission convenes public hearings and briefings with expert witnesses on OSCE-related issues; issues public reports concerning implementation of OSCE commitments in participating States; publishes a monthly Digest with up-to-date information on OSCE developments and Commission activities; and organizes official delegations to participating States and OSCE meetings to address and assess democratic, economic, and human rights developments firsthand.

The Organisation for Security and Cooperation in Europe (OSCE) is engaged in standard setting in fields including military security, economic and environmental cooperation, and human rights and humanitarian concerns. In addition, the OSCE undertakes a variety of preventive diplomacy initiatives designed to prevent, manage and resolve conflict within and among the participating States.

The OSCE has its main office in Vienna, Austria, where weekly meetings of the Permanent Council are held. In addition, specialized seminars and meetings are convened in various locations and periodic consultations among Senior Officials, Ministers and Heads of State or Government are held.

Principles Guiding Relations Between Participating States

- Sovereign equality, respect for the rights inherent in sovereignty;
- Refraining from threat or use of force;
- Inviolability of frontiers;
- Territorial integrity of States;
- Peaceful settlement of disputes;
- Non-intervention in internal affairs;
- Respect for human rights and fundamental freedoms, including the freedom of thought, conscience, religion or belief;
- Equal rights and self-determination of peoples;
- Co-operation among States;
- Fulfilment in good faith of obligations under international law.

The OSCE provides a forum for consultation and negotiation among the participating States. The OSCE decision-making bodies are:

- The Permanent Council—the main regular decision-making body of the Organisation, convenes weekly in Vienna to discuss current developments in the OSCE area and to make appropriate decisions.
- The Forum for Security Co-operation—meets weekly in Vienna to discuss and make decisions regarding military aspects of security in the OSCE area, in particular confidence- and security-building measures.
- The Senior Council/Economic Forum—convenes once a year in Prague to focus on economic and environmental factors that affect security in the OSCE area.
- Summits—OSCE Heads of State or Government meet periodically to set priorities and provide orientation at the highest political level. Each Summit is preceded by a review conference, where the implementation of OSCE commitments is reviewed and Summit documents are negotiated.
- Ministerial Council—a meeting of OSCE Foreign Ministers is convened in those years when no Summit takes place to review OSCE activities and to make appropriate decisions.

Structures and Institutions

The Organisation has developed several structures and institutions to follow-up on the political decisions negotiated by the participating States:

- Chairman-in-Office—The Minister of Foreign Affairs of an OSCE participating State, selected each year, bears overall responsibility for executive action and co-ordination of OSCE activities. He/she is assisted by the Ministerial Troika, supported by the Secretary General.
- Parliamentary Assembly—gathers over 300 parliamentarians from OSCE participating States, with the aim of

promoting parliamentary involvement in the activities of the Organisation.

- Secretariat—under the direction of the Secretary General, provides operational support to the Organisation. The Secretariat's mandate involves: support of OSCE field activities; maintaining contacts with international and non-governmental organisations; co-ordinating OSCE economic and environmental activities; OSCE activities in the politico-military field; administrative, financial and personnel services; conference and language services; information technology and press and public information.
- Office for Democratic Institutions and Human Rights—is the principal institution responsible for the promotion of human rights and democracy in the OSCE area.
- High Commissioner on National Minorities—seeks early resolution of ethnic tensions that might endanger peace, stability or friendly relations between OSCE participating States.
- Representative on Freedom of the Media—observes media development in OSCE participating States and provides early warning on violations of freedom of expression.
- Court of Conciliation and Arbitration—created to settle disputes among OSCE participating States that are parties to the Convention on Conciliation and Arbitration within the OSCE.
- Arms Control and Confidence and Security-Building Measures—the OSCE Chairman-in-Office has appointed Personal Representatives for the implementation of Articles II, IV and V of Annex 1-B of the Dayton Peace Accords.

Dayton Peace Accord is a General Framework Agreement for Peace in Bosnia and Herzegornia signed in December 1995. It was signed recognising the need for a comprehensive settlement to bring an end to the tragic conflict in the region and for promoting enduring peace and stability.

5.5: MIDDLE EAST REGIONAL ARRANGEMENTS

ARAB LEAGUE

Arab League, informal name of the League of Arab States, a voluntary association of independent countries whose peoples are mainly Arabic speaking. Its stated purposes are to strengthen ties among the member states, coordinate their policies, and promote their common interests.

The Arab League was founded in Cairo in 1945 by Egypt, Iraq, Lebanon, Saudi Arabia, Syria, Transjordan (Jordan, as of 1950), and Yemen. Countries that later joined are: Algeria (1962), Bahrain (1971), Comoros (1993), Djibouti (1977), Kuwait (1961), Libya (1953), Mauritania (1973), Morocco (1958), Oman (1971), Qatar (1971), Somalia (1974), Southern Yemen (1967), Sudan (1956), Tunisia (1958), and the United Arab Emirates (1971). The Palestine Liberation Organisation was admitted in 1976. Egypt's membership was suspended in 1979 after it signed a peace treaty with Israel; the league's headquarters was moved from Cairo, Egypt, to Tunis, Tunisia. In 1987 Arab leaders decided to renew diplomatic ties with Egypt. Egypt was readmitted to the league in 1989 and the league's headquarters was moved back to Cairo.

The Arab League is involved in political, economic, cultural, and social programs designed to promote the interests of member states. The Arab League has served as a forum for member states to coordinate their policy positions and deliberate on matters of common concern, settling some Arab disputes and limiting conflicts such as the Lebanese civil wars of 1958. The Arab League has served as a platform for the drafting and conclusion of almost all landmark documents promoting economic integration among member states, such as the creation of the Joint Arab Economic Action Charter, which set out the principles for economic activities of the league. It has played an important role in shaping school curricula, and preserving manuscripts and Arab cultural heritage. The Arab League has launched literacy campaigns, and reproduced intellectual works, and translated modern technical terminology for the use of member states. It encourages measures against crime and drug abuse and deals with labour issues (particularly among the emigrant Arab workforce).

The Arab League has also fostered cultural exchanges between member states, encouraged youth and sports programs, helped to advance the role of women in Arab societies, and promoted child welfare activities.

The Egyptian government first proposed the Arab League in 1943. Egypt and some of the other Arab states wanted closer cooperation without the loss of self-rule that would result from total union. The original charter of the Arab League created a regional organisation of sovereign states that was neither a union nor a federation. Among the goals the league set for itself were winning independence for all Arabs still under alien rule, and to prevent the Jewish minority in Palestine (then governed by the British) from creating a Jewish state. The members eventually formed a joint defense council, an economic council, and a permanent military command.

Subsidiary Bodies of the Arab League

- Council (Internal Regulations of the Council [1951] and Internal Regulations of the Committees [1951]:
  - Arab Women's Committee
  - Committee of Arab Experts on Cooperation
  - Communications Committee
  - Conference of Liason Officers
  - Cultural Committee
  - Health Committee
  - Human Rights Committee
  - Information Committee
  - Legal Committee
  - Organisation of Youth Welfare
  - Permanent Committee for Administrative and Financial Affairs
  - Political Committee
  - Social Committee
- General Secretariat (Internal Regulations of the Secretariat-General of the League [1953]):
- Defense and Economic Cooperation Bodies:
  - Arab Unified Military Command

  - Economic Council
  - Joint Defense Council
  - Permanent Military Commission
- Arab Deterrent Force
- Other Institutions of the League:
  - Administrative Tribunal of the Arab League
  - Arab Fund for Technical Assistance to African and Arab Countries (AFTAAAC)
  - Special Bureau for Boycotting Israel
- Specialized Organisations:
  - Arab Administrative Development Organisation
  - Arab Centre for the Study of Arid Zones and Dry Lands (ACSAD)
  - Arab Industrial Development and Mining Organisation
  - Arab Labour Organisation
  - Arab League Educational, Cultural, and Scientific Organisation (ALESCO)
  - Arab Maritime Transport Academy, Alexandria
  - Arab Organisation for Agricultural Development
  - Arab Organisation for Social Defense against Crime
  - Arab Postal Union
  - Arab Satellite Communication Organisation (ARABSAT)
  - Arab States Broadcasting Union (ASBU)
  - Arab Telecommunications Union
  - Banque arabe pour le developpement economique en Afrique (BANDEA) (Arab Bank for Economic Development)
  - Council of Arab Ministers of the Interior
  - Inter-Arab Investment Guarantee Corporation
- Other Related Organisations:
  - Arab Fund for Economic and Social Development (AFESD)

- Arab Monetary Fund
- Council for Arab Economic Unity
- Organisation of Arab Petroleum Exporting Countries (OAPEC)

ARAB MONETARY FUND (AMF)

Arab Monetary Fund is a Regional Arab Organisation, Founded 1976, and has started operations in 1977. The fund aims at contributing to the achievement of the following objectives:

- Correcting disequilibria in the balances of payments of member States.
- Striving for the removal of restrictions on current payments between member States.
- Establishing policies and modes of Arab monetary co-operation.
- Rendering advice, whenever called upon to do so, with regard to policies related to the investment of the financial resources of member States in foreign markets.
- Promoting the development of Arab financial markets.
- Paving the way towards the creation of a unified Arab currency.
- Promote trade among member States.

For the realisation of its goals, the Fund shall employ the following means:

1. Providing short-term and medium-term credit facilities to member States with a view to assisting in financing their overall balance of payments deficits.
2. Liberalising and promoting trade and the resulting current payments and encouraging capital movements between member States.
3. Allocating from its resources, paid in the currencies of the member States, sufficient funds to provide the necessary credits to settle their current payments among them, in accordance with the rules and regulations to be laid down by the Board of Governors and within

the framework of a special account to be opened by the Fund for that purpose.

4. Managing any funds placed under the charge of the Fund by a member State or States.
5. Holding periodic consultations with member States on their economic conditions and the policies they pursue in support of the realisation of the goals of the Fund and the States concerned.
6. Conducting the research required to achieve the goals of the Fund.
7. Providing technical assistance to banking and monetary institutions in member States.

The member States shall co-operate among themselves and with the Fund for the realisation of the goals of the Fund and each member shall, in particular:

1. Reduce the restrictions on current payments among member States and the restrictions on the transfer of capital and the transfer of profits therefrom, with a view to the total elimination of the said restrictions.
2. Endeavour to achieve the necessary degree of co-ordination between Arab economic policies, particularly financial and monetary, in a manner that will contribute to Arab economic integration and assist in creating the necessary conditions for the establishment of a unified Arab currency.

The Fund shall co-operate with similar Arab institutions to achieve its objectives, likewise, when necessary, it shall co-operate with similar international organisations.

The Fund shall provide technical assistance and services in the financial and monetary sphere to member States, which conclude economic agreements aimed at attaining a monetary union between them as on of the stages leading the realisation of the goals of the Fund.

Top management of the AMF consists of the Board of Governors (General Assembly), and the board of executive directors chaired by the Director General Chairman of the board.

GULF COOPERATION COUNCIL (GCC)

The Cooperation Council for the Arab States of the Gulf (GCC) is a regional organisation created in May 1981 by Bahrain, Kuwait, Oman, Qatar, Saudi Arabia and United Arab Emirates. Behind the creation was a general perception by these states of their vulnerability arising from their oil wealth in contrast to their small and dispersed populations (28 million), their vast surface area (2.6 million km^2) and their limited military capabilities in a generally instable region.

On 21st Rajab 1401 AH corresponding to 25th May 1981, their Majesties and Highnesses, the leaders of the United Arab Emirates, State of Bahrain, Kingdom of Saudi Arabia, Sultanate of Oman, State of Qatar and State of Kuwait met in Abu Dhabi, United Arab Emirates, where they reached a cooperative framework joining the six states to effect coordination, integration and inter-connection among the Member States in all fields in order to achieve unity, according to article 4 of the GCC Charter. Article 4 also emphasized the deepening and strengthening of relations, links and areas of cooperation among their citizens. The underpinnings which are clearly provided for in the preamble of the GCC Charter, confirm the special relations, common qualities and similar systems founded on the creed of Islam, faith in a common destiny and sharing one goal, and that the cooperation among these states would serve the sublime objectives of the Arab nation.

The decision was not a product of the moment but an institutional embodiment of a historical, social and cultural reality. Deep religious and cultural ties link the six states, and strong kin relations prevail among their citizens. All these factors, enhanced by one geographical entity extending from sea to desert, have facilitated contacts and interaction among them, and created homogeneous values and characteristics.

Therefore, while, on one hand, the GCC is a continuation, evolution and institutionalisation of old prevailing realities, it is, on the other, a practical answer to the challenges of security and economic development in the area. It is also a fulfilment of the aspirations of its citizens towards some sort of Arab regional unity.

The basic objectives are to:

- Formulating similar regulations in various fields such as economy, finance, trade, customs, tourism, legislation, and administration;
- Fostering scientific and technical progress in industry, mining, agriculture, water and animal resources;
- Establishing scientific research centres;
- Setting up joint ventures;
- Encouraging cooperation of the private sector;
- Strengthening ties between their people.

Organisational Structure

The Supreme Council is the highest authority of the GCC formed of the Heads of Member States. Its presidency rotates according to the Arabic alphabetical order of the names of Member States. It convenes one regular session every year. However, extraordinary sessions may be convened at the request of any Member State seconded by another. In 1998, during the 19th summit held in Abu Dhabi, the Supreme Council decided to hold a consultative meeting in between two summits every year. Meetings of the Supreme Council are considered valid if attended by two-thirds of the Member States, at which each has one vote. Resolutions on substantive matters are issued by unanimous approval of the members present, while a majority is enough to approve those of procedural nature.

The Consultative Commission. Formed of thirty GCC citizens (five from each Member States) chosen according to their experience and qualification for a period of three years. The Consultative Commission is charged with studying matters referred to it by the Supreme Council.

Commission for the Settlement of Disputes. Formed by the Supreme Council for every case on an ad-hoc basis in accordance with the nature of the dispute.

The Ministerial Council. It is composed of the Ministers of Foreign Affairs or other ministers acting on their behalf. Presidency of the Ministerial Council is entrusted with the Member State that presided the last ordinary session of the

Supreme Council, or when necessary, with the Member State that is next to preside the Supreme Council. The Ministerial Council convenes every three months, and may hold extraordinary meetings upon the request of one Member State seconded by another. A meeting is considered valid if attended by two-thirds of the Member States.

Among other jurisdictions, the Ministerial Council is authorised to propose policies, lay out recommendations, and encourage and coordinate the already existing activities in all fields. Resolutions adopted by other ministerial committees are referred to the Ministerial Council, which in turn would refer the relevant matters, along with appropriate recommendations, to the Supreme Council for approval. The Ministerial Council is also charged with arranging the Supreme Council meetings and preparing their agenda. Procedures of voting are similar to those applicable at the Supreme Council.

The Secretariat-General. It is charged, among other functions, with preparing studies related to cooperation, co-ordination, and integrated plans and programmes for joint work. It is also entrusted with the preparation of periodic reports on the work of the GCC, follow up implementation of the resolutions, prepare reports and studies when requested by the Supreme Council or the Ministerial Council. The Secretariat also makes preparation for meetings and prepare the agendas and draft resolutions for the Ministerial Council.

The Organisational body of the Secretariat-General is comprised of the following:

- A Secretary-General appointed by the Supreme Council for a period of three years renewable only once.
- Three Assistant Secretaries-General for political, economic and military affairs, as well as the head of the GCC delegation to Brussels, who are appointed by the Ministerial Council for three renewable years, upon nomination of the Secretary-General.
- Directors-general of the Secretariat-General sectors as well as other staff that are appointed by the Secretary-General.

The administrative structure of the Secretariat General consists of a number of sectors: Political Affairs, Economic

Affairs, Military Affairs, Human and Environment Affairs, Legal Affairs, Office of the Secretary-General, Finance and Administrative Affairs, Patent Bureau, Administrative Development Unit, Internal Auditing Unit, and Information Centre, in addition to the GCC Delegation in Brussels and the Telecommunications Bureau in Bahrain.

ISLAMIC DEVELOPMENT BANK GROUP

Islamic Development Bank (IDB) Group, is a multilateral development financing institution, established to foster social and economic development of it's member countries and Muslim communities world-wide. It is an international financial institution established in pursuance of the Declaration of Intent issued by the Conference of Finance Ministers of Muslim Countries held in Jeddah in Dhul Q'adah 1393H, corresponding to December 1973. The Inaugural Meeting of the Board of Governors took place in Rajab 1395H, corresponding to July 1975, and the Bank was formally opened on 15 Shawwal 1395H corresponding to 20 October 1975.

Objectives

In line with its overall objectives of fostering economic development and social progress, the Bank finances productive projects and programs in both public and private sectors in member countries. It invests in economic and social infrastructure projects, provides technical assistance to member countries and assist in the promotion of foreign trade, especially capital goods. The Bank also assists Muslim communities in non-member countries and undertakes shari'ah-based research studies in Islamic economics and banking through special funds established for this purpose.

IDB finances development projects in member countries through a number of shari'ah-compatible modes such as Loan, Leasing, Instalment Sale, Istisna'a, Equity Participation, Lines of Financing, etc. Besides, its trade financing schemes, such as Import Trade Financing Operations (ITFO), Export Financing Scheme (EFS), and Islamic Banks' Portfolio (IBP), Unit Investment Fund (UIF), etc., promote trade among member countries.

Purpose and Functions

The purpose of the Bank is to foster the economic development and social progress of member countries and Muslim communities individually as well as jointly in accordance with the principles of Shari'ah i.e., Islamic Law.

The functions of the Bank are to participate in equity capital and grant loans for productive projects and enterprises besides providing financial assistance to member countries in other forms for economic and social development. The Bank is also required to establish and operate special funds for specific purposes including a fund for assistance to Muslim communities in non-member countries, in addition to setting up trust funds.

The Bank is authorized to accept deposits and to mobilize financial resources through Shari'ah compatible modes. It is also charged with the responsibility of assisting in the promotion of foreign trade, especially in capital goods, among member countries; providing technical assistance to member countries; and extending training facilities for personnel engaged in development activities in Muslim countries to conform to the Shari'ah.

Membership

The present membership of the Bank consists of 55 countries. The basic condition for membership is that the prospective member country should be a member of the Organisation of the Islamic Conference, pay its contribution to the capital of the Bank and be willing to accept such terms and conditions as may be decided upon by the IDB Board of Governors.

Head Office and Regional Offices

The Bank's principal office is in Jeddah in the Kingdom of Saudi Arabia. Two regional offices were opened in 1994; one in Rabat, Morocco, and the other in Kuala Lumpur, Malaysia. In July 1996, the board of Executive Directors also approved the establishment of an IDB Representative Office at Almaty, Kazakhstan, to serve as a link between IDB member countries and Central Asian Republics. The office became operational in July 1997 and is now a full-fledged Regional Office. The

Bank also has field representatives in eleven member countries. These are: Indonesia, Iran, Kazakhstan, Libya, Pakistan, Senegal, Sudan, Gambia, Guinea Bissau, Muritania and Algeria.

Organisation

The Board of Governors is the highest policy making body, which elects the Board of Executive Directors and the President. The Board of Executive Directors ensures that the Bank operates in accordance with the policies laid out by the Board of Governors. The President as the Chief Executive, is responsible for the day to day operation of the Bank.

The Bank's organisation structure is dynamic and subject to change like any other organisation. At present, there are three Vice Presidents reporting directly to the President. In addition, some departments/offices report to the President directly.

Regional Offices

The Bank has two regional offices. One in Rabat, Morocco, and the other in Kuala Lumpur, Malaysia. In addition, the Bank has one representative office in Almaty, Kazakstan and a Biosaline Agriculture Centre in Dubai, the UAE.

The main functions of the regional offices are to:

- act as the Bank's liaison office for the member countries in that region
- assist in project identification and follow-up
- market the Bank's financing modes and explain its policies and procedures
- assist in recruitment of staff
- assist in private sector development activities
- assist in mission preparation and organisation
- prepare short-list of consultants
- liaise with other regional and international organisations located in its region and represent the Bank in regional conferences and seminars

The Islamic Corporation for Insurance of Investments and Export Credit (ICIEC)

The Islamic Corporation for Insurance of Investments and Export Credits (ICIEC) is a 50% owned subsidiary of the

Islamic Development Bank a AAA rated institution, established on 1st August 1994, as an international institution with full juridical personality. ICIEC offers Islamic compatible insurance products for investments and export credit.

The objective of ICIEC, as defined in its Articles of Agreement, is to enlarge the scope of trade transactions and the flow of investments among Member States. In fulfillment of this objective ICIEC provides, in accordance with the principles of Shariah:

(a) Export Credit Insurance and reinsurance to cover the non-payment of export receivables resulting from commercial (buyer) or non-commercial (country) risks and

(b) Foreign Investment Insurance and reinsurance against country risks, mainly the risks of exchange transfer restrictions, expropriation, war and civil disturbance and breach of contract by the host government.

Islamic Research & Training Institute (IRTI)

IRTI is member of the Islamic Development Bank Group. The purpose of IRTI is to undertake research for enabling the economic, financial and banking activities in Muslim countries to conform to Shari'ah and to extend training facilities to personnel engaged in economic development activities in the Bank's member countries.

The purpose of the Institute is to undertake research for enabling the economic, financial and banking activities in Muslim countries to conform to Shari'ah and to extend training facilities to personnel engaged in economic development activities in the Bank's member countries.

IRTI has been assigned following functions:

- to organize and conduct basic and applied research with a view to developing models and methods for the application of Shari'ah in the field of economics, finance and banking;
- to provide for the training and development of professional personnel in Islamic Economics to meet the needs of research and Shari'ah-observing agencies;

- to train personnel engaged in development activities in the Bank's member countries;
- to establish an information center to collect, systematize and disseminate information in fields related to its activities and
- to undertake any other activities which may advance its purpose.

Islamic Corporation for the Development of Private Sector (ICD)

Mission of ICD is to complement the role played by the Islamic Development Bank through the development and promotion of the private sector as a vehicle for economic growth and prosperity. Its vision is to become a premier Islamic multilateral financial institution for the development of the private sector.

ICD focuses on the following objectives:

- Identifying opportunities in the private sector that could function as engines of growth;
- Providing a wide range of Shari'a-compatible financial products and services;
- Expanding access to Islamic capital markets by private companies in IsDB member countries.

In achieving these objectives, ICD seeks to play a role in:

- Mobilizing funds for private sector investment;
- Acting as a catalyst in privatisation programs and restructuring of companies in member countries by providing advisory services to both public and private sectors;
- Encouraging the development of Islamic capital markets.

World Waqf Foundation

To activate the role of Waqf as a socio-economic institution in order to contribute to the plans and programmes of sustainable development that aim at civilisational uplifiting of Muslim Peoples and communities and end the suffering of the poor are amongst the main objectives of World Waqf

Foundation. It functions in co-ordination with the Islamic Development Bank Group.

ORGANISATION OF ISLAMIC COUNTRIES (OIC)

The Organisation of the Islamic Conference (OIC) is an inter-governmental organisation grouping of fifty-six States. These States decided to pool their resources together, combine their efforts and speak with one voice to safeguard the interest and ensure the progress and well-being of their peoples and those of other Muslims in the world over.

The Organisation was established in Rabat, Kingdom of Morocco, on 12 Rajab 1389H (25 September 1969) when the First meeting of the leaders of the Islamic world was held in this city in the wake of the criminal arson perpetrated on 21 August 1969 by Zionist elements against Al-Aqsa Mosque, in occupied Jerusalem. It was indeed in order to defend the honour, dignity and faith of the Muslims, to face this bitter challenge launched in the holy city of Al-Quds so dear to them and against the Mosque of Al-Aqsa, the first Qibla and third holiest Shrine of Islam, that the leaders of the Muslim world, at their Summit in Rabat, seized that event—which brought about unanimous worldwide condemnation and reprobation—to think together of their common cause and muster the force required to overcome their differences, unite and lay the foundations of this large grouping of States, that is, the Organisation of the Islamic Conference which they entrusted, in absolute priority, with liberating Jerusalem and Al-Aqsa from Zionist occupation.

Six months after that historical meeting, i.e. in Muharram 1390H (March 1970), the First Islamic Conference of Ministers of Foreign Affairs held in Jeddah set up a permanent General Secretariat, to ensure a liaison among Member States and charged it to coordinate their action. The Conference appointed its Secretary General and chose Jeddah as the Headquarters of the Organisation, pending the liberation of Jerusalem, which would be the permanent Headquarters.

Two and a half years after Rabat, in Muharram 1392H (February 1972), the Islamic Conference of Foreign Ministers, meeting in its Third Session, adopted the Charter of the Organisation, whose purpose is to strengthen solidarity and cooperation among Islamic States in the political, economic, cultural, scientific and social fields.

Under the Charter, the Organisation aims to:

- Strengthen:
  -Islamic solidarity among Member States;
  -Cooperation in the political, economic, social, cultural and scientific fields,
  -The struggle of all Muslim people to safeguard their dignity, independence and—national rights.
- Coordinate action to:
  -Safeguard the Holy Places;
  -Support the struggle of the Palestinian people and assist them in recovering their—rights and liberating their occupied territories.
- Work to:
  -Eliminate racial discrimination and all forms of colonialism;
  -Create a favorable atmosphere for the promotion of cooperation and understanding between Member States and other countries.

The Charter also enumerates principles which OIC Member States undertake to inspire themselves from, in order to achieve the objectives of the Organisation.

The Charter also enumerates the principles governing OIC activities, namely:

- Full equality among Member States.
- Observation of the right to self determination and non-interference in the internal affairs of Member States.
- Observation of the sovereignty, independence and territorial integrity of each State.
- The settlement of any dispute that might arise among Member States by peaceful means such as negotiations, mediation, conciliation and arbitration.
- A pledge to refrain, in relations among Member States, from resorting to force or threatening to resort to the use of force against the unity and territorial integrity or the political independence of any one of them.

In order to achieve its objectives, the Organisation has main bodies, secondary organs, institutions and specialized committees.

Principal Bodies

The Islamic Summit Conference. The Islamic Summit Conference is the supreme body of the OIC entrusted with defining strategies for the OIC policies and actions. It convenes once every three years.

The Islamic Conference of Foreign Ministers (ICFM). The ICFM considers the means of implementing the general policy of the organisation and adopts resolutions accordingly. It meets in regular sessions once a year. There are also ICFM special sessions as required by circumstances.

The General Secretariat. It carries out duties entrusted to it by the above conferences as the Organisation's executive organ. The headquarters are in Jeddah, Saudi Arabia. The General Secretariat is headed by a Secretary General elected by the ICFM for a period of four years, renewable once only.

The International Islamic Court of Justice. The establishment of the Court has been decided by the Third Islamic Summit. It is envisioned to have 7 members elected by the Islamic Conference of Foreign Ministers and to have headquarters in Kuwait City, the State of Kuwait.

Subsidiary Organs

The Statistical, Economic and Social Research and Training Centre for Islamic Countries, (SESRTCIC), Ankara, Turkey

The Research Centre for Islamic History, Art and Culture, (IRCICA), Istanbul, Turkey

The Islamic Institute of Technology, (IIT), Dhaka, Bangladesh

The Islamic Centre for Development of Trade, (ICDT), Casablanca, Morocco

The Islamic Fiqh Academy, Jeddah, Saudi Arabia

The Islamic Solidarity Fund, Jeddah, Saudi Arabia

The International Commission for the Preservation of the Islamic Heritage Istanbul, Turkey

Islamic University of Niger

Islamic University of Uganda

Specialised Institutions

The Islamic Development Bank, (IDB), Jeddah, Saudi Arabia

The Islamic Educational, Scientific and Cultural Organisation, (ISESCO), Rabat, Morocco

The International Islamic News Agency, (IINA), Jeddah, Saudi Arabia

The Islamic States Broadcasting Organisation, (ISBO), Jeddah, Saudi Arabia

Affiliated Institutions

The Islamic Chamber of Commerce and Industry, (ICCI), Karachi, Pakistan

The Islamic Committee of the International Crescent, (ICIC), Benghazi, Libya

The Organisation of the Islamic Shipowners Association, (OISA), Jeddah, Saudi Arabia

The International Association of Islamic Banks, Cairo, Egypt

The Organisation of Islamic Capitals and Cities, (OICC), Makkah Al-Mukarramah, Saudi Arabia

The Sports Federation of Islamic Solidarity Games, Riyadh, Saudi Arabia

The World Federation of International Arabo-Islamic Schools, Jeddah, Saudi Arabia.

APPENDICES

APPENDIX-1

LIST OF MEMBER COUNTRIES OF IMPORTANT ORGANISATIONS

African Union

Algeria
Angola
Benin
Botswana
Burkina-Faso
Burundi
Cameroon
Cape-Verde
Central African Republic
Chad
Comoros
Congo
Côte d'Ivoire
Democratic Republic of Congo
Djibouti
Egypt
Erithrea
Equatorial Guinea
Ethiopia
Gabon
Gambia
Ghana
Republic of Guinea
Guinea-Bissau
Kenya
Lesotho
Liberia
Libyan Arab Jamahiriya
Madagascar
Malawi
Mali
Mauritania
Mauritius
Mozambique
Namibia
Niger
Nigeria
Rwanda
SADR
Sao Tome and Principe
Senegal
Seychelles
Sierra Leone
Somalia
South Africa
Sudan
Swaziland
Tanzania
Togo
Tunisia
Uganda
Zambia
Zimbabwe.

African Development Bank Group

Algeria
Angola
Benin
Botswana
Burkina-Faso
Burundi
Cameroon
Cape-Verde
Central African Republic
Chad
Comoros
Congo
Côte d'Ivoire
Democratic Republic of Congo
Djibouti
Egypt
Erithrea
Equatorial Guinea
Ethiopia
Gabon
Gambia
Ghana
Republic of Guinea
Guinea-Bissau
Kenya
Lesotho
Liberia
Libyan Arab Jamahiriya
Madagascar
Malawi
Mali

Mauritania	Sao Tome and Principe	Swaziland
Mauritius	Senegal	Tanzania
Morocco	Seychelles	Togo
Mozambique	Sierra Leone	Tunisia
Namibia	Somalia	Uganda
Niger	South Africa	Zambia
Nigeria	Sudan	Zimbabwe.
Rwanda		

Non-Regional Member Countries

Argentina	France	Norway
Austria	Germany	Portugal
Belgium	India	Saudi Arabia
Brazil	Italy	Spain
Canada	Japan	Sweden
China	Korea	Switzerland
Denmark	Kuwait	United Kingdom
Finland	Netherlands	United States.

ALADI

Argentina, Brazil, Mexico, Chile, Colombia, Peru, Uruguay, Venezuela, Bolivia, Ecuador, and Paraguay.

Andean Group

Bolivia, Colombia, Chile, Ecuador, Peru and Venezuela.

AMU

Algeria, Libya, Mauritania, Morocco, Tunisia.

APEC

Brunei Darussalam; Canada; Chile; People's Republic of China; Hong Kong, China; Indonesia; Japan; Republic of Korea; Malaysia; Mexico; New Zealand; Papua New Guinea; Peru; The Republic of the Philippines; The Russian Federation; Singapore; Chinese Taipei; Thailand; United States of America; Viet Nam.

Arab League

Algeria	Bahrain	Comoros	Djibouti
Egypt	Iraq	Jordan	Kuwait
Lebanon	Libya	Mauritania	Morocco
Oman	Palestine	Qatar	Saudi Arabia
Somalia	Sudan	Syria	Tunisia
United Arab Emirates	Yemen		

Arab Monetary Fund

Jordan, United Arab Emirates, Bahrain, Tunisia, Algeria, Djibouti, Saudi Arabia, Sudan, Syria, Somalia, Iraq, Oman, Palestine, Qatar, Kuwait, Lebanon, Libya, Egypt, Morocco, Mauritania, Yemen, Comoros.

ASEAN

Brunei Darussalam, Cambodia, Indonesia, Laos, Malaysia, Myanmar, Philippines, Singapore, Thailand, Vietnam.

Asian Development Bank

Afghanistan (1966)
Australia (1966)
Austria (1966)
Azerbaijan (1999)
Bangladesh (1973)
Belgium (1966)
Bhutan (1982)
Cambodia (1966)
Canada (1966)
China, People's Republic of (1986)
Cook Islands (1976)
Denmark (1966)
Fiji Islands (1970)
Finland (1966)
France (1970)
Germany (1966)
Hong Kong, China (1969)
India (1966)
Indonesia (1966)
Italy (1966)
Japan (1966)
Kazakhstan (1994)
Kiribati (1974)
Korea, Republic of (1966)
Kyrgyz Republic (1994)
Lao People's Democratic Republic (1966)
Luxembourg (2003)
Malaysia (1966)
Maldives (1978)
Marshall Islands, Republic of the (1990)
Micronesia, Federated States of (1990)
Mongolia (1991)
Myanmar (1973)
Nauru (1991)
Nepal (1966)
New Zealand (1966)
Norway (1966)
Pakistan (1966)
Palau (2003)
Papua New Guinea (1971)
Philippines (1966)
Portugal (2002)
Samoa (1966)
Singapore (1966)
Solomon Islands (1973)
Spain (1986)
Sri Lanka (1966)
Sweden (1966)
Switzerland (1967)
Taipei,China (1966)
Tajikistan (1998)
Thailand (1966)
The Netherlands (1966)
Timor-Leste (2002)
Tonga (1972)
Turkey (1991)
Turkmenistan (2000)
Tuvalu (1993)
United Kingdom (1966)
United States (1966)
Uzbekistan (1995)
Vanuatu (1981)
Viet Nam, Socialist Republic of (1966)

BIMST-EC

Bangladesh, Bhutan, India, Myanmar, Nepal, Sri Lanka, Thailand.

CACM

Guatemala, Honduras, Nicaragua, El Salvador, and Costa Rica.

CARICOM

Antigua and Barbuda
The Bahamas *(The Bahamas is a member of the Community but not the Common Market)*
Barbados
Belize
Dominica
Grenada
Guyana
Haiti
Jamaica
Montserrat
St. Kitts and Nevis
Saint Lucia
St. Vincent and the Grenadines
Suriname
Trinidad and Tobago

CIS

Armenia, Azerbaijan, Belarus, Georgia, Kazakhstan, Kyrgyzstan, Moldova, Russia, Tajikistan, Turkmenistan, Ukraine, and Uzbekistan.

COMECON

Albania, Bulgaria, Cuba, Czechoslovakia, East Germany, Hungary, Mongolia, Poland, Romania, Soviet Union, and Vietnam.

COMESA

Angola	Burundi	Comoros	D.R.Congo	Djibouti
Egypt	Eritrea	Ethiopia	Kenya	Madagascar
Malawi	Mauritius	Namibia	Rwanda	Seychelles
Sudan	Swaziland	Uganda	Zambia	Zimbabwe

Commonwealth

Antigua and Barbuda
Australia
The Bahamas
Bangladesh
Barbados
Belize
Botswana
Brunei Darussalam
Cameroon
Canada
Cyprus
Dominica
Fiji Islands
The Gambia
Ghana
Grenada
Guyana
India
Jamaica
Kenya
Kiribati
Lesotho
Malawi
Malaysia
Maldives
Malta
Mauritius
Mozambique
Namibia
Nauru
New Zealand
Nigeria
Pakistan
Papua New Guinea
St Kitts and Nevis
St Lucia
St Vincent and the Grenadines
Samoa
Seychelles
Sierra Leone
Singapore
Solomon Islands
South Africa
Sri Lanka
Swaziland
Tonga
Trinidad and Tobago
Tuvalu
Uganda
United Kingdom
United Republic of Tanzania
Vanuatu
Zambia

EAC

Kenya, Uganda and the United Republic of Tanzania.

ECOWAS

Benin, Burkina Faso, Cape Verde, Cote d'Ivoire , The Gambia, Ghana, Guinea, Guinea-Bissau, Liberia, Mali, Niger, Nigeria, Senegal, Sierra Leone, and Togo.

European Union

Austria	Germany	Netherlands
Belgium	Greece	Portugal
Denmark	Ireland	Spain
Finland	Italy	Sweeden
France	Luxembourg	United Kingdom

New Members

Cyprus	Latvia	Slovakia
Czech Republic	Lithuania	Slovania
Estonia	Malta	
Hungary	Poland	

G-7/8

France, the United States, Britain, Germany, Japan, Italy, Canada and Russia.

G-15

Algeria, Argentina, Brazil, Chile, Egypt, India, Indonesia, Jamaica, Kenya, Malaysia, Mexico, Nigeria, Peru, Senegal, Venezuela and Zimbabwe.

G-20

Argentina, Australia, Brazil, Canada, China, France, Germany, India, Indonesia, Italy, Japan, Korea México, Russia, Saudi Arabia, South Africa, Turkey, the United Kingdom, the United States and the European Union.

G-77

Afganistan	Belize	Burkina Faso
Algeria	Benin	Burundi
Angola	Bhutan	Cambodia
Antigua and Barbuda	Bolivia	Cameroon
Argentina	Bosnia and Herzegovina	Cape Verde
Bahamas	Botswana	Central African Republic
Bahrain	Brazil	Chad
Bangladesh	Brunei Darussalam	Chile
Barbados		

China
Colombia
Comoros
Congo
Costa Rica
Côte d'Ivoire
Cuba
Cyprus
Democratic People's Republic of Korea
Democratic Republic of the Congo
Djibouti
Dominica
Dominican Republic
Ecuador
Egypt
El Salvador
Equatorial Guinea
Eritrea
Ethiopia
Fiji
Gabon
Gambia
Ghana
Grenada
Guatemala
Guinea
Guinea-Bissau
Guyana
Haiti
Honduras
India
Indonesia
Iran (Islamic Republic of)
Iraq
Jamaica
Jordan
Kenya
Kuwait
Lao People's Democratic Republic
Lebanon
Lesotho
Liberia
Libyan Arab Jamahiriya
Madagascar
Malawi
Malaysia
Maldives
Mali
Malta
Marshall Islands
Mauritania
Mauritius
Micronesia (Federated States of)
Mongolia
Morocco
Mozambique
Myanmar
Namibia
Nepal
Nicaragua
Niger
Nigeria
Oman
Pakistan
Palau
Palestine
Panama
Papua New Guinea
Paraguay
Peru
Philippines
Qatar
Romania
Rwanda
Saint Kitts and Nevis
Saint Lucia
Saint Vincent and the Grenadines
Samoa
Sao Tome and Principe
Saudi Arabia
Senegal
Seychelles
Sierra Leone
Singapore
Solomon Islands
Somalia
South Africa
Sri Lanka
Sudan
Suriname
Swaziland
Syrian Arab Republic
Thailand
Timor-Leste
Togo
Tonga
Trinidad and Tobago
Tunisia
Turkmenistan
Uganda
United Arab Emirates
United Republic of Tanzania
Uruguay
Vanuatu
Venezuela
Viet Nam
Yemen
Zambia
Zimbabwe

IAEA

Afghanistan
Albania
Argentina
Australia
Austria
Belarus
Brazil
Bulgaria
Canada
Cuba
Denmark
Dominican Republic
Egypt
El Salvador
Ethiopia
France
Germany
Greece

Guatemala
Haiti
Holy See
Hungary
Iceland
India
Indonesia
Israel
Italy
Japan
Republic of Korea
Monaco
Morocco
Myanmar
Netherlands
New Zealand
Norway
Pakistan
Paraguay
Peru
Poland
Portugal
Romania
Russian Federation
Serbia and Montenegro
South Africa
Spain
Sri Lanka
Sweden
Switzerland
Thailand
Tunisia
Turkey
Ukraine
United Kingdom
United States
Venezuela
Vietnam
Belgium
Ecuador
Finland
Islamic Republic of Iran
Luxembourg
Mexico
Philippines
Sudan
Iraq
Chile
Colombia
Ghana
Senegal
Lebanon
Mali
Democratic Republic of the Congo
Liberia
Saudi Arabia
Algeria
Bolivia
Côte d'Ivoire
Libyan Arab Jamahiriya
Syrian Arab Republic
Uruguay
Cameroon
Gabon
Kuwait
Nigeria
Costa Rica
Cyprus
Jamaica
Kenya
Madagascar
Jordan
Panama
Sierra Leone
Singapore
Uganda
Liechtenstein
Malaysia
Niger
Zambia
Ireland
Bangladesh
Mongolia
Mauritius
Qatar
United Arab Emirates
United Republic of Tanzania
Nicaragua
Namibia
China
Zimbabwe
Estonia
Slovenia
Armenia
Croatia
Czech Republic
Lithuania
Slovakia
The Former Yugoslav Republic of Macedonia
Kazakhstan
Marshall Islands
Uzbekistan
Yemen
Bosnia and Herzegovina
Georgia
Latvia
Malta
Republic of Moldova
Burkina Faso
Angola
Benin
Tajikistan
Azerbaijan
Central African Republic
Eritrea
Botswana
Honduras
Seychelles
Kyrgyzstan

ICC

Afghanistan
Albania
Algeria
Andorra
Angola
Antigua and Barbuda
Argentina
Armenia
Australia
Austria
Bahamas
Bahrain
Bangladesh
Barbados
Belgium
Belize
Benin
Bolivia
Bosnia and Herzegovina
Botswana
Brazil
Bulgaria
Burkina Faso
Burundi
Cambodia
Cameroon
Canada
Cape Verde
Central African Republic
Chad
Chile
Colombia
Comoros
Congo
Costa Rica
Cote d'Ivoire
Croatia
Cyprus
Czech Republic
Democratic Republic of Congo
Denmark
Djibouti
Dominica
Dominican Repbulic
East Timor
Ecuador
Egypt
Eritrea
Estonia
Fiji
Finland
France
Gabon
Gambia
Georgia
Germany
Ghana
Greece
Guinea
Guinea-Bissau
Guyana
Haiti
Honduras
Hungary
Iceland
Iran (Islamic Republic of)
Ireland
Israel
Italy
Jamaica
Jordan
Kenya
Kuwait
Kyrgyzstan
Latvia
Lesotho
Liberia
Liechtenstein
Lithuania
Luxembourg
Macedonia (F.Y.R)
Madagascar
Malawi
Mali
Malta
Marshall Islands
Mauritius
Mexico
Monaco
Mongolia
Morocco
Mozambique
Namibia
Nauru
Netherlands
New Zealand
Niger
Nigeria
Norway
Oman
Panama
Paraguay
Peru
Philippines
Poland
Portugal
Republic of Korea
Republic of Moldova
Romania
Russian Federation
Saint Lucia
Saint Vincent and the Grenadines
Samoa
San Marino
Sao Tome and Principe
Senegal
Serbia and Montenegro
Seychelles
Sierra leone
Slovakia
Slovenia
Solomon Islands
South Africa
Spain
Sudan
Sweden
Switzerland
Syrian Arab Republic
Tajikistan
Tanzania (United Rep.)

Thailand
Trinidad and Tobago
Uganda
Ukraine
United Arab Emirates
United Kingdom
United States of America
Uruguay
Uzbekistan
Venezuela
Yemen
Zambia
Zimbabwe

Interpol

Afghanistan | Albania | Algeria | Andorra | Angola | Antigua & Barbuda | Argentina | Armenia | Aruba | Australia | Austria | Azerbaijan

Bahamas | Bahrain | Bangladesh | Barbados | Belarus | Belgium | Belize | Benin | Bolivia | Bosnia-Herzegovina | Botswana | Brazil | Brunei | Bulgaria | Burkina-Faso | Burundi

Cambodia | Cameroon | Canada | Cape Verde | Central African Republic | Chad | Chile | China | Colombia | Comoros | Congo | Congo (Democratic Rep.) | Costa Rica | Côte d'Ivoire | Croatia | Cuba | Cyprus | Czech Republic

Denmark | Djibouti | Dominica | Dominican Republic

East Timor | Ecuador | Egypt | El Salvador | Equatorial Guinea | Eritrea | Estonia | Ethiopia

Fiji | Finland | Former Yugoslav Republic of Macedonia | France

Gabon | Gambia | Georgia | Germany | Ghana | Greece | Grenada | Guatemala | Guinea | Guinea Bissau | Guyana

Haiti | Honduras | Hungary

Iceland | India | Indonesia | Iran | Iraq | Ireland | Israel | Italy

Jamaica | Japan | Jordan

Kazakhstan | Kenya | Korea (Rep. of) |Kuwait | Kyrgyzstan

Laos | Latvia | Lebanon | Lesotho | Liberia | Libya | Liechtenstein | Lithuania | Luxembourg

Madagascar | Malawi | Malaysia | Maldives | Mali | Malta | Marshall Islands | Mauritania | Mauritius | Mexico | Moldova | Monaco | Mongolia | Morocco | Mozambique | Myanmar

Namibia | Nauru | Nepal | Netherlands | Netherlands Antilles | New Zealand | Nicaragua | Niger | Nigeria | Norway

Oman

Pakistan | Panama | Papua New Guinea |Paraguay | Peru | Philippines | Poland | Portugal

Qatar

Romania | Russia | Rwanda

St Kitts & Nevis | St Lucia | St Vincent & the Grenadines | Sao Tome & Principe | Saudi Arabia | Senegal | Serbia & Montenegro | Seychelles | Sierra Leone | Singapore | Slovakia | Slovenia | Somalia | South Africa | Spain | Sri Lanka | Sudan | Suriname | Swaziland | Sweden | Switzerland | Syria

Tanzania | Thailand | Togo | Tonga | Trinidad & Tobago | Tunisia | Turkey

Uganda | Ukraine | United Arab Emirates | United Kingdom | United States | Uruguay | Uzbekistan

Venezuela | Vietnam

Yemen

Zambia | Zimbabwe

IOM

. Albania
· Algeria
· Angola
· Argentina
· Armenia
· Australia
· Austria
· Azerbaijan
· Bangladesh
· Belgium
· Belize
· Benin
· Bolivia
· Bulgaria
· Burkina Faso
· Cambodia
· Canada
· Cape Verde
· Chile
· Colombia
· Congo
· Costa Rica
· Côte d'Ivoire
· Croatia
· Cyprus
· Czech Republic
· Democratic Republic of the Congo
· Denmark
· Dominican Republic
· Ecuador
· Egypt
· El Salvador
· Finland
· France
· Gambia
· Georgia
· Germany
· Greece
· Guatemala
· Guinea
· Guinea-Bissau
· Haiti
· Honduras
· Hungary

- Iran (Islamic Republic of)
- Ireland
- Israel
- Italy
- Japan
- Jordan
- Kazakhstan
- Kenya
- Kyrgyzstan
- Latvia
- Liberia
- Lithuania
- Luxembourg
- Madagascar
- Mali
- Malta
- Mauritania
- Mexico
- Morocco
- Netherlands
- New Zealand
- Nicaragua
- Nigeria
- Norway
- Pakistan
- Panama
- Paraguay
- Peru
- Philippines
- Poland
- Portugal
- Republic of Korea
- Republic of Moldova
- Romania
- Rwanda
- Senegal
- Serbia and Montenegro
- Sierra Leone
- Slovakia
- Slovenia
- South Africa
- Sri Lanka
- Sudan
- Sweden
- Switzerland
- Tajikistan
- Thailand
- Tunisia
- Uganda
- Ukraine
- United Kingdom of Great Britain and Northern Ireland
- United Republic of Tanzania
- United States of America
- Uruguay
- Venezuela
- Yemen
- Zambia
- Zimbabwe

IOR-ARC

Australia, Bangladesh, India, Indonesia, Iran, Kenya, Madagascar, Malaysia, Mauritius, Mozambique, Oman, the Seychelles, Singapore, South Africa, Sri Lanka, Tanzania, Thailand, the United Arab Emirates, and Yemen

IPU

Albania, Algeria, Andorra, Angola, Argentina, Armenia, Australia, Austria, Azerbaijan

Bahrain, Bangladesh, Belarus, Belgium, Benin, Bolivia, Bosnia and Herzegovina, Botswana, Brazil, Bulgaria, Burkina Faso, Burundi

Cambodia, Cameroon, Canada, Cape Verde, Chile, China, Colombia, Congo, Costa Rica, Côte d'Ivoire, Croatia, Cuba, Cyprus, Czech Republic

Democratic People's Republic of Korea, Denmark, Djibouti

Ecuador, Egypt, El Salvador, Estonia, Ethiopia

Fiji, Finland, France

Gabon, Germany, Ghana, Greece, Guatemala, Guinea

Hungary

Iceland, India, Indonesia, Iran (Islamic Republic of), Ireland, Israel, Italy

Japan, Jordan

Kazakhstan, Kenya, Kuwait, Kyrgyzstan

Lao People's Democratic Republic, Latvia, Lebanon, Libyan Arab Jamahiriya, Liechtenstein, Lithuania, Luxembourg

Malaysia, Mali, Malta, Mauritania, Mauritius, Mexico, Monaco, Mongolia, Morocco, Mozambique

Namibia, Nepal, Netherlands, New Zealand, Nicaragua, Niger, Nigeria, Norway

Pakistan, Panama, Papua New Guinea, Peru, Philippines, Poland, Portugal

Republic of Korea, Republic of Moldova, Romania, Russian Federation, Rwanda

Samoa, San Marino, Sao Tome and Principe, Saudi Arabia, Senegal, Serbia and Montenegro, Singapore, Slovakia, Slovenia, South Africa, Spain, Sri Lanka, Sudan, Suriname, Sweden, Switzerland, Syrian Arab Republic

Tajikistan, Thailand, The former Yugoslav Republic of Macedonia, Togo, Tunisia, Turkey

Uganda, Ukraine, United Arab Emirates, United Kingdom, United Republic of Tanzania, Uruguay, Uzbekistan

Venezuela, Viet Nam

Yemen

Zambia, Zimbabwe

ISA

Albania
Algeria
Angola
Antigua & Barbuda
Argentina
Armenia
Australia
Austria
Bahamas
Bahrain
Bangladesh
Barbados
Belgium
Belize
Benin
Bolivia
Bosnia & Herzegovina
Botswana
Brazil
Brunei Darussalam
Bulgaria
Cameroon
Canada
Cape Verde
Chile
China
Comoros
Cook Islands
Costa Rica
Côte d'Ivoire

Croatia
Cuba
Cyprus
Czech Republic
DRC
Djibouti
Dominica
Egypt
Equatorial Guinea
European Community
Fiji
Finland
France
Gabon
Gambia
Georgia
Germany
Ghana
Greece
Grenada
Guatemala
Guinea
Guinea-Bissau
Guyana
Haiti
Honduras
Hungary
Iceland
India
Indonesia
Iraq
Ireland
Italy
Jamaica
Japan
Jordan
Kenya
Kiribati
Kuwait
Lao
Lebanon
Lithuania
Luxembourg
Madagascar
Maldives
Malaysia
Mali
Malta
Marshall Islands
Mauritania
Mauritius
Mexico
Micronesia
Monaco
Mongolia
Mozambique
Myanmar
Namibia
Nauru
Nepal
Netherlands
New Zealand
Nicaragua
Nigeria
Norway
Oman
Pakistan
Palau
Panama
Papua New Guinea
Paraguay
Philippines
Poland
Portugal
Qatar
Republic of Korea
Romania
Russian Federation
Saint Kitts and Nevis
Saint Lucia
Saint Vincent &the Grenadines
Samoa
Sao Tome and Principe
Saudi Arabia
Senegal
Serbia and Montenegro
Seychelles
Sierra Leone
Singapore
Slovakia
Slovenia
Somalia
Solomon Islands
South Africa
Spain
Sri Lanka
Sudan
Suriname
Sweden
Macedonia
Togo
Tonga
Trinidad & Tobago
Tunisia
Tuvalu
Uganda
Ukraine
UK & Northern Ireland
Tanzania
Uruguay
Vanuatu
Vietnam
Yemen
Zambia
Zimbabwe

Islamic Development Bank Group

Afghanistan
Albania
Algeria
Azerbaijan Republic
Kingdom of Bahrain
Bangladesh
Republic of Benin
Brunei Darussalam
Burkina Faso
Republic of Cameroon
Republic of Chad
Union of Comoros
Republic of Côte d'Ivoire
Republic of Djibouti
Arab Republic of Egypt
Republic of Gabon
Republic of the Gambia

Republic of Guinea
Republic of Guinea Bissau
Republic of Indonesia
Islamic Republic of Iran
Republic of Iraq
Hashemite Kingdom of Jordan
Republic of Kazakhstan
State of Kuwait
Kyrgyz Republic
Republic of Lebanon
Libya
Malaysia
Republic of Maldives
Republic of Mali
Islamic Republic of Mauritania
Kingdom of Morocco
Republic of Mozambique
Republic of Niger
Sultanate of Oman
Islamic Republic of Pakistan
State of Palestine
State of Qatar
Kingdom of Saudi Arabia
Republic of Senegal
Republic of Sierra Leone
Republic of Somalia
Republic of Sudan
Republic of Suriname
Syrian Arab Republic
Republic of Tajikistan
Republic of Togo
Republic of Tunisia
Republic of Turkey
Republic of Turkmenistan
Republic of Uganda
United Arab Emirates
Republic of Uzbekistan
Republic of Yemen

ISO

Albania	Correspondent members
Algeria	Member bodies
Angola	Correspondent members
Antigua and Barbuda	Subscriber members
Argentina	Member bodies
Armenia	Member bodies
Australia	Member bodies
Austria	Member bodies
Azerbaijan	Member bodies
Bahrain	Member bodies
Bangladesh	Member bodies
Barbados	Member bodies
Belarus	Member bodies
Belgium	Member bodies
Benin	Subscriber members
Bolivia	Correspondent members
Bosnia and Herzegovina	Member bodies
Botswana	Member bodies
Brazil	Member bodies
Brunei Darussalam	Correspondent members
Bulgaria	Member bodies
Burundi	Subscriber members
Cambodia	Subscriber members
Canada	Member bodies
Chile	Member bodies
China	Member bodies
Colombia	Member bodies
Congo, The Democratic Republic of	Correspondent members
Costa Rica	Member bodies
Croatia	Member bodies

Cuba	Member bodies
Cyprus	Member bodies
Czech Republic	Member bodies
Côte-d'Ivoire	Member bodies
Denmark	Member bodies
Dominica	Subscriber members
Dominican Republic	Subscriber members
Ecuador	Member bodies
Egypt	Member bodies
El Salvador	Correspondent members
Eritrea	Subscriber members
Estonia	Correspondent members
Ethiopia	Member bodies
Fiji	Subscriber members
Finland	Member bodies
France	Member bodies
Germany	Member bodies
Ghana	Member bodies
Greece	Member bodies
Grenada	Subscriber members
Guatemala	Correspondent members
Guyana	Subscriber members
Honduras	Subscriber members
Hong Kong, China	Correspondent members
Hungary	Member bodies
Iceland	Member bodies
India	Member bodies
Indonesia	Member bodies
Iran, Islamic Republic of	Member bodies
Iraq	Member bodies
Ireland	Member bodies
Israel	Member bodies
Italy	Member bodies
Jamaica	Member bodies
Japan	Member bodies
Jordan	Member bodies
Kazakhstan	Member bodies
Kenya	Member bodies
Korea, Democratic People's Republic	Member bodies
Korea, Republic of	Member bodies
Kuwait	Member bodies
Kyrgyzstan	Correspondent members
Latvia	Correspondent members
Lebanon	Correspondent members
Lesotho	Subscriber members
Libyan Arab Jamahiriya	Member bodies
Lithuania	Correspondent members

Luxembourg	Member bodies
Macau, China	Correspondent members
Madagascar	Correspondent members
Malawi	Correspondent members
Malaysia	Member bodies
Malta	Member bodies
Mauritius	Member bodies
Mexico	Member bodies
Moldova, Republic of	Correspondent members
Mongolia	Member bodies
Morocco	Member bodies
Mozambique	Correspondent members
Namibia	Correspondent members
Nepal	Correspondent members
Netherlands	Member bodies
New Zealand	Member bodies
Nicaragua	Correspondent members
Niger	Subscriber members
Nigeria	Member bodies
Norway	Member bodies
Oman	Member bodies
Pakistan	Member bodies
Palestine	Subscriber members
Panama	Member bodies
Papua New Guinea	Correspondent members
Paraguay	Correspondent members
Peru	Correspondent members
Philippines	Member bodies
Poland	Member bodies
Portugal	Member bodies
Qatar	Member bodies
Romania	Member bodies
Russian Federation	Member bodies
Rwanda	Correspondent members
Saint Lucia	Correspondent members
Saudi Arabia	Member bodies
Senegal	Correspondent members
Serbia and Montenegro	Member bodies
Seychelles	Correspondent members
Singapore	Member bodies
Slovakia	Member bodies
Slovenia	Member bodies
South Africa	Member bodies
Spain	Member bodies
Sri Lanka	Member bodies
Sudan	Correspondent members
Swaziland	Correspondent members

Sweden	Member bodies
Switzerland	Member bodies
Syrian Arab Republic	Member bodies
Tanzania, United Republic of	Member bodies
Thailand	Member bodies
The former Yugoslav Republic of Macedonia	Member bodies
Trinidad and Tobago	Member bodies
Tunisia	Member bodies
Turkey	Member bodies
Turkmenistan	Correspondent members
USA	Member bodies
Uganda	Correspondent members
Ukraine	Member bodies
United Arab Emirates	Member bodies
United Kingdom	Member bodies
Uruguay	Member bodies
Uzbekistan	Member bodies
Venezuela	Member bodies
Viet Nam	Member bodies
Yemen	Correspondent members
Zambia	Correspondent members
Zimbabwe	Member bodies

LAFTA

Argentina, Bolivia Brazil, Chile, Colombia, Ecuador, Mexico, Paraguay, Peru, Uruguay, and Venezuela.

MERCUSOR

Argentina, Bolivia, Brazil, Chile, Paraguay, and Uruguay.

NAFTA

Canada, Mexico and United States of America.

NAM

Afghanistan	Algeria	Angola
Bahamas	Bahrain	Bangladesh
Barbados	Belize	Benin
Bhutan	Bolivia	Botswana
Brunei Darussalam	Burkina Faso	Burundi
Cambodia	Cameroon	Cape Verde
Central African Republic	Chad	Chile
Colombia	Comoros	Congo
Congo Democratic Rep of	Cote d'Ivoire	Cuba
Cyprus	Djibouti	Ecuador
Egypt	Equatorial Guinea	Eritrea
Ethiopia	Gabon	Gambia
Ghana	Grenada	Guatemala

Guinea	Guinea-Bissau	Guyana
Honduras	India	Indonesia
Iran Islamic Rep of	Iraq	Jamaica
Jordan	Kenya	Korea Democratic People's Rep of
Kuwait	Lao People's Democratic Rep	Lebanon
Lesotho	Liberia	Libyan Arab Jamahirya
Madagascar	Malawi	Malaysia
Maldives	Mali	Malta
Mauritania	Mauritius	Mongolia
Morocco	Mozambique	Myanmar
Namibia	Nepal	Nicaragua
Niger	Nigeria	Oman
Pakistan	Palestine	Panama
Papua New Guinea	Peru	Philippines
Qatar	Rwanda	Saint Lucia
Sao Tome and Principe	Saudi Arabia	Senegal
Seychelles	Sierra Leone	Singapore
Somalia	South Africa	Sri Lanka
Sudan	Suriname	Swaziland
Syrian Arab Republic	Thailand	Togo
Trinidad and Tobago	Tunisia	Turkmenistan
Uganda	United Arab Emirates	Tanzania United Rep of
Uzbekistan	Vanuatu	Venezuela
Viet Nam	Yemen	*Yugoslavia
Zambia	Zimbabwe	

SUSPENDED

NATO

Belgium, Bulgaria, Canada, Czechoslovakia, Denmark, Estonia, France, Germany, Greece, Hungary, Iceland, Italy, Latvia, Lithuania, Luxembourg, Netherlands, Norway, Poland, Portugal, Romania, Slovakia, Slovania, Spain, Turkey, U.K. and U.S.

Nordic Council

Åland , Denmark, Faeroes, Finland, Greenland, Iceland, Norway and Sweden

OAS

Antigua and Barbuda, Argentina, Barbados, Bahamas, Belize, Bolivia, Brazil, Canada, Chile, Colombia, Costa Rica, Cuba (the current Government of Cuba is excluded from participation in the OAS), Dominican Republic, Dominica and Saint Lucia, Ecuador, El Salvador, Grenada, Guatemala, Guyana, Haiti, Honduras, Jamaica, Mexico, Nicaragua, Panama, Paraguay, Peru,

Saint Vincent and the Grenadines, St. Kitts and Nevis, Surinam, Trinidad and Tobago, United States of America, Uruguay and Venezuela.

OECD

Australia
Austria
Belgium
Canada
Czech Republic
Denmark
Finland
France
Germany
Greece
Hungary
Iceland
Ireland
Italy
Japan
Korea
Luxembourg
Mexico
Netherlands
New Zealand
Norway
Poland
Portugal
Slovak Republic
Spain
Sweden
Switzerland
Turkey
United Kingdom
United States

OIC

Afghanistan
Albania,
Algeria,
Azerbaijan,
Bahrain,
Bangladesh,
Benin,
Brunei Dar-us-Salaam,
Burkina Faso
Cameroon,
Chad,
Comoros,
Cote d'Ivoire,
Djibouti,
Egypt,
Gabon,
Gambia,
Guinea,
Guinea-Bissau,
Guyana,
Indonesia,
Iran,
Iraq,
Jordan,
Kazakhstan,
Kuwait,
Kyrghyzistan,
Lebanon,
Libya,
Malaysia
Maldives,
Mali,
Mauritania,
Morocco,
Mozambique,
Niger,
Nigeria,
Oman,
Pakistan,
Palestine,
Qatar,
Saudi Arabia,
Senegal,
Sierra Leone,
Somalia,
Sudan,
Surinam,
Syrian
Tajikistan,
Togo,
Tunisia,
Turkey,
Turkmenistan,
Uganda,
United Arab Emirates,
Uzbekistan,
Yemen.

OPEC

Algeria, Indonesia, Iran, Iraq, Kuwait, Libya, Nigeria, Qatar, Saudi Arabia, the United Arab Emirates and Venezuela.

OSCE

Albania
Andorra
Armenia
Austria
Azerbaijan
Belarus
Belgium
Bosnia and Herzegovina
Bulgaria
Canada
Croatia
Cyprus
Czech Republic
Denmark

Estonia
Finland
France
Georgia
Germany
Greece
Holy See
Hungary
Iceland
Ireland
Italy
Kazakhstan
Kyrgyzstan
Latvia
Liechtenstein
Lithuania
Luxembourg
Malta
Moldova
Monaco
Netherlands
Norway
Poland
Portugal
Romania
Russian Federation
San Marino
Serbia and Montenegro
Slovak Republic
Slovenia
Spain
Sweden
Switzerland
Tajikistan
The former Yugoslav Republic of Macedonia
Turkey
Turkmenistan
Ukraine
United Kingdom
United States of America
Uzbekistan

SADC

Angola
Botswana
D.R.Congo
Lesotho
Malawi
Mauritius
Mozambique
Namibia
Seychelles
South Africa
Swaziland
Tanzania
Zambia
Zimbabwe

SAARC

Bangladesh, Bhutan, India, Maldives, Nepal, Pakistan and Sri Lanka.

UNCTAD

Afghanistan*
Albania*
Algeria*
Andorra
Angola*
Antigua and Barbuda
Argentina*
Armenia*
Australia*
Austria*
Azerbaijan*
Bahamas
Bahrain*
Bangladesh*
Barbados*
Belarus*
Belgium*
Belize
Benin*
Bhutan*
Bolivia*
Bosnia and Herzegovina
Botswana*
Brazil*
Brunei Darussalam
Bulgaria*
Burkina Faso*
Burundi*
Cambodia
Cameroon*
Canada*
Cape Verde
Central African Republic*
Chad*
Chile*
China*
Colombia*
Comoros
Congo*
Costa Rica*
Côte d´Ivoire*
Croatia*
Cuba*
Cyprus*
Czech Republic*
Democratic People´s Republic of Korea*
Democratic Republic of the Congo*
Denmark*
Djibouti
Dominica*
Dominican Republic*
Ecuador*
Egypt*
El Salvador*
Equatorial Guinea*
Eritrea

Estonia
Ethiopia*
Fiji
Finland*
France*
Gabon*
Gambia
Georgia*
Germany*
Ghana*
Greece*
Grenada*
Guatemala*
Guinea*
Guinea-Bissau
Guyana*
Haiti*
Holy See
Honduras*
Hungary*
Iceland*
India*
Indonesia*
Iran (Islamic Republic of)*
Iraq*
Ireland*
Israel*
Italy*
Jamaica*
Japan*
Jordan*
Kazakhstan
Kenya*
Kiribati
Kuwait*
Kyrgyzstan
Lao People´s Democratic Republic
Latvia*
Lebanon*
Lesotho*
Liberia*
Libyan Arab Jamahiriya*
Liechtenstein*
Lithuania*
Luxembourg*
Madagascar*
Malawi
Malaysia*
Maldives
Mali*
Malta *
Marshall Islands
Mauritania*
Mauritius*
Mexico*
Micronesia (Federated States of)
Monaco
Mongolia*
Morocco*
Mozambique*
Myanmar*
Namibia*
Nauru
Nepal*
Netherlands*
New Zealand*
Nicaragua *
Niger
Nigeria*
Norway*
Oman*
Pakistan*
Panama*
Papua New Guinea*
Paraguay*
Peru*
Philippines*
Poland*
Portugal*
Qatar*
Republic of Korea*
Republic of Moldova*
Romania *
Russian Federation*
Rwanda
Saint Kitts and Nevis
Saint Lucia
Saint Vincent and the Grenadines
Samoa
San Marino
Sao Tome and Principe*
Saudi Arabia*
Senegal*
Serbia and Montenegro*
Seychelles
Sierra Leone *
Singapore*
Slovakia*
Slovenia*
Solomon Islands
Somalia*
South Africa*
Spain*
Sri Lanka*
Sudan *
Suriname*
Swaziland
Sweden *
Switzerland*
Syrian Arab Republic*
Tajikistan
Thailand *
Timor Leste
The Former Yugoslav Republic of Macedonia*
Togo*
Tonga
Trinidad and Tobago*
Tunisia*
Turkey *
Turkmenistan
Tuvalu
Uganda*
Ukraine*
United Arab Emirates*
United Kingdom of Great Britain and Northern Ireland*
United Republic of Tanzania*
United States of America*

Uruguay *
Uzbekistan
Vanuatu
Venezuela*
Viet Nam *
Yemen*
Zambia*
Zimbabwe*

The members of the Trade and Development Board are marked with an "*".

WCO

Albania
Algeria
Andorra
Angola
Argentina
Armenia
Australia
Austria
Azerbaijan
Bahamas
Bahrain
Bangladesh
Barbados
Belarus
Belgium
Benin
Bermuda
Bhutan
Bolivia
Botswana
Brazil
Brunei Darussalam
Bulgaria
Burkina Faso
Burundi
Cambodia
Cameroon
Canada
Cape Verde
Central African Republic
Chile
China
Colombia
Comoros
Congo (Republic of the)
Costa Rica
Côte d'Ivoire
Croatia
Cuba
Cyprus
Czech Republic
Democratic Republic of the Congo
Denmark
Ecuador
Egypt
Eritrea
Estonia
Ethiopia
Fiji
Finland
France
Gabon
Gambia
Georgia
Germany
Ghana
Greece
Guatemala
Guinea
Guyana
Haiti
Hong Kong, China
Hungary
Iceland
India
Indonesia
Iran (Islamic Republic of)
Iraq
Ireland
Israel
Italy
Jamaica
Japan
Jordan
Kazakhstan
Kenya
Korea (Republic of)
Kuwait
Kyrgyzstan
Latvia
Lebanon
Lesotho
Liberia
Libyan Arab Jamahiriya
Lithuania
Luxembourg
Macau, China
Madagascar
Malawi
Malaysia
Maldives
Mali
Malta
Mauritania
Mauritius
Mexico
Moldova
Mongolia
Morocco
Mozambique
Myanmar
Namibia
Nepal
Netherlands
Netherlands Antilles
New Zealand
Nicaragua
Niger
Nigeria Norway
Oman
Pakistan
Panama
Papua New Guinea
Paraguay
Peru
Philippines
Poland

Portugal
Qatar
Romania
Russian Federation
Rwanda
Samoa
Saudi Arabia
Senegal
Serbia and Montenegro
Seychelles
Sierra Leone
Singapore
Slovakia
Slovenia
South Africa
Spain
Sri Lanka
Sudan
Swaziland
Sweden
Switzerland
Syrian Arab Republic
Tajikistan
Tanzania
Thailand
The Former Yugoslav Republic of Macedonia
Timor-Leste
Togo
Trinidad and Tobago
Tunisia
Turkey
Turkmenistan
Uganda
Ukraine
United Arab Emirates
United Kingdom
United States
Uruguay
Uzbekistan
Venezuela
Vietnam
Yemen
Zambia
Zimbabwe

World Bank Group

Member	IBRD	IFC	IDA	MIGA	ICSID
Afghanistan	•	•	•	•	•
Albania	•	•	•	•	•
Algeria	•	•	•	•	•
Angola	•	•	•	•	
Antigua and Barbuda	•	•			
Argentina	•	•	•	•	•
Armenia	•	•	•	•	•
Australia	•	•	•	•	•
Austria	•	•	•	•	•
Azerbaijan	•	•	•	•	•
Bahamas, The	•	•		•	•
Bahrain	•	•		•	•
Bangladesh	•	•	•	•	•
Barbados	•	•	•	•	•
Belarus	•	•		•	•
Belgium	•	•	•	•	•
Belize	•	•	•	•	
Benin	•	•	•	•	•
Bhutan	•	•	•		
Bolivia	•	•	•	•	•
Bosnia and Herzegovina	•	•	•	•	•
Botswana	•	•	•	•	•
Brazil	•	•	•	•	
Brunei Darussalam	•				•
Bulgaria	•	•		•	•
Burkina Faso	•	•	•	•	•
Burundi	•	•	•	•	•
Cambodia	•	•	•	•	

Member	IBRD	IFC	IDA	MIGA	ICSID
Cameroon	•	•	•	•	•
Canada	•	•	•	•	
Cape Verde	•	•	•	•	
Central African Republic	•	•	•	•	•
Chad	•	•	•	•	•
Chile	•	•	•	•	•
China	•	•	•	•	•
Colombia	•	•	•	•	•
Comoros	•	•	•		•
Congo, Democratic Republic of	•	•	•	•	•
Congo, Republic of	•	•	•	•	•
Costa Rica	•	•	•	•	•
Cote d'Ivoire	•	•	•	•	•
Croatia	•	•	•	•	•
Cyprus	•	•	•	•	•
Czech Republic	•	•	•	•	•
Denmark	•	•	•	•	•
Djibouti	•	•	•		
Dominica	•	•	•	•	
Dominican Republic	•	•	•	•	
Ecuador	•	•	•	•	•
Egypt, Arab Republic of	•	•	•	•	•
El Salvador	•	•	•	•	•
Equatorial Guinea	•	•	•	•	
Eritrea	•	•	•	•	
Estonia	•	•		•	•
Ethiopia	•	•	•	•	
Fiji	•	•	•	•	•
Finland	•	•	•	•	•
France	•	•	•	•	•
Gabon	•	•	•	•	•
Gambia, The	•	•	•	•	•
Georgia	•	•	•	•	•
Germany	•	•	•	•	•
Ghana	•	•	•	•	•
Greece	•	•	•	•	•
Grenada	•	•	•	•	•
Guatemala	•	•	•	•	•
Guinea	•	•	•	•	•
Guinea-Bissau	•	•	•		
Guyana	•	•	•	•	•
Haiti	•	•	•	•	
Honduras	•	•	•	•	•
Hungary	•	•	•	•	•
Iceland	•	•	•	•	•

Member	IBRD	IFC	IDA	MIGA	ICSID
India	•	•	•	•	
Indonesia	•	•	•	•	•
Iran, Islamic Republic of	•	•	•	•	
Iraq	•	•	•		
Ireland	•	•	•	•	•
Israel	•	•	•	•	•
Italy	•	•	•	•	•
Jamaica	•	•		•	•
Japan	•	•	•	•	•
Jordan	•	•	•	•	•
Kazakhstan	•	•	•	•	•
Kenya	•	•	•	•	•
Kiribati	•	•	•		
Korea, Republic of	•	•	•	•	•
Kuwait	•	•	•	•	•
Kyrgyz Republic	•	•	•	•	
Lao People's Democratic Republic	•	•	•		
Latvia	•	•	•	•	•
Lebanon	•	•	•	•	•
Lesotho	•	•	•	•	•
Liberia	•	•	•		•
Libya	•	•	•	•	
Lithuania	•	•		•	•
Luxembourg	•	•	•	•	•
Macedonia, FYR of	•	•	•	•	•
Madagascar	•	•	•	•	•
Malawi	•	•	•	•	•
Malaysia	•	•	•	•	•
Maldives	•	•	•		
Mali	•	•	•	•	•
Malta	•			•	•
Marshall Islands	•	•	•		
Mauritania	•	•	•	•	•
Mauritius	•	•	•	•	•
Mexico	•	•	•		
Micronesia, Federated States of	•	•	•	•	•
Moldova	•	•	•	•	
Mongolia	•	•	•	•	•
Morocco	•	•	•	•	•
Mozambique	•	•	•	•	•
Myanmar	•	•	•		
Namibia	•	•		•	
Nepal	•	•	•	•	•
Netherlands	•	•	•	•	•
New Zealand	•	•	•		•

Member	IBRD	IFC	IDA	MIGA	ICSID
Nicaragua	•	•	•	•	•
Niger	•	•	•		•
Nigeria	•	•	•	•	•
Norway	•	•	•	•	•
Oman	•	•	•	•	•
Pakistan	•	•	•	•	•
Palau	•	•	•	•	
Panama	•	•	•	•	•
Papua New Guinea	•	•	•	•	•
Paraguay	•	•	•	•	•
Peru	•	•	•	•	•
Philippines	•	•	•	•	•
Poland	•	•	•	•	
Portugal	•	•	•	•	•
Qatar	•			•	
Romania	•	•		•	•
Russian Federation	•	•	•	•	
Rwanda	•	•	•	•	•
Samoa	•	•	•	•	•
San Marino	•				
Sao Tome and Principe	•		•		
Saudi Arabia	•	•	•	•	•
Senegal	•	•	•	•	•
Serbia and Montenegro	•	•	•	•	
Seychelles	•	•		•	•
Sierra Leone	•	•	•	•	•
Singapore	•	•	•	•	•
Slovak Republic	•	•	•	•	•
Slovenia	•	•	•	•	•
Solomon Islands	•	•	•		•
Somalia	•	•	•		•
South Africa	•	•	•	•	
Spain	•	•	•	•	•
Sri Lanka	•	•	•	•	•
St. Kitts and Nevis	•	•	•	•	•
St. Lucia	•	•	•	•	•
St. Vincent and the Grenadines	•		•	•	•
Sudan	•	•	•	•	•
Suriname	•			•	
Swaziland	•	•	•	•	•
Sweden	•	•	•	•	•
Switzerland	•	•	•	•	•
Syrian Arab Republic	•	•	•	•	
Tajikistan	•				

APPENDIX-2

Charter of The United Nations

INTRODUCTORY NOTE

The Charter of the United Nations was signed on 26 June 1945, in San Francisco, at the conclusion of the United Nations Conference on International Organisation, and came into force on 24 October 1945. The Statute of the International Court of Justice is an integral part of the Charter.

Amendments to Articles 23, 27 and 61 of the Charter were adopted by the General Assembly on 17 December 1963 and came into force on 31 August 1965. A further amendment to Article 61 was adopted by the General Assembly on 20 December 1971, and came into force on 24 September 1973. An amendment to Article 109, adopted by the General Assembly on 20 December 1965, came into force on 12 June 1968.

The amendment to Article 23 enlarges the membership of the Security Council from eleven to fifteen. The amended Article 27 provides that decisions of the Security Council on procedural matters shall be made by an affirmative vote of nine members (formerly seven) and on all other matters by an affirmative vote of nine members (formerly seven), including the concurring votes of the five permanent members of the Security Council.

The amendment to Article 61, which entered into force on 31 August 1965, enlarged the membership of the Economic and Social Council from eighteen to twenty-seven. The subsequent amendment to that Article, which entered into force on 24 September 1973, further increased the membership of the Council from twenty-seven to fifty-four.

The amendment to Article 109, which relates to the first paragraph of that Article, provides that a General Conference of Member States for the purpose of reviewing the Charter may be held at a date and place to be fixed by a two-thirds vote of the members of the General Assembly and by a vote of any nine members (formerly seven) of the Security Council. Paragraph 3 of Article 109, which deals with the consideration of a possible review conference during the tenth regular session of the General Assembly, has been retained in its original form in its reference to a "vote, of any seven members of the Security Council", the paragraph having been acted upon in 1955 by the General Assembly, at its tenth regular session, and by the Security Council.

PREAMBLE

We the peoples of the United Nations Determined

- to save succeeding generations from the scourge of war, which twice in our lifetime has brought untold sorrow to mankind, and
- to reaffirm faith in fundamental human rights, in the dignity and worth of the human person, in the equal rights of men and women and of nations large and small, and
- to establish conditions under which justice and respect for the obligations arising from treaties and other sources of international law can be maintained, and
- to promote social progress and better standards of life in larger freedom,
- AND FOR THESE ENDS
- to practice tolerance and live together in peace with one another as good neighbours, and
- to unite our strength to maintain international peace and security, and
- to ensure, by the acceptance of principles and the institution of methods, that armed force shall not be used, save in the common interest, and
- to employ international machinery for the promotion of the economic and social advancement of all peoples,

Have Resolved to Combine Our Efforts to Accomplish These Aims

Accordingly, our respective Governments, through representatives assembled in the city of San Francisco, who have exhibited their full powers found to be in good and due form, have agreed to the present Charter of the United Nations and do hereby establish an international organisation to be known as the United Nations.

CHAPTER I
PURPOSES AND PRINCIPLES

Article 1

The Purposes of the United Nations are:

To maintain international peace and security, and to that end: to take effective collective measures for the prevention and removal of threats to the peace, and for the suppression of acts of aggression or other breaches of the peace, and to bring about by peaceful means, and in conformity with the principles of justice and international law, adjustment or settlement of international disputes or situations which might lead to a breach of the peace;

To develop friendly relations among nations based on respect for the principle of equal rights and self-determination of peoples, and to take other appropriate measures to strengthen universal peace;

To achieve international co-operation in solving international problems of an economic, social, cultural, or humanitarian character, and in promoting and encouraging respect for human rights and for fundamental freedoms for all without distinction as to race, sex, language, or religion and

To be a centre for harmonizing the actions of nations in the attainment of these common ends.

Article 2

The Organisation and its Members, in pursuit of the Purposes stated in Article 1, shall act in accordance with the following Principles.

The Organisation is based on the principle of the sovereign equality of all its Members.

All Members, in order to ensure to all of them the rights and benefits resulting from membership, shall fulfill in good faith the obligations assumed by them in accordance with the present Charter.

All Members shall settle their international disputes by peaceful means in such a manner that international peace and security, and justice, are not endangered.

All Members shall refrain in their international relations from the threat or use of force against the territorial integrity or political independence of any state, or in any other manner inconsistent with the Purposes of the United Nations.

All Members shall give the United Nations every assistance in any action it takes in accordance with the present Charter, and shall refrain from giving assistance to any state against which the United Nations is taking preventive or enforcement action.

The Organisation shall ensure that states which are not Members of the United Nations act in accordance with these Principles so far as may be necessary for the maintenance of international peace and security.

Nothing contained in the present Charter shall authorize the United Nations to intervene in matters which are essentially within the domestic jurisdiction of any state or shall require the Members to submit such matters to settlement under the present Charter; but this principle shall not prejudice the application of enforcement measures under Chapter Vll.

CHAPTER II
MEMBERSHIP

Article 3

The original Members of the United Nations shall be the states which, having participated in the United Nations Conference on International Organisation at San Francisco, or having previously signed the Declaration by United Nations of 1 January 1942, sign the present Charter and ratify it in accordance with Article 110.

Article 4

1. Membership in the United Nations is open to all other peace-loving states which accept the obligations contained in the present Charter and, in the judgment of the Organisation, are able and willing to carry out these obligations.

2. The admission of any such state to membership in the United Nations will be effected by a decision of the General Assembly upon the recommendation of the Security Council.

Article 5

A Member of the United Nations against which preventive or enforcement action has been taken by the Security Council may be suspended from the exercise of the rights and privileges of membership by the General Assembly upon the recommendation of the Security Council. The exercise of these rights and privileges may be restored by the Security Council.

Article 6

A Member of the United Nations which has persistently violated the Principles contained in the present Charter may be expelled from the Organisation by the General Assembly upon the recommendation of the Security Council.

CHAPTER III
ORGANS

Article 7

There are established as the principal organs of the United Nations:

- a General Assembly
- a Security Council
- an Economic and Social Council
- a Trusteeship Council
- an International Court of Justice
- and a Secretariat

Such subsidiary organs as may be found necessary may be established in accordance with the present Charter.

Article 8

The United Nations shall place no restrictions on the eligibility of men and women to participate in any capacity and under conditions of equality in its principal and subsidiary organs.

CHAPTER IV
THE GENERAL ASSEMBLY

COMPOSITION

Article 9

The General Assembly shall consist of all the Members of the United Nations.

Each Member shall have not more than five representatives in the General Assembly.

FUNCTIONS and POWERS

Article 10

The General Assembly may discuss any questions or any matters within the scope of the present Charter or relating to the powers and functions of any organs provided for in the present Charter, and, except as provided in Article 12, may make recommendations to the Members of the United Nations or to the Security Council or to both on any such questions or matters.

Article 11

The General Assembly may consider the general principles of co-operation in the maintenance of international peace and security, including the principles governing disarmament and the regulation of armaments, and may make recommendations with regard to such principles to the Members or to the Security Council or to both.

The General Assembly may discuss any questions relating to the maintenance of international peace and security brought before it by any Member of the United Nations, or by the Security Council, or by a state which is not a Member of the United Nations in accordance with Article 35, paragraph 2, and, except as provided in Article 12, may make recommendations with regard to any such questions to the state or states concerned or to the Security Council or to both. Any such question on which action is necessary shall be referred to the Security Council by the General Assembly either before or after discussion.

The General Assembly may call the attention of the Security Council to situations which are likely to endanger international peace and security.

The powers of the General Assembly set forth in this Article shall not limit the general scope of Article 10.

Article 12

While the Security Council is exercising in respect of any dispute or situation the functions assigned to it in the present

Charter, the General Assembly shall not make any recommendation with regard to that dispute or situation unless the Security Council so requests.

The Secretary-General, with the consent of the Security Council, shall notify the General Assembly at each session of any matters relative to the maintenance of international peace and security which are being dealt with by the Security Council and shall similarly notify the General Assembly, or the Members of the United Nations if the General Assembly is not in session, immediately the Security Council ceases to deal with such matters.

Article 13

The General Assembly shall initiate studies and make recommendations for the purpose of:

(a) promoting international co-operation in the political field and encouraging the progressive development of international law and its codification;

(b) promoting international co-operation in the economic, social, cultural, educational, and health fields, and assisting in the realisation of human rights and fundamental freedoms for all without distinction as to race, sex, language, or religion.

The further responsibilities, functions and powers of the General Assembly with respect to matters mentioned in paragraph 1 (b) above are set forth in Chapters IX and X.

Article 14

Subject to the provisions of Article 12, the General Assembly may recommend measures for the peaceful adjustment of any situation, regardless of origin, which it deems likely to impair the general welfare or friendly relations among nations, including situations resulting from a violation of the provisions of the present Charter setting forth the Purposes and Principles of the United Nations.

Article 15

The General Assembly shall receive and consider annual and special reports from the Security Council; these reports shall include an account of the measures that the Security

Council has decided upon or taken to maintain international peace and security.

The General Assembly shall receive and consider reports from the other organs of the United Nations.

Article 16

The General Assembly shall perform such functions with respect to the international trusteeship system as are assigned to it under Chapters XII and XIII, including the approval of the trusteeship agreements for areas not designated as strategic.

Article 17

The General Assembly shall consider and approve the budget of the Organisation.

The expenses of the Organisation shall be borne by the Members as apportioned by the General Assembly.

The General Assembly shall consider and approve any financial and budgetary arrangements with specialized agencies referred to in Article 57 and shall examine the administrative budgets of such specialized agencies with a view to making recommendations to the agencies concerned.

VOTING

Article 18

Each member of the General Assembly shall have one vote.

Decisions of the General Assembly on important questions shall be made by a two-thirds majority of the members present and voting. These questions shall include: recommendations with respect to the maintenance of international peace and security, the election of the non-permanent members of the Security Council, the election of the members of the Economic and Social Council, the election of members of the Trusteeship Council in accordance with paragraph 1 (c) of Article 86, the admission of new Members to the United Nations, the suspension of the rights and privileges of membership, the expulsion of Members, questions relating to the operation of the trusteeship system, and budgetary questions.

Decisions on other questions, including the determination of additional categories of questions to be decided by a two-thirds majority, shall be made by a majority of the members present and voting.

Article 19

A Member of the United Nations which is in arrears in the payment of its financial contributions to the Organisation shall have no vote in the General Assembly if the amount of its arrears equals or exceeds the amount of the contributions due from it for the preceding two full years. The General Assembly may, nevertheless, permit such a Member to vote if it is satisfied that the failure to pay is due to conditions beyond the control of the Member.

PROCEDURE

Article 20

The General Assembly shall meet in regular annual sessions and in such special sessions as occasion may require. Special sessions shall be convoked by the Secretary-General at the request of the Security Council or of a majority of the Members of the United Nations.

Article 21

The General Assembly shall adopt its own rules of procedure. It shall elect its President for each session.

Article 22

The General Assembly may establish such subsidiary organs as it deems necessary for the performance of its functions.

CHAPTER V

THE SECURITY COUNCIL

COMPOSITION

Article 23

The Security Council shall consist of fifteen Members of the United Nations. The Republic of China, France, the Union of Soviet Socialist Republics, the United Kingdom of Great Britain and Northern Ireland, and the United States of America shall be permanent members of the Security Council. The General Assembly shall elect ten other Members of the United Nations to be non-permanent members of the Security Council, due regard being specially paid, in the first instance to the contribution of Members of the United Nations to the maintenance of international peace and security and to the other purposes of the Organisation, and also to equitable geographical distribution.

The non-permanent members of the Security Council shall be elected for a term of two years. In the first election of the non-permanent members after the increase of the membership of the Security Council from eleven to fifteen, two of the four additional members shall be chosen for a term of one year. A retiring member shall not be eligible for immediate re-election.

Each member of the Security Council shall have one representative.

FUNCTIONS and POWERS

Article 24

In order to ensure prompt and effective action by the United Nations,its Members confer on the Security Council primary responsibility for the maintenance of international peace and security, and agree that in carrying out its duties under this responsibility the Security Council acts on their behalf.

In discharging these duties the Security Council shall act in accordance with the Purposes and Principles of the United Nations. The specific powers granted to the Security Council for the discharge of these duties are laid down in Chapters VI, VII, VIII, and XII.

The Security Council shall submit annual and, when necessary, special reports to the General Assembly for its consideration.

Article 25

The Members of the United Nations agree to accept and carry out the decisions of the Security Council in accordance with the present Charter.

Article 26

In order to promote the establishment and maintenance of international peace and security with the least diversion for armaments of the world's human and economic resources, the Security Council shall be responsible for formulating, with the assistance of the Military Staff Committee referred to in Article 47, plans to be submitted to the Members of the United Nations for the establishment of a system for the regulation of armaments.

VOTING

Article 27

Each member of the Security Council shall have one vote.

Decisions of the Security Council on procedural matters shall be made by an affirmative vote of nine members.

Decisions of the Security Council on all other matters shall be made by an affirmative vote of nine members including the concurring votes of the permanent members; provided that, in decisions under Chapter VI, and under paragraph 3 of Article 52, a party to a dispute shall abstain from voting.

PROCEDURE

Article 28

The Security Council shall be so organized as to be able to function continuously. Each member of the Security Council shall for this purpose be represented at all times at the seat of the Organisation.

The Security Council shall hold periodic meetings at which each of its members may, if it so desires, be represented by a member of the government or by some other specially designated representative.

The Security Council may hold meetings at such places other than the seat of the Organisation as in its judgment will best facilitate its work.

Article 29

The Security Council may establish such subsidiary organs as it deems necessary for the performance of its functions.

Article 30

The Security Council shall adopt its own rules of procedure, including the method of selecting its President.

Article 31

Any Member of the United Nations which is not a member

of the Security Council may participate, without vote, in the discussion of any question brought before the Security Council whenever the latter considers that the interests of that Member are specially affected.

Article 32

Any Member of the United Nations which is not a member of the Security Council or any state which is not a Member of the United Nations, if it is a party to a dispute under consideration by the Security Council, shall be invited to participate, without vote, in the discussion relating to the dispute. The Security Council shall lay down such conditions as it deems just for the participation of a state which is not a Member of the United Nations.

CHAPTER VI

PACIFIC SETTLEMENT OF DISPUTES

Article 33

The parties to any dispute, the continuance of which is likely to endanger the maintenance of international peace and security, shall, first of all, seek a solution by negotiation, enquiry, mediation, conciliation, arbitration, judicial settlement, resort to regional agencies or arrangements, or other peaceful means of their own choice.

The Security Council shall, when it deems necessary, call upon the parties to settle their dispute by such means.

Article 34

The Security Council may investigate any dispute, or any situation which might lead to international friction or give rise to a dispute, in order to determine whether the continuance of the dispute or situation is likely to endanger the maintenance of international peace and security.

Article 35

Any Member of the United Nations may bring any dispute, or any situation of the nature referred to in Article 34, to the attention of the Security Council or of the General Assembly.

A state which is not a Member of the United Nations may bring to the attention of the Security Council or of the General Assembly any dispute to which it is a party if it accepts in advance, for the purposes of the dispute, the obligations of pacific settlement provided in the present Charter.

The proceedings of the General Assembly in respect of matters brought to its attention under this Article will be subject to the provisions of Articles 11 and 12.

Article 36

The Security Council may, at any stage of a dispute of the nature referred to in Article 33 or of a situation of like nature, recommend appropriate procedures or methods of adjustment.

The Security Council should take into consideration any procedures for the settlement of the dispute which have already been adopted by the parties.

In making recommendations under this Article the Security Council should also take into consideration that legal disputes should as a general rule be referred by the parties to the International Court of Justice in accordance with the provisions of the Statute of the Court.

Article 37

Should the parties to a dispute of the nature referred to in Article 33 fail to settle it by the means indicated in that Article, they shall refer it to the Security Council.

If the Security Council deems that the continuance of the dispute is in fact likely to endanger the maintenance of international peace and security, it shall decide whether to take action under Article 36 or to recommend such terms of settlement as it may consider appropriate.

Article 38

Without prejudice to the provisions of Articles 33 to 37, the Security Council may, if all the parties to any dispute so request, make recommendations to the parties with a view to a pacific settlement of the dispute.

CHAPTER VII

ACTION WITH RESPECT TO THREATS TO THE PEACE, BREACHES OF THE PEACE, AND ACTS OF AGGRESSION

Article 39

The Security Council shall determine the existence of any threat to the peace, breach of the peace, or act of aggression and shall make recommendations, or decide what measures shall be taken in accordance with Articles 41 and 42, to maintain or restore international peace and security.

Article 40

In order to prevent an aggravation of the situation, the Security Council may, before making the recommendations or deciding upon the measures provided for in Article 39, call upon the parties concerned to comply with such provisional measures as it deems necessary or desirable. Such provisional measures shall be without prejudice to the rights, claims, or position of the parties concerned. The Security Council shall duly take account of failure to comply with such provisional measures.

Article 41

The Security Council may decide what measures not involving the use of armed force are to be employed to give effect to its decisions, and it may call upon the Members of the United Nations to apply such measures. These may include complete or partial interruption of economic relations and of rail, sea, air, postal, telegraphic, radio, and other means of communication, and the severance of diplomatic relations.

Article 42

Should the Security Council consider that measures provided for in Article 41 would be inadequate or have proved to be inadequate, it may take such action by air, sea, or land forces as may be necessary to maintain or restore international peace and security. Such action may include demonstrations, blockade, and other operations by air, sea, or land forces of Members of the United Nations.

Article 43

All Members of the United Nations, in order to contribute to the maintenance of international peace and security, undertake to make available to the Security Council, on its call and in accordance with a special agreement or agreements, armed forces, assistance, and facilities, including rights of passage, necessary for the purpose of maintaining international peace and security.

Such agreement or agreements shall govern the numbers and types of forces, their degree of readiness and general location, and the nature of the facilities and assistance to be provided.

The agreement or agreements shall be negotiated as soon as possible on the initiative of the Security Council. They shall be concluded between the Security Council and Members or between the Security Council and groups of Members and shall be subject to ratification by the signatory states in accordance with their respective constitutional processes.

Article 44

When the Security Council has decided to use force it shall, before calling upon a Member not represented on it to provide armed forces in fulfilment of the obligations assumed under Article 43, invite that Member, if the Member so desires, to participate in the decisions of the Security Council concerning the employment of contingents of that Member's armed forces.

Article 45

In order to enable the United Nations to take urgent military measures, Members shall hold immediately available national air-force contingents for combined international enforcement action. The strength and degree of readiness of these contingents and plans for their combined action shall be determined within the limits laid down in the special agreement or agreements referred to in Article 43, by the Security Council with the assistance of the Military Staff Committee.

Article 46

Plans for the application of armed force shall be made by the Security Council with the assistance of the Military Staff Committee.

Article 47

There shall be established a Military Staff Committee to advise and assist the Security Council on all questions relating to the Security Council's military requirements for the maintenance of international peace and security, the employment and command of forces placed at its disposal, the regulation of armaments, and possible disarmament.

The Military Staff Committee shall consist of the Chiefs of Staff of the permanent members of the Security Council or their representatives. Any Member of the United Nations not permanently represented on the Committee shall be invited by the Committee to be associated with it when the efficient discharge of the Committee's responsibilities requires the participation of that Member in its work.

The Military Staff Committee shall be responsible under the Security Council for the strategic direction of any armed forces placed at the disposal of the Security Council. Questions relating to the command of such forces shall be worked out subsequently.

The Military Staff Committee, with the authorisation of the Security Council and after consultation with appropriate regional agencies, may establish regional sub-committees.

Article 48

The action required to carry out the decisions of the Security Council for the maintenance of international peace and security shall be taken by all the Members of the United Nations or by some of them, as the Security Council may determine.

Such decisions shall be carried out by the Members of the United Nations directly and through their action in the appropriate international agencies of which they are members.

Article 49

The Members of the United Nations shall join in affording mutual assistance in carrying out the measures decided upon by the Security Council.

Article 50

If preventive or enforcement measures against any state are taken by the Security Council, any other state, whether a Member of the United Nations or not, which finds itself confronted with special economic problems arising from the carrying out of those measures shall have the right to consult the Security Council with regard to a solution of those problems.

Article 51

Nothing in the present Charter shall impair the inherent right of individual or collective self-defence if an armed attack occurs against a Member of the United Nations, until the Security Council has taken measures necessary to maintain international peace and security. Measures taken by Members in the exercise of this right of self-defence shall be immediately reported to the Security Council and shall not in any way affect the authority and responsibility of the Security Council under the present Charter to take at any time such action as it deems necessary in order to maintain or restore international peace and security.

CHAPTER VIII
REGIONAL ARRANGEMENTS

Article 52

Nothing in the present Charter precludes the existence of regional arrangements or agencies for dealing with such matters relating to the maintenance of international peace and security as are appropriate for regional action provided that such arrangements or agencies and their activities are consistent with the Purposes and Principles of the United Nations.

The Members of the United Nations entering into such arrangements or constituting such agencies shall make every effort to achieve pacific settlement of local disputes through such regional arrangements or by such regional agencies before referring them to the Security Council.

The Security Council shall encourage the development of pacific settlement of local disputes through such regional arrangements or by such regional agencies either on the initiative of the states concerned or by reference from the Security Council.

This Article in no way impairs the application of Articles 34 and 35.

Article 53

The Security Council shall, where appropriate, utilize such regional arrangements or agencies for enforcement action under its authority. But no enforcement action shall be taken under regional arrangements or by regional agencies without the authorisation of the Security Council, with the exception of measures against any enemy state, as defined in paragraph 2 of this Article, provided for pursuant to Article 107 or in regional arrangements directed against renewal of aggressive policy on the part of any such state, until such time as the Organisation may, on request of the Governments concerned, be charged with the responsibility for preventing further aggression by such a state.

The term enemy state as used in paragraph 1 of this Article applies to any state which during the Second World War has been an enemy of any signatory of the present Charter.

Article 54

The Security Council shall at all times be kept fully informed of activities undertaken or in contemplation under regional arrangements or by regional agencies for the maintenance of international peace and security.

CHAPTER IX

INTERNATIONAL ECONOMIC AND SOCIAL CO-OPERATION

Article 55

With a view to the creation of conditions of stability and well-being which are necessary for peaceful and friendly relations among nations based on respect for the principle of equal rights and self-determination of peoples, the United Nations shall promote:

a. higher standards of living, full employment, and conditions of economic and social progress and development;

b. solutions of international economic, social, health, and related problems; and international cultural and educational cooperation and

c. universal respect for, and observance of, human rights and fundamental freedoms for all without distinction as to race, sex, language, or religion.

Article 56

All Members pledge themselves to take joint and separate

action in co-operation with the Organisation for the achievement of the purposes set forth in Article 55.

Article 57

The various specialized agencies, established by intergovernmental agreement and having wide international responsibilities, as defined in their basic instruments, in economic, social, cultural, educational, health, and related fields, shall be brought into relationship with the United Nations in accordance with the provisions of Article 63.

Such agencies thus brought into relationship with the United Nations are hereinafter referred to as specialized agencies. OL

Article 58

The Organisation shall make recommendations for the co-ordination of the policies and activities of the specialized agencies.

Article 59

The Organisation shall, where appropriate, initiate negotiations among the states concerned for the creation of any new specialized agencies required for the accomplishment of the purposes set forth in Article 55.

Article 60

Responsibility for the discharge of the functions of the Organisation set forth in this Chapter shall be vested in the General Assembly and, under the authority of the General Assembly, in the Economic and Social Council, which shall have for this purpose the powers set forth in Chapter X.

CHAPTER X

THE ECONOMIC AND SOCIAL COUNCIL

COMPOSITION

Article 61

The Economic and Social Council shall consist of fifty-four Members of the United Nations elected by the General Assembly.

Subject to the provisions of paragraph 3, eighteen members of the Economic and Social Council shall be elected each year for a term of three years. A retiring member shall be eligible for immediate re-election.

At the first election after the increase in the membership of the Economic and Social Council from twenty-seven to fifty-four members, in addition to the members elected in place of the nine members whose term of office expires at the end of that year, twenty-seven additional members shall be elected. Of these twenty-seven additional members, the term of office of nine members so elected shall expire at the end of one year, and of nine other members at the end of two years, in accordance with arrangements made by the General Assembly.

Each member of the Economic and Social Council shall have one representative.

FUNCTIONS and POWERS

Article 62

The Economic and Social Council may make or initiate studies and reports with respect to international economic, social, cultural, educational, health, and related matters and may make recommendations with respect to any such matters to the General Assembly to the Members of the United Nations, and to the specialized agencies concerned.

It may make recommendations for the purpose of promoting respect for, and observance of, human rights and fundamental freedoms for all.

It may prepare draft conventions for submission to the General Assembly, with respect to matters falling within its competence.

It may call, in accordance with the rules prescribed by the United Nations,international conferences on matters falling within its competence.

Article 63

The Economic and Social Council may enter into agreements with any of the agencies referred to in Article 57, defining the terms on which the agency concerned shall be brought into relationship with the United Nations. Such agreements shall be subject to approval by the General Assembly.

It may co-ordinate the activities of the specialized agencies through consultation with and recommendations to such agencies and through recommendations to the General Assembly and to the Members of the United Nations.

Article 64

The Economic and Social Council may take appropriate steps to obtain regular reports from the specialized agencies. It may make arrangements with the Members of the United Nations and with the specialized agencies to obtain reports on the steps taken to give effect to its own recommendations and to recommendations on matters falling within its competence made by the General Assembly.

It may communicate its observations on these reports to the General Assembly.

Article 65

The Economic and Social Council may furnish information to the Security Council and shall assist the Security Council upon its request.

Article 66

The Economic and Social Council shall perform such functions as fall within its competence in connexion with the carrying out of the recommendations of the General Assembly.

It may, with the approval of the General Assembly, perform services at the request of Members of the United Nations and at the request of specialized agencies.

It shall perform such other functions as are specified elsewhere in the present Charter or as may be assigned to it by the General Assembly.

VOTING

Article 67

Each member of the Economic and Social Council shall have one vote.

Decisions of the Economic and Social Council shall be made by a majority of the members present and voting.

PROCEDURE

Article 68

The Economic and Social Council shall set up commissions in economic and social fields and for the promotion of human rights, and such other commissions as may be required for the performance of its functions.

Article 69

The Economic and Social Council shall invite any Member of the United Nations to participate, without vote, in its deliberations on any matter of particular concern to that Member.

Article 70

The Economic and Social Council may make arrangements for representatives of the specialized agencies to participate, without vote, in its deliberations and in those of the commissions established by it, and for its representatives to participate in the deliberations of the specialized agencies.

Article 71

The Economic and Social Council may make suitable arrangements for consultation with non-governmental organisations which are concerned with matters within its competence. Such arrangements may be made with international organisations and, where appropriate, with national organisations after consultation with the Member of the United Nations concerned.

Article 72

The Economic and Social Council shall adopt its own rules of procedure, including the method of selecting its President.

The Economic and Social Council shall meet as required in accordance with its rules, which shall include provision for the convening of meetings on the request of a majority of its members.

CHAPTER XI

DECLARATION REGARDING NON-SELF-GOVERNING TERRITORIES

Article 73

Members of the United Nations which have or assume responsibilities for the administration of territories whose peoples have not yet attained a full measure of self-government recognize the principle that the interests of the inhabitants of these territories are paramount, and accept as a sacred trust the obligation to promote to the utmost, within the system of international peace and security established by the present Charter, the well-being of the inhabitants of these territories, and, to this end:

a. to ensure, with due respect for the culture of the peoples concerned, their political, economic, social, and educational advancement, their just treatment, and their protection against abuses;

b. to develop self-government, to take due account of the political aspirations of the peoples, and to assist them in the progressive development of their free political institutions, according to the particular circumstances of each territory and its peoples and their varying stages of advancement;

c. to further international peace and security;

d. to promote constructive measures of development, to encourage research, and to co-operate with one another and, when and where appropriate, with specialized international bodies with a view to the practical achievement of the social, economic, and scientific purposes set forth in this Article and

e. to transmit regularly to the Secretary-General for information purposes, subject to such limitation as security and constitutional considerations may require, statistical and other information of a technical nature relating to economic, social, and educational conditions in the territories for which they are respectively responsible other than those territories to which Chapters XII and XIII apply.

Article 74

Members of the United Nations also agree that their policy in respect of the territories to which this Chapter applies, no less than in respect of their metropolitan areas, must be based on the general principle of good-neighbourliness, due account being taken of the interests and well-being of the rest of the world, in social, economic, and commercial matters.

CHAPTER XII

INTERNATIONAL TRUSTEESHIP SYSTEM

Article 75

The United Nations shall establish under its authority an international trusteeship system for the administration and supervision of such territories as may be placed thereunder by subsequent individual agreements. These territories are hereinafter referred to as trust territories.

Article 76

The basic objectives of the trusteeship system, in accordance with the Purposes of the United Nations laid down in Article 1 of the present Charter, shall be:

a. to further international peace and security;

b. to promote the political, economic, social, and educational advancement of the inhabitants of the trust territories, and their progressive development towards self-government or independence as may be appropriate to the particular circumstances of each territory and its peoples and the freely expressed wishes of the peoples concerned, and as may be provided by the terms of each trusteeship agreement;

c. to encourage respect for human rights and for fundamental freedoms for all without distinction as to race, sex, language, or religion, and to encourage recognition of the interdependence of the peoples of the world and

d. to ensure equal treatment in social, economic, and commercial matters for all Members of the United Nations and their nationals, and also equal treatment for the latter in the administration of justice, without prejudice to the attainment of the foregoing objectives and subject to the provisions of Article 80.

Article 77

The trusteeship system shall apply to such territories in the following categories as may be placed thereunder by means of trusteeship agreements:

a. territories now held under mandate;
b. territories which may be detached from enemy states as a result of the Second World War and
c. territories voluntarily placed under the system by states responsiblefor their administration.

It will be a matter for subsequent agreement as to which territories in the foregoing categories will be brought under the trusteeship system and upon what terms.

Article 78

The trusteeship system shall not apply to territories which have become Members of the United Nations, relationship among which shall be based on respect for the principle of sovereign equality.

Article 79

The terms of trusteeship for each territory to be placed under the trusteeship system, including any alteration or amendment, shall be agreed upon by the states directly concerned, including the mandatory power in the case of territories held under mandate by a Member of the United Nations, and shall be approved as provided for in Articles 83 and 85.

Article 80

Except as may be agreed upon in individual trusteeship agreements, made under Articles 77, 79, and 81, placing each territory under the trusteeship system, and until such agreements have been concluded, nothing in this Chapter shall be construed in or of itself to alter in any manner the rights whatsoever of any states or any peoples or the terms of existing international instruments to which Members of the United Nations may respectively be parties.

Paragraph 1 of this Article shall not be interpreted as giving grounds for delay or postponement of the negotiation and conclusion of agreements for placing mandated and other territories under the trusteeship system as provided for in Article 77.

Article 81

The trusteeship agreement shall in each case include the terms under which the trust territory will be administered and designate the authority which will exercise the administration of the trust territory. Such authority, hereinafter called the administering authority, may be one or more states or the Organisation itself.

Article 82

There may be designated, in any trusteeship agreement, a strategic area or areas which may include part or all of the trust territory to which the agreement applies, without prejudice to any special agreement or agreements made under Article 43.

Article 83

All functions of the United Nations relating to strategic areas, including the approval of the terms of the trusteeship agreements and of their alteration or amendment shall be exercised by the Security Council.

The basic objectives set forth in Article 76 shall be applicable to the people of each strategic area.

The Security Council shall, subject to the provisions of the trusteeship agreements and without prejudice to security considerations, avail itself of the assistance of the Trusteeship Council to perform those functions of the United Nations under the trusteeship system relating to political, economic, social, and educational matters in the strategic areas.

Article 84

It shall be the duty of the administering authority to ensure that the trust territory shall play its part in the maintenance of international peace and security. To this end the administering authority may make use of volunteer forces, facilities, and assistance from the trust territory in carrying out the obligations towards the Security Council undertaken in this regard by the administering authority, as well as for local defence and the maintenance of law and order within the trust territory.

Article 85

The functions of the United Nations with regard to trusteeship agreements for all areas not designated as strategic, including the approval of the terms of the trusteeship agreements and of their alteration or amendment, shall be exercised by the General Assembly.

The Trusteeship Council, operating under the authority of the General Assembly shall assist the General Assembly in carrying out these functions.

CHAPTER XIII
THE TRUSTEESHIP COUNCIL

COMPOSITION

Article 86

The Trusteeship Council shall consist of the following Members of the United Nations:

a. those Members administering trust territories;

b. such of those Members mentioned by name in Article 23 as are not administering trust territories and

c. as many other Members elected for three-year terms by the General Assembly as may be necessary to ensure that the total number of members of the Trusteeship Council is equally divided between those Members of the United Nations which administer trust territories and those which do not.

Each member of the Trusteeship Council shall designate one specially qualified person to represent it therein.

FUNCTIONS and POWERS

Article 87

The General Assembly and, under its authority, the Trusteeship Council, in carrying out their functions, may:

a. consider reports submitted by the administering authority;

b. accept petitions and examine them in consultation with the administering authority;

c. provide for periodic visits to the respective trust territories at times agreed upon with the administering authority and

d. take these and other actions in conformity with the terms of the trusteeship agreements

Article 88

The Trusteeship Council shall formulate a questionnaire on the political, economic, social, and educational advancement of the inhabitants of each trust territory, and the administering authority for each trust territory within the competence of the General Assembly shall make an annual report to the General Assembly upon the basis of such questionnaire.

VOTING

Article 89

Each member of the Trusteeship Council shall have one vote.

Decisions of the Trusteeship Council shall be made by a majority of the members present and voting.

PROCEDURE

Article 90

The Trusteeship Council shall adopt its own rules of procedure, including the method of selecting its President.

The Trusteeship Council shall meet as required in accordance with its rules, which shall include provision for the convening of meetings on the request of a majority of its members.

Article 91

The Trusteeship Council shall, when appropriate, avail itself of the assistance of the Economic and Social Council and of the specialized agencies in regard to matters with which they are respectively concerned.

CHAPTER XIV
THE INTERNATIONAL COURT OF JUSTICE

Article 92

The International Court of Justice shall be the principal judicial organ of the United Nations. It shall function in accordance with the annexed Statute, which is based upon the Statute of the Permanent Court of International Justice and forms an integral part of the present Charter.

Article 93

All Members of the United Nations are ipso facto parties to the Statute of the International Court of Justice.

A state which is not a Member of the United Nations may become a party to the Statute of the International Court of Justice on conditions to be determined in each case by the General Assembly upon the recommendation of the Security Council.

Article 94

Each Member of the United Nations undertakes to comply with the decision of the International Court of Justice in any case to which it is a party.

If any party to a case fails to perform the obligations incumbent upon it under a judgment rendered by the Court, the other party may have recourse to the Security Council, which may, if it deems necessary, make recommendations or decide upon measures to be taken to give effect to the judgment.

Article 95

Nothing in the present Charter shall prevent Members of the United Nations from entrusting the solution of their differences to other tribunals by virtue of agreements already in existence or which may be concluded in the future.

Article 96

The General Assembly or the Security Council may request the International Court of Justice to give an advisory opinion on any legal question.

Other organs of the United Nations and specialized agencies, which may at any time be so authorized by the General

Assembly, may also request advisory opinions of the Court on legal questions arising within the scope of their activities.

CHAPTER XV
THE SECRETARIAT

Article 97

The Secretariat shall comprise a Secretary-General and such staff as the Organisation may require. The Secretary-General shall be appointed by the General Assembly upon the recommendation of the Security Council. He shall be the chief administrative officer of the Organisation.

Article 98

The Secretary-General shall act in that capacity in all meetings of the General Assembly, of the Security Council, of the Economic and Social Council, and of the Trusteeship Council, and shall perform such other functions as are entrusted to him by these organs. The Secretary-General shall make an annual report to the General Assembly on the work of the Organisation.

Article 99

The Secretary-General may bring to the attention of the Security Council any matter which in his opinion may threaten the maintenance of international peace and security.

Article 100

In the performance of their duties the Secretary-General and the staff shall not seek or receive instructions from any government or from any other authority external to the Organisation. They shall refrain from any action which might reflect on their position as international officials responsible only to the Organisation.

Each Member of the United Nations undertakes to respect the exclusively international character of the responsibilities of the Secretary-General and the staff and not to seek to influence them in the discharge of their responsibilities.

Article 101

The staff shall be appointed by the Secretary-General under regulations established by the General Assembly.

Appropriate staffs shall be permanently assigned to the

Economic and Social Council, the Trusteeship Council, and, as required, to other organs of the United Nations. These staffs shall form a part of the Secretariat.

The paramount consideration in the employment of the staff and in the determination of the conditions of service shall be the necessity of securing the highest standards of efficiency, competence, and integrity. Due regard shall be paid to the importance of recruiting the staff on as wide a geographical basis as possible.

CHAPTER XVI
MISCELLANEOUS PROVISIONS

Article 102

Every treaty and every international agreement entered into by any Member of the United Nations after the present Charter comes into force shall as soon as possible be registered with the Secretariat and published by it.

No party to any such treaty or international agreement which has not been registered in accordance with the provisions of paragraph 1 of this Article may invoke that treaty or agreement before any organ of the United Nations.

Article 103

In the event of a conflict between the obligations of the Members of the United Nations under the present Charter and their obligations under any other international agreement, their obligations under the present Charter shall prevail.

Article 104

The Organisation shall enjoy in the territory of each of its Members such legal capacity as may be necessary for the exercise of its functions and the fulfilment of its purposes.

Article 105

The Organisation shall enjoy in the territory of each of its Members such privileges and immunities as are necessary for the fulfilment of its purposes.

Representatives of the Members of the United Nations and officials of the Organisation shall similarly enjoy such privileges and immunities as are necessary for the independent exercise of their functions in connexion with the Organisation.

The General Assembly may make recommendations with a view to determining the details of the application of paragraphs 1 and 2 of this Article or may propose conventions to the Members of the United Nations for this purpose.

CHAPTER XVII
TRANSITIONAL SECURITY ARRANGEMENTS

Article 106

Pending the coming into force of such special agreements referred to in Article 43 as in the opinion of the Security Council enable it to begin the exercise of its responsibilities under Article 42, the parties to the Four-Nation Declaration, signed at Moscow, 30 October 1943, and France, shall, in accordance with the provisions of paragraph 5 of that Declaration, consult with one another and as occasion requires with other Members of the United Nations with a view to such joint action on behalf of the Organisation as may be necessary for the purpose of maintaining international peace and security.

Article 107

Nothing in the present Charter shall invalidate or preclude action, in relation to any state which during the Second World War has been an enemy of any signatory to the present Charter, taken or authorized as a result of that war by the Governments having responsibility for such action.

CHAPTER XVIII
AMENDMENTS

Article 108

Amendments to the present Charter shall come into force for all Members of the United Nations when they have been adopted by a vote of two thirds of the members of the General Assembly and ratified in accordance with their respective constitutional processes by two thirds of the Members of the United Nations, including all the permanent members of the Security Council.

Article 109

A General Conference of the Members of the United Nations for the purpose of reviewing the present Charter may be held at a date and place to be fixed by a two-thirds vote of the members of the General Assembly and by a vote of any nine members of the Security Council. Each Member of the United Nations shall have one vote in the conference.

Any alteration of the present Charter recommended by a two-thirds vote of the conference shall take effect when ratified in accordance with their respective constitutional processes by two thirds of the Members of the United Nations including all the permanent members of the Security Council.

If such a conference has not been held before the tenth annual session of the General Assembly following the coming into force of the present Charter, the proposal to call such a conference shall be placed on the agenda of that session of the General Assembly, and the conference shall be held if so decided by a majority vote of the members of the General Assembly and by a vote of any seven members of the Security Council.

CHAPTER XIX
RATIFICATION AND SIGNATURE

Article 110

The present Charter shall be ratified by the signatory states in accordance with their respective constitutional processes.

The ratifications shall be deposited with the Government of the United States of America, which shall notify all the signatory states of each deposit as well as the Secretary-General of the Organisation when he has been appointed.

The present Charter shall come into force upon the deposit of ratifications by the Republic of China, France, the Union of Soviet Socialist Republics, the United Kingdom of Great Britain and Northern Ireland, and the United States of America, and by a majority of the other signatory states. A protocol of the ratifications deposited shall thereupon be drawn up by the Government of the United States of America which shall communicate copies thereof to all the signatory states.

The states signatory to the present Charter which ratify it after it has come into force will become original Members of the United Nations on the date of the deposit of their respective ratifications.

Article 111

The present Charter, of which the Chinese, French, Russian, English, and Spanish texts are equally authentic, shall remain deposited in the archives of the Government of the United States of America. Duly certified copies thereof shall be transmitted by that Government to the Governments of the other signatory states.

IN FAITH WHEREOF the representatives of the Governments of the United Nations have signed the present Charter.

DONE at the city of San Francisco the twenty-sixth day of June, one thousand nine hundred and forty-five.

BIBLIOGRAPHY

Adisheshiah Malcom, *Regional Economic Arrangements* (New Delhi: India International Centre, 1989).

A.D.V. de S. (ed.), *Globalization and South Asia: Retrospect and Prospect* (Sri lanka Association for the Advancement of Science, 1999, Colombo).

Adil Najam, "Global Governance and International Organization", *Foreign Affairs*, Anthology (New York: Council on Foreign Affairs 2003).

Ahmad, S. Hasan, *The United Nations and the Colonies* (London, Asia. Pub. House, 1974).

Almond Gabriel A. and James S. Coleman (eds.), *The Politics of Developing Areas* (Princeton University Press, 1960).

Amer, Ramses, *The United Nations & Foreign Military Interventions: A Comparative Study of the Application of the Charter* (Coronet Books, 1992).

Anne O. Krueger, "Whither the World Bank and the IMF?" *Journal of Economic Literature* 36 (December 1998).

Anne-Marie Slaughter, "The Real New World Order," *Foreign Affairs* 76:5 (Sept.-Oct. 1997).

Another Attempt At Safta, *The Hindu*, January 8, 2004.

Arend, Anthony C. and Robert J. Beck, *International Law and the Use of Force: Beyond the UN Charter Paradigm* (London, New York, Routledge, 1993).

Armstead J. Holmes, Jr., "The ICC: History Development and Status" (*Santa Clara Law Review*: Summer, 1998).

Arnold-Forster, William, *The United Nations Charter examined* (London: Labour Party, 1946).

Asante S.K.B., *Regionalism and Africa's Development: Expectations, Realities and Challenges* (London: Macmillan, 1998).

Asante, S.K.B., "What Really is African Union", (*West Africa,* 7-13 July, 2003).

Balassa, Bela, *The Theory of Economic Integration–III* (Homewood, Richard Irwin, 1961).

Baldwin, R., "The Causes of Regionalism", *World Economy,* [20(7), 1997].

Barbara Crossette, "World Criminal Court Having a Painful Birth" (*New York Times,* August 13,1997).

Bartram S. Brown, "Unilateralism, Multilateralism and the ICC", in Stewart Patrick and Shepard Foreman (ed.), *Multilateralism and US Foreign policy: Ambivalent Engagement* (Lynne Rienner, 2001).

Baru, S., "Regional Economic Cooperation: Threat or Opportunity?" in Gunewardena, V. (ed), *Regional Cooperation and Integration: Perspective from Europe and South Asia* (European Commission to Sri Lanka, 1998, Colombo).

Basset, N.P., *Constitution of the United Nations of the World* (Boston, Christopher Publishing House, 1944).

Batra, T.S., *International Institutions: the UN Charter and the International Court of Justice,* 2nd ed. (New Delhi, Bookhive, 1987).

Bennet A. Leroy, *International Organization,* (Englewood Cliffs, Prentice-Hall, 1995).

Bentwich, Norman, *A Commentary on the Charter of the United Nations* (London: Routledge & Keegan Paul, 1951).

Blum, Yehuda Zvi, *Eroding the United Nations Charter* (Dordrecht, Netherlands; Boston, MA: M. Nijhoff; 1993).

Borgese, Elizabeth Mann, *A Constitution for the World* (Santa Barbara, CA: Center for the Study of Democratic Institutions, 1965).

Bowett D.W., *The Law of International Institutions* (University Paper-backs, London, Metheun, 1964).

Boyd A., *The United Nations: Piety, Myth and Truth* (Penguin, 1964).

Brage C., *The New Regionalism and its Consequence* (Washington DC, World Bank, 1994).

Bregman, A, *Appeasement Charter? A Study of the Dumbarton Oaks Proposals* (London: Love; 1945).

Brierly, James Leslie, *The Covenant and the Charter* (Cambridge, [England]: The University Press, 1947).

Cassese, Antonio (ed.), *The Current Legal Regulation of the Use of Force* (Dordrecht, Netherlands; Boston, MA: M. Nijhoff; 1986).

Cassese, Antonio, *Legal Restraints on the Use of Force 40 Years After the UN Charter* (Dordrecht, Netherlands: M. Nijhoff; 1986).

CGG (The Commission On Global Governance), *Our Global Neighborhood* (New York: Oxford University Press 1995).

Cecil Viscount, *A Great Experiment* (London: New York, 1941).

Chadwick F. Alger, "Methodological Innovation Research on International Organizations", in James A. Robinson (ed), *Political Science* Annual, 1969-70, Vol. 2 (Indianapolis, Ind: Bobbs-Mervill, 1969).

Chadwick F. Alger, "A Decade of Quantitative and Field Research on International Organization", (*International Organization,* Vol. 24, 1970).

Chadwick, John, *International Organization* (Methuen Educational Ltd., London, 1965).

Chaudhri, Mohammed Ahsen, *United Nations Peace Mechanisms and Rules* (Karachi, Pakistan: Council for Pakistan Studies, 1973).

Chaudhuri, Sanjib, *Amendments to the Charter of United Nations, with Specific Proposals* (Calcutta: World Constitution Office, 1953).

Chevalier, Stuart, *The World Charter and the Road to Peace* (Los Angeles, CA.: Ritchie; 1946).

Chowdhury, Subrata Roy, *Military Alliances and Neutrality in War and Peace* (Bombay: Orient Longman, 1966).

Ciobanu, Dan, *Financial Obligations of States under Article 19 of the UN Charter* (Milano: A. Giuffre; 1973).

Clark, Grenville and Louis B. Sohn, *Peace through Disarmament and Charter Revision; Detailed Proposals for Revision of the United Nations Charter* (Dublin, N.H., 1953).

Clark, Grenville, *A Plan for Peace* (New York: Harper; 1950).

Clark, Grenville, Louis B. Sohn and Robert Henkle Reno, *A Digest of Peace through Disarmament and Charter Revision; Detailed Proposals for Revision of the United Nations Charter* (New York: Institute for International Order, 1953).

Claud Innis Jr., *Swords in Ploughshares* (New York: Random House, 1984).

Claud Innis, "International Organization: The process and the Institutions", in D. Sius (ed.), *International Encyclopaedia of the Social Sciences,* Vol. 8 (New York: Macmillan and Free Press, 1968).

Constitutive Act of the African Union.

David A. Kay (ed.), *The United Nations Political System,* (London: John Wily, 1967).

David Williams, "Constructing the Economic Space: The World Bank and the Making of *Homo Oeconomicus,*" *Millennium* 28:1 (1999).

Davis H.E. (ed.), *Pioneers in the World Order* (New York, 1928).

De Melo and Arvind Panagria (eds.), *New Dimensions of Regional Integration* (Cambridge University Press, 1994).

De Silva, K.M., " SAARC and the Future of South Asia: A View from the Periphery", *South Asian Survey,* Vol. 6. No. 2, 1999.

Deutsch, K.W., *Political Community at the International Level* (New York, 1954).

Du Bois, W.E.B., "Pan-Africanism", *Voice of Africa,* June 1961.

Dubey, M., *New Regionalism and the Countries of the South* (South Centre, 1997, Geneva).

Eagleton, Clyde, *Covenant of the League of Nations and the Charter of the United Nations; Points of Difference* (Washington, D.C.: G.P.O.; 1946).

Eduardo Faleiro, "South Asian Economic Cooperation", *South Asia Politics,* August, 2003.

Edward H. Carr, *The Twenty Years' Crisis, 1919-1939* (Harper Collins, 1981).

Efimov, Gennadii Konstantinovich, *UN Charter as an Instrument of Peace* (Moscow: Nauka Publishers; 1986).

Eichelberger, Clark Mell, *The United Nations Charter: What Was Done at San Francisco* (New York: American Association for the United Nations, Inc., 1945).

El-Ayouty, Yassin, *The United Nations and decolonization: the Role of Afro-Asia* (The Hague: Martinus Nijhoff; 1971).

Elias, T.O., *The United Nations Charter and the World Court* (Lagos: Nigerian Institute of Advanced Legal Studies; 1989).

European Union Information Brochure, "Africa and the European Union", May 2003.

European Union, Encyclopaedia Article; *The Columbia Encyclopaedia*, VI Edition, 2000.

Everyman's United Nations—A Basic History of the Organization, United Nations Publication.

Fakher, Hossein, *The Charter and Organization of the U.N* (Teheran: Ettela'at; 1951).

Fanshawe, Maurice, *The Charter Explained* (London: United Nations Association of Great Britain and Northern Ireland; 6th ed., 1951).

Foroutan, F., "Regional Integration in Sub-Saharan Africa: Past Experience and Future Prospects", in De Melo and Arvind Panagria (eds.), *New Dimensions of Regional Integration* (Cambridge University Press, 1994).

Gerbet, G., "Rise and Development", *International social Science Journal*, Vol. 29, No. 1, 1977.

Ghose, S. and Mukherjee, S. (eds.), *Emerging South Asian Order: Hopes and Concerns* (Media South Asia, 1996, Calcutta).

Gonsalves, E and Jetly, N. (eds.), *The Dynamics of South Asia: Regional Cooperation and SAARC* (Sage, 1999, New Delhi).

Gonzalez Felipe, "European Union and Globalization" (Foreign Policy, Summer 1999).

Goodrich L.M., "From League of Nations to United Nations", *International Organization,* 1947.

Goodrich, Leland Matthew, *Charter of the United Nations:*

Commentary and Documents (New York: Columbia University Press; 3rd ed., 1969).

Goodspeed Stephen S., *The Nature and Function of International Organization,* (New York: Oxford University Press, 1959).

Graham, Robert A, *Our Way to Peace in the Atomic Age: A Study of the United Nations Charter* (New York, The America Press; 1949).

Gregg Robert W., "The Un Regional Economic Commissions and Integration in the Underdeveloped Regions", *International Organization,* Vol. XX, No. 2, 1966.

Gunewardena, V. (ed.), *Regional Cooperation and integration: Perspective from Europe and South Asia* (European Commission to Sri lanka, 1998, Colombo).

Haas, Ernest B., "The Study of Regional Integration: Reflections on the Joy and Anguish of Pre-Theorizing", *International Organization* (Cambridge), Vol. 24, Autumn 1970.

Haga, Shiro, *Introduction to the U.N., with Article by Article Explanation of the Charter* (Tokyo: Japan United Nations Association; 1948).

Haile, Minasse, *United Nations Consideration of Domestic Questions and of their International Effects* (Ann Arbor, MI.: University Microfilms; 1967).

Hanreider Wolfram, "International Organizations and International System", *The Journal of Conflict Resolution,* Vol. 10, No. 3.

Hoffman Stanley, "International Organizations and International System", *International Organization,* Vol. 24 (1973).

Holmes, A.H, *Three Points of View of U.N. Charter Revision* (Cambridge, MA: New England Conference on U.N. Revision, 19549).

Holsti Ole R. and M. Randorph Siverson, *Change in the International System* (West View Press, Boulder, Colorado, 1980).

Hunter Miller D., *The Drafting of the Covenant* (New York: London, 1928).

Huntington Samuel P., "Trans-national Organizations in the World Politics", *World Politics,* Vol. XXV, No. 3, April 1973.

Ian Black, "The EU's Growing Pains" (Foreign Policy, March-April, 2001).

Indian Council of World Affairs, *Revision of the United Nations Charter: A Symposium* (New Delhi: 1956).

International Criminal Court, *Human Rights Watch World Report,* 1999 (HRW).

International Justice: International Criminal Court, *Human Rights Watch World Report,* 2001 (HRW).

Inter-Parliamentary Union, *The Problem of Revision of the United Nations Charter* (Monaco, 1954).

Jacob Phillip E. and Alexine L. Atherton, *The Dynamics of International Organization* (Dorsey Press, Homewood, Illinois, 1965).

Jacob Phillip E., "Organizing the Nations in the 70s", *Orbis,* Special Issue, 1971.

James A. Caporaso, "The European Union and Forms of the State: Westphalian, Regulatory, or Post-Modern?" *Journal of Common Market Studies* 34:1 (March 1996).

Jenks C. Wilfred, *The World Beyond the Charter* (London, George Allen and Unwin, 1969).

Jenks, Clarence Wilfred, *The World beyond the Charter in Historical Perspective: A Tentative Synthesis of Four Stages of World Organization* (London: George Allen and Unwin; 1969).

John Mccormick, *The European Union: Politics and Policies,* 2nd edn. (Westview, 1999).

John Mearsheimer, "The False Promise of International Institutions," *International Security* 19:3 (Winter 1994/95).

John S. Duffield, "NATO's Functions After the Cold War," *Political Science Quarterly* 109:5 (Winter 1994-95).

Jordon Dinic "The African Union: A historic Watershed for the African Continent", *Review of International Affairs,* Oct-Dec, 2002.

Kalegama, S., "SAARC: from Association to a Community—A Small Country Perspective", *South Asian Survey,* Vol. 6, No. 2, 1999.

Karen A. Mingst and Margaret P. Karns, *The United Nations in the Post-Cold War Era*, (Boulder: Westview Press, 2000).

Kelly-Kate Pease, *International Organizations: Perspectives on Governance in the Twenty-First Century* (Prentice-Hall, 2000).

Kelsen, Hans, *The law of the United Nations: A Critical Analysis of Its Fundamental Problems* (London: Stevens; 1950).

Kennes Walter, "Developing Countries and Regional Integration", *The Courier ACP-EU,* No. 165, Sept.-Oct, 1997.

Khare, Subhas Chandra, *Use of Force under U.N. Charter* (New Delhi, India: Metropolitan; 1st ed., 1985).

Krasner Stephen D. (ed.), *International regimes,* (Ithaca, N.Y.: Comell University Press, 1983).

Kratochwil Fredrich and John Gerard Ruggie, "International Organization: A State of the Art or an Art of the State", *International Organization,* Vol. 40, No. 4, 1986.

Krugman, P., "Regionalism Vs Multi lateralism; An Analytical Notes", in DeMelo and Panagariya (eds.), *New Dimensions in Regional Cooperation* (Cambridge University Press, 1994).

Landau, A., "Multilateralism and Regionalism International Economic Relations" in Daniel C. Bach (ed.) *Regionalisation in Africa: Integration and Disintegration* (Indiana University Press, 1999)

L. Alan Winters, "The European Community: A Case of Successful Integration?" in De Melo and Arvind Panagria (eds.), *New Dimensions of Regional Integration* (Cambridge University Press, 1994).

Lama, M.P., " Add Spark to SAARC", *The Times of India,* January 6, 2004.

Leonard Larry L., *International Organization* (New York: McGraw-Hill, 1951).

Luard Evan (ed.), *The Evolution of International Organization* (Thames and Hudson, London, 1966).

Maier, Franklin L, *World Peace by Covenant: the United Nations Considered as an International Organization for Securing World Peace* (New York: Exposition Press; 1955).

Maitland Donald, "The European Union: The Way Ahead", (International Relations, May 2001).

Mangone Gerard J., *A Short History of International Organization*, (McGraw Hill, New York, 1854).

Mathews K., "Birth of AU", *Africa Quarterly*, Vol. 41. Nos 1 & 2: Jan. to June, 2001.

Matnoush H. Arsanjani, "The Rome Statute of the International Criminal Court", *American Journal of International Law*, 1999.

Mc Cormick, John, *The European Union: Politics and Policies*, (Westview Press, 1996).

Miller Linda B. (ed.), *Dynamics of World Politics*, (Prentice Hall, 1963).

Mistry, P.S., " Regional Integration and Development: Panacea or Pitfalls?" (RIS Occasional Paper, No. 47, New Delhi, 1995).

Mitrany, David, *The United Nations Charter; The Text and A Commentary* (London: National Peace Council; 1945).

Morley, Felix, *The Charter of the United Nations: An Analysis* (New York: American Enterprise Association, Inc., 1946).

Mukherjee, Sakti Pada, *Reflections on League Covenant, United Nations and International Court of Justice* (Calcutta: Alpha Pub. Concern; 1967).

Muni, S.D., "Regionalism Beyond the Regions: South Asia Outside SAARC", in Gonsalves, E. and Jetly, N. (eds.), *The Dynamics of South Asia: Regional Cooperation and SAARC*, (Sage, 1999, New Delhi).

Myers D.P., *Handbook of the League of Nations*, (Geneva, Boston, 1935).

Naidu, Mumulla Venkat Rao, *The United Nations Force: Legal Theory and Political Practice* (Ann Arbor, Mich.: University Microfilms; 1967).

Narayan, C.V.L., *Analysis of the Principles and System of International Trusteeship in the Charter; A Study of the Origin, Principles and Application in International Law* (Geneva: Imp. Populaires; 1951).

Nawaz, M.K., *The Legal Principles Governing Friendly Relations and Cooperation among States in the Spirit of the United Nations Charter* (Leyden: A.W. Sijthoff; 1966).

Nepad, Oau, Abuja, Nigeria, October 2001.

Newcombe, Hanna, *Alternative Approaches to World Government* (Clarkson, Canada: Canadian Peace Research Institute; 1967).

Nicholas H.G., *The United Nations as a Political Institution* (London, 1959).

Nye J.S., *Peace in Parts: Integration and Conflict in Regional Organization* (Little Brown, 1971).

Nye, Joseph S. and Robert Keohane, *Transnational Relations and Two Faces of World Politics* (Harvard University Press, Cambridge, 1970).

Official Websites of the Respective Organizations.

Panagariya, A. "Trade Policy in South Asia: Recent Liberalization and Future Agenda", *World Economy*, June, 1999.

Pant, V.P., "Economics of Regional Cooperation", *South Asia Forum*, Winter, 1981.

Pigato, M. et al., *South Asia's Integration into the World Economy* (The World Bank, 1997, Washington D.C.).

Pinder, John, *U.N. Reform: Proposals for Charter Amendment* (London: Federal Union; 2nd ed. 1953).

Plischke E. (ed.), *Systems of Integrating the International Community* (Princeton, 1964).

Potter P.B., *Introduction to the Study of International Organization* (New York, 1948).

Pyzel, Robert, *The Task that Lies Before Us: A Counter Proposal for the Charter of the United Nations* (New York, N.Y.: J. M. Barrett Corporation; 1945).

Rajan, M.S, *United Nations and domestic jurisdiction* (2nd ed. London: Asia Publishing House; 1961).

Rana A.P., "Regionalism as an Approach to International Order: A Conceptual Overview", *International Studies* (New Delhi, Vol. 13, 1979).

Rao, Bhaskar N., "SAARC or no SAARC, We are Neighbours", *South Asia Politics,* February, 2003.

Redmond, J., The Expanding European Union: Past, Present, Future (Lynne Rienner Publishers, 1998).

Report on "Comparative Political Analysis of International Organizations", presented at Sixth World Congress, IPSA (Geneva, 1964).

Roachester Martin J., "The rise and fall of the international organization as a field of study", *International Organization,* Vol. 40, No. 4, 1986.

Robert W. Cox, "Multilateralism and World Order," in Robert W. Cox with Timothy J. Sinclair, *Approaches to World Order* (Cambridge: Cambridge University Press, 1996).

Robinson, Jacob, *Human Rights and Fundamental Freedoms in the Charter of the United Nations: A Commentary* (New York: Institute of Jewish Affairs of the American Jewish Congress and World Jewish Congress; 1946).

Ross Herbert, "The African Union and the NEPAD in 2002: A Pivotal Year", *South African Yearbook of International Affairs,* 2002/03.

Ross, Alf, *Constitution of the United Nations: Analysis of Structure and Function* (New York: Rinehart; 1950).

Russell, Ruth B, *The United Nations: Patterns of Constitutional Development, Development of Peacekeeping Rules; Two Papers* (Washington, D.C.: Brookings Institution; 1965).

S. Rajaratnam, "ASEAN: The Way Ahead", in *The ASEAN Reader,* Institute of South-East Asian Studies (Singapore, 1992).

Sarah B. Sewall and Carl Kaysen, eds., *The United States and the International Criminal Court* (Rowman and Littlefield, 2000).

Sarah B. Sewall and Carl Kaysen (eds.), *The United States and the International Criminal Court* (Rowman and Littlefield, 2000).

Sideri S., "Globalisation and Regional Integration", *European Journal of Development Research,* 9(1), 1997.

Simma, Bruno (ed.), *Charter of the United Nations: A Commentary* (Oxford; New York: Oxford University Press; 1994).

Sirte Decleration, Sirte, Great Socialist People's Libyan Arab, (Jamahariya, 9-9-1999).

Soper T., *Evolving Commonwealth* (Pergomon Press, 1965).

Stassen, Harold E., *The Stassen Draft Charter for a New United Nations 1985* (Philadelphia, Pa.: Glenview Foundation; 1985).

Stassen, Harold Edward, United Nations: A Working Paper for Restructuring Minneapolis (MN.: Lerner Publications Co.; 1994).

Steinberg, Samuel, *The UN: Structure, Achievements, and problems including the UN Charter and Universal Declaration of Human Rights* (New York: Oxford Book Co; 1968).

Stuart Croft et.al., "The Enlargement of NATO," in *The Enlargement of Europe* (Manchester University Press, 1999).

Sud, Usha Roy, *United Nations and the Non-Self-Governing Territories* (Jullundur: University Publishers; 1965).

Thanat Khoman, "ASEAN Conception and Evolution", in *The ASEAN Reader* (Institute of South-East Asian Studies, Singapore, 1992).

Tharp Paul A. (ed.), *Regional International Organizations: Structures and Functions* (St. Martin's Press, New York, 1971).

The African Union Directory 2002, First Heads of State Summit (Millenium African Publication, Port Louis, 2002).

The Islamabad Declaration, adopted by the 12th SAARC Summit.

The United Nations System and Its Functions: Selected Readings (Van Nostrand Political Science Series, 1968).

Thomas, Norman Mattoon, *A Socialist Look at the United Nations* (Syracuse, NY: Syracuse University Press; 1945).

Toussaint, Charmian Edwards, *The Trusteeship System of the United Nations* (NY: Praeger; 1956).

Treaty of South Asian Association for Regional Cooperation.

Vernon Nash, "World Order Through World Law," in *Nash, The World Must Be Governed* (Harper and Brothers, 1949).

Wallace M. and D. Singer, "Intergovernmental Organization in the Global System, 1815-1964", *International Organization,* Vol. 24, No. 2 (1970).

Walter F.P., "The League of Nations", in Evan Luard (ed.), *The Evolution of International Organization* (Thames and Hudson, London, 1966).

Wilcox, Francis Orlando, *Proposals for Changes in the United Nations* (Washington, D.C.: Brookings Institution; 1955).

Williams, John E, *A New Charter for the United Nations* (Bushey, England: World Union Press; 1965).

Williamson, J.A., *A Notebook of Commonwealth History* (MacMillan, 1967).

Yearbook of International Organization, 31st Edition, Vol. 1, 1994/95.